COLOSSIANS

Jerry L. Sumney

Colossians

A Commentary

Westminster John Knox Press
LOUISVILLE • LONDON

© 2008 Jerry L. Sumney

All rights reserved. No part of this book may be reproduced or transmitted in any form or by any means, electronic or mechanical, including photocopying, recording, or by any information storage or retrieval system, without permission in writing from the publisher. For information, address Westminster John Knox Press, 100 Witherspoon Street, Louisville, Kentucky 40202-1396.

Scriptural quotations outside Colossians, unless otherwise indicated, are from the New Revised Standard Version Bible. Copyright © 1989 National Council of the Churches of Christ in the United States of America. Used by permission. All rights reserved.

Book design by Jennifer K. Cox

First edition
Published by Westminster John Knox Press
Louisville, Kentucky

This book is printed on acid-free paper that meets the American National Standards Institute Z39.48 standard. ∞

PRINTED IN THE UNITED STATES OF AMERICA

08 09 10 11 12 13 14 15 16 17 — 10 9 8 7 6 5 4 3 2 1

Library of Congress Cataloging-in-Publication Data

Sumney, Jerry L.
    Colossians : a commentary / Jerry L. Sumney.
        p. cm.—(The New Testament library)
    Includes bibliographical references (p.   ) and index.
    ISBN 978-0-664-22142-3 (alk. paper)
      1. Bible. N.T. Colossians—Commentaries. I. Title.
BS2715.53.S86 2008
227'.707—dc22
                    2008008395

To
Victor Paul Furnish
Richard Oster
Harvey L. Floyd

CONTENTS

PREFACE

Writing a commentary on Colossians has been an enjoyable learning experience. Writing any commentary imposes the discipline of studying every text in a book and making decisions about the meaning of each word. It also requires a more direct exchange with the text than do most other genres. This immediate focus on the text has benefited both my studies and my teaching. The task of writing this commentary has stretched me to read in new areas of research and to think about the early church in clearer ways. I hope the fruit of these studies is greater clarity in our understanding of Colossians.

Every commentator stands on the shoulders of previous commentators and interpreters—and my debt to my predecessors is profound. The bibliographies and citations illustrate the deep and sustained conversations I have had with these interpreters as well as with the text itself. The keen observations and careful arguments of others have shown me things I would have missed and helped to position me to make my own contribution to the reading of this ancient letter.

I owe thanks to many people who have helped make this book possible. I thank the editorial board of the New Testament Library for their invitation and their wise advice as I began writing. I am particularly thankful to John Carroll. He has been tireless in his efforts to make this a better, clearer, and more useable commentary. Every reader will benefit from his work with me. Any errors and problems that remain in the book, however, are my responsibility. I thank Lexington Theological Seminary for its generous sabbatical policy, which gave me time to complete this work. The trustees of this seminary have continued to recognize the value of sabbaticals to the faculty, the institution, and the larger church. I am also grateful for the seminary's Bosworth Library, which houses a wonderful collection for New Testament studies and boasts a helpful staff, many of whom have helped me gain access to material as I worked on this book. I also thank colleagues who have thoughtfully engaged my prior work on Colossians and so have enriched my understanding of the letter.

This commentary is dedicated to the three teachers who have been most influential in shaping my exegetical and interpretive skills at different stages of my academic career: Victor Paul Furnish of Southern Methodist University, Richard Oster of Harding University Graduate School of Religion in Memphis, and

Harvey L. Floyd of David Lipscomb University. My *Doktorvater,* Victor Furnish, exemplifies the ways kindness and rigor can be combined in graduate studies. He modeled how one could be a scholar and teacher who would take time to be with students, even while facing pressing academic responsibilities. His patient insistence on excellence honed my exegetical and analytical skills. Richard Oster, director of my master's thesis, helped guide me through my initial wrestling with critical method. Though laboring under a very heavy teaching load, he gave careful and demanding attention to each student's work and created a space for honest, searching, and thoughtful conversation (with a welcome light-heartedness) that allowed me to construct a lasting faith. Harvey Floyd, my undergraduate major professor, introduced me to careful scholarship that came to expression in energetic teaching. His example set me on the path to a life of study and teaching. I am thankful to each of these teachers and scholars who have contributed so much to my life and to the work I have done in this commentary. I hope this book honors their labors and that they will be able to see how they have contributed something good to, perhaps even through, it.

JERRY L. SUMNEY
LEXINGTON THEOLOGICAL SEMINARY

ABBREVIATIONS

AB	Anchor Bible
ABD	*Anchor Bible Dictionary*. Edited by D. N. Freedman. 6 vols. New York, 1992
ACNT	Augsburg Commentaries on the New Testament
AGSU	Arbeiten zur Geschichte des Spätjudentums und Urchristentums
ANTC	Abingdon New Testament Commentaries
BAGD	Bauer, W., W. F. Arndt, F. W. Gingrich, and F. W. Danker. *Greek-English Lexicon of the New Testament and Other Early Christian Literature*. 2d ed. Chicago, 1979
BBB	Bonner biblische Beiträge
BDAG	Bauer, W., F. W. Danker, W. F. Arndt, and F. W. Gingrich. *A Greek-English Lexicon of the New Testament and Other Early Christian Literature*. 3d ed. Chicago, 2000
BDF	Blass, F. A., A. Debrunner, and R. W. Funk. *A Greek Grammar of the New Testament and Other Early Christian Literature*. Chicago, 1961
BETL	Bibliotheca ephemeridum theologicarum lovaniensium
Bib	*Biblica*
BibLeb	*Bibel und Leben*
BSac	*Bibliotheca sacra*
BZNW	Beihefte zur Zeitschrift für die neutestamentliche Wissenschaft
CBQ	*Catholic Biblical Quarterly*
CGTC	Cambridge Greek Testament Commentary
ÉBib	Études bibliques
EvQ	*Evangelical Quarterly*
EvT	*Evangelische Theologie*
Hermeneia	Hermeneia: A Critical and Historical Commentary on the Bible
HNT	Handbuch zum Neuen Testament
HTR	*Harvard Theological Review*

ICC	International Critical Commentary
Int	*Interpretation*
JBL	*Journal of Biblical Literature*
JETS	*Journal of the Evangelical Theological Society*
JJS	*Journal of Jewish Studies*
JSNT	*Journal for the Study of the New Testament*
JSNTSup	Journal for the Study of the New Testament: Supplement Series
JTS	*Journal of Theological Studies*
KEK	Kritisch-Exegetischer Kommentar über das Neue Testament (Meyer-Kommentar)
KJV	King James Version
LSJM	Liddell, H. G., R. Scott, and H. S. Jones, assisted by R. McKenzie et al. *A Greek-English Lexicon.* 9th ed. with revised supplement. Oxford, 1996
LTQ	*Lexington Theological Quarterly*
MM	Moulton, J. H., and G. Milligan. *The Vocabulary of the Greek Testament*, 1930. Reprint, Peabody, Mass., 1997
MNTC	Moffatt New Testament Commentary
NCB	New Century Bible
NEB	New English Bible
Neot	*Neotestamentica*
Nestle-Aland[26]	Eberhard Nestle and Erwin Nestle, with K. Aland et al., eds. *Novum Testamentum Graece.* 26th ed. Stuttgart, 1979
NHC	Nag Hammadi Codices
NICNT	New International Commentary on the New Testament
NIGTC	New International Greek Testament Commentary
NIV	New International Version
NJB	New Jerusalem Bible
NovT	*Novum Testamentum*
NovTSup	Novum Testamentum Supplements
NPNF[1]	*Nicene and Post-Nicene Fathers*, Series 1
NRSV	New Revised Standard Version
NTS	*New Testament Studies*
OGIS	*Orientis graeci inscriptiones selectae.* Edited by W. Dittenberger. 2 vols. Leipzig, 1903–1905
PG	Patrologia graeca. Edited by J.-P. Migne. 162 vols. Paris, 1857–1886
PGL	*Patristic Greek Lexicon.* Edited by G. W. H. Lampe. Oxford, 1968
QD	Quaestiones disputatae
ResQ	*Restoration Quarterly*

RevExp	*Review and Expositor*
RSV	Revised Standard Version
SBLDS	Society of Biblical Literature Dissertation Series
SBLSBS	Society of Biblical Literature Sources for Biblical Studies
SJLA	Studies in Judaism in Late Antiquity
SJT	*Scottish Journal of Theology*
SNTSMS	Society of New Testament Studies Monograph Series
SP	Sacra pagina
StPatr	Studia patristica
SUNT	Studien zur Umwelt des Neuen Testaments
TDNT	*Theological Dictionary of the New Testament.* Edited by G. Kittel and G. Friedrich. Translated by G. W. Bromiley. 10 vols. Grand Rapids, 1964–1976
ThSt	Theologische Studiën
TLNT	*Theological Lexicon of the New Testament.* C. Spicq. Translated and edited by J. D. Ernest. 3 vols. Peabody, Mass., 1994
UBS⁴	*The Greek New Testament.* Edited by B. Aland, K. Aland, et al. 4th rev. ed. United Bible Societies, U.S.A. Stuttgart, 1983
WBC	Word Biblical Commentary
WTJ	*Westminster Theological Journal*
WUNT	Wissenschaftliche Untersuchungen zum Neuen Testament
ZBK	Züricher Bibelkommentare
ZNW	*Zeitschrift für die neutestamentliche Wissenschaft und die Kunde der älteren Kirche*
ZTK	*Zeitschrift für Theologie und Kirche*

BIBLIOGRAPHY

Reference Works

Bauer, Walter. *A Greek-English Lexicon of the New Testament and Other Early Christian Literature*. Revised and edited by Frederick W. Danker, W. F. Arndt, F. W. Gingrich. Chicago, Ill.: University of Chicago Press, 2000.

Blass, F., and A. Debrunner. *A Greek Grammar of the New Testament and Other Early Christian Literature*. Translated by Robert W. Funk. Cambridge: Cambridge University Press, 1961.

Freedman, David N. *Anchor Bible Dictionary*. 6 vols. New York: Doubleday, 1992.

Kittel, Gerhard, and Gerhard Friedrich, eds. *Theological Dictionary of the New Testament*. Translated by Geoffrey W. Bromiley. 10 vols. Grand Rapids: Eerdmans, 1964–1976.

Liddell, Henry G., and Robert Scott. *A Greek-English Lexicon*. 9th ed. Edited by H. J. Jones and R. McKenzie. Oxford: Clarendon Press, 1996.

Moulton, James H., and George Milligan. *The Vocabulary of the Greek New Testament*. London: Hodder & Stoughton, 1930.

Spicq, Ceslas. *Theological Lexicon of the New Testament*. Translated and edited by James D. Ernest. 3 vols. Peabody, Mass.: Hendrickson, 1994.

Strack, Hermann L., and Paul Billerbeck. *Kommentar zum Neuen Testament aus Talmud und Midrasch*. 6 vols. Munich: Beck, 1922–61.

Commentaries

Abbott, T. K. *A Critical and Exegetical Commentary on the Epistles to the Ephesians and to the Colossians*. ICC. Edinburgh: T&T Clark, 1897.

Aletti, Jean-Noël. *Saint Paul Épître aux Colossiens: Introduction, Traduction et Commentaire*. ÉBib 20. Paris: Éditions J. Gabalda, 1993.

Barth, Markus, and Helmut Blanke. *Colossians*. AB 34B. New York: Doubleday, 1994.

Beare, Francis W. "The Epistle to the Colossians: Introduction and Exegesis." Pages 133–241 in *The Epistle to the Philippians, The Epistle to the Colossians,*

The First and Second Epistles to the Thessalonians, The First and Second Epistles to Timothy and The Epistle to Titus, The Epistle to the Hebrews. Vol. 11 of *The Interpreter's Bible.* Edited by George A. Buttrick. Nashville: Abingdon, 1955.

Bruce, F. F. "Commentary on the Epistle to the Colossians: The English Text with Introduction, Exposition and Notes." Pages 160–312 in *Commentary on the Epistles to the Ephesians and Colossians.* By E. K. Simpson and F. F. Bruce. NICNT. Grand Rapids: Eerdmans, 1957.

Caird, George B. *Paul's Letters from Prison: Ephesians, Philippians, Colossians, Philemon, in the Revised Standard Version.* Oxford: Oxford University Press, 1976.

Calvin, Jean. *The Epistles of Paul the Apostle to the Galatians, Ephesians, Philippians, and Colossians.* Calvin's Commentaries. Grand Rapids: Eerdmans, 1965.

Dibelius, Martin. *An die Kolosser, Epheser, an Philemon.* HNT 12. 3rd ed. Tübingen: Mohr (Siebeck), 1953.

Dunn, James D. G. *The Epistles to the Colossians and to Philemon: A Commentary on the Greek Text.* NIGTC. Grand Rapids: Eerdmans, 1996.

Harris, Murray J. *Colossians and Philemon.* Exegetical Guide to the Greek New Testament. Grand Rapids: Eerdmans, 1991.

Hay, David M. *Colossians.* ANTC. Nashville: Abingdon, 2000.

Horgan, Maurya P. "The Letter to the Colossians." Pages 876–82 in *The New Jerome Biblical Commentary.* Edited by Raymond E. Brown, Joseph A. Fitzmyer, and Roland E. Murphy. Englewood Cliffs, N.J.: Prentice Hall, 1990.

Hübner, Hans. *An Philemon, An die Kolosser, An die Epheser.* HNT 12. Tübingen: Mohr, 1997.

Lightfoot, Joseph B. *Saint Paul's Epistles to the Colossians and to Philemon.* Rev. ed. New York: Macmillan, 1879. Repr. Grand Rapids: Zondervan, 1959.

Lincoln, Andrew T. "The Letter to the Colossians." Pages 553–669 in *The Second Letter to the Corinthians, The Letter to the Galatians, The Letter to the Ephesians, The Letter to the Philippians, The Letter to the Colossians, The First and Second Letters to Timothy and the Letter to Titus, The Letter to Philemon.* Vol. 11 of *The New Interpreter's Bible.* Edited by Leander E. Keck. Nashville: Abingdon, 2000

Lindemann, Andreas. *Der Kolosserbrief.* ZBK, NT 10. Zurich: Theologischer Verlag Zürich, 1983.

Lohmeyer, Ernst. *Die Briefe an die Kolosser und an Philemon.* KEK. Göttingen: Vandenhoeck & Ruprecht, 1956.

Lohse, Eduard. *A Commentary on the Epistles to the Colossians and to Philemon.* Hermeneia. Philadelphia: Fortress, 1971.

MacDonald, Margaret Y. *Colossians and Ephesians*. SP. Collegeville, Minn.: Liturgical Press, 2000.

Martin, Ralph P. *Colossians and Philemon*. NCB. London: Marshall, Morgan & Scott, 1974.

Meyer, Heinrich A. W. *A Critical and Exegetical Handbook to the Epistles to the Philippians and Colossians, and to Philemon*. Meyer's Critical and Exegetical Handbook to the New Testament. New York: Funk & Wagnalls, 1885.

Moule, C. F. D. *The Epistles of Paul the Apostle to the Colossians and Philemon*. CGTC. Cambridge: Cambridge University Press, 1957.

Pokorný, Petr. *Colossians: A Commentary*. Peabody, Mass.: Hendrickson, 1991.

O'Brien, Peter T. *Colossians, Philemon*. WBC. Waco, Tex.: Word, 1982.

Scott, E. F. *The Epistles of Paul to the Colossians, to Philemon, and to the Ephesians*. MNTC. New York: Harper & Brothers, 1930.

Schweizer, Eduard. *The Letter to the Colossians: A Commentary*. Minneapolis: Augsburg, 1976.

Stagg, Frank. "Colossians." Pages 1235–39 in *Mercer Commentary on the Bible*. Edited by Watson Mills and Richard F. Wilson. Macon, Ga.: Mercer University Press, 1995.

Thompson, Marianne Meye. *Colossians and Philemon*. Two Horizons New Testament Commentary. Grand Rapids: Eerdmans, 2005.

Thurston, Bonnie B. *Reading Colossians, Ephesians, and 2 Thessalonians: A Literary and Theological Commentary*. Reading the New Testament. New York: Crossroad, 1995.

Walsh, Brian J., and Sylvia C. Keesmaat. *Colossians Remixed: Subverting the Empire*. Downers Grove, Ill.: InterVarsity, 2004.

Other Studies

Anderson, Charles P. 1966. "Who Wrote the 'Epistle from Laodicea'?" *JBL* 85: 436–40.

Arnold, Clinton E. 1994. "Jesus Christ: Head of the Church (Colossians and Ephesians)." Pages 346–66 in *Jesus of Nazareth: Lord and Christ; Essays on the Historical Jesus and New Testament Christology*. Edited by Joel B. Green and Max Turner. Grand Rapids: Eerdmans.

———. 1996. *The Colossian Syncretism: The Interface between Christianity and Folk Belief at Colossae*. Grand Rapids: Baker.

Attridge, Harold W. 1994. "On Becoming an Angel: Rival Baptismal Theologies at Colossae." Pages 483–98 in *Religious Propaganda and Missionary Competition in the New Testament World: Essays Honoring Dieter Georgi*. Edited by L. Bormann, K. Del Tredici, and A. Standhartinger. NovTSup 74. Leiden: Brill.

Balch, David. 1988. "Household Codes." Pages 25–50 in *Greco-Roman Literature and the New Testament: Selected Forms and Genres.* Edited by David E. Aune. SBLSBS 21. Atlanta: Scholars.

Balchin, John F. 1985. "Colossians 1:15–20: An Early Christian Hymn? The Arguments from Style." *Vox evangelica* 15: 65–94.

Bammel, Ernst. 1961. "Versuch zu Col 1:15–20." *ZNW* 52: 88–95.

Bandstra, Andrew J. 1974. "Did the Colossian Errorists Need a Mediator?" Pages 329–43 in *New Dimensions in New Testament Study.* Edited by Richard N. Longenecker and Merrill C. Tenney. Grand Rapids: Zondervan.

Barclay, John M. G. 1997. *Colossians and Philemon.* T&T Clark Study Guides. New York: T&T Clark.

Bauman-Martin, Betsy J. 2004. "Women on the Edge: New Perspectives on Women in the Petrine *Haustafel.*" *JBL* 123: 253–79.

Beasley-Murray, Paul. 1980. "Colossians 1:15–20: An Early Christian Hymn Celebrating the Lordship of Christ." Pages 169–83 in *Pauline Studies: Essays Presented to Professor F. F. Bruce on His 70th Birthday.* Edited by Donald A. Hagner and Murray J. Harris. Grand Rapids: Eerdmans [Paternoster].

Behr, John. 1996. "Colossians 1:13–20: A Chiastic Reading." *St. Vladimir's Theological Journal* 40: 247–64.

Bevere, Allen R. 2003. *Sharing in the Inheritance: Identity and the Moral Life in Colossians.* JSNTSup 226. New York: Sheffield Academic Press.

Bieder, Werner. 1952. *Die Kolossische Irrlehre und die Kirche von Heute.* ThSt 33. Zurich: Evangelischer Verlag.

Bornkamm, Günther. 1973. "The Heresy of Colossians." Pages 123–47 in *Conflict at Colossae: A Problem in the Interpretation of Early Christianity Illustrated by Selected Modern Studies.* Edited by Fred O. Francis and Wayne A. Meeks. SBLSBS 4. Missoula, Mont.: Scholars Press.

Bratcher, Robert G., and Eugene A. Nida. 1977. *A Translator's Handbook on Paul's Letters to the Colossians and to Philemon.* Stuttgart: United Bible Societies.

Brown, Jeannine K. 2006. "Just a Busybody? A Look at the Greco-Roman Topos of Meddling for Defining ἀλλοτριεπίσκοπος [*allotriepiskopos*] in 1 Peter 4:15." *JBL* 125: 549–68.

Brunt, P. A. 1997. "Laus Imperii." Pages 25–35 in *Paul and Empire: Religion and Power in Roman Imperial Society.* Edited by Richard A. Horsley. Harrisburg, Pa.: Trinity Press International.

Bussmann, Claus. 1983. "Gibt es chistologische Begründungen für eine Unterordnung der Frau im Neuen Testament?" Pages 254–62 in *Die Frau im Urchristentum.* Edited by Gerhard Dautzenberg, Helmut Merklein, and Karlheinz Müller. QD 95. Freiburg: Herder.

Campbell, Douglas A. 1996. "Unravelling Colossians 3.11b." *NTS* 42: 120–32.

Cannon, George E. 1983. *The Use of Traditional Materials in Colossians.* Macon, Ga.: Mercer University Press.

Carr, Wesley. 1981. *Angels and Principalities: The Background, Meaning, and Development of the Pauline Phrase hai archai kai hai exousia.* New York: Cambridge University Press. Repr. 2005.

Carter, Warren. 2004. "Going All the Way? Honoring the Emperor and Sacrificing Wives and Slaves in 1 Peter 2.12–3.6." Pages 14–33 in *A Feminist Companion to the Catholic Epistles and Hebrews.* Edited by Amy-Jill Levine and Maria Mayo Robbins. Cleveland, Ohio: Pilgrim Press.

Cerfaux, Lucien. 1985. "L'influence des 'Mystères' sur les Épîtres de S. Paul aux Colossians et aux Éphèsiens." Pages 279–85 in *Recueil Lucien Cerfaux: Études d'exégèse et d'histoire religieuse.* Vol. 3. BETL 71. Leuven: Leuven University Press.

Crouch, James E. 1972. *The Origin and Intention of the Colossian Haustafel.* Göttingen: Vandenhoeck & Ruprecht.

Dahl, Nils A. 1976. *Jesus in the Memory of the Early Church.* Minneapolis: Augsburg.

Deichgräber, Reinhard. 1967. *Gotteshymnus und Christushymnus in der frühen Christenheit: Untersuchungen zu Form, Sprache und Stil der frühchristlichen Hymnen.* SUNT 5. Göttingen: Vandenhoeck & Ruprecht.

Delebecque, Edouard. 1989. "Sur un problème de temps chez Saint Paul (Col 3,1–4)." *Bib* 70: 389–95.

Detwiler, David F. 2001. "Church Music and Colossians 3:16." *BSac* 158: 347–69.

Dibelius, Martin. 1973. "The Isis Initiation in Apuleius and Related Initiatory Rites." Pages 61–121 in *Conflict at Colossae: A Problem in the Interpretation of Early Christianity Illustrated by Selected Modern Studies.* Edited by Fred O. Francis and Wayne O. Meeks. SBLSBS 4. Missoula, Mont.: Scholars Press.

Downing, F. Gerald. 2003. "Paul's Drive for Deviants." *NTS* 49: 360–71.

Dudrey, Russ. 1999. "'Submit Yourselves to One Another': A Socio-Historical Look at the Household Code of Ephesians 5:15–6:9." *ResQ* 41: 27–44.

Elliott, Neil. 2004. "Strategies of Resistance and Hidden Transcripts in the Pauline Communities." Pages 97–122 in *Hidden Transcripts and the Arts of Resistance: Applying the Work of James C. Scott to Jesus and Paul.* Edited by Richard A. Horsley. Semeia 48. Atlanta: Society of Biblical Literature.

Fee, Gordon D. 1994. *God's Empowering Presence: The Holy Spirit in the Letters of Paul.* Peabody, Mass.: Hendrickson.

Fiorenza, Elisabeth Schüssler. 1975. "Wisdom Mythology and the Christological Hymns of the New Testament." Pages 17–41 in *Aspects of Wisdom in Judaism and Early Christianity.* Edited by Robert L. Wilken. Notre Dame, Ind.: University of Notre Dame Press.

Fitzmyer, Joseph A. 1989. "Another Look at κεφαλή [*kephalē*] in 1 Corinthians 11.3." *NTS* 35: 503–11.

Fossum, Jarl. 1989. "Colossians 1:15–18a in the Light of Jewish Mysticism and Gnosticism." *NTS* 35: 183–201.

Francis, Fred O. 1973. "Humility and Angelic Worship in Col. 2:18." *Studia theologica* 16 (1962): 109–34. Repr. as pages 163–95 in *Conflict at Colossae: A Problem in the Interpretation of Early Christianity Illustrated by Selected Modern Studies*. Edited by Fred O. Francis and Wayne A. Meeks. SBLSBS 4. Missoula, Mont.: Scholars Press.

———. 1977. "The Christological Argument of Colossians." Pages 192–208 in *God's Christ and His People: Studies in Honour of Nils Alstrup Dahl*. Edited by Jacob Jervell and Wayne A. Meeks. Oslo: Universitetsforlaget.

Francis, Fred O., and Wayne A. Meeks, eds. 1973. *Conflict at Colossae: A Problem in the Interpretation of Early Christianity Illustrated by Selected Modern Studies*. SBLSBS 4. Missoula, Mont.: Scholars Press.

Furnish, Victor P. 1992. "Colossians, Epistle to the." Pages 1090–96 in vol. 1 of *The Anchor Bible Dictionary*. Edited by David N. Freedman. New York: Doubleday.

Gardner, Paul D. 1983. "'Circumcised in Baptism—Raised through Faith': A Note on Col 2:11–12." *WTJ* 45: 172–77.

Garnsey, Peter, and Richard Saller. 1997. "Patronal Power Relations." Pages 96–103 in *Paul and Empire: Religion and Power in Roman Imperial Society*. Edited by Richard A. Horsley. Harrisburg, Pa.: Trinity Press International.

Gehring, Roger W. 2004. *House Church and Mission: The Importance of Household Structures in Early Christianity*. Peabody, Mass.: Hendrickson.

Georgi, Dieter. 1997. "God Turned Upside Down." Pages 148–57 in *Paul and Empire: Religion and Power in Roman Imperial Society*. Edited by Richard A. Horsley. Harrisburg, Pa.: Trinity Press International.

Gewiess, Josef. 1962. "Die apologetische Methode des Apostels Paulus in Kampf gegen die Irrlehre in Kolossä." *BibLeb* 3: 258–70.

Goldenberg, David. 1998. "Scythian-Barbarian: The Permutations of a Classical Topos in Jewish and Christian Texts of Late Antiquity." *JJS* 49: 87–102.

Gorday, Peter. 2000. *Colossians, 1–2 Thessalonians, 1–2 Timothy, Titus, Philemon*. Ancient Christian Commentary on Scripture: New Testament, vol. 9. Downers Grove, Ill.: InterVarsity.

Gordon, Richard. 1997. "The Veil of Power." Pages 126–37 in *Paul and Empire: Religion and Power in Roman Imperial Society*. Edited by Richard A. Horsley. Harrisburg, Pa.: Trinity Press International.

Gräbe, Petrus J. 2005. "Salvation in Colossians and Ephesians." Pages 287–304 in *Salvation in the New Testament: Perspectives on Soteriology*. Edited by Jan G. van der Watt. NovTSup 121. Leiden: Brill.

Grässer, Erich. 1967. "Kol 3,1–4 als Beispiel einer Interpretation secundum homines recipientes." *ZTK* 64: 139–68.

Gunton, Colin. 1996. "Atonement and the Project of Creation: An Interpretation of Colossians 1:15–23." *Dialog* 35: 35–41.

Hartman, Lars. 1987. "Code and Context: A Few Reflections on the Parenesis of Col 3:6–4:1." Pages 237–47 in *Tradition and Interpretation in the New Testament: Essays in Honor of E. Earle Ellis.* Edited by Gerald F. Hawthorne and Otto Betz. Grand Rapids: Eerdmans.

———. 1988. "Some Unorthodox Thoughts on the 'Household-Code Form.'" Pages 219–32 in *The Social World of Formative Christianity and Judaism: Essays in Tribute to Howard Clark Kee.* Edited by Jacob Neusner et al. Philadelphia: Fortress.

Hay, David. 1973. *Glory at the Right Hand: Psalm 110 in Early Christianity.* Nashville: Abingdon.

Heen, Erik M. 2004. "The Role of Symbolic Inversion in Utopian Discourse: Apocalyptic Reversal in Paul and in the Festival of the Saturnalia/Kronia." Pages 123–44 in *Hidden Transcripts and the Arts of Resistance: Applying the Work of James C. Scott to Jesus and Paul.* Edited by Richard A. Horsley. Semeia 48. Atlanta: Society of Biblical Literature.

Hengel, Martin. 1980. "Hymn and Christology." Pages 173–97 in vol. 3 of *Studia Biblica 1978.* Edited by Elizabeth A. Livingstone. JSNTSup 3. Sheffield: JSOT Press.

Hester, James D. 1968. *Paul's Concept of Inheritance; A Contribution to the Understanding of Heilsgeschichte.* Scottish Journal of Theology Occasional Papers 14. Edinburgh: Oliver & Boyd.

Hinson, E. Glenn. 1973. "The Christian Household in Colossians 3:18–4:1." *RevExp* 70: 495–506.

Hollenbach, Bruce. 1979. "Colossians 2:23: Which Things Lead to the Fulfillment of the Flesh." *NTS* 25: 254–61.

Hooker, Morna D. 1973. "Were There False Teachers in Colossae?" Pages 315–31 in *Christ and Spirit in the New Testament: Studies in Honour of Charles Francis Digby Moule.* Edited by Barnabas Lindars and Stephen S. Smalley. Cambridge: Cambridge University Press.

Hoppe, Rudolf. 1992. "Theologie in den Deuteropaulinen (Kolosser- und Epheserbrief)." Pages 163–86 in *Monotheismus und Christologie: Zur Gottesfrage im hellenistischen Judentum und im Urchristentum.* Edited by J. Gnilka et al. QD 138. Freiburg: Herder.

Horsley, Richard A. 1997. "Paul's Anti-Imperial Gospel: Introduction." Pages 140–47 in *Paul and Empire: Religion and Power in Roman Imperial Society.* Edited by Richard A. Horsley. Harrisburg, Pa.: Trinity Press International.

———. 2003. "Subverting Disciplines: The Possibilities and Limitations of Postcolonial Theory for New Testament Studies." Pages 90–105 in *Toward a New Heaven and a New Earth: Essays in Honor of Elisabeth Schüssler Fiorenza.* Edited by Fernando F. Segovia. Maryknoll, N.Y.: Orbis.

———. 2004. "Introduction—Jesus, Paul, and the 'Arts of Resistance': Leaves from the Notebook of James C. Scott." Pages 1–26 in *Hidden Transcripts and the Arts of Resistance: Applying the Work of James C. Scott to Jesus and Paul.* Edited by Richard A. Horsley. Semeia 48. Atlanta: Society of Biblical Literature.

———, ed. 2004. *Hidden Transcripts and the Arts of Resistance: Applying the Work of James C. Scott to Jesus and Paul.* Semeia 48. Atlanta: Society of Biblical Literature.

Hubbard, Moyer V. 2005. "Urban Uprisings in the Roman World: The Social Setting of the Mobbing of Sosthenes." *NTS* 51: 416–28.

Jefford, Clayton N. 1997. "Household Codes and Conflict in the Early Church." *StPatr* 31: 121–27.

Jensen, Joseph. 1978. "Does *Porneia* Mean Fornication? A Critique of Bruce Malina." *NovT* 20: 161–84.

Johnston, George. 1984. "'Kingdom of God' Sayings in Paul's Letters." Pages 143–56 in *From Jesus to Paul: Studies in Honour of Francis Wright Beare.* Edited by Peter Richardson and John C. Hurd. Waterloo, Ont.: Wilfrid Laurier University Press.

Judge, Edwin A. 2003. "Did the Churches Compete with Cult Groups?" Pages 501–24 in *Early Christianity and Classical Culture: Comparative Studies in Honor of Abraham J. Malherbe.* Edited by John T. Fitzgerald, Thomas H. Olbricht, and L. Michael White. NovTSup 110. Leiden: Brill.

Käsemann, Ernst. 1982. "A Primitive Christian Baptismal Liturgy." Pages 149–68 in *Essays on New Testament Themes.* Philadelphia: Fortress.

Kim, Jung Hoon. 2004. *The Significance of Clothing Imagery in the Pauline Corpus.* JSNTSup 268. New York: T&T Clark.

Kittel, G., and G. Friedrich, eds. 1964–76. *Theological Dictionary of the New Testament.* Translated by G. W. Bromiley. 10 vols. Grand Rapids: Eerdmans.

Kreitzer, Larry. 2004. "Living in the Lycus Valley: Earthquake Imagery in Colossians, Philemon and Ephesians." Pages 81–94 in *Testimony and Interpretation: Early Christology in Its Judeo-Hellenistic Milieu; Studies in Honour of Petr Pokorný.* Edited by Jirí Mrázek and Jan Roskovec. JSNTSup 272. New York: T&T Clark.

Kremer, Jacob. 1956. *Was an den Leiden Christi noch Mangelt: Eine interpretationsgeschichtliche und exegetische Untersuchung zu Kol 1,24b.* BBB. Bonn: Hanstein.

Lamarche, Paul. 1975. "Structure de l'épître aux Colossiens." *Bib* 56: 453–63.

Lampe, G. W. H. 1964. "The New Testament Doctrine of *Ktisis.*" *SJT* 17: 449–62.

Leppä, Outi. 2003. *The Making of Colossians: A Study on the Formation and Purpose of a Deutero-Pauline Letter.* Publication of the Finnish Exegetical Society 86. Göttingen: Vandenhoeck & Ruprecht.

Levison, John R. 1989. "2 *Apoc. Bar.* 48:42–52:7 and the Apocalyptic Dimension of Colossians 3:1–6." *JBL* 108: 93–108.

Lewis, Edwin. 1948. "Paul and the Perverters of Christianity: Revelation through the Epistle to the Colossians." *Int* 2: 143–57.

Lightfoot, Joseph B. 1973. "The Colossian Heresy." Pages 13–59 in *Conflict at Colossae: A Problem in the Interpretation of Early Christianity Illustrated by Selected Modern Studies.* Edited by Fred O. Francis and Wayne A. Meeks. SBLSBS 4. Missoula, Mont.: Scholars Press.

Lincoln, Andrew T. 1981. *Paradise Now and Not Yet: Studies in the Role of the Heavenly Dimension in Paul's Thought with Special Reference to His Eschatology.* SNTSMS 43. New York: Cambridge University Press.

———. 1999. "The Household Code and Wisdom Mode of Colossians." *JSNT* 74: 93–112.

Lohse, Eduard. 1968. "Pauline Theology in the Letter to the Colossians." *NTS* 15: 211–20.

———. 1970. "Die Mitarbeiter des Apostels Paulus im Kolosserbrief." Pages 189–194 in *Verborum Veritas: Festschrift für Gustav Stählin zum 70. Geburtstag.* Edited by Otto Böcher and Klaus Haacker. Wuppertal: Theologischer Verlag Rolf Brockhaus.

Löwe, Hartmut. 1980. "Bekenntnis, Apostelamt und Kirche im Kolosserbrief." Pages 299–314 in *Kirche: Festschrift für Günther Bornkamm zum 75. Geburtstag.* Edited by D. Lührmann and Georg Strecker. Tübingen: Mohr (Siebeck).

Luttenberger, Joram. 2005. "Der gekreuzigte Schuldschein: Ein Aspekt der Deutung des Todes Jesu im Kolosserbrief." *NTS* 51: 80–95.

MacDonald, Margaret Y. 2003. "Early Christian Women Married to Unbelievers." Pages 14–28 in *A Feminist Companion to the Deutero-Pauline Epistles.* Edited by Amy-Jill Levine and Marianne Blickenstaff. Cleveland, Ohio: Pilgrim.

———. 2007. "Slavery, Sexuality and House Churches: A Reassessment of Colossians 3.18–4.1 in Light of New Research on the Roman Family." *NTS* 53: 94–113.

McGuire, Anne. 1990. "Equality and Subordination in Christ: Displacing the Powers of the Household Code in Colossians." Pages 65–86 in *Religion and Economic Ethics.* Edited by Joseph F. Gower. Annual Publication of the College Theology Society 31. Lanham, Md.: University Press of America.

Maier, Harry O. 2005. "A Sly Civility: Colossians and Empire." *JSNT* 27: 323–49.

Malina, Bruce. 1972. "Does *Porneia* Mean Fornication?" *NovT* 14: 10–17.

Martin, Clarice. 1991. "The *Haustafeln* (Household Codes) in African American Biblical Interpretation: 'Free Slaves' and 'Subordinate Women.'" Pages 206–31 in *Stony the Road We Trod: African American Biblical Interpretation.* Edited by Cain Hope Felder. Minneapolis: Fortress.

Martin, Dale. 1990. *Slavery as Salvation: The Metaphor of Slavery in Pauline Christianity.* New Haven: Yale University Press.

Martin, Troy W. 1995. "But Let Everyone Discern the Body of Christ (Col 2:17)." *JBL* 114: 249–55.

———. 1996. *By Philosophy and Empty Deceit: Colossians as a Response to a Cynic Critique.* JSNTSup 118. Sheffield: Sheffield Academic Press.

Meeks, Wayne A. 1977. "In One Body: The Unity of Humankind in Colossians and Ephesians." Pages 209–21 in *God's Christ and His People: Studies in Honour of Nils Alstrup Dahl.* Edited by Jacob Jervell and Wayne A. Meeks. Oslo: Universitetsforlaget.

———. 1983. *The First Urban Christians: The Social World of the Apostle Paul.* New Haven: Yale University Press.

———. 1993. "'To Walk Worthily of the Lord': Moral Formation in the Pauline School Exemplified by the Letter to Colossians." Pages 37–58 in *Hermes and Athena: Biblical Exegesis and Philosophical Theology.* Edited by Eleonore Stump and Thomas P. Flint. University of Notre Dame Studies in the Philosophy of Religion 7. Notre Dame, Ind.: University of Notre Dame Press.

Metzger, Bruce M. 1975. *A Textual Commentary on the Greek New Testament.* Rev. ed. Stuttgart: United Bible Societies.

Mollenkott, Virginia Ramey. 2003. "Emancipative Elements in Ephesians 5.21–33: Why Feminist Scholarship Has (Often) Left Them Unmentioned, and Why They Should be Emphasized." Pages 37–58 in *A Feminist Companion to the Deutero-Pauline Epistles.* Edited by Amy-Jill Levine and Marianne Blickenstaff. Cleveland, Ohio: Pilgrim.

Moule, C. F. D. 1973. "'The New Life' in Colossians." *RevExp* 70: 481–93.

Moxnes, Halvor. 2003. "Asceticism and Christian Identity in Antiquity: A Dialogue with Foucault and Paul." *JSNT* 26: 3–29.

Müller, Karlheinz. 1983. "Die Haustafel des Kolosserbriefes und das antike Frauenthema: Eine kritische Rückschau auf alte Ergebnisse." Pages 263–319 in *Frau im Urchristentum.* Edited by Gerhard Dautzenberg, Helmut Merklein, and Karlheinz Müller. QD 95. Freiburg: Herder.

Munro, Winsome. 1972. "Col. III. 18-IV. 1 and Eph. V. 21-VI. 9: Evidences of a Late Literary Stratum?" *NTS* 18: 434–47.

Nash, Robert Scott. 1989. "Heuristic *Haustafeln*: Domestic Codes as Entrance to the Social World of Early Christianity; The Case of Colossians." Pages 25–50 in vol. 2 of *Religious Writings and Religious Systems.* Edited by Jacob Neusner, Ernest S. Frerichs, and Amy-Jill Levine. Atlanta: Scholars Press.

Nock, A. D. 1933. "The Vocabulary of the NT." *JBL* 52: 131–39.

Olbricht, Thomas H. 1996. "The Stoicheia and the Rhetoric of Colossians: Then and Now." Pages 308–28 in *Rhetoric, Scripture and Theology: Essays from the Pretoria Conference.* JSNTSup 121. Sheffield: Sheffield Academic Press.

Osiek, Carolyn, and David L. Balch. 1997. *Families in the New Testament World: Households and House Churches.* Louisville: Westminster John Knox.

———, ed. 2003. *Early Christian Families in Context: An Interdisciplinary Dialogue.* Grand Rapids: Eerdmans.

Osiek, Carolyn, Margaret Y. MacDonald, and Janet H. Tulloch. 2006. *A Woman's Place: House Churches in Earliest Christianity.* Minneapolis: Fortress.

Økland, Jorunn. 2003. "Sex Slaves of Christ: A Response to Halvor Moxnes." *JSNT* 26: 31–34.

Percy, Ernst. 1946. *Die Probleme der Kolosser—und Epheserbriefe.* Lund: Gleerup.

Portefaix, Lilian. 2003. "'Good Citizenship' in the House of God: Women's Position in the Pastorals Reconsidered in the Light of Roman Rule." Pages 147–58 in *A Feminist Companion to the Deutero-Pauline Epistles.* Edited by Amy-Jill Levine and Marianne Blickenstaff. Cleveland, Ohio: Pilgrim Press.

Price, S. R. F. 1997. "Rituals and Power." Pages 47–71 in *Paul and Empire: Religion and Power in Roman Imperial Society.* Edited by Richard A. Horsley. Harrisburg, Pa.: Trinity Press International.

Robinson, James M. 1957. "A Formal Analysis of Colossians 1:15–20." *JBL* 76: 270–87.

Rowland, Christopher. 1983. "Apocalyptic Visions and the Exaltation of Christ in the Letter to the Colossians." *JSNT* 19: 73–83.

Sappington, Thomas J. 1991. *Revelation and Redemption at Colossae.* JSNTSup 53. Sheffield: JSOT Press.

Schenk, Wolfgang. 1983. "Christus, das Geheimnis der Welt, als dogmatisches und ethisches Grundprinzip des Kolosserbriefes." *EvT* 43: 138–55.

Schubert, Paul. 1939. *Form and Function of the Pauline Thanksgivings.* BZNW 20. Berlin: Töpelmann.

Schweizer, Eduard. 1963. "Die Sünde in den Gliedern." Pages 437–39 in *Abraham Unser Vater: Juden und Christen im Gespräch über die Bibel; Festschrift für Otto Michel zum 60. Geburtstag.* Edited by Otto Betz, Martin Hengel, and Peter Schmidt. AGSU 5. Leiden: Brill.

———. 1976. "Christianity of the Circumcised and Judaism of the Uncircumcised." Pages 245–60 in *Jews, Greeks and Christians: Religious Cultures in Late Antiquity; Essays in Honor of William David Davies.* Edited by Robert Hamerton-Kelly and Robin Scroggs. SJLA 21. Leiden: Brill.

———. 1979. "Traditional Ethical Patterns in the Pauline and Post-Pauline Letters and Their Development (Lists of Vices and House-tables)." Pages 195–209 in *Text and Interpretation*. Edited by E. Best and R. McL. Wilson. Cambridge: Cambridge University Press.

———. 1988. "Slaves of the Elements and Worshipers of Angels: Gal 4:3, 9 and Col 2:8, 18, 20." *JBL* 107: 455–68.

Scott, James C. 1990. *Domination and the Arts of Resistance: Hidden Transcripts*. New Haven: Yale University Press.

Shogren, Gary S. 1988. "Presently Entering the Kingdom of Christ: The Background and Purpose of Col 1:12–14." *JETS* 31: 173–80.

Standhartinger, Angela. 1999. *Studien zur Entstehungsgeschichte und Intention des Kolosserbriefs*. NovTSup 94. Leiden: Brill.

———. 2000. "The Origin and Intention of the Household Code in the Letter to the Colossians." *JSNT* 79: 117–30.

———. 2003. "The Epistle to the Congregation in Colossae and the Invention of the 'Household Code.'" Pages 88–121 in *A Feminist Companion to the Deutero-Pauline Epistles*. Edited by Amy-Jill Levine and Marianne Blickenstaff. Cleveland, Ohio: Pilgrim.

Stirewalt, Martin Luther, Jr. 1977. "The Form and Function of the Greek Letter-Essay." Pages 175–206 in *The Romans Debate*. Edited by Karl P. Donfried. Minneapolis: Augsburg.

Stroumsa, Gedaliahu G. 1983. "Form(s) of God: Some Notes on Metatron and Christ." *HTR* 76: 269–88.

Sumney, Jerry L. 1990. *Identifying Paul's Opponents: The Question of Method in 2 Corinthians*. JSNTSup 40. Sheffield: Sheffield Academic Press.

———. 1999. *"Servants of Satan," "False Brothers," and Other Opponents of Paul*. JSNTSup188. Sheffield: Sheffield Academic Press.

———. 2002a. "The Argument of Colossians." Pages 339–52 in *Rhetorical Argumentation in Biblical Texts: Essays from the Lund 2000 Conference*. Edited by Anders Eriksson, Thomas H. Olbricht, and Walter Übelacker. Emory Studies in Early Christianity 8. Harrisburg, Pa.: Trinity Press International.

———. 2002b. "New Testament Perspectives on Ministry." Pages 27–43 in *The Order of the Ministry: Equipping the Saints*. Edited by Jerry L. Sumney. Lexington, Ky.: Lexington Theological Seminary.

———. 2005. "The Function of Ethos in Colossians." Pages 301–15 in *Rhetoric, Ethic, and Moral Persuasion: Essays from the 2002 Heidelberg Conference*. Edited by Thomas H. Olbricht and Anders Eriksson. Emory Studies in Early Christianity 11. New York: T&T Clark.

———. 2006. "'I Fill Up What Is Lacking in the Afflictions of Christ': Paul's Vicarious Suffering in Colossians." *CBQ* 68: 664–80.

Swart, Gerhard. 1966. "Eschatological Vision of Exhortation to Visible Christian Conduct? Notes on the Interpretation of Colossians 3:4." *Neot* 33: 169–77.

Tannehill, Robert C. 1967. *Dying and Rising with Christ: A Study in Pauline Theology.* BZNW 32. Berlin: Töpelmann.

Thornton, T. C. G. 1989. "Jewish New Moon Festivals, Galatians 4:3–11 and Colossians 2:16." *JTS* 40 NS: 97–100.

Thurston, Bonnie B. 1999. "Paul's Associates in Colossians 4:7–17." *ResQ* 41: 45–53.

Van der Horst, P. W. 1972. "Observations on a Pauline Expression." *NTS* 19: 181–87.

Vawter, Bruce. 1971. "The Colossians Hymn and the Principle of Redaction." *CBQ* 33: 62–81.

Wedderburn, A. J. M., and Andrew T. Lincoln. 1993. *The Theology of the Later Pauline Letters.* Cambridge: Cambridge University Press.

Weiser, Alfons. 1983. "Die Rolle der Frau in der urchristlichen Mission." Pages 158–81 in *Die Frau im Urchristentum.* Edited by Gerhard Dautzenberg, Helmut Merklein, and Karlheinz Müller. QD 95. Freiburg: Herder.

Weiss, Herold. 1972. "The Law in the Epistle to the Colossians" *CBQ* 34: 294–314.

White, John L. 1972. *The Form and Function of the Body of the Greek Letter: A Study of the Letter-Body in the Non-literary Papyri and in Paul the Apostle.* SBLDS 2. Missoula, Mont.: Scholars Press.

———. 1986. *Light from Ancient Letters.* Philadelphia: Fortress.

Wicker, Kathleen O'Brien. 1975. "First Century Marriage Ethics: A Comparative Study of the Household Codes and Plutarch's Conjugal Precepts." Pages 141–53 in *No Famine in the Land: Studies in Honor of John L. McKenzie.* Edited by J. W. Flanagan and A. W. Robinson. Missoula, Mont.: Scholars Press.

Wilson, Walter T. 1997. *The Hope of Glory: Education and Exhortation in the Epistle to the Colossians.* NovTSup 88. Leiden: Brill.

Winter, Bruce W. 2003. *Roman Wives, Roman Widows: The Appearance of New Women and the Pauline Communities.* Grand Rapids: Eerdmans.

Wright, N. T. 1990. "Poetry and Theology in Colossians 1.15–20." *NTS* 36: 444–68.

Yates, Roy. 1970. "Note on Colossians 1:24." *EvQ* 42: 88–92.

———. 1980. "Christ and the Powers of Evil in Colossians." Pages 461–68 in vol. 3 of *Studia Biblica 1978.* Edited by Elizabeth A. Livingstone. JSNTSup 3. Sheffield: JSOT Press.

———. 1991. "The Christian Way of Life: The Paraenetic Material in Colossians 3:1–4:6." *EvQ* 63: 241–51.

Zanker, Paul. 1997. "The Power of Images." Pages 72–86 in *Paul and Empire: Religion and Power in Roman Imperial Society.* Edited by Richard A. Horsley. Harrisburg, Pa.: Trinity Press International.

———. 1988. *The Power of Images in the Age of Augustus.* Ann Arbor: University of Michigan Press.

INTRODUCTION

Colossians gives present-day readers a glimpse of the world of the first-century church. We catch sight of the kinds of people who were in the church and the kinds of problems and questions they faced. This letter also acquaints us with the place of the church in the world and how believers practiced their faith in various life settings. At the same time, we see the church struggling with questions about which *religious* practices were consistent with the new faith its members had come to own. But these images remain less than crystal clear. Many historical questions persist: When was Colossians written? What problems does it address? Who wrote it? While Colossians makes powerful affirmations about Christ's identity and how believers' participation "in Christ" does and should affect their lives, we will better understand such statements if we have greater clarity about the situation the letter addresses.

Interpreters have given matters related to the setting of Colossians extensive attention without reaching consensus. This introduction can do little more than familiarize readers with the issues and give the most important reasons for the positions taken here. As will become clear, some disagreements lead to notable differences in interpretation. Other disagreements bear more on our understanding of the development of the church and its relationship with the surrounding culture than on the interpretation of Colossians itself.

Colossians is traditionally included among the Prison Epistles (along with Philippians, Ephesians, and Philemon), letters that all have Paul writing from prison. Interpreters sometimes assume that all four epistles were composed during the same imprisonment, but only Philemon and Colossians contain material that supports this idea—and other matters make this timing questionable. Still, all four of the Prison Epistles allow Paul's identity as a prisoner for the gospel to shape their messages.

Authorship and Date

For more than a century and a half, interpreters have raised doubts about whether Paul wrote Colossians. The style and vocabulary of Colossians appear markedly different from the undisputed Pauline Letters.[1] Colossians has many terms that appear nowhere else in Paul or, for that matter, in the rest of the New Testament.[2] Furthermore, the pleonastic style of Colossians distinguishes it from the undisputed letters; Paul seldom multiplies adjectives and other modifiers the way Colossians characteristically does. But the situation that Colossians addresses may account for some of its distinctive stylistic features, just as it may explain the differences in vocabulary.[3] All of Paul's Letters (including Philemon) have terms that appear in no other letter, though often not in the abundance with which they appear in Colossians. Moreover, Colossians has many characteristic Pauline phrases (e.g., "in the Lord," 3:18, 20; "with Christ," 2:12, 20; for more examples, see the list in Lohse 85–87). Given the different problems that each of Paul's Letters addresses, differences in vocabulary and style do not constitute sufficient reason to reject Pauline authorship.

One other formal difference merits notice. Colossians is the earliest New Testament letter to contain a "household code" (3:18–4:1), a formalized list of duties for various positions within a first-century household. This literary form appears in the slightly later Ephesians (which is dependent upon Colossians) and then in other later New Testament letters (Titus 2:3–10; 1 Pet 2:18–3:7). Interpreters often see the presence of the household code as evidence that Colossians was written after Paul's death, because it seems to introduce a firm hierarchy, a kind of structure that Paul elsewhere resists. My reading in the commentary, however, will suggest that this understanding of the code's instructions in Colossians misses their intent. The inserted qualifications (e.g., "in the Lord," 3:18) and other hints within the code cued the initial readers to view these socially imposed structures as constructions that stand in conflict with the will of God, even if believers must continue to live within these institutional constraints. The presence of this literary form, then, does not necessarily show that Paul was not the author of this letter.

Beyond these more formal differences, Colossians' theology differs from the undisputed letters in its themes and emphases. Specific features of the occasion of the letter can account for some of these differences, but others may reflect developments beyond the theological stances Paul takes in the undisputed letters. Colossians does not, for example, dwell on the theme of justification by faith. Its prominence in Galatians and Romans, and to some extent in Philippians, has led some interpreters (including Martin Luther) to identify justification

---

1. The undisputed letters of Paul (i.e., the letters most interpreters agree were written by Paul) include Romans, 1 and 2 Corinthians, Galatians, Philippians, 1 Thessalonians, and Philemon.

2. These include *areskeia* ("pleasing," 1:10); *katabrabeuō* ("condemn" or "judge," 2:18); *embateuō* ("enter into," 2:18); *plēsmonē* ("fullness," 2:23); *antanaplēroō* ("fill up," 1:24); *aischrologia* ("obscene speech," 3:8).

3. Abbott (lii) asserts that there are no more words found only in Colossians than one should expect given the new topic of discussion.

as the essential and central Pauline theme. Thus, one might argue, since Colossians does not develop this theme, it was probably not written by Paul. This view of justification by faith, however, exaggerates its centrality in Paul's theology. As important as this theme has been in the history of the church, including its early efforts to understand itself in relation to the Old Testament and the synagogue, this metaphor is not as dominant in Paul's thought as has often been claimed. When not faced with issues that elicit the judicial metaphor of justification, Paul uses many nonjuridical images (e.g., reconciliation, release from sin, and adoption) to speak of the believer's relationship with God. Therefore, the relative lack of attention to justification by faith does not suggest that the letter was penned by someone other than Paul. Other theological issues, however, present more of a challenge to maintaining Pauline authorship.

In comparison with the undisputed Pauline Letters, the near absence of references to the Holy Spirit in Colossians stands out. The only direct mention of the Spirit appears in 1:8, where the writer notes that the readers' love comes from the Spirit. The adjective "spiritual" (*pneumatikos*) also appears in 1:9 and 3:16. In these places *pneumatikos* may refer to understanding gained through the Spirit (1:9) and to songs inspired by the Spirit (3:16), but these statements may be more generic references to "spiritual understanding" and "spiritual songs" (see the commentary on these verses). Compared to the attention Paul gives the Spirit in 1 and 2 Corinthians, Galatians, and Romans, Colossians represents a significant departure. In those undisputed letters, the Spirit plays a major role in Paul's eschatology and ethics; it is the gift of God that ensures believers of their relationship with God and enables them to live for God. The Spirit has no such prominence in Colossians, even though affirmations about the presence of the Spirit could address some of the letter's central concerns. Still, nothing Colossians says about the Spirit conflicts with the understanding of the Spirit found in the undisputed letters. Thus, while the shift may be attributable to a difference in the letter's occasion, Colossians represents a considerable modification to the emphasis Paul gives the role of the Spirit in believers' lives.

Colossians also uses the image of the body of Christ in a way the undisputed letters do not. In the undisputed letters, Paul only uses this metaphor to describe local churches, but Colossians refers to the worldwide church as the body of Christ, with the cosmic Christ as its head (1:18). Paul certainly maintains that the church is one throughout the world and in its many manifestations, but he does not use "body" to express that idea in the undisputed letters. Even if the metaphor was already present in the preformed liturgical piece in which it appears (though many think the author of Colossians inserted it [e.g., Lohse 42–43, 52; Schweizer 57–60; Dunn 85, 94–95]), retaining it represents a departure from Paul's customary usage. Contextually, Colossians' use of "body" for the universal church follows from the liturgical piece's cosmic Christology (1:15–20), and utilizing it does not signify a dramatic change in ecclesiology, since Paul had already identified individual congregations as manifestations of the body of Christ. Still, Paul's uses of "body" remain more localized (e.g., 1 Cor 12:12–31) than the cosmic image found in Colossians.

The change in this expression of ecclesiology in Colossians does not, however, imply that the church has moved toward adopting a hierarchical structure. Colossians' ecclesiology is not structured according to offices (elder, deacon, etc.), which suggests that the letter belongs to a time before the changes in church structure that are evident in Ephesians and the Pastorals. In Colossians, all members of the church share the ministries of teaching and admonishing (3:16) and are distinguished more by gifts and commissions than by office (4:17). So this aspect of its ecclesiology seems consistent with that of the undisputed letters, even as it expands Paul's use of the body metaphor. This suggests that Colossians was written either during Paul's lifetime or shortly after his death.

Colossians grounds its response to the teaching it opposes in a cosmic Christology. Colossians envisions Christ as a heavenly being who has always been God's mediating agent in relation to the cosmos. God worked through Christ to create the cosmos, as well as to reconcile the church (1:15–20). Believers' identity as the people of God is rooted in their identification with the Christ in whom all the fullness of deity lives and in whom they receive and experience all knowledge of God (2:9). Such assertions are not unique to Colossians. Interpreters have sometimes claimed that such an exalted Christology indicates that a writing is late, but the church made claims about the exaltation of Christ from its earliest days. Paul's Letters, our earliest evidence for the nascent church's faith, manifest a belief in an exalted and cosmic Christ who has initiated the last days. Beyond the Pauline affirmations of the position of Christ at God's right hand and as judge and king (e.g., Rom 8:34; 1 Cor 15:23–28), Paul quotes a preformed hymnic piece in Phil 2:6–11 that asserts the preexistence and exaltation of Christ. This confessional piece appears in a letter penned in the 50s and was apparently so widely accepted that Paul can use it to ground exhortations to the church without supporting its affirmations about Christ with any arguments. Similarly, the Gospels envision the return of the exalted Christ at the Parousia (e.g., Matt 24:30; Mark 13:26; Luke 21:27). Thus, viewing Christ as an exalted savior formed an important part of the earliest church's proclamation.

Colossians does expand upon some christological claims that earlier Pauline Letters only mention without elaboration. Particularly, Colossians describes more fully Christ's role as the one through whom God created the cosmos. This protological aspect of Christ's agency is present, but less explicit, in the undisputed letters. For Colossians, Christ has been the one who mediated God's acts and words to the cosmos from the beginning of creation; Christ is the one through whom all beings came into existence, and Christ remains the one who sustains the cosmos so it does not disintegrate into chaos (1:15–17). While Paul affirms that the preexistent Christ served as the mediator or agent of God's presence before the incarnation (1 Cor 10:4), the undisputed letters do not assert so baldly that Christ was God's agent of creation, even though Paul intimates this belief in 1 Cor 8:6. Paul affirms that Christ was and is the image of God, but Colossians' more detailed explication of Christ's role as God's agent of creation may represent a development in the church's Christology. Since Paul affirms that Christ possesses "equality with God" (Phil 2:6) and that all came into existence through him (1 Cor 8:6), he could well accept Colossians' fuller statement about Christ's work in creation. But Paul does not extend his Christology in this direction within the undisputed letters.

This christological development carries significant weight in Colossians. The letter's assertion that beings in heavenly places offer nothing that members of the church do not already possess rests on the claim that Christ is not only the ruler of these spiritual powers (which the undisputed letters affirm), but also their creator. This christological claim does not contradict Paul's Christology, but does expand its expression. This expansion may take place after Paul's death, but could easily emerge within his lifetime, even within his own thought. Thus, Colossians' cosmic Christology does not exclude the possibility that Paul wrote this letter.

Many interpreters identify Colossians' eschatology as one of its greatest departures from the theology of the undisputed letters. In a way found in no earlier letter, Colossians focuses steadfastly on believers' present possession of eschatological blessings. In addition to asserting that believers' hope already exists in the heavens (1:5) and that they have already been filled (2:9), Colossians says that they have already been raised with Christ (3:1). Throughout the letter, the author proclaims that believers possess the fullness of God's blessings in the present. Some interpreters have taken this to mean that Colossians has lost, or nearly lost, the future aspect of its eschatology (e.g., Lohse 177–78). While it is true that the future aspect of eschatological expectation seldom comes to explicit expression, this view ignores various statements that demonstrate the importance that a future act of God has for Colossians' interpretation of the place of believers in the present (1:22; 3:4, 25).

The expectation of Christ's return emerges clearly in chapter 3. The opening exhortation of the chapter refers to the second coming, when Christ and believers will be revealed in glory (3:4). The original readers of Colossians knew well that they did not possess this glory in the present. They also knew that Christ's rule over the powers had not been fully realized. The reference to coming judgment does more than support the letter's exhortations; it also reminds those who suffer unjustly, most particularly slaves, that a future reward awaits those who endure faithfully.

At the same time, Colossians does not manifest the urgency about the timing of the Parousia that 1 Thessalonians, for example, has. In this, Colossians mirrors a shift in emphasis about the second coming that appears in other New Testament writings as well. Rather than proclaiming that the end is soon, Colossians places emphasis on the certainty of the end.[4] Philippians may signal this same change as Paul reflects on the possibility of his death before the Parousia (1:20–26).

Colossians focuses on the present possession of eschatological blessings primarily to combat the teaching it opposes. Some teachers are trying to convince the letter's recipients that believers in Christ need additional spiritual and visionary experiences to fully receive God's forgiveness and blessings and to truly be God's people. In the face of a teaching that denies believers these gifts, Colossians argues that the baptized already possess all spiritual blessings in Christ. In this polemic, Colossians does not add the qualifier that they possess all blessings *that are available in the present*. The writer assumes that the readers expect a future act of God that will bring a fuller manifestation of God's will and a vindication of God's people despite the disadvantages they have accepted as believers. It is difficult, perhaps impossible, to determine whether the distinctive emphasis in Colossians' eschatology reflects more a difference in beliefs about the Parousia than a response to the problem the letter addresses. Both factors probably play a role.

Some cooling of the expectation of an imminent end occurred during Paul's lifetime. Beginning with his earliest extant letter, 1 Thessalonians, Paul tried to calm concerns about the Parousia's delay by shifting the Thessalonians' focus to its certainty, rather than its immediacy (4:13–5:11). As I have already noted, his musings in Philippians about his own death before that day indicate that by the time he writes that letter, Paul does not expect the end immediately. Furthermore, Paul also makes some unqualified statements about believers' present possession of eschatological blessings (e.g., 1 Cor 1:5) and he can speak of the present existence of the eschatological realm (2 Cor 5:1). The undisputed letters, however, balance such affirmations of present enjoyment of eschatological blessings with statements about future fulfillment in ways that Colossians does not.

The eschatological emphasis of Colossians, then, differs from that found in the undisputed letters. But again, the difference is not such that it contradicts Paul's eschatology or would be impossible for Paul. Yet it does not quite sound like Paul. What Thompson (3) says with respect to the place of justification by faith in Colossians applies equally well to this and other aspects of Colossians' theology: "The problem is not that Colossians fails to treat a typically Pauline theme, but that Colossians fails to treat this theme in a typically Pauline manner." The way Colossians treats these themes might have developed within Paul's own thought, or they could reflect the hand of another author. Still, Colossians does not manifest the more substantial changes in outlook visible in the Pastorals, or even in Ephesians.

---

4. Other New Testament writings add that the end is not only certain but will come suddenly and unexpectedly (see, e.g., Mark 13; 2 Pet 3:8–10).

Colossians' similarity to Paul's thought, alongside a noticeable shade of difference from it, leads a number of interpreters to suggest that the letter was written by an associate of Paul during Paul's lifetime. According to this view, a colleague wrote with Paul's knowledge and approval, though having a freer hand than Paul's secretary usually had.[5] Giving such freedom to a trusted associate was not unknown in the ancient world. This solution has the potential to explain the differences from other Pauline Letters that we have seen in Colossians to this point. But we need to explore one other aspect of Colossians' thought before arriving at a conclusion about the book's authorship.

Colossians devotes a great deal of attention (proportionately) to establishing Paul's position as the trustworthy and authoritative apostle of the whole church. It gives extended consideration to his sufferings for the church as evidence of Paul's status and dependability. Colossians is certainly not alone in emphasizing Paul's apostleship and suffering, and their meaning for the church. Paul dedicates much of 2 Corinthians to the task of establishing his position as an authoritative apostle. He reminds the Corinthians that his suffering was for their benefit and argues that his suffering embodies the gospel (e.g., 2:14–16; 4:11). But Colossians approaches the topic of Paul's sufferings from a somewhat different angle. In the first place, when Colossians says that Paul's sufferings "fill up what is lacking in the afflictions of Christ" (1:24), it goes beyond Paul's descriptions of those sufferings (see the commentary for the meaning of this statement). Paul could have described his sufferings in this way without diminishing the significance of Christ's death, but he does not do so in the undisputed letters.

Furthermore, when Paul speaks of suffering for the church, he usually has in mind a particular congregation for which he suffers. But in Colossians, Paul suffers for the whole church, especially for those he has never met (2:1). This expansion of the meaning of Paul's sufferings for the church best fits a time after his death. Again, Paul might be willing to make such a claim, because he believes his ministry plays a role in the unfolding of the eschatological scheme (e.g., Rom 9–11), but he does not elsewhere say that his ministry benefits those he has never met and never will meet. Finally, though the occasion of writing to a church he did not personally establish would provide some reason for dwelling on his ethos (that is, his character and the understanding of himself that he wants the readers to have), the amount of space Colossians devotes to this subject is unusual for a letter in which his authority is not under attack. However, the need to establish his authority and reliability *for the whole church* becomes particularly important if he has died without having had contact with the recipients of this letter.

---

5. E.g., Schweizer 23–25; Dunn 37–38. Both these commentators suggest that Timothy is the author who wrote with Paul's approval, and even had Paul add his own signature.

Colossians' discussion of Paul's sufferings fits well within theologies of martyrdom that appear in various Jewish and Christian (as well as pagan) sources (see the commentary on 1:24). These are martyrdom traditions that Paul knows and occasionally employs in his letters, and thus it is not surprising that his associates know and use them. While Colossians' statements about Paul's suffering are possible before his death, they gain power and persuasiveness if he has already met a martyr's fate.

While no single assertion, theological affirmation, or perspective in Colossians is impossible for Paul, the cumulative effect of the shifts in meaning and emphasis in so many areas suggests that an associate penned this letter soon after Paul's death. The interpretation of Paul's sufferings in Colossians tips the balance slightly in favor of this conclusion.

Pseudonymity (writing in someone else's name) in the ancient world was not the equivalent of forgery in the modern world. Philosophical schools and groups within Judaism had a long tradition of writing in the name of a revered leader. Philosophers composed letters purportedly written by Socrates 400 years after his death, and Jewish and Christian apocalyptic writers penned works in the names of characters from Genesis and the prophets of Israel even longer after their deaths. School exercises in the first century included learning to write in the style of revered leaders and thinkers (see, e.g., Quintilian, *Inst. orat.* 10.1–2; 10.8.71). Pseudonymous writings extended the influence and authority of the person imitated, even as they brought that person's authority to bear on a new situation.

Colossians draws on Paul's recognized authority and asserts it for the whole church. For Colossians, Paul and his associates possess the true gospel that brings salvation and secures a relationship with God. Colossians represents a first step in establishing and maintaining Paul's authority after his death. The letter asserts that Paul's ministry and martyrdom—and his authority—extend to the whole church. Colossians even instructs churches to exchange his letters (4:16). Paul's commendation of the people mentioned throughout the letter, then, confers on them significant authority. Those named in the closing and elsewhere as faithful leaders become the people the authoritative Paul approves as faithful.

Questions about authorship have no effect on whether a New Testament writing is authoritative for the church. We do not know who wrote many of the books of the New Testament (e.g., the Synoptic Gospels and Hebrews), as well as of the Old Testament (e.g., 1 and 2 Kings and 1 and 2 Chronicles). These writings are authoritative because the church has heard the word of God in them and has built its life on the faith they proclaim and shape. Pseudonymity does nothing to change that.[6] Indeed, recognizing that a letter is pseudonymous clar-

---

6. If Timothy wrote this letter, as some suggest (see the discussion above), this lessens the impact of questions about pseudonymity because the greeting lists him as a cowriter. But this hypothesis must remain only a possibility, not a probability; no evidence directly supports it.

ifies the context that gave rise to it and thus aids us in understanding it. This, in turn, may help us make more faithful use of the epistle in the church.

The closeness of Colossians' thought to the theology found in the undisputed Pauline Letters, in addition to its establishment of Paul as the apostle of the whole church, suggests that the letter was composed soon after Paul's death, perhaps even in the wake of this loss to the church. These factors commend a date of 62–64 for the letter's composition. Perhaps an early date would also help explain why Colossians draws so heavily on Philemon. If Paul wrote Philemon shortly before his death, the author of Colossians can assume that the people mentioned in that letter are known to his readers and recognized as faithful. Alternatively, the recipients of Colossians may know the letter of Philemon. In this case, the names support the claim that Paul composed Colossians. In either case, the author clearly constructs Colossians so that he addresses churches that know (or at least know of) the same people the recipients of Philemon know. The recipients of Colossians, then, can also rely on these people for proper guidance in the practice of their faith.

Destination

The original and most direct audience of Colossians remains difficult to identify. If Paul is not the letter's author, the churches of Colossae are probably not its actual recipients. A devastating earthquake struck the Lycus valley sometime between 60 and 62 C.E. In that earthquake both Laodicea and Hierapolis sustained significant damage, and Laodicea (which Tacitus called one of the famous cities of Asia) later boasted of rebuilding without imperial aid (*Ann.* 14.27). Not until the fourth century do we hear about the damage Colossae sustained. Eusebius (as found in Jerome's translation of *Chron. Olymp.* 210.4) says that the earthquake destroyed Colossae as well as Laodicea and Hierapolis. If a substantial part of the city of Colossae, located about a hundred miles east of Turkey's western coast on the Lycus River (a tributary of the Meander), remained standing when this letter was written, it had nevertheless declined to the point that it had little importance. Indeed, Pliny the Elder mentions it as an unimportant and declining city (*Nat.* 5.41.145). The nearby cities of Hierapolis and Laodicea (both within fifteen miles of Colossae) were both larger and more prosperous, in part because of their locations and proximity to natural resources. This region of Phrygia, particularly Colossae, was known for its wool industry. Because these three cities were near the river, they also served as transportation centers that connected the inner parts of Turkey to the coast and the major city of Ephesus. Shipping and commerce, along with the wool industry, fueled their economies. The region's warm mineral springs also drew tourists and those seeking cures for disease, particularly to Hierapolis. The populations of these cities were diverse because of their locations on the trade route, a diversity that included a substantial Jewish population. Josephus reports that Antiochus the

Great (223–187 B.C.E.) transplanted two thousand Jewish families to Lydia and Phrygia (*Ant.* 12.3.4).

If Colossae was heavily damaged or destroyed by the earthquake and not rebuilt, addressing the letter to the church in that city could facilitate its acceptance after Paul's death. With the city gone, its church would not exist to dispute having received it during Paul's lifetime. But we cannot be certain that Colossae sustained the same level of damage its neighboring cities suffered. Notably, however, neither Revelation nor Papias (as pieced together from Eusebius) mentions a church in Colossae, though they do mention its neighboring cities. Even if the Christian community in Colossae was not the actual recipient, the letter probably addresses churches in that region because it specifically mentions the churches in Laodicea and Hierapolis.[7] Furthermore, the author's greeting of people whom Paul mentioned in Philemon also points to this region, because churches in that area would be more likely to know these people. Lohse (181) may be correct that Colossians addresses the whole of Asia Minor. The actual intended readers of Colossians constitute a broader group than the churches in a single city, as its instruction to have the church in Laodicea read it indicates. Lindemann (36) suggests that the Laodiceans are the letter's actual intended recipients, but this is more specific than the evidence allows and too narrow a readership. While, to be sure, the problem Colossians addresses is quite specific, we do not know precisely who was tempted to adopt the teaching the author opposes or how widespread it was.

The False Teaching

Interpreters continue to debate the character of the teaching that Colossians opposes. Even though the letter provides some direct statements about that teaching, much about it is difficult to discern.[8] Various hypotheses about this teaching identify its adherents as syncretists who incorporate elements of mystery cults (Dibelius 1973), gnostics (Bornkamm 1973), Jews who claim superiority over the church (Dunn 33–35), and non-Christian Cynics (T. Martin 1996). In the face of these multiple and contradictory reconstructions, Morna Hooker argues that the letter has no opponents in view.[9]

Most hypotheses about the opponents of Colossians contend that they venerate angels. Clinton Arnold finds this view particularly suggestive for Asia Minor because of archaeological evidence that folk religion in that region relied

---

7. Alternatively, mentioning these cities might promote the letter's acceptance elsewhere, since the Christians in other regions would know few people in the named cities. Thus, they would have no way to verify whether it had been sent to them during Paul's lifetime.

8. The following discussion of the opponents of Colossians relies on Sumney 1999: 188–213.

9. "Were There False Teachers in Colossae?" in *God's Christ and His People*, ed. B. Lindars and S. Smalley (Oslo: Universitetsforlaget, 1977), 192–208.

heavily on worship of such beings (Arnold 1996). But evidence of such practices in the social environment does not necessarily indicate that this is the particular problem Colossians addresses. Reconstructions proposing that these teachers venerate angels have built on the phrase "worship of angels" in 2:18. In the literary context and the construction of the sentence, however, this phrase does not mean that the opponents worship angels but that they engage in angelic worship (Francis 1973: 163–96). Just as the phrase "the worship of the church" designates the worship that the church performs (not that someone worships the church), so this phrase in Colossians indicates that these teachers see angelic worship in their visions and want the church to adopt those worship practices (see the commentary on 2:18).

If we begin with explicit statements about the other teaching, we see that its advocates urge acceptance of some food and drink regulations and the observance of holy days, at least some of which they draw from Judaism (e.g., observance of the Sabbath; see 2:16–17, 21–23). They observe these regulations as a means to attain heavenly visions in which they see angels worship, and they probably join in that angelic worship directed to God (2:18). Less direct statements about these teachers show how they argue that Christians who do not adopt these practices and attain these visions do not have as close a relationship with God as those who have such experiences. In fact, these teachers go so far as to assert that such mystic flights are necessary for forgiveness of sins. This judgment against others in the church is the crux of the problem (2:16). To counter the other teachers' judgments against people who have not experienced these visions, Colossians makes the certainty of forgiveness and of the proper relationship with God its central theme. The writer assures readers that participation in Christ through baptism grants believers forgiveness and all God's other blessings (e.g., 1:12–14, 20–23; 2:9–12, 13–15; 3:1). The writer of Colossians does not object to receiving or seeking heavenly visions or ascents. After all, Paul had visions and other ecstatic experiences; thus, Colossians can hardly reject them. What the author rejects is the insistence that those experiences are mandatory, whether as evidence that one has been granted forgiveness and the proper relationship with God or as the experience required to attain that forgiveness and relationship. These visionaries probably do not intend to oppose Paul or his teaching, but Colossians regards their beliefs as a violation of a central tenet of the gospel.

In no uncertain terms, Colossians rejects these teachers; its evaluations of them and their teaching have a sharp edge. But the polemic does not reach the pitch of 2 Corinthians or Galatians, letters that address churches where a teaching that Paul opposes has begun to make significant inroads or has caused recurrent problems. Thus, the visionaries challenged in Colossians have probably not yet won over the readers. Moreover, the letter does not reprimand its readers for adopting the other teaching but only warns them against accepting it. Still, it appears that the recipients have begun to doubt their salvation. Though many are tempted to adopt the other teaching and its practices, most have resisted to this point. Colossians uses its Christology and eschatology to assure its readers of their salvation and to convince them that the other teaching offers them no spiritual benefit that they do not already possess in Christ.

Reception and Textual Witnesses for the Letter

Although no ancient authors raise questions about the authorship of Colossians, early writers do not certainly allude to it as early as allusions appear from most other Pauline Letters, including Ephesians and the Pastorals. The *Epistle of Barnabas* (12.7) may allude to Col 1:16 when it affirms that "all things are in him and for him," but Barnabas does not attribute this assertion to Colossians, and the wording is not precisely that of Colossians (see the discussion of possible allusions to Colossians in second-century writings in Barth and Blanke 117–18). Both Tertullian (200–250) and Origen (185–254), however, refer to Colossians by name. In his *On Modesty* (12), Tertullian explicitly cites Colossians, attributing it to Paul, and he alludes to the letter later in the same work (19). He cites Colossians again in *Against Marcion* 5.19.1, where he also calls it by name. Origen attributes a passage from Colossians to "the apostle" in *De principiis* 1.1.8. Colossians was also part of Marcion's (110–160) canon, as seen from the Marcionite Prologues. While our first extant record of these prologues is Codex Fuldensis (6th century), most scholars think they have an earlier origin though perhaps they do not come from Marcion himself. Still, they reflect the collection he proposed as the canon in about 150. These second-century references indicate that Colossians was widely accepted as a Pauline letter from early in the second century.

Colossians appears in some of the earliest and most reliable manuscripts of the New Testament. Colossians is present in P[46], a collection of leaves of papyrus from about 200 C.E., that is our earliest witness for many writings of the New Testament. Colossians is also in the two important fourth-century codices B (Codex Vaticanus) and ℵ (Codex Sinaiticus). Beyond these witnesses, Colossians appears in some fifth-century documents, including Codex A (Alexandrinus) and C (Ephraemi Rescriptus). The latter manuscript has the sermons of a later preacher copied over the New Testament writings, but the biblical text has been recovered. Colossians appears as well in many later manuscripts and translations in collections of Paul's Letters. Thus, while there are a number of textual problems in Colossians, good evidence for its text remains available to help us establish its original text.

Theological Themes

All the theological themes Colossians develops serve as means to help its readers recognize that they gain nothing of value from what the other teaching offers. The writer's focus on Christology and realized eschatology contributes to his argument against the view that all believers must attain visionary or mystical experiences to enjoy the fullness of God's blessings. At the same time, he develops an understanding of spirituality that centers on the conduct of one's life in the world, rather than on ecstatic or exalted spiritual experiences.

Soteriology

Soteriology is the central topic of Colossians. The writer's Christology emphasizes the exalted position of Christ to assure readers that their identification with Christ provides them with forgiveness and the proper relationship with God. The extensive attention Colossians gives to developing its Christology does not indicate that the readers have a defective Christology but that they have not recognized the implications of their Christology and of their identification with the exalted and cosmic Christ. Christology stands at the heart of this epistle, but always in the service of soteriological claims.

Colossians gives extraordinary attention to forgiveness of sins. The undisputed Pauline Letters do not make forgiveness a major theme in their discussions of salvation. Usually Paul does not even speak of sin in the plural. Rather than viewing sin as individual evil acts, Paul commonly sees it as a power that captures and imprisons (e.g., Rom 7:7–25). But Colossians resolutely makes forgiveness of sins a central element of its soteriology. This emphasis emerges, in large part, because the teaching the letter opposes asserts that believers without visionary experiences still bear the guilt of their sins.[10]

Colossians interprets various metaphors for salvation in terms of forgiveness. When introducing the liturgical confession about Christ in 1:15–20, the writer uses four metaphors for salvation. He says believers have been made God's heirs, rescued from the powers of darkness, transferred into the kingdom of God's Son, and redeemed. The writer then interprets redemption as the forgiveness of sins. The christological affirmations in 1:15–20 support these assertions about believers' place with God, and most immediately about their forgiveness. When the poetic liturgy concludes by proclaiming Christ's defeat of the powers, the author immediately applies Christ's victory to the readers' lives, asserting that though they were once estranged from God, they now are reconciled through Christ's death and, therefore, stand guiltless in judgment. Thus, assurances of forgiveness frame the christological confession of 1:15–20.

The topic of forgiveness appears again in Colossians' explication of believers' secure relationship with God in 2:9–15. The writer makes forgiveness of their trespasses a corollary of being raised with Christ (v. 13). Their trespasses had brought them death, but now believers have been given life through receiving

---

10. Colossians warns against accepting the other teachers' judgments in 2:4, 8, 16–17.

forgiveness in Christ. Verses 14–15 develop the theme of forgiveness by interpreting the cross as the means by which Christ makes forgiveness possible. In the crucifixion—which here must include the resurrection—the record of believers' sin and the decree of their guilt are erased through Christ's defeat of the powers. No power or person, then, has the authority to bring charges against those who have been raised with Christ in baptism. The forgiveness that believers have received becomes, in turn, the basis for the later exhortation that they forgive one another (3:13).

Colossians always ties forgiveness and its corollaries to identification with Christ. All relationship with God, all forgiveness, all security from hostile spiritual forces, and all spiritual blessings come to believers through their participation in the life of Christ, which God grants them in baptism. Participation in Christ, and nothing else, grants access to all God's blessings. Colossians identifies being "in Christ" as the sphere of salvation (see esp. 2:9–15; also 3:3). Therefore, Colossians has a participationist soteriology. Believers are God's people because they have been incorporated into Christ and thus have been identified with him. Their place in Christ determines their identity and their relationship with God. They have died to their old lives and been raised to new life in Christ and therefore participate in the new eschatological reality that God offers through Christ. As a result, they can live a life of service to God without fear that hostile spiritual powers might disrupt that relationship, and without fear of condemnation. The only condition attached to their continuing participation in Christ is faithfulness to the gospel they have already received from Epaphras, the founder of their church and coworker with Paul.

Colossians also commonly interprets salvation as release from hostile spiritual powers. The apocalyptic eschatology characteristic of the early church assumed the existence of powers in the cosmos that actively oppose God's will and seek to harm God's people. These powers have seized control of the world and taken its inhabitants captive. Moreover, they encourage evil and destructive behavior and thus diminish people's lives. Through cooperation with these powers and participation in sinful acts, people separate themselves from God. Humans cannot free themselves from their captivity to these powers; liberation requires an act of God.

Colossians proclaims that Christ has freed believers from the power of these beings, declaring that Christ has defeated them and so reclaimed believers for God (2:14–15, 20). Christ has not only rescued believers but also transferred them into his own realm. Therefore, they no longer serve those hostile powers but are citizens of a different kingdom (1:12–14), in which they are heirs with Christ, properly qualified to receive all God's blessings. Believers are also freed from their fear of these beings because Christ, who has defeated the powers, protects them. As a result of their participation in Christ's eschatological kingdom, believers can serve God wholeheartedly, knowing that these beings cannot disrupt their relationship with God. Furthermore, these beings have no spiritual blessings to offer people who have been incorporated into Christ. Even nonhostile spiritual powers (e.g., angels) have no gift to offer that believers do not already enjoy in Christ. For Colossians, identification with Christ brings all spiritual gifts.

Colossians' proclamation of Christ's victory over the powers and of believers' release from them does not imply that those powers have no continuing influence in the world. The readers of Colossians know well that their membership in the church has led to conflict with the world around them; indeed, the virtues and way of life that Colossians identifies as appropriate for believers have brought social and economic disadvantage. Members of the church have often experienced difficulties, and even persecution, when their new way of life in Christ prompted them to reject the practices and customs of the broader culture. Believers must endure these troubles because the powers that Christ has defeated continue to determine the structures of the world and society. Christ's victory will not be fully evident in the world until the Parousia, when all will acknowledge the lordship of Christ.

Colossians proclaims its message of Christ's victory with language that echoes Rome's claims about itself. Rome claimed to bring peace and good news (a gospel). It interpreted its dominance as the will of the gods, exercised for the good of the world. Rome even called its emperor "Lord" and identified him (or his predecessors) as a son of a god who deserved veneration (*Res. gest.* 12–13; Appian, *Bell. civ.* 5.130). Through these claims, Rome asserted that heavenly powers had authorized the way the empire structured society.

The early church experienced the dominance of Rome and the societal structures it supported as neither good news nor the will of God. Rather, the structures of the world conflicted with the church's beliefs and practices; therefore, Rome's interpretation of the world differed sharply from the church's. Even as Colossians proclaims that the powers upholding these systems have been defeated, it must provide guidance to its readers on how to live in a world still determined by them. The letter's proclamation of salvation does not remove believers from this difficult situation, but it does promise them that God will render judgment on the injustices of this world; a reward lies ahead for the faithful, while judgment awaits those who afflict them.

The new life and new understanding of the cosmos that believers possess relativizes recognized social, ethnic, and economic distinctions to the point that such differences no longer determine the way believers value one another (3:11). Thus, the church's teaching and life reflect a set of values that run counter to the rest of society. While living out such beliefs may present many problems, the blessings of community and relationship with God (among other things) mark this manner of life as a participation in salvation.

Therefore, in addition to defining salvation in terms of forgiveness of sins, participation in Christ, and release from the powers, Colossians maintains that salvation entails adopting a manner of life consistent with the character of God. Participation in Christ requires believers to conform their lives to Christ, who is the image of God (1:15; 3:9–10). This new way of life is both a demand and a gift. Their faith must include adopting this manner of life, and these demands enhance their lives as individuals and as a community.

Christology

Christology provides the primary support for Colossians' assertions about the security of believers' salvation. The center of the letter's theological thought is found in the interplay between Christology and soteriology, that is, between who Christ is and what that means for believers' relationship with God. Colossians emphasizes Christ's exalted place with God: Christ reigns over the cosmos and all that is in it (2:10–11). Christ attains this position, in part, by defeating the powers that oppose God's will (1:18–20; 2:15). Thus, God exalts him to the highest place in heaven (3:1). In all of this, Christ works as God's agent. Furthermore, the fullness of God's nature dwells in Christ (1:19; 2:9). With this fullness, Christ comes into the world with the power of God to accomplish God's purposes. Christ realizes these purposes most evidently in his cross and resurrection, where God both defeats the powers and secures all blessings for those who identify with Christ (2:14–15). Therefore, both Christ's nature and his work fit him for this exalted position.

Colossians goes beyond affirmations of the presence of God in Christ's salvation-bestowing acts; it also identifies Christ as God's agent in creation. Israel's Wisdom literature had earlier identified Wisdom as the one through whom God created the world (e.g., Prov 3:19; Wis 7:22; 8:6; 14:2). Colossians transfers the mediating of creation to the preexistent Christ. The preformed liturgical piece in 1:15–20 asserts that Christ is the one through whom all things were created and by whom the cosmos is sustained. This description of Christ's work, which predates the writing of Colossians, makes him the highest being in the cosmos not only because he lived before anything came into being but also because all came into existence through him and continues to exist through his power.

Colossians identifies Christ with God even more fully than its expressions of Christ's exaltation imply. While its statements about Christ's nature press beyond anything in the undisputed letters, these explications do not necessarily conflict with the understanding of Christ found in earlier Pauline writings. Paul's own descriptions of the nature of Christ contain unresolved tensions,[11]

---

11. We see such a tension in Paul's Christology by comparing Rom 1:4, where Paul says Christ was "declared to be Son of God" through the resurrection, with Phil 2:6, which affirms Christ's preexistence in the "form of God." Even if these statements can be reconciled, they approach the identity of Christ from significantly different angles.

and some trajectories of his proclamations about Christ cohere with the ampli-
fications evident in Colossians (see particularly Phil 2:6–8). Paul's unelabo-
rated statement in 1 Cor 8:6, where he says that all things are "through Christ,"
suggests that he credits Christ with a role in creating, and perhaps sustaining,
the cosmos. Therefore, the more elaborate statement in Colossians does not represent a substantial departure from some directions of Paul's own thought. The
affirmations about Christ in 1 Corinthians, Philippians, and Colossians all contributed to the church's development of the doctrine of the Trinity.

Colossians identifies this preexistent Christ who mediated creation as God's
agent of salvation. It is this cosmic Christ who effects salvation and constitutes
the eschatological realm in which believers reside; their lives are hidden with
him (3:3) because he is not just the ruler of the cosmos but also the head of the
church (1:18). Believers identify with this most powerful of beings in baptism,
where they become members of his body and are raised to share this exalted
Christ's relationship with God. Believers also gain all knowledge of God in
Christ because that knowledge resides fully in him (2:3). This exalted understanding of Christ therefore assures believers that they lack no spiritual blessing, because they have been incorporated into him.

In Colossians, then, Christ is the means through which God exercises sovereignty in the world. Christ mediates God's power and presence to the world
in creation, redemption, and the consummation of all things. The full and final
victory of God will be a manifestation of Christ that includes the glorification
of those identified with him (3:4). God's love, presence, and justice thus come
to fullest expression in this one who is "the image of the unseen God" (1:15).

Eschatology

Colossians emphasizes believers' present possession of eschatological blessings. The author asserts that they have already been raised with Christ (2:12–13;
3:1) and have already been made full (2:10). While Paul often speaks of receiving new life in Christ (e.g., Rom 6:1–4), he does not explicitly use resurrection
language to speak of the present existence of believers in the undisputed letters.
Despite its distinctive use of resurrection language, however, Colossians, too,
looks forward to a future eschatological act to manifest God's will for the world
(3:1–4, 25).

Colossians' claims that believers already possess the blessings of the eschatological age cluster around its most direct statements against the visionaries'
teaching. Though they appear in a few other places, the clearest assertions about
present enjoyment of eschatological blessings serve to counter the teaching that
believers need certain experiences and practices to supplement what they have
received in baptism. This clustering suggests that the letter's emphasis on realized eschatology plays an important role in the author's rejection of the false

teaching. Contrary to the visionaries' teaching, believers need no additional spiritual experiences to gain or affirm their forgiveness and relationship with God; rather, they already have full access to God's blessings in Christ through baptism. Thus, the letter's emphasis on realized eschatology reflects its rhetorical exigence[12] (more, perhaps, than it indicates a significant shift from Paul's eschatological outlook).

Colossians also declares that the eschatological blessings that believers will receive at the Parousia now exist in heaven. The letter's use of spatial imagery to describe the eschatological blessings (e.g., these blessings are already "laid up in the heavens," 1:5) complements its emphasis on the present possession of those gifts but does not indicate that it lacks a future orientation.

Some apocalyptic works combine spatial imagery with clear expectations of a future consummation. For example, *2 Baruch* speaks of eschatological realities that exist now but will not be revealed until the consummation (4:2–7; 48:42–52; see the commentary on Col 3:4). Colossians' allusions to coming judgment (1:23, 27, 28; 3:6, 24–25; 4:1) also manifest a lively expectation of a future act of God.[13] Given the direct reference to a future revelation of Christ in 3:4, the author expects the Parousia to include judgment, as the passing reference to the coming wrath of God in 3:6 confirms.

Thus, Colossians retains a significant future element in its eschatology. Indeed, the letter's understanding of the church's place in the world requires a future act of God. The epistle proclaims Christ as the victor over all powers, but that victory is not yet evident in the structure and conduct of the world. The author recognizes the tensions between his proclamations about Christ and believers' place in him, on the one hand, and the actual lived experience of believers who must still contend with a hostile world, on the other. The world's refusal to recognize the lordship of Christ demands a future eschatological act, a time when Christ's lordship will be evident and believers' true identity, now hidden, will be manifested (3:4).

The absence of urgency about the imminence of the end does distinguish Colossians from many of the undisputed letters. Paul conditions his advice about marriage in 1 Corinthians 7 on the expectation that the "time has grown short" (v. 29). In this passage, he anticipates the Parousia in the near future. Interpreters often assume that all the undisputed letters reflect this expectation. In Philippians, however, Paul considers the possibility of his death before the Parousia (1:21–26; see also 2 Cor 5:1–10). The timing of the consummation has

12. The letter's exigence includes the situation of the reader and author, and most particularly what leads the writer to compose the document.
13. These statements about being prepared for judgment are much like statements in the undisputed letters that expect judgment at the Parousia (see, e.g., Phil 1:10).

lost some of its importance here; he does say that "the Lord is near" (Phil 4:5), but this timing carries no weight in the letter. Still, Paul probably continues to expect that the Parousia lies in the not-too-distant future. Colossians contains only one passage suggesting that its author expects the end to come soon. In its closing exhortations—the same place Paul speaks of the end's timing in Philippians—Colossians encourages its readers to "redeem the time" (4:5). This injunction seems to imply an expectation that the Parousia is drawing near. Nevertheless, the timing of the Parousia does not shape Colossians' message; it stands in the background, without playing a significant role in the letter's argument. Therefore, while *certainty* of the Parousia holds an important place in Colossians, its *immediacy* does not.

Spirituality

Questions about the nature of Christian spirituality underlie much of the argument of Colossians. The false teachers advocate an understanding of spirituality that emphasizes extraordinary experiences, particularly visions. They make such otherworldly experiences central to Christian life and a relationship with God, and their moderately ascetic practices ("Do not hold, Do not taste, and Do not touch," 2:21) have the goal of producing these heavenly flights. The primary thing the recipient gains from these visions is a personal, individual experience of God that provides assurance of one's own salvation. The individualistic nature of their pursuit is evident in their condemnation of believers who have not attained such states. These extraordinary experiences may enrich the individual who has the vision, but they offer nothing to the church community. Even when these teachers try to incorporate elements of the angelic worship they observe into the church's worship, the focus remains on what the individual gains from the vision, because they continue to condemn believers who have not attained such experiences. Thus, the teachers' spirituality is oriented primarily toward the individual.

Such an understanding of spirituality and contact with a god is common in the Greco-Roman cultural environment, where religious experiences often had an individualistic orientation. The experience of a god attained through initiation into a mystery religion is a good example. These cults held many open services and publicly proclaimed myths about their gods, but the ceremony in which a person attained a closer association with the god was closed and private. In these initiations, the only persons present were the priests and initiates, and the rites involved secret rituals and activities that the initiates swore not to reveal (Apuleius, *Metam.* 11.48). Such initiation ceremonies offered a personal and ecstatic experience of the god. Various ancient writers testify about the power of these experiences to bring hope and goodness to life; they give the initiated a feeling of importance in the cosmos and hope of life beyond death (see, e.g., Cicero, *Leg.* 2.14.36; Apuleius, *Metam.* 11.47–48; Julian, *Symp.* 336C).[14] All of this comes through a mystical and ecstatic experience of a god. This private experience, however, does nothing for other people or a community. It does not enrich others' knowledge of the god or bring noninitiates closer to the god. Benefit accrues only to the one initiated.

This way of cultivating a spiritual connection with the gods defined spirituality for many in the Greco-Roman world. A similar framework for understanding religious experiences also seems to condition how the visionaries that Colossians opposes think about spirituality. They expect each person to have an experience that does little for the rest of the community beyond establishing such visions as a requirement for others.

Other ways of understanding and using mystical and visionary experiences, however, were common in this era. While such experiences are intensely personal by their very nature, they may also serve the good of a community. Many apocalyptic writings tell of visionary experiences, but without demanding that all the faithful seek such experiences of God; the recipients, instead, return with messages for their communities that offer hope and encouragement (e.g., Revelation, *1 Enoch*, and other apocalyptic texts that relate visionary experiences). In these settings, such experiences serve a wider good, not just the salvation or exaltation of the one who has the vision. Similarly, Paul's own vision of the risen Christ conveys his commission to spread the gospel—though he recognized the danger of pride associated with receiving such experiences (2 Cor 12:7–10). Thus, the writer of Colossians can tap resources that help him define the role of visionary experiences in a manner different from much of the surrounding culture.

Colossians does not reject the validity of visions but does shift the focus so that extraordinary experiences are not a necessary element of spirituality. For Colossians, spirituality consists largely of discerning how to live as a Christian amid the complexities of life. When this writer exhorts readers to "seek the things above" (3:1), he depicts this pursuit as putting sin out of their lives and adopting the virtues appropriate to their new life in Christ. Thus, he redefines seeking the "things above" in a dramatic and unexpected way, directing attention to behavior in this world rather than to what one may experience in some other realm. The author's understanding of spirituality begins with the assumption that believers have been raised with Christ and so already possess the gifts that come from being in the presence of God. Believers can attain no higher status or more important experience than possessing life in Christ—and this is a life shared with the whole body of believers. The only exalted experience they

---

14. See also Walter Burkert, *Ancient Mystery Cults* (Cambridge, Mass.: Harvard University Press, 1987), 23–29.

need to look for will come at the Parousia, when they will all be revealed together with Christ (3:4).

For Colossians, then, Christian spirituality comes to expression in one's manner of life, not the attainment of otherworldly experiences. Seeking the "things above" means adopting virtues that serve the good of the community, because the instructions that accompany this exhortation involve relations within the community (see the commentary on 3:5–11, 12–17). Since the injunction "Seek the things above" introduces the main body of ethical instructions, the letter presents all its ethical exhortations as expressions of the spirituality it advocates. Colossians, thus, reorients the thought of its readers by making proper ethical living, particularly in the context of the gathered church, the central manifestation of Christian spirituality. Proper behavior therefore constitutes the primary way believers live out their exalted position as persons raised with the one who sits at God's right hand in the highest heaven.

The central theological themes of Colossians assure readers of their place with God and of the full sufficiency of their identification with Christ for attaining that position. Through various means, then, this letter maintains that believers need nothing beyond their participation in Christ to confidently possess forgiveness and salvation—indeed, the fullness of God's eschatological blessings.

COMMENTARY

COLOSSIANS 1:1–2

Epistolary Greeting

The greetings of the Pauline Letters follow the standard form found in other Hellenistic letters. The Pauline greetings also often reflect the situation the letter addresses. Such flexibility is not unusual for the greeting of a Hellenistic letter. Writers enlarged or shortened the greeting to meet the need of the moment. Paul sometimes expands his greetings to emphasize some aspect of his identity or relationship with the recipients (e.g., his apostolic authority [Gal 1:1–5] or his close personal relationship with the recipients [Phlm 1–2]). The greeting of Colossians indicates that "Paul" is exercising his apostolic commission in the writing of this letter. In a pseudonymous letter, using the designation "apostle" establishes the letter's authority for the readers who now receive it. Since the church receives the letter in the context of worship, perhaps the greeting also invokes, or assures the recipients of, the presence of God among them (see Schweizer 27).

1:1 Paul, an apostle of Christ Jesus by the will of God, and Timothy, the brother, 2 to the holy[a] and faithful brothers and sisters[b] in Christ[c] who are in Colossae; grace and peace from God our Father be with you.[d]

a. This phrase might be rendered "to the saints and faithful brothers and sisters." However, the single article *tois* seems to govern both *hagiois* and *pistois*.

b. The Greek text has only "brothers" (*adelphois*), but the writer clearly means all members of the congregation.

c. Codex A, the original hand of D, and some later manuscripts add *Iēsou* here, but the preponderance of manuscript evidence is with the shorter reading. The reading in the text is also to be preferred because it is the shorter reading, and it is more likely that a copyist added "Jesus" than that it was dropped from the text.

d. A number of manuscripts, including ℵ, A, and C, add after *hēmōn* ("our") the phrase *kai kyriou Iēsou christou* ("and the Lord Jesus Christ"). This assimilates Colossians to the more-common greeting in the Pauline Letters. Some form of the expression "and the Lord Jesus Christ" is found in every other letter in the Pauline corpus. So the temptation for a copyist to insert it, either accidentally or intentionally, would have been great. That it dropped out seems much less likely, especially since the reading without the addition is also widely known (it is in B, D [among others], and many early translations).

[1:1] This greeting begins with Paul establishing his apostolic credentials by noting both whose apostle he is (Christ Jesus') and how he came to be one (by God's will). With this brief phrase, Colossians both establishes Paul's authority and places him under the will of God. This combination signals that Paul holds this position only because of the gracious act of God on his behalf. Indeed, for Paul, a person can only become an apostle if God commissions him or her directly (see 1 Cor 15:8–10). So apostleship is a gift from God, one of the gifts that contributes to the building up of the church (cf. 1 Cor 12:28–30; also Eph 4:11–12). The presence of this title does not indicate that Paul's authority or claim to be an apostle is under attack. Rather, its use points to the official character of the letter and establishes its authority. This assertion of authority would be necessary whether Paul himself is writing to the Colossians, whom he has never visited,[1] or whether another has appropriated Paul's name to claim his authority for the matters to be discussed.[2]

Readers who do not know Paul might take offense at this only slightly veiled assertion of authority. If so, attributing his apostleship to the will of God not only secures its validity but also makes his claim more acceptable. When Plutarch gives advice on how to avoid resentment when praising oneself, he recommends attributing one's success to the will of the gods (*On Inoffensive Self-Prase*, in *Mor.* 542). Naming God as the source and reason for Paul's apostleship, then, lessens the offense of asserting apostolic authority even as it indicates that he has God's approval.

In contrast to the claim of office made for Paul, Timothy is simply "the brother." Since the Colossians themselves are called "brothers" in the next verse, "brother" does not designate any official position or role (contra Barth and Blanke 138–39), as "fellow worker" (Col 4:11; Rom 16:21) and "fellow servant" (Col 1:7) do later in the letter. In the undisputed letters, Paul refers to Timothy in the greetings of 2 Corinthians and Philemon as simply "the brother" (in 1 Corinthians Paul refers to Sosthenes in the same way). This characterization of Timothy in relation to Paul perhaps places him on a more equal footing with Paul than do the Pastorals, where Timothy is called Paul's child (1 Tim 1:2, 18; 2 Tim 1:2; 2:1). Calling Timothy "brother" clearly identifies him with the letter's recipients, to whom the writer immediately ascribes the same designation. This commonality with Timothy helps to strengthen the relationship between Paul and the recipients, whom the writer grants the same status as the known associate and companion of the apostle.

---

1. Lightfoot (131) comments that Paul uses the title because he "interposes by virtue of his Apostolic commission."

2. This whole first line of the Colossians greeting is exactly the same as that of 2 Corinthians and Ephesians and very similar to 1 Corinthians (which only adds *klētos* ["called"] immediately before *apostolos* ["apostle"]).

[2] As discussed in the introduction, this letter addresses (at least, purport-edly) the Christian community in a rather small and insignificant city. Colos-sians, however, envisions a broader audience than just the churches of Colossae because the writer instructs these readers to forward the letter to the nearby town of Laodicea (4:16). Still, Colossians is a letter, not a theological treatise. This letter clearly addresses the situation the author understands the readers to be facing.[3]

The writer first describes the letter's recipients as *hagiois*. This term could be construed as a noun, in which case the author begins by calling them "saints." Use of *hagios* in Pauline greetings favors this view: every other time this word appears in a Pauline greeting, it is the substantive. However, the writer of Colossians appends a second title, "faithful brothers." The grammat-ical construction in Colossians is distinctive because a single definite article ("the") governs both *hagiois* and *pistois* (faithful), as well as the noun "broth-ers." In this construction, *hagiois* and *pistois* serve better as adjectives modi-fying the noun "brothers." Thus the translation would be: "holy and faithful brothers [and sisters]." Whether the author intends to call them "saints and faithful brothers [and sisters]" or "holy and faithful brothers [and sisters]," this beginning assigns to the readers laudable attributes that he hopes to reinforce by writing this letter.

Calling the recipients "holy" draws upon several nuances of the word as it is used in the Bible and in the early church.[4] Throughout the Old Testament, Israel is holy because God has chosen or elected them (e.g., Exod 19:6; Lev 11:44; 1 Sam 2:2; 2 Chr 8:11; 31:18; Jer 2:3). Those texts voice two primary meanings for holiness: separateness or distinctiveness and possessing a moral character. As God's chosen people, the Israelites must separate themselves from the profane to maintain their relationship with God. As they reflect God's dis-tinctiveness in that relationship, they must also reflect God's moral character and so live holy lives. Thus Israel could not divorce its election from the requirement to be holy, in both senses. Similarly, the church as elected by God cannot separate its election from moral behavior, as Colossians' later use of "holy" in its instructions for living indicates (3:12).

When the writer calls the readers "faithful," as well as "holy," it is surely hortatory as well as descriptive (just as it was when he called them "holy"); that is, he calls them to be faithful even as he asserts that they are. By designating them as "faithful," he does more than acknowledge that they have put their trust in Christ; he also encourages them to remain faithful to the gospel they have

---

3. See the discussion of M. L. Stirewalt Jr. 1977.

4. Aletti (47) says we cannot know the connotation of "holy" because it is used in so many ways, though, he adds, use of the term in 1:22 and 3:1–4:1 may allow us to say more. However, it seems unnecessary to limit a term of such broad use to a single nuance or connotation.

received. In the face of new and defective teaching, such encouragement is especially appropriate for a letter that aims to secure the readers' steadfastness to the gospel that they have already received.[5]

The writer does not call the Colossians a "church" but instead addresses them as "brothers [and sisters]." Paul does not call the recipients of a letter "brothers" in any greeting among the undisputed letters (Hübner 43). Neither, however, does Paul always refer to those addressed as the "church." The greetings of neither Romans nor Philippians include the term *ekklēsia* (church), though Paul does call the members of those communities "saints." Thus, the absence of the term *ekklēsia* may have no significance, especially if the letter is pseudonymous, in which case we should expect changes from the Pauline pattern (even if unintentional). While the absence of "church" could be more than just an accident (contra Meyer 209), the writer probably does not intend to begin the letter with a polemical accent by dividing the church into the faithful believers and those listening to the false teachers (contra Lindemann 17). Still, no other letter in the Pauline corpus uses the term "brothers" as an address of the recipients. Perhaps the writer has Paul use the more personal address "brothers" because Paul does not know them personally, and thus the writer seeks to establish a connection with them (so Abbott 193). More important, this address calls the readers to recognize that as members of the Christ-confessing community, they are bound together in a fundamental relationship expressed with this familial language (so Aletti 46). This is no small thing; they are "brothers," just as is Timothy. So they have a close and personal relationship with an apostle and those who are near him. Furthermore, use of this familial language entails significant expectations about the ways they relate to one another.

The intimate, familial relationship shared among the recipients and with "Paul" is grounded "in Christ." This phrase bases these relationships on the saving work of God in Christ. It also designates the sphere in which believers live; they reside in the realm governed by Christ. Throughout the entire letter, the writer will develop the significance of this assertion. Much of the reason he writes involves defining what it means to be "in Christ."

The concluding benediction of Pauline greetings is an adaptation of the common greeting in Hellenistic letters and some Jewish letters. In Hellenistic letters, the greeting often closes with *chairein*, "Greetings." The Pauline formula uses *charis* (grace), a change of only a few letters but an important change in thought worlds. This change specifically invokes the grace of God as a blessing and so puts the readers in a new context, a context determined by the grace

5. Lightfoot (132) comments that calling these recipients "faithful brothers" "obliquely hints at the defection" of some to the other teaching. This is probably reading too much into these words.

that comes through Christ. In place of the common wish for health following *chairein*, the Pauline greetings employ "peace." Such language also appears in some Jewish letters of the era;[6] the idea of peace found in the Old Testament therefore probably lies behind its use in the Pauline Letters. This peace was not just psychological well-being; it also signals a relationship with God that includes personal wholeness, a social dimension, and a commitment to living a moral life (O'Brien 5–6). Such meanings are mostly implicit here because this is a stereotypical formula (similar to our "God bless you"; see Bratcher and Nida, 1977, 5).

All of the Pauline Letters except 1 Thessalonians and Colossians name "God our [or the] Father and the Lord Jesus Christ" as the source of the grace and peace mentioned in the benediction. First Thessalonians mentions neither the "Father" nor "Christ" but has simply "Grace and peace." The Pastorals change the standard form found in other Pauline Letters but still indicate that the blessings come from the "Father" and "Christ." Colossians alone has these blessings come from only "God our Father." Perhaps the author does not mention Christ for a third time in this greeting because the phrase that immediately precedes the benediction ends with a reference to Christ.[7] This omission implies no diminution of Christ; the poetic material in 1:15–20 will shortly supply an exalted Christology. The omission of Christ in this formula does, however, cast serious doubt on the thesis that the main issue of Colossians centers on Christology: in that case the author would hardly have lessened Christ's role in the community's experience of God by failing to mention him in this part of the letter's greeting.

The greeting, then, serves several purposes. First, it establishes Paul's position as an apostle, an apostle whose commission comes from God. This commission puts Paul in a good position from which to address the recipients' questions and problems. The greeting also attributes a rather high status to the implied readers: they are holy and faithful. These complimentary designations describe the readers and also call them to live up to those characteristics. In addition to these descriptions, the greeting identifies them as siblings and thus reminds them that they share an intimate connection with one another that is grounded in Christ. Perhaps this begins to hint that they should be of a single mind on the matters causing the problems that the letter addresses. The attribution of all these identities prepares the (implied and actual) readers to receive the letter's content more favorably.

---

6. See 2 Macc 1:1, where greetings and peace are both included.

7. Lohse's assertion (11) that Paul leaves out "Christ" for the sake of maintaining variety in his greetings seems unlikely.

COLOSSIANS 1:3–23

Introductory Thanksgiving and Prayer

After the greeting, Colossians moves into a period of thanksgiving such as we usually find in Pauline Letters.[8] These periods of thanksgiving and prayer are ordinarily fairly short (among the undisputed letters they average just less than 125 words in length with none being more than 195 words) and distinct. In nearly all the letters in the Pauline corpus the writer signals the beginning of the section that follows the thanksgiving with either a disclosure formula (e.g., 2 Cor 1:8 RSV ["We do not want you to be unaware"]; also Rom 1:16; Phil 1:12; 1 Thess 2:1; 2 Tim 1:15) or an exhortation (e.g., 1 Cor 1:10 NRSV ["Now I appeal to you"]; also 2 Thess 2:1; Phlm 8). These formulas help the reader identify the transition to the body of the letter. No such transition marker appears in Colossians. The introductory thanksgiving/prayer of Colossians is much longer than in other Pauline Letters, extending through 1:23. The last phrase of 1:23 changes from the preceding second-person plural (you) to first-person singular (I). This first-person perspective continues as a new sentence and paragraph begin in 1:24. The passage beginning in 1:24 interprets the suffering of Paul as something that brings benefits to the readers. This thought is clearly distinct from the thanksgiving and thus marks the beginning of a new thought unit. Though there is some justification for ending the thanksgiving at either 1:11 or 1:14, it is preferable to extend this opening section through 1:23. The flow of thought and web of connections throughout this section indicate that the whole of 1:3–23 is a unified prayer of thanksgiving and intercession that introduces the major themes of the letter.[9]

As has long been recognized, the thanksgivings in Paul's Letters "telegraph" the themes that he will develop in the rest of the letter. The thanksgiving prayer of Colossians serves much the same function. In the language of rhetorical criticism, Col 1:3–23 is the exordium, a passage that introduces the audience to the subject and begins leading them to a favorable disposition toward the speaker (or in this case the writer). The most prominent theme in 1:3–23 is that Chris-

---

8. The only exceptions are Galatians and perhaps 2 Cor 10–13, if the redactor has not eliminated that thanksgiving; 2 Cor 1 has a blessing that serves the same purpose as a thanksgiving in that letter.

9. See, e.g., Lohse 13; Pokorný 36; Aletti 49–51; Barth and Blanke 148. Lamarche (454–56) makes 1:20 the last verse of the introductory section, with 1:21–23 beginning the next section and presenting the major themes that will appear through 2:15. While it is correct that 1:21–23 sets out the matters to be discussed in the following section, these verses seem to fit better with what has gone before, especially given the clear transition at 1:24.

tians can be certain that they have a secure relationship with God and that they already possess God's blessings because they are in Christ.

This long introductory prayer may be subdivided into five interrelated parts: 1:3–8, 9–11b, 11c–14, 15–20, and 21–23. Verses 3–8 contain the initial thanksgiving. The prayer continues with intercession in vv. 9–11(b). Verses 11c-14 serve both as an initial conclusion for vv. 3–11b and as the introduction to the poetic material in vv. 15–20. Standing in this central place in the opening of the letter, vv. 11c-14 introduce themes that will be further elaborated in 1:21–23, the verses that set out the primary thesis of Colossians and give theme and structure to much of the rest of the letter.

1:3–8 The Initial Thanksgiving

1:3 We give thanks to God,[a] the Father of our Lord Jesus Christ, every time we pray for you, 4 because we have heard about your faith in Christ Jesus and the love you have for all the saints 5 because of the hope stored up for you in the heavens. You heard before about this hope in the Word of truth, that is, the gospel 6 that has come and remains present among you, just as it has gone out into the whole world.[b] It is bearing fruit and growing there just as it has been with you from the day you heard it and came to know the grace of God in truth. 7 This is the message you learned from Epaphras our beloved fellow slave who is a faithful servant of Christ for you.[c] 8 He has told us about your love in the Spirit.

a. In the Pauline Letters, it is unusual for God to be called the Father of Christ, and in other places where this does occur, a *kai* ("and") is found between *theos* ("God") and *patēr* ("Father"). Within the Pauline materials, God is called the Father of Christ only in 2 Cor 1:3; Eph 1:3; 5:20. In each case there is a *kai* between God and Father. For Col 1:3, a *kai* is found in א, A, a corrector of C, and several other manuscripts. An alternative reading adds *tō*; this reading is present in the original hand of D and in F and G. The reading adopted here appears in P⁶¹, B, and the original hand of C. It can account for the other readings more easily, and it is the difficult reading (cf. Metzger 619).

b. *Kathōs kai en panti tō kosmō* may modify the preceding phrase ("present among you") or the one following ("bearing fruit and growing"). Many translations (including the NRSV) and the UBS 4th and Nestle-Aland 26th editions group it with the following phrase. However, Abbott (197, 199) and Barth and Blanke (157) argue that it should modify the preceding phrase and so be a statement about the spread of the gospel. This latter reading is accepted here because it makes the statement less repetitive, though as Barth and Blanke note, it remains rather infelicitous.

c. "For us" or "on our behalf" has the clear support from the early Greek manuscripts (including P⁴⁶, א, A, and B). However, the Nestle-Aland 26th and UBS 4th editions choose "you" rather than "us." Metzger (619–20) explains this decision by saying that the editorial committee was impressed by how widespread this reading was within patristic witnesses and early translations. He adds that *hēmōn* ("us") may have been introduced because of the influence of the *hēmōn* in the preceding clause. See the discussion of v. 7 below.

Long, elaborate sentences are a feature of the style of Colossians, and the initial thanksgiving exemplifies this: 1:3–8 is a single sentence.[10] Though some interpreters find a chiasmus (e.g., Lamarche 453–54) or some less exact concentric structure (e.g., Aletti 50, 55) in vv. 3–8, it seems best simply to say that several themes are repeated with varying degrees of emphasis. The audience would not have experienced such repetition as tedious, and it enabled the author to make his points more clearly. Most of those who experienced Colossians heard it rather than read it. Thus, the writer must formulate the letter's message so that it is persuasive and memorable for those who hear it. A writer could accomplish this through the repetition of themes and, at times, this was done by using concentric structures.

[3] Verses 3–8 contain the author's report of Paul's thanksgiving for the Colossians and give grounds for his thankfulness about them. As is the case with nearly all the letters in the Pauline corpus (1 Thessalonians, Philemon, and 2 Timothy are the only exceptions), this thanksgiving begins by using the first-person plural ("we"). Thus, the thanksgiving formally comes from Paul and Timothy, the other person mentioned in the greeting. However, the "we" in such thanksgivings refers primarily to Paul since others mentioned in the greetings are invisible for most of the letter.[11] That is certainly the case here; Timothy plays no prominent role in Colossians.

The author addresses the thanksgiving to God, whom he identifies as the "Father of our Lord Jesus Christ." Other Pauline thanksgivings insert "and" (*kai*) between "God" and "Father," but not Colossians. Perhaps the omission of *kai* stems from the borrowing of language from a confession or other formula commonly used in early Christian worship (so Lohse 15; O'Brien 10) or adds an emphasis on Christ, who will be the focus in vv. 13–20. This omission may, however, simply reflect the author's customary way of speaking of God. The absence of "and" does allow a distinctive understanding of the relationship between God and Christ. If the word were present, the phrase would designate God as the God of Christ, an affirmation that clearly puts Christ in a subordinate position. Omission of the "and" may therefore lessen the element of subordination in the statement because God is the Father but not the God of Christ. In the first century the position of father certainly included holding a superior place in relation to one's son, but in comparison with being someone's God, the role of father is less exalted. At the same time, identifying God as the Father of Christ may also emphasize the relationship between them.

---

10. The other sentences in the introductory section are also lengthy: vv. 9–(16) 20; vv. 21–23.
11. As Lohse (14) comments, this "we" really refers to "the apostle as an individual."

The church probably borrowed the identification of God as "Father" from Judaism. In the Old Testament and other Jewish texts, this designation of God meant that God is the one who bequeathed the inheritance to Israel, the one who cares for Israel as a parent cares for a child, and the one who is worthy of honor and obedience (Num 26:53–56; 1 Chr 29:10–13; Isa 61:7–10; 63:16; Jer 3:19; 31:9).[12] The themes of inheritance (e.g., Col 1:12, 15) and discerning who is worthy of obedience (e.g., 2:4–5, 8) play important roles in Colossians.

The writer identifies Jesus as "Lord" in v. 3. The church assigned this title to Jesus at a very early date because it identified Jesus as the one at the right hand of God, the one who rules for God and executes the will of God. Although 1:15–20 will emphasize the significance of Jesus, Colossians, like other Pauline Letters, already names Jesus "Lord" in the greeting or the opening of the thanksgiving. The combination of calling Jesus "Lord" here and in the poetic material of 1:15–20 shows that Colossians has a developed and fairly high Christology, but omission of "and" between "God" and "Father" probably does not signal that this letter's Christology is higher or more developed than that of some other Pauline Letters, particularly Philippians.

The author writes that Paul gives thanks "every time" he prays for the recipients. The phrase "every time" is a rendering of the adverb "always" (*pantote*). This expression is often translated "praying always." At times this phrase has been mistakenly understood to be a comment about Paul's vigilance in prayer. But stating that one "prays always" for another person is a common form of hyperbole found in both Jewish and pagan letters (O'Brien 10). While "always" (*pantote*) links grammatically to "praying," its intention is to signal that Paul's remembrance of the recipients regularly gives him cause to offer God thanks.[13] The phrase reveals more about Paul's care for the Colossians than about his prayer habits.

The entire opening section of the letter (vv. 3–23) serves to establish good relations with the Colossians. This statement of Paul's remembrance of them in prayer introduces this *philophronēsis* ("kind treatment" designed to gain favor with the readers). Verse 3, that is, begins providing evidence of Paul's goodwill toward the recipients by drawing attention to the good feelings he has when he remembers them in prayer.

[4–6] Verses 4–6 articulate the grounds for the thanks that Paul renders when he prays about the Colossians. These verses continue the building of a warm relationship between Paul and the Colossians. For other readers, it shows Paul

12. See Marianne Meye Thompson, *The Promise of the Father: Jesus and God in the New Testament* (Louisville: Westminster John Knox, 2000), 18, 35–55.

13. Lightfoot (133) argues that *pantote* goes with *peri hymōn*. That reading does capture an important dimension of the meaning and has the proximity of the two parts to commend it. However, Eph 5:20 took the adverb "always" to be attached to "praying," and it seems more in line with Pauline usage to take it with a form of a verb.

to be a person of goodwill and so helps to construct an image of Paul that will lead readers to trust him.

Verses 4 and 5 contain the Pauline triad "faith, hope, and love." Well known from 1 Cor 13, this triad also appears in 1 Thess 1:3, where the three parts appear in the same order as in Col 1:4–5. Since there is no compelling evidence that Paul was the first to put these three together, this combination may have been in use before Paul took it up. As we will see, these terms do not all mean the same things here that they do in 1 Corinthians. This could be evidence that the triad had a wider currency in the Pauline communities than the direct evidence of the Pauline Letters suggests, even though the three elements appear together nowhere in the New Testament outside the Pauline corpus.[14]

Paul had only heard about their faith and love because he had never visited this church. His report about them came from Epaphras. This element draws readers other than the Colossians to identify with the purported readers because they, like the Colossians, have not met Paul and yet are being called on to obey his instructions.

The Colossians' faith, the first ground of the author's thanksgiving, is "in Christ Jesus." The phrase "in Christ Jesus" can be understood in two ways: it may specify the object or content of their faith (so Pokorný 39–40), or it may designate the sphere in which believers live, the sphere in which they receive salvation and life (most commentators). Grammatical considerations favor the second alternative. In Paul, the object of the verb "believe" (*pisteuein*) is usually designated with a genitive or with the prepositions *pros* or *eis*. But Colossians uses the preposition *en*. Use of this preposition counts against seeing Christ as the object of their faith, but does not render the view untenable. Pauline usage, however, may not be determinative for Colossians, especially if the letter is pseudonymous. In any case, it seems unwise to make a hard and fast division between these alternatives. Both belief in and dependence upon Christ are important for Colossians as it combats views the author thinks diminish the person and work of Christ. At the same time, a central element of Colossians' response to the other teaching is the assertion that those who confess Christ are securely "in Christ" and so need not concern themselves with the teachers' evaluations of their relationship with God. So the writer may be thinking broadly enough to include both of these meanings. It is, after all, faith in Christ that brings one into that sphere of security in which God grants reconciliation and holiness.

The "love" the Colossians manifest for "all the saints" (their fellow believers) is the second ground the writer gives for his thanksgiving to God. The New Testament often calls members of the church "saints" or "holy ones." Such a designation denotes something of what it means to be in the church. Being holy indicates that one is set apart by God and that one lives a holy or moral life.

14. However, in Jas 2:5 the inheritance (and thus hope) are linked with faith and love (cf. Rev 2:19).

Holiness is so central to the meaning of being a believer that the early church found it appropriate to refer to one another as "saints." Having love for others is an important element of this holy life. As those who exist within the sphere of Christ and who approach God through Christ, believers live lives that express their identity as "saints" by loving others; love demonstrates their faith in Christ. Just as being holy and being loving are inseparable, so having faith and loving others are inseparable. Having this faith in or residing in the sphere of Christ means, by definition, that one will be loving. "Faith is always lived as much with the lips as with the heart (Rom 10:9), as much with the hands and feet as with the brain" (Schweizer 33).

The third member of the triad, "hope," also appears in v. 5. Though this may be another, separate ground of thanksgiving (so Abbott 197), it is more likely that this "hope stored up for you in the heavens" serves as the basis for their faith and love.[15] So "hope" designates the content of their hope rather than the disposition of being hopeful. By contrast, when Paul uses "hope" in the trio in 1 Cor 13, the word clearly refers to a disposition rather than to the object of hope. While Colossians' use of "hope" thus differs from what is found in 1 Corinthians, the understanding of hope in Col 1:5 is not un-Pauline. Philippians 3:20 ("our citizenship is in the heavens" [my trans.]) illustrates that Paul, too, can talk about the possessions that believers already have in the heavens.[16] In Colossians, this hope probably refers both to the blessings enjoyed by those who are already in heaven, in the presence of Christ the Savior, and to the blessings Christians will receive at the Parousia. For the purpose of the letter as a whole, the author needs to assert that the eschatological blessings already exist. The recipients can be certain about receiving these gifts because they do already exist and are waiting with Christ for them. Therefore, their salvation is certain.[17] Since the other teaching placed the readers' forgiveness and salvation in question, this meaning of "hope" offers comfort by assuring the recipients about those blessings.

Colossians nearly always uses spatial imagery to speak of the hope that believers possess. In view of the recipients' need for assurance that their salvation is secure, this was a necessary emphasis. Some interpreters take the emphasis on spatial imagery, as opposed to temporal imagery (e.g., hoping for the blessings to come at the end time), to indicate that Colossians possesses a realized eschatology allowing for little or no temporal aspect. The emphasis on the

15. See the arguments from syntax and context in Lightfoot 133–34. Barth and Blanke (154) note that Paul's thanksgivings usually deal with things for which he is thankful within that church rather than something beyond it.

16. Hübner (45) sees Phil 3:20 as the root for the shift to the meaning of hope found in Colossians.

17. Barth and Blanke (155) assert that *apokeimai* ("laid up") in the New Testament always carries with it a sense of certainty. It appears elsewhere in the New Testament only in Luke 19:20; 2 Tim 4:8; Heb 9:27.

spatial element does not, however, mean that the temporal aspect is absent. The ideas of a present realm of existence (spatial imagery) and of a time-oriented existence (temporal imagery) are intertwined in the hope of 1:5.[18] The certainty of the present existence of these blessings strengthens the attractiveness of attaining them in the future. Both spatial and temporal orientations have important meanings, and Colossians develops both in ways that are mutually enriching. Both orientations contribute to the message of Colossians because it must assure its recipients that the blessings God has for them are already awaiting them and, at the same time, offer them a hope for a future in which they will receive those blessings. Thus they can be certain that God has prepared these blessings for them and still see the need to heed exhortations about living in the way God expects of those who hope to receive those blessings.

When the writer says the readers had "heard before" about this hope, he implies a contrast between the gospel they received from Epaphras and the recent, less valuable, and less true teaching that now troubles them. The writer asserts that the message to which they first responded admitted them to the ranks of the saints and brought them new life in Christ. This message is "the Word of truth." Again, this may signal a contrast with the false teaching they are now hearing. But this expression is rooted in the Old Testament description of the word of God as the word of truth. In Ps 119:43 God's word is the "word of truth," and in 119:160 the totality of God's word is truth. In other places the term "truth" (*'ĕmet*) refers to the way one lives (e.g., Ps 25:5; Hos 4:1). Thus, it can designate the totality of the word of God or the way God calls people to live.[19] These Old Testament texts sometimes contrast the falseness of worship of other gods with the truth of worship of the one God (see esp. Dan 8:12). If the readers detect this nuance, they may hear a contrast with the false teaching they face, a contrast that intimates an equivalence between idol worship and the teaching they need to reject.

"Truth" (*alētheia*) in the New Testament, including the Letters of Paul, often connotes God's will and word (e.g., Rom 2:8; Gal 2:5). In Col 1:5 "gospel" stands in apposition to the expression "Word of truth." Thus, this "Word of truth" is the gospel. In Colossians, the gospel is the message that God has acted in Christ to rescue those with faith from the powers of evil, to forgive their sins, and to effect reconciliation with God (1:12–14) and thus gain for them life with God. So the gospel they had heard from Epaphras brought them news of the hope that God preserves for them in heaven—a hope grounded in the resurrected Christ, who now resides in the heavens and preserves blessings for believers until the Parousia.

18. Hübner 47; cf. Pokorný 40–41. Aletti (60–61) sees significant future reference even in the use of hope here. He sees faith, love, and hope to have the temporal aspects of past, present, and future respectively.

19. See G. Quelle, *TDNT* 1:234–36.

The gospel the Colossians had heard before "remains present among" them (v. 6). The expression "remains present among" (*pareinai eis*) is fairly common in classical usage; it often means that something has come and that it remains there. The readers' faith and love are evidences that the gospel "remains present among" them.

The writer says that this gospel and the reality it creates are present not only in Colossae but also "in the whole world." While this is hyperbole,[20] the author probably has in mind the world of the Roman Empire. The point is not that every person within the sphere of the empire has heard the gospel, but rather that the message the Colossians accepted is the same message that is preached everywhere. This assertion establishes the universality, and implies the universal validity, of the gospel that Epaphras has preached to them. The writer may have asserted the gospel's universality as a contrast to the local false teaching. But Paul often mentions the universality of the gospel in his thanksgivings, so this may be more a reflection of Paul's customary practice.[21]

It is difficult to translate v. 6 because of its repetition of "just as" (*kathōs*). The first "just as" probably belongs with the first phrase of v. 6: the gospel is present among the readers just as it is present in the whole world.[22] This statement about the spread of the gospel to the whole world may reveal something about the writer's eschatology, particularly if he is drawing on elements of Paul's eschatology. Paul had regarded his mission to the Gentiles as a necessary prelude to the Parousia. Perhaps Colossians also understands the spread of the gospel to the whole world to mean that the conditions have been fulfilled, and therefore the Lord may return at any time.[23] Such a meaning reveals a more active temporal aspect in the eschatology of Colossians than many interpreters grant. But if this statement of the gospel reaching the whole world does draw on Paul's eschatology, then the writer sees God's plan moving forward. Consequently, adherence to the true gospel is even more urgent.

Whether or not the author has this eschatological scheme in mind, his emphasis on the same gospel being preached everywhere with the same results is important. These assertions draw other readers beyond Colossae into the circle addressed by the letter. All believers have heard and received the same

---

20. Barth and Blanke (158) call it "popular oriental hyperbole." Cf. Acts 17:6; 19:27; 1 Thess 1:8; 2 Cor 2:14.

21. See Lohse 19. He cites 1 Thess 1:8–9; Rom 1:8 as examples among the undisputed letters along with 2 Thess 1:3 among the disputed letters.

22. So a comma would come after *estin*. The UBS[4] and Nestle-Aland[26] place a comma instead after *eis hymin* ("among you") and so attach both uses of *kathōs* ("just as") to bearing fruit and growing.

23. Schweizer (35–36) presents an eschatological understanding of the passage. The writer of Colossians probably does not hold that truth is universal, while error arises locally. Although this is a perspective that the church adopts soon (e.g., Irenaeus, *Haer.* 3.3; 5.20.1; Eusebius, *Hist. eccl.* 4.24), there is little evidence that it was a widespread view before the end of the first century.

gospel. Therefore, what the Paul of the letter says to the purported original recipients in Colossae about this gospel has relevance for all readers.

The second "just as" in v. 6 speaks of the gospel "bearing fruit and growing" and asserts that it does these things both among the Colossians and in the whole world. Notably it is the gospel, not the Colossians, that is bearing fruit and growing. This keeps the emphasis on what God is doing. "Bearing fruit" (*karpophoroumenon*) is a very unusual form. This is its only occurrence in the New Testament in the middle voice (i.e., the subject of the verb performs the act on or for oneself) and it appears in only one other place in extant ancient Greek.[24] Many commentators have argued that the use of the middle voice indicates that there is an "inherent energy" in the gospel.[25] This is probably reading more into the voice of the verb than it will bear. Rather, it implies that God works through the gospel to produce the fruit.

Attempts to discern precisely the difference between the gospel's bearing fruit and growing have produced differing results. John Chrysostom (*Homilies on Colossians* 1 [*NPNF*[1] 13:259]) contended that bearing fruit meant doing good works, while growing meant the spread of the message to more people, a view followed by O'Brien (13) and Pokorný (43). While agreeing that "growing" indicates that the message reaches more people, others contend that fruit-bearing means inner, personal growth (e.g., Lightfoot 135; Abbott 198). Both these understandings of fruit-bearing put more emphasis on the acts of the people who receive the gospel than on what the gospel itself is doing. Yet, to this point, it is God's action through the gospel that the writer has set center stage. Furthermore, the polyvalence of the metaphor does not support such a precise meaning. Rather, this is a case of hendiadys (saying a single thing with two terms) used for emphasis. The basic meaning is that the gospel is working powerfully throughout the world. That working includes spiritual growth, good deeds, and spreading to increasing numbers of people, among other things the gospel might produce. Identifying this as a simple case of hendiadys also reduces the oddity of mentioning fruit-bearing before growing.

Since this active and powerful gospel is at work among the letter's recipients, just as it is throughout the world, they are drawn into God's working in the world. And they were not slow to respond to this message; the gospel has been bearing fruit and growing among them "from the day you heard." If this

---

24. Barth and Blanke 159; the other example is an inscription (no. 918 in E. Hicks et al., *The Collection of Ancient Greek Inscriptions in the British Museum*, 4 vols. [Oxford: Clarendon, 1874–1916] which they cite from BAGD). So perhaps it is not so unusual that it would have been considered strange on a public marker.

25. See, e.g., Lightfoot 135 and many who follow him. Lightfoot looks to Moulton's note on the "dynamic middle" to support this reading (Moulton so characterizes this use of the middle in his editing of G. B. Winer, *A Treatise on the Grammar of New Testament Greek*, trans. and ed. W. F. Moulton, 2nd ed. [Edinburgh: T&T Clark, 1877], 318–19 n. 5).

statement has a polemical edge, it would be that the gospel was working powerfully among the recipients before the other teaching arose. But since this affirmation appears in the thanksgiving, the author is probably simply commending them for their ready acceptance of the gospel when it was first preached to them. Such a compliment helps the writer establish good relations with the recipients and connects them with the message the author advocates throughout the letter.

The Colossians not only heard the gospel, but also "came to know" it. This signifies more than that they understood it mentally. The knowledge spoken of here is experiential knowledge, knowledge that comes from having participated in the experience of God's presence that the gospel mediates.[26] What the implied readers came to hear and know is "the grace of God in truth."[27] The same message has been referred to in vv. 5–6 as "the Word of truth," "the gospel," and "the grace of God in truth," and it includes the "hope stored up in the heavens" (v. 5). The repetition of "truth" suggests that this message stands in contrast to the new message the recipients are hearing. The writer asserts that they have received the true gospel and must not turn to another. The blessings of the fruit, the growth, and the experience of the gospel all belong to the readers through the message they first received. The other teaching adds nothing to this richness. Since the other teaching prescribes additional requirements that its adherents claim are necessary to attain forgiveness and so be granted a place with God, even calling the original message God's "grace" amounts to a rejection of that view.

[7–8] Verses 7–8 provide further definition of the message the Colossians had received "in truth," specifying that the true word from God is the message that Epaphras had preached to them. Within the story implied in the text, Epaphras, himself a resident of Colossae (4:12), is the evangelist who brought the gospel to Colossae. Whether the letter was written by Paul or a later disciple, this verse probably reveals some genuine historical information. If the letter is authentic, Epaphras would be known to the readers firsthand. On the other hand, if Colossians is pseudonymous, Epaphras must have been a well-known evangelist in western Asia Minor for his name to be recognizable to readers in the decades following Paul's death. Since Paul's identification of Epaphras as a fellow prisoner in Phlm 24 is insufficient reason to give him this leading role in Colossians, the best hypothesis remains that he was a known evangelist from this region. It is not possible to know whether this Epaphras is the same person as the Epaphroditus mentioned in Phil 2:25 and 4:18, even though Epaphras is an abbreviated form of Epaphroditus.

---

26. While there is no basic difference in the meaning of *ginōskō* ("to know") and its compound form *epiginōskō*, the compound form may suggest some emphasis here. Barth and Blanke (161) think its use may indicate a complete knowledge in contrast to fragmentary knowledge.

27. So *tēn charin* ("the grace") serves as the object of both verbs in this clause.

Verse 7 begins with the third use of "just as" (*kathōs*) in the space of two verses. Together these three uses of "just as" indicate that the Colossians received the same gospel that has been preached in the whole world, that it is having the same effects there as elsewhere, and that this productive and world-wide message is the one that Epaphras brought them. These assertions, which the "just as" expressions bring together, provide powerful legitimation for the writer's gospel because he claims that he advocates this very message; and this is in implicit contrast to the teaching the readers are hearing from the visionaries. By comparison, that other teaching has not proved itself and, Colossians asserts, it is not the message on which the readers' identity as participants in the realm of Christ is founded.

By recalling the Colossians' initial reception of the gospel, the author again asserts that they do not need the visionaries' teaching; they have already received from Epaphras the true gospel that brings the grace of God. Thus, as the writer has already intimated, they now possess all the blessings of God that are available at present, and the future gifts of God are already reserved for them.

The association the text establishes between Paul and Epaphras functions in two ways. First, it increases the status of Epaphras by associating him with an apostle, a move that further authenticates Epaphras's gospel.[28] But second, it also draws Paul and the readers into a closer and more friendly relationship because this association connects Paul with someone they know and trust. Rhetoricians recommended that speakers mention their associations with people their audiences know and trust because the hearers will grant some of that trust and goodwill to the friend of their friend. That Epaphras is "beloved" by Paul draws the two yet closer together. The enhanced status the writer gives Epaphras is of a strange sort, however: "Paul" calls him "our fellow slave." Being a slave was not a position of status, even though slaves in powerful households might wield considerable power and were given deference that poor freed people never received. But even these powerful slaves were still slaves. Paul and his fellow slave Epaphras have God (or Christ) as their master. It is possible that calling Epaphras a "fellow slave" puts him on the same level as Paul (Barth and Blanke 164). On the other hand, Paul may stand over Epaphras much as a regional bishop stands over pastors. In this model, Paul is the servant of Christ, and then Epaphras is Paul's fellow servant (Hübner 49). But this model implies a more developed idea of apostolic succession than we find elsewhere in Colossians, especially since the status of each is enhanced by his association with the other. Still, Epaphras does work under Paul's direc-

---

28. Lindemann (20) asserts that this securing of status for Epaphras may indicate that he was the author of Colossians. While this is not impossible, such a hypothesis cannot be proved, as Lindemann acknowledges. The association of Epaphras with Paul has a function different from having the readers accept a writing they know to be pseudepigraphic.

tion and with Paul's authorization. This connection with Paul gives Epaphras's teaching the stamp of apostolicity, an important mark both during and after Paul's lifetime.

The identification of Paul as a slave (*doulos*) is an interesting turn. This is not a word commonly used for leaders, apostles, or evangelists in the New Testament. (In fact, within the Pauline corpus, "fellow slave" [*syndoulos*] appears only in Colossians.) The more-common term used for such people is "servant" (*diakonos*, from which we derive the word "deacon"). These words have overlapping semantic fields, but *doulos* implies more servility than *diakonos* and most often refers to slavery.[29] *Diakonos*, on the other hand, was used more often in contexts that do not imply that the person is servile or of the slave class. Plato even used *diakonos* for those who hold public office, and through the Hellenistic period, philosophers continued to describe themselves as "servants of God."[30] Paul often refers to himself as a "servant" (*diakonos*), whether of God or of his churches, but he refers to himself as a "slave" (*doulos*) only three times within the undisputed letters (2 Cor 4:5; Gal 1:10; Phil 1:1).[31] The difference between these two words can be seen in Mark 10:32–45, the episode in which James and John ask Jesus for the highest positions in the kingdom. Jesus responds that those who want to be great in the kingdom must be "servants" (*diakonoi*), and the one who wants to be the greatest must become the "slave" (*doulos*) of all.[32]

Such a designation for leaders, even apostles, in the church speaks an important word about what it means to be called to such offices. Leaders are to see themselves as slaves of God. Paul even says in 2 Cor 4:5 that he is a slave of the Corinthians. This understanding of the place of the church's leaders excludes the possibility of claiming status and privilege based upon that position. It calls for leaders to understand themselves as those who work in service to the church rather than as those in charge who demand deference. The description of Paul and Epaphras as "slaves" may indicate that Colossians rejects hierarchy and envisions a collective mutuality as the proper way for the community to function (Standhartinger 1999, 241–42). This language for leaders certainly required the readers to adopt understandings of community and leadership that were contrary to those of other institutions in their world; such language calls them to envision a type of leadership that is consistent with the gospel rather than with cultural expectations.

---

29. See Karl Rengstorf, *TDNT* 2:261–80. That *doulos* means slave is particularly clear in the following passages within the Pauline corpus: 1 Cor 7:21–23; Eph 6:5; Col 3:11, 22; Phlm 16. In these passages the term refers to a person who is literally a slave.

30. Plato, *Leg.* 955cd; Epictetus, *Diatr.* 3.22.69; 3.24.65. See Hermann Beyer, *TDNT* 2:82–83.

31. The title "*doulos* [slave] of God" is also used of Paul in Titus 1:1. See also 2 Tim 2:24, where Timothy is referred to as a "slave of the Lord."

32. Matthew 20:20–28 and Mark 10:44 also use *doulos* throughout for those who want to be leaders.

Colossians also describes Epaphras as a "faithful servant of Christ," employing the more-common term *diakonos* (v. 7). Since the writer mentions Epaphras in connection with the gospel's arrival in Colossae, his faithfulness to Christ probably refers to his preaching and, perhaps more to the point, to the correct content of his message. There is a textual problem in this part of v. 7. Some manuscripts read "for [on behalf of] *us*," while others have "for [on behalf of] *you*." The difference between these two readings in Greek is one letter (*hymōn*, "you," or *hēmōn*, "us"). Commentators have overwhelmingly chosen "on *our* behalf."[33] This reading designates Epaphras as a representative of the Pauline mission: he came to Colossae preaching the authentic gospel as authorized by the apostle Paul. However, if the reading is "for *you*," it means that Epaphras's preaching was for the benefit of the Colossians.[34] Thus both readings ("us" and "you") fit well in the context. Nevertheless, the reading "for you" alleviates some of the tension the expression "for us" creates because the latter reading has a servant of one person working on behalf of, nearly at the behest of, someone else. This is not impossible, but neither is it probable.

In addition to performing his duties as a servant of Christ for the Colossians, Ephaphras has also brought news to Paul about their "love in the Spirit." This is the second time within the span of four verses that the writer has spoken of the recipients' love. In v. 4 their love is for "all the saints," and this seems to be the most likely object of their love here as well.[35] While the writer specifies the *object* of their love in v. 4, he comments about the *nature* of their love in v. 8; it is "in the Spirit." This could mean that they have a spirit of love or even spiritual love,[36] but it probably refers instead to the Holy Spirit as the source of their love, even though this is the only direct mention of the Spirit in Colossians. That the Spirit appears so seldom in Colossians is surprising because it plays such a major role in the undisputed Paulines, particularly as a primary component of the eschatological blessings that believers now possess. Colossians constantly asserts that believers now possess significant blessings in Christ, so one would expect the Spirit to have some prominence. Perhaps the minimal role the Spirit plays in Colossians reveals more about what the author thinks he needs to discuss to persuade his readers than it does about his pneumatology or eschatology. In any case, the writer asserts in v. 8 that the Spirit of God is the source of their love for fellow believers. This passing comment shows that the character of God—and their experience of that character mediated by the Spirit—is the

33. A rare exception is Lindemann 19.

34. It is possible that this reading means that Epaphras represents the Colossians to Paul, but this seems rather unlikely.

35. Contra Lindemann (19–20), who argues that it is love for Paul, which is why it must be in spirit; after all, they do not know him physically, through direct contact.

36. Barth and Blanke (166) observe that when the writer of Colossians wants to speak of something being spiritual, he uses the adjective rather than this sort of paraphrastic expression.

basis for their love within the community; they reflect God's love in the ways they treat one another. Furthermore, this statement implies that they are empowered by God's Spirit to love one another.

In vv. 3–8 the writer grounds his thanksgiving for the readers in their faith and love. He uses hope, the third element in the well-known triad, to shift the focus of the thanksgiving to a description of the broad scope and powerful action of the gospel. Its scope extends even to the heavens, where God's blessings already await the faithful. These declarations about the gospel also enlarge the circle of those whom the letter addresses because the gospel the Colossians have received is the same message that believers everywhere have heard and accepted. Thus, what Paul says to the Colossians is relevant for other readers as well. Finally, the writer notes that the love they have for one another is formed and empowered by the Spirit.

1:9–12 Intercession for the Colossians

1:9 For that reason, from the time we heard about you, we have not stopped praying for you and asking that you be filled with the knowledge of his will in all spiritual wisdom and understanding, 10 so that you[a] may live a life worthy of the Lord, pleasing [to him] in every way: bearing fruit in every good work and growing by means of the knowledge of God, 11 being empowered with all strength according to the might of his glory, that you may have all patience and be long-suffering, and 12 giving thanks with joy to the Father[b] who qualifies[c] you[d] to receive a share of the inheritance of the saints in light.

a. The subject *hymas* ("you") has been added for the infinitive *peripatēsai* ("to walk, live") by the Byzantine (Koine) tradition. However, the sentence functions well with the subject left unexpressed, and it seems more probable that it would have been added for clarity than that it would have been deleted.

b. It is unusual in the Pauline corpus for God to be referred to simply as "the Father." So some copyists have added *theō* ("God") before *tō patri* ("the Father"; e.g., א) while other later copyists added *tou christou* ("Christ"; 303, 451, 2492). It also seems unlikely that the *hama* ("together with") found in P[46] and B is original because it breaks the flow of this list of participles and is not present in other important witnesses.

c. Perhaps because *hikanoō* ("to be fitted, sufficient, qualified") is found only one other time in the New Testament (2 Cor 3:6), it has been replaced in the original hand of D and in F and G by the more-common verb *kaleō* (*kalesanti*, "called"). That the reading seemed problematic to early copyists can be seen by the conflation in B, which has *kalesanti kai hikanōsanti* ("called and qualified").

d. The reading *hymas* ("you") is supported by א and B. The alternative reading, *hēmas* ("us"), is found in A, C, D, and F. *Hymas* better fits the context of the intercessory prayer; it may have been changed to *hēmas* through assimilation to the *hēmas* at the beginning of v. 13 (Metzger 620).

The prayer that began in 1:3 as a report about the things for which Paul thanks God when he thinks of the Colossians now assumes the form of intercession. Translators and interpreters are divided over where this section should end; some think this subsection goes through v. 11 (or 11c), while others assert that it continues through v. 14 and so introduces the following poetic material.[37] The change from the description of what the author does in vv. 9–11 (i.e., intercedes for the readers) to a summons to give thanks in v. 12 could suggest that these are separate sections (so Schweizer 40). However, such a division creates syntactical and thematic problems. First, the participle "giving thanks" (*eucharistountes*) in v. 12 is the fourth in a series of participles that begins in v. 10 and explicates what it means to be pleasing to the Lord. It is unlikely that v. 11c or v. 12 begins a new thought unit within this series of participles. A larger turn in thought comes at the beginning of v. 13, but even this statement about the work of God is directly dependent on what has been said about God in v. 12.

Part of the difficulty readers experience when trying to understand the flow of thought in this section is that 1:12–14 serves two distinct and important functions. These verses continue the intercession begun in v. 9 *and* introduce the poetic material that follows in 1:15–20. Readers must keep both functions in view to understand this section of Colossians. In the intercession of vv. 9–11 "the senders are praying that the recipients might be able to thank God in the manner demonstrated in 1:11b-14, because in Christ, God has acted" in the way 1:15–20 depicts in poetic form (Pokorný 46). While the poetic material in vv. 15–20 continues the thought of vv. 9–14, the distinct literary form of vv. 15–20 gives us reason to distinguish those verses from the preceding material for analysis. But this artificial separation must not lead us to miss the necessary interconnectedness.

[9–12] Many parallels tie together vv. 3–8 and vv. 9–12. Both subsections speak of constant prayer for the recipients, both have "from the time we heard" and "bearing fruit and growing," both speak of knowledge, of giving thanks, of a possession kept in the heavens, of the saints, and of "the Father" (though in v. 3 it is the Father of Christ while in v. 12 it is the Father of believers).[38] Both sections also use the word "all" several times.

The opening words of v. 9, "For that reason . . . ," tie vv. 9–12 to the preceding section. The writer prays for the Colossians because he has heard of their "love in the Spirit" (v. 8). This immediate cause of his prayer for them cannot

37. E.g., Hübner (50–51) and Schweizer (39–40) break the section at the end of v. 11. Nestle-Aland[26] begins a new paragraph with v. 11d so that the initial words of the new section are *meta charas* ("with joy"). Most other recent commentators take the section through v. 14, as do the RSV, NIV, and NRSV. The UBS[4] has a minor break without beginning a new sentence at the end of v. 11 but includes vv. 12–14 within a section that begins at v. 9. Abbott (201) continues the section through v. 12, and this is the way the NEB and NJB break the text.

38. In addition, v. 8 has love in *the Spirit* while v. 9 has *spiritual* knowledge.

be separated from the faith mentioned in v. 4. Verses 9–11 are an extension of the preceding verses, with vv. 3–8 focusing on present success and vv. 9–11 giving attention to the readers' spiritual needs (Hay 44). The writer says that these prayers began the day he heard about the Colossians, again indicating that he does not know the recipients and relies on what Epaphras has told him about them. Paul's unfamiliarity with, perhaps absence from, them has already been mentioned three times. In a pseudonymous letter, this attention to absence may serve as a metaphor for the churches existing without the physical presence of Paul. Thus, the actual recipients have the same relationship with Paul that the implied recipients had. By implication, then, the later readers should also read the letter as one that possesses the authority of the apostle.

The writer says that Paul has prayed for them "from the time we heard" and has "not stopped" in this prayer. Perhaps this signals an intensity in the prayer (Dunn 69), but it may simply be an example of the predilection of Colossians to speak in exaggerated terms and to repeat themes (see vv. 3, 6). Moreover, rather than indicating intensity, the use of both "praying" and "asking" seems to be another case of hendiadys (one thing being said with two words), another stylistic feature of Colossians. It may be that the "and" (*kai*) between these two words is explanatory and so indicates that this prayer is not prompted by the author's worry about the readers but by the good news he has heard about them (Barth and Blanke 173).[39]

The content of this prayer is that they may be filled with knowledge of God's will,[40] with spiritual wisdom and understanding, and that this may lead to living in a way that pleases God. Use of the passive, "be filled" (*plērōthēte*), indicates that God is the actor. This statement implies that the Colossians do not attain this knowledge for themselves; God grants it to them. The divine passive represents a subtle rejection of the other teaching, which prescribed means for its adherents to attain heavenly knowledge and experiences for themselves. The reference to fullness probably also implies that Paul's gospel brings with it what the other teachers claim to offer.

The writer wants the readers to be filled, not just with knowledge but also with a particular kind of knowledge. As was the case with the verb in v. 6, the augmented form of the noun "knowledge" (*epignōsis*) is used in v. 9. This form does not, however, have a meaning different from the unaugmented form (*gnōsis*) in Colossians.[41] Furthermore, the presence of the terms "knowledge" and "wisdom"

---

39. Aletti (70) notes that the combination "praying and asking" does not appear in the undisputed letters.

40. This is expressed with a purpose clause that begins with *hina*.

41. Lightfoot (138), on the other hand, argues that *epignōsis* means more-thorough knowledge, while Abbott (201–2) asserts that the augmented form "lends itself better to the expression of practical knowledge." But such differences in nuance do not appear to be the case in the usage of Paul or that of Colossians and Ephesians; see Rudolf Bultmann, *TDNT* 1:706–7.

here and throughout Colossians does not point to problems stemming from a particular type of heresy (e.g., Gnosticism), because many religions and philosophies spoke of their teachings as "knowledge." The qualifying phrases that follow specify the kind of knowledge that the writer has in mind. He wants the Colossians to have knowledge of the will of God. This is not just knowledge about God but also knowledge about God's will for how they should live, as we see from v. 10. The Dead Sea Scrolls often make this connection between knowledge of God and doing God's will. In the Dead Sea Scrolls, knowledge of God includes the obligation to do God's will.[42] Colossians expresses a similar idea here. This necessary connection between possessing knowledge of God and having an obligation to live in accord with it does not allow for the distinction often made between faith and works, with faith being all that is necessary for a relationship with God. The Pauline Letters constantly link knowledge of God and faith, on the one hand, and holy living, on the other. For Paul, faith and the faithful life are two sides of a single coin, and failure to live the faithful life is evidence that a person does not really have faith.[43] This same inextricable connection is present in Colossians. From early in chapter 2, the writer will describe the proper life for believers as an embodiment of baptism. When he speaks of "knowledge of the will of [God]" in 1:9, we may have our first intimation of that emphasis on the connection between belief and manner of living.

The prepositional phrase "in all[44] spiritual wisdom and understanding" delineates further the sort of knowledge the writer wants God to give the readers. In the Greek text the adjective "spiritual" (*pneumatikē*) follows the word "understanding" and so may modify either "understanding" or both "understanding" and "wisdom," as the translation above renders it.[45] However, since the visionaries offer the Colossians another means to knowledge and probably wisdom, our writer does not want the readers to have "*all* wisdom." That is, he does not want them to have every sort of wisdom, especially that of the other teachers; he wants them to have *spiritual* wisdom. By calling the wisdom and understanding "spiritual," he implies that it comes from the Spirit of God.

The writer intends no significant distinction between wisdom and understanding. Since Colossians for stylistic effect often accumulates terms that have the same basic meaning, this is another instance of hendiadys. In addition, wisdom and knowledge often appear together in the LXX. Even the expression "wis-

42. See 1QS 1.5; 3.1; 8.6–9; 1QS^b 1.2; 1QH 4.21, 24; also Lohse 25–26 and Schweizer 41–42 for other specific references.

43. This link can be seen in Rom 6:1–4, 12–14; Gal 5:13–16; Phil 1:27–28; 2:12–14. See the discussion in Victor P. Furnish, *Theology and Ethics in Paul* (Nashville: Abingdon, 1968), 207–27.

44. Hübner (50) notes that the "all" here is typical of Colossians (e.g., 1:28; 3:16) but is not common in Paul's genuine letters. Dunn (72) sees this use of "all" as part of the "rather florid style" of vv. 9–12.

45. Similarly, the "all" that precedes wisdom modifies both nouns.

dom and understanding" (*sophia kai synesis*) is found regularly. In the LXX these terms are often synonymous (e.g., Exod 31:3–6) and appear in connection with both the Spirit and doing God's will, understood as keeping the Law.[46] So these terms are used together in the LXX in ways that are quite similar to the way Colossians employs them here; they point to a full understanding of God's will that leads one to act according to that will. Thus, the language that begins this prayer of intercession suggests a necessary connection between living the life of holiness and possessing knowledge of God. This intimation becomes explicit in the next phrase.

The purpose of attaining the wisdom and understanding that come from the Spirit is "to live a life worthy of the Lord" (v. 10).[47] The connection between knowledge of God and right conduct is found throughout Scripture and Jewish apocalyptic writings. The actual verb used in this phrase is "walk" (*peripateō*), which often means the manner in which people conduct their lives.[48] The expression has its roots in the Old Testament, where we find such expressions as "walk in the way of righteousness" (Prov 8:20—spoken by "Wisdom"), and in such ideas as the two-ways (Ps 1). But it comes to Colossians more directly from Paul; in every undisputed letter except Philemon, he uses this verb to mean manner of life.[49] So this is a common Pauline expression. The formulation of the phrase in Colossians is similar to what we find in 1 Thessalonians. In 1 Thess 2:12 Paul urges the recipients to "walk worthily of God" (my trans.), and in 4:1 he says it is necessary for the readers to "walk and to please [*areskein*] God." "Walking in a manner worthy of" God, then, is a Pauline expression for how believers should live their lives, even though the precise formulation in Colossians does not appear elsewhere in the Pauline corpus. The distinctive element in the formulation of the statement in Colossians is that one lives a life worthy of the *Lord*. "Lord" refers to both God and Christ in the Pauline corpus. In Col 1:10 it probably refers to Christ because this expression is part of the introduction of the poetic material in vv. 15–20 and because the Father is explicitly mentioned in v. 12.[50]

---

46. Barth and Blanke (175 n. 12) give the following examples: Exod 31:3; 35:31, 35; Deut 4:6; 1 Chr 22:12; 2 Chr 1:10–13; 2:12; Isa 11:2; 29:14; Dan 2:21. Exodus 31:3; 35:31; and Isa 11:2 associate wisdom and understanding with the Spirit of God, and Deut 4:6 and 1 Chr 22:12 relate them to keeping God's law, and so doing God's will. In Dan 2:21 they are gifts received from God.

47. Lightfoot (139) and Abbott (203) see "walk worthily" as a consequence of attaining this knowledge rather than as the purpose. However, Sappington (112–37) has shown that in some Jewish apocalyptic writings the goal of attaining knowledge of God is living a life of obedience to God.

48. Although *peripateō* did not have this meaning in classical Greek, by the Hellenistic period it was being used with this meaning and is occasionally found in the LXX (e.g., Prov 8:20; Eccl 11:9).

49. E.g., Rom 6:4; 8:4; 1 Cor 3:3; 7:17; 2 Cor 4:2; 5:7; Gal 5:16; Phil 3:17, 18; 1 Thess 2:12; 4:1 [2x], 12.

50. Barth and Blanke (177) assert that "Lord" always refers to Christ in Colossians. However, Aletti (73) may be correct when he says that the author does not really want to distinguish between the two at this point.

It is a lofty goal indeed to live a life worthy of the Lord. It demands that the believer's whole self be given in "undivided obedience" to Christ (Lohse 28). This expression, borrowed from Pauline paraenesis, means a life that corresponds to the gospel (Pokorný 48). This life is not only a responsibility but also a gift; believers are given knowledge of God's will, which presents them with the possibility of living in ways that please Christ (and thus also God). Colossians does not explicitly state whom this life will please. The statement could mean that the conduct of the readers should be pleasing to the Christian community or the larger world, but that seems unlikely, in part, because of the word used. "Pleasing" (*areskeia*), a New Testament *hapax legomenon*,[51] usually has negative connotations, indicating that a person is obsequious. That is not the proper disposition for Christians to cultivate among themselves or toward outsiders. In some Jewish writers of this period, however, this word is used for pleasing God, and in these contexts it carries no derogatory implications (e.g., Philo, *Spec.* 1.176, 300; *Abr.* 130). I have supplied "to him" in the translation above to indicate that believers live to please Christ. An additional reason for identifying Christ as the one who is pleased is that this is part of an intercessory prayer; it makes sense that the writer prays that they may be pleasing to Christ, the one through whom he implicitly addresses this petition, which introduces a section identifying Christ as the mediator of all God's work in the world.

The ambitious goal that Colossians sets before the readers is that they may be pleasing to Christ "in every way." While this is a comprehensive goal, it is also vague, so the writer proceeds to fill this idea with content. He specifies four elements of the life he is commending or four modes in which it is manifested: bearing fruit in good works, growing in knowledge of God, being empowered by God, and giving thanks (Aletti 67). These means are expressed in a series of parallel participial phrases that take us through the beginning of v. 12.

The first two ways in which one lives a life pleasing to God echo language used earlier in the thanksgiving. In v. 6 the writer asserts that the gospel is bearing fruit and growing; in v. 10 the Colossians themselves need to bear fruit and grow. Perhaps this indicates that the gospel finds its real fulfillment in the way it works in people, leading them to live worthy lives (Hübner 51).

The recipients are to manifest this worthy life by bearing fruit in every good work. Doing good works is both a central part and a consequence of the pleasing life. "Good works" may, as in some rabbinic literature, include such acts as helping the poor and visiting the sick and distressed (e.g., *t. Pe'ah* 4, 19 (24) [in the Tosefta]; *b. Sukkah* 49[b]; Strack-Billerbeck 4:536–38). The writer would hardly

---

51. The cognate verb *areskō* is found only 14 times in the Pauline corpus and only 3 additional times elsewhere in the New Testament. Given the range of contexts in which it appears, it is not possible to assert anything about a customary Pauline usage.

exclude such things, since he speaks of "*every* good work." But the more direct reference is to the various exhortations the writer gives throughout Colossians. As defined in 3:17, these good works encompass everything the believer does.

Growth comes by means of the knowledge of God; the readers are able to grow in this life and to perform good works because they have received the knowledge of God, for which the author prays in v. 9. Rather than enjoining them to learn more about God (which Colossians does take occasion to do in other places), this verse speaks of the way in which the knowledge of God that the readers already possess should work in their lives. This is the understanding of most critical commentators,[52] even though the leading English translations seldom render the dative phrase "knowledge of God" in a way that indicates that meaning. The NRSV, RSV, NIV, NJB, and NEB all translate this phrase by inserting the preposition "in" before "the knowledge of God." While possible, this translation does not capture the sense of the instrumental dative.[53] As an instrumental dative, this phrase reinforces the pattern already seen in the way vv. 9 and 10 are related: knowledge of the will of God leads the recipients to obey the will of God. Given that emphasis, the knowledge of God to which the writer refers is not esoteric knowledge about God, but knowledge that expresses itself in appropriate conduct, in performing "every good work."[54]

The third element of this exhortation to worthy living offers comfort and security. The Colossians are not simply admonished to live such lives; they are also empowered by God to do so. The writer proclaims that they are "empowered with all strength according to the might of his glory" (v. 11). The structure of this clause parallels that of the first ("bearing fruit in every good work") in this series of participial clauses that define what it means to live in a manner worthy of the Lord. Both begin with the preposition "in" (*en*), which is followed by a form of the adjective "all." Then each has a noun followed by a participle, though in v. 10 there is an adjective between the noun and the participle. The parallel structure suggests that the elements in the phrases function in parallel ways. In Greek the initial phrase in v. 11 is "with all strength"; in v. 10 the initial phrase of the construction is "in every good work." If these prepositional phrases have the same function, then "in all strength" does not express the means by which the readers endure, but rather announces the topic that the

---

52. O'Brien (23) is an exception.

53. Alternatively, this could be read as a dative of reference ("with respect to knowledge of God, growing") and so make the three phrases "good works," "knowledge of God," and "all strength" parallel. Thus, the readers are to be pleasing with respect to each of these things.

54. Sappington (183) argues that in some Jewish apocalyptic writings knowledge is viewed as a way to salvation. If some of that outlook informs the teaching that Colossians opposes, this verse rejects that function of knowledge in favor of seeing it as what enables appropriate living even while salvation comes through Christ.

clause addresses, just as the prepositional phrase did in v. 10. Thus the topic in v. 11 is possessing strength,, and the meaning is that in the matter of having strength, the readers are enabled by the power of God's glory. The somewhat awkward "all" in the phrase is a part of the pleonastic style that characterizes vv. 9–12, in which "all" appears five times. The repetitious sound of the opening phrases (translated more woodenly "being empowered[55] in all power") signals a Semitic influence, as does the expression "strength of his glory" (Dunn 73). The word used for God's power here, *kratos,* appears only four times in the Pauline corpus (cf. Eph 1:19; 6:10; 1 Tim 6:16),[56] and Col 1:11 seems to be its earliest occurrence.

Apart from Jewish and Christian texts, there are few references in ancient Greek to divine "glory" (*doxa*). In classical usage *doxa* often referred to a person's reputation or renown.[57] The word does appear in a few inscriptions where it seems to refer to a god's holiness. In Josephus and Philo, "glory" sometimes denotes honor and splendor. From these uses, *doxa* develops the meanings of light, glory, and radiance, meanings found only in Jewish and Christian writings.[58] "Glory" can refer to God's presence, power, and radiance in the LXX. For example, when Moses asks to see God, it is the "glory" of God that he is allowed to see, and then only a glimpse of the back side of that glory (Exod 33:22–23). This divine radiance possesses so much power that it causes Moses' face to shine, or in the language of the LXX, to be glorified (*dedoxastai*; Exod 34:29). In Colossians, "glory" seems to refer broadly to God's majesty and power, God's reputation as radiant power. So the strength that enables readers to live in a worthy manner derives from the power inherent in these overwhelming characteristics of God's nature. These emphatic assertions about the enabling power of God anticipate the coming statements that oppose what the visionaries teach about angelic powers and rulers.

After asserting that the readers are empowered by this mighty force, the writer reveals the purpose of this empowering: that they may live with "patience and long-suffering." Interpreters disagree about the nuances present in each of these words, with some suggesting that *hypomonē* points to endurance until the eschaton (e.g., Barth and Blanke 182), while others maintain that *makrothymia* has this force (e.g., Sappington 182). In some instances, *hypomonē* seems to indicate standing fast while under attack (e.g., 4 Macc 5:23; 17:17; Josephus,

55. The verb *dynamoō* occurs only here and in Heb 11:34 in all the New Testament. In addition P[46] and B replace *endynamoō* ("put on") with *dynamoō*.

56. It appears six other times in the New Testament. In all except one, Heb 2:14, it refers to the strength or power of God. In Heb 2:14 it is used to speak of the power of the devil. So all of its New Testament usages involve superhuman power.

57. E.g., Demosthenes, *Or.* 2.15; 3.24. See Gerhard Kittel, *TDNT* 2:234–35.

58. E.g., Josephus, *Life* 273; *Ant.* 16.158; Philo, *Leg.* 2.107. See Kittel, *TDNT* 2:233–37.

Ant. 2.7),[59] and *makrothymia* seems closer to the general virtue of patience.[60] Whatever the shades in meaning, these words are basically synonyms. Thus, the writer again employs hendiadys to make his point emphatically. He asserts that God strengthens the readers to endure with faith whatever difficulties they face, whether those difficulties involve persecution or false teaching. The emphatic proclamation of God's power seems disproportionate to what it enables: patience. Colossians contains no clear indications that the readers are experiencing violent or organized civic persecution, but we should not underestimate the devastating effects of social and economic persecution that members of the church regularly faced. This type of persecution requires empowered patience because it is an ongoing part of life. After all, such persecution could well involve painful privation even of enough to eat. Furthermore, the recipients' need for patience may derive in part from the presence of the other teaching and their waiting for the second coming. Perhaps this declaration of God's power also prepares for the coming assertion that God is the one who has done the work to qualify the readers to receive the heavenly blessings.

The last two words of v. 11, "with joy," may be taken with either the preceding ("endurance and patience with joy") or the following clause ("giving thanks with joy"). A good case can be made for either option. Paul often calls for joy in the face of persecution; mention of joy in connection with endurance therefore coheres with Pauline thought. Though social and economic persecution was a daily reality for many in the early church, interpreting that experience is not a focus at this point in Colossians. Thus, the writer probably does not highlight the need for joy in the face of persecution.

The structure of the phrase makes the reading "giving thanks with joy" preferable. This reading recognizes the parallel with two of the other clauses in this series of four participial clauses. The first and third clauses ("bearing fruit in every good work" and "being empowered with all strength") begin with a prepositional phrase using *en* ("in" or "with") as the initial word in the clause. The second clause does not begin this way because the author has kept together "bearing fruit and growing" so that it echoes those words in v. 6. The phrase "with joy" does use a different preposition (*meta*), but the placement of the prepositional phrase at the beginning of the clause conforms to the pattern of two of the three other clauses that define the worthy life. Thus, "with joy" describes the way the readers give thanks to God.

The participle *eucharistountes* ("giving thanks") may function as an imperative. Käsemann (149–68) argues that because it is imperative, it serves as the

---

59. See F. Hauck, *TDNT* 4:581–88.

60. It is one of the fruits of the Spirit in Gal 5:22 and appears in the Pauline corpus in references to the patience of God (Rom 2:4; 9:22).

introduction for a hymn, which he begins in v. 12. If *eucharistountes* is imperative in function, then the three preceding participles (bearing fruit, growing, and being empowered) should also be understood as imperatives since they all relate to "live a life worthy of the Lord" in the same way.[61] But even if these participles do function as imperatives, the evidence does not support the claim that the early church used such an imperative as a formal introduction to a hymn. While cognates of *eucharisteō* may sometimes introduce confessional material in Philo and in later Christian settings,[62] there are no examples in the New Testament where the word serves this purpose. And while there are poetic and confessional elements in vv. 12–14, the author of Colossians constructs these verses to prepare for the hymnic material of vv. 15–20.[63] Still, the participles do have a hortatory function, even though grammatically they are not imperatives. As the writer reports his intercession for the recipients, he certainly intends that his requests to God also serve as exhortations to the readers to do the things for which he prays. That is, when he prays that God will give them these things, he wants his mention of those characteristics of "living worthily" to encourage the readers to pursue them. This hortatory function fits the author's understanding of the recipients' need to remain in the teaching they had received and to reject the new teaching.

Since *eucharistountes* is a summons to give thanks, just as the other participles summon the readers to bear fruit, grow, and be empowered, there is no break in thought as v. 12 begins. Paul offers his thanks to "the Father." This absolute use of Father, with no possessive qualifier (e.g., "our" or "of Jesus Christ"), is unusual in the Pauline corpus. Romans 6:4 refers to the Father with no further designation, but there it is clear that the child involved is Christ. The absolute use in Colossians leaves us momentarily wondering whom the writer envisions as the children, but the immediate mention of an inheritance to be granted to Christians indicates that God is their parent; God has adopted believers and made them heirs. This absolute use of Father may be prayer language (Lindemann 22). Romans 8:15 supports this understanding when it says that believers cry out to God as "Abba! Father!" in their prayers. Calling God by the name "Father" (rather than "Mother") here broadly reflects the patriarchal cul-

---

61. Barth and Blanke (178–79) suggest that these participles are imperative because they are in the nominative case rather than in the accusative, which would be the proper case for them in their relationship to the infinitive *peripatēsai* ("to live"). However, their translation does not reflect this grammatical decision.

62. See Käsemann 153–54; and Günther Bornkamm, "Das Bekenntnis im Hebräerbrief," in *Studien zu Antike und Urchristentum* (Munich: Chr. Kaiser, 1963), 196–97.

63. To demonstrate that 1:12–14 and 1:15–20 were not linked before the writing of Colossians, Sappington (195) gives the following differences between them: vv. 12–14 are prose while vv. 15–20 are poetry; vv. 12–14 speak of the congregation but vv. 15–20 of cosmic matters; and vv. 12–14 are in first-person plural while vv. 15–20 are about the redeemer and so use third person.

ture of the first century, but this identification is culturally required in this verse because of the connection with inheritance. The father was the parent who determined who would receive the inheritance. So for the image of believers being heirs of God to have its full impact, God must be the one with authority to distribute the estate: God must be the Father.

According to v. 12, God has qualified the readers to be heirs of God's inheritance.[64] In contrast to the other teaching, which advocates the observance of regulations as a condition of receiving visions and even of receiving forgiveness from God, this statement asserts that it is God who prepares the readers for God's gifts. They are not heirs because of their observances or visions but because God has adopted them and made them heirs.

In v. 12, the "you" in the phrase "who qualifies you to receive a share" (over against "who rescued *us*," v. 13) may highlight the distinction between Jews and Gentiles. Thus the Gentiles have now been brought into the inheritance of the Jews (so, e.g., Barth and Blanke 184). But this understanding is unlikely because v. 12 is still part of the thanksgiving in which the writer often distinguishes between the senders and recipients, not between Jews and Gentiles. If the primary contrast were between Jews and Gentiles, we would expect the writer to describe the inheritance the readers receive as the inheritance of Israel rather than of "the saints." Though the imagery the writer employs draws on ideas associated with God granting Israel an inheritance, that is not the inheritance the readers receive. Furthermore, the writer uses the second person because the recipients need to hear that they specifically have been made heirs. Besides, when the language changes to first person in v. 13, the writer is citing a preformed statement, and the change in person facilitates the transition to the poetic material in vv. 15–20.

God has qualified the readers, and all believers, for "a share of the inheritance." This language transports us to the exodus and the land of Israel as an inheritance for Israel from God. The land is often called the inheritance of Israel (e.g., Deut 3:18; 19:14; Josh 13:7).[65] So this is a known way to speak of receiving the blessings that God has reserved for God's people. Jeremiah 13:25 and

---

64. The verb *hikanoō* is found only here and in 2 Cor 3:6 in the New Testament. In 2 Cor 3:6 Paul uses this verb to assert that God has made "us" (referring primarily to himself, but including other apostles) sufficient or qualified them for their ministry. The cognate adjective (*hikanos*) appears seven times in the Pauline corpus, with a wide range of meanings.

65. This language is also used of the land when it is noted that the Levites are not to be given property as the other tribes are (e.g., Deut 10:9; 18:1–2). The LXX translation of Deut 18:1–2 uses both nouns that describe the inheritance in Colossians (*meris* and *klēros*), and the Lord is said to be the inheritance of Levites. However, this language is rare in the Pauline corpus. *Meris* ("share") appears only five times in the New Testament, and within the Pauline corpus *meris* appears only here and in 2 Cor 6:15, which many likewise identify as a preformed piece. Thus this vocabulary may support the notion that v. 13 contains preformed material.

Isa 57:6 use these terms for the individual's inherited plot. These words sometimes also refer to eschatological blessings in Daniel and other Jewish literature of the era.[66] Other New Testament writings and some scrolls from Qumran
characterize salvation as an inheritance.[67] The writer of Colossians may phrase
this statement as he does ("share of the inheritance") to indicate that each will
have an appropriate portion of the inheritance, or it may be another case of
pleonasm, just as the writer uses multiple adjectives to express the same basic
idea. Whichever is the case, the real point is that God has identified the readers
(and by extension all who believe in Christ [cf. v. 13]) as the people who will
receive the eschatological blessings; they are among those whom God will save.
Drawing on the Old Testament meaning of inheritance, the author pictures salvation as an inalienable possession that comes to one through God's grace and
election (Hester 22–29).

This inheritance is with "the saints in light." These saints are either angels
or the faithful people who are already with God, because the expression "in
light" refers to God's dwelling place. Interpreters who opt for the meaning of
angels point to the Dead Sea Scrolls, where angels are often called holy ones
(e.g., 1QS 9.7; so Lohse 36 and Pokorný 52). This understanding of "saints"
fits well in a polemic against teachers who require others to have visions in
which they see angels. Yet Paul often uses the term "saints" (*hagioi*) for believers, and every use of the word in Colossians other than this one clearly has
humans in view. The assertion that the departed saints already possess the inheritance and that the readers' share of it is secured by God offers encouragement
in the face of the other teaching, a teaching that places in doubt the readers'
relationship with God.[68] Here, and often in Colossians, the writer uses spatial

66. See Dan 12:13; Wis 5:5. The concept of inheritance is used for heavenly blessings also in
2 Macc 2:4; 2 Esd 7:17, 96.

67. See 1QS 11.7–8; 1QH 11.10–12; Rom 8:23; and among later writings Eph 1:14 and Heb
9:15. James D. Hester (34–36) notes that the concept of inheritance is more individualized at Qumran than it is in the Old Testament texts. This is also the case in Colossians. However, Gary S.
Shogren (180) contends that 1:13 is not about the individual but about the church. It seems better
to hold both the individual and the corporate meanings in view just as we must hold Christ's death
and resurrection, which confer the blessings, together with the individual's baptism, which appro-
priates them. The New Testament uses *klēronomia* and *klēronomos* more often than the vocabulary
used here. But even these words are relatively uncommon: *klēronomia* is used 14 times in the New
Testament, in the Pauline corpus only in Gal 3:18 among the undisputed letters, and among the disputed only in Col 3:24 and Eph 1:14, 18; 5:5. *Klēronomos* appears only 15 times in the New Testament, within the Pauline corpus only in Rom (4:13, 14; 8:17 [2x]) and Gal (3:29; 4:1, 7) in the
undisputed letters, with only one additional reference in the disputed letters (Titus 3:7). So this is
not a common image in the New Testament. This is especially clear when we observe that some
uses of these words refer to literal inheritances and heirs.

68. As Dunn (77) comments, however the "saints" are identified, this passage conveys a sense
of possessing great privilege, though his stress on the distinction between Jews (who already possessed it) and Gentiles is doubtful.

rather than temporal imagery to speak of eschatological blessings. In accord with this imagery, Colossians places more emphasis on realized elements of eschatology in this passage.

In vv. 9–11 the writer connects knowledge of God and proper living. When he speaks of the believer's life as living in a manner that is worthy of the Lord, he invests ethical living with extraordinary dignity. Christians are called to live lives that reflect the character of God and to do so with a consistency that honors the God who is always faithful. The writer designates the doing of good works and attaining yet more knowledge of God as ways in which this worthy living should come to expression. He also declares that God's own power enables believers to live such lives. Thus, God both calls them to this life and enables them to fulfill that call. A final element of the living worthily, giving thanks, appears in v. 12 (along with the last two words of v. 11 in Greek: "with joy"). This feature of worthy living both completes the immediate characterization of that life and begins the transition to the poetic material in vv. 15–20.

1:13–14 God's Saving Acts

1:13 God[a] rescued us from the power of darkness and transferred us into the kingdom of his beloved Son, 14 in whom we have redemption, that is, the forgiveness of sins.

a. The word translated "God" here is the relative pronoun *hos* ("who"). In the structure of the sentence in Greek, it is clear that the antecedent of this pronoun is "the Father" of v. 12.

Verses 13–14 (along with v. 12) serve a dual function, both advancing the thought begun in v. 9 (especially by continuing the description of the life that is pleasing to God)[69] and introducing the poetic material of vv. 15–20. These are compatible functions because all of 1:3–23 prepares the recipients for the core of the letter's argument. Verses 13–14 prepare for the transition from prose to the poetic style of vv. 15–20 by incorporating confessional materials into the description of the God to whom thanks is rendered. This confessional material may well derive from a baptismal setting. From the perspective of the letter's argument, the poetic material in vv. 15–20 is not the central feature of 1:3–23. Rather, the poetic section provides support for the assertions in vv. 12–14; it supplies the grounds for the readers' confidence that they belong among the

---

69. Ralph Martin (53) contends that vv. 12–14 are not part of the prayer because Paul never closes intercessions with thanksgiving. However, the syntactical connections between vv. 9–11 and v. 12 suggest the contrary. Furthermore, Martin's argument assumes that Paul is the author. Since this is disputed, it is better not to base arguments so singularly on a comparison with Paul's undisputed letters.

heirs (v. 12), have been rescued and transferred into the kingdom (v. 14), and have had their sins forgiven (v. 14). Thus while 1:15–20 has figured prominently in later discussions of Christology, affirming those statements about Christ is not the writer's primary point.

Verse 12 provides the transitional link between the description of (and implied exhortation to live) the life that is worthy of the Lord and the description of the work of Christ in the poetic material. The former (vv. 9–12) explains how the readers should live, while vv. 15–20 serve as evidence that God has granted believers all the blessings mentioned in vv. 12–14 (i.e., inheritance, rescue, transfer, redemption, and forgiveness). Verses 13–14 continue to identify God as the one who acts to bring about salvation (v. 12) and prepare the way for the exalted claims about Christ in vv. 15–20. As v. 13 asserts, it is God who rescues believers and transfers them into the realm where the work of Christ is effective. The poetic features in v. 12 show that the author is adjusting his style to ease the transition to the longer poetic section. The relative clauses and change to first-person plural in v. 13 anticipate the incorporation of liturgical material in vv. 13–14. The references to forgiveness of sins, Jesus as the "beloved Son," the contrast between light and darkness, and the language of transfer and rescue—all point to a baptismal context. Thus vv. 13–14 seem to draw on preformed baptismal material,[70] perhaps confessional material. These verses contain the letter's first clear allusion to baptism, a rite that plays a prominent role in the rest of Colossians. Thus, the writer introduces a central image and element of his argument with this confessional material.

[13] "The Father" is the antecedent of the relative pronoun ("who"), which begins v. 13. Thus, God is the actor in v. 13; God rescues believers from the grasp of darkness and transfers them into the kingdom. The image of God as one who rescues God's people from the grip of an overwhelming power is firmly rooted in the exodus, an event that is central to Israel's understanding of God. Colossians takes up and broadens that understanding of God so that God rescues believers from oppression not by a nation, but by cosmic powers, the ruling powers of darkness. This statement envisions people imprisoned by these powers in a realm dominated by evil.[71] Those who have been captured by evil—and this includes all people—are incapable of freeing themselves because these powers possess such strength. Since humans are unable to free themselves from this predicament, God has acted to free them. Both "rescued" and "transferred" are

---

70. Interestingly, the language of 1:12–14 is similar to the description of conversion found in Acts 26:18.

71. Darkness as an image for evil appears in the Dead Sea Scrolls (the War Scroll is replete with this imagery; cf. the opening section, 1QM 1.1–17; 13.10–17; 14.16–17; 15.8–9; 16.11; see also 1QS 2.6–8; 3.3; 3.17–4.1; 11.10; 4Q 177 frg. 14–16; 4Q 286 frg. 7 2.1–5) and throughout the New Testament (Eph 5:11; 6:12; 1 Thess 5:5; 2 Pet 2:4; 1 John 2:11), so the writer can assume that will be understood when it is used here.

in the aorist tense: these acts of God have already occurred. God accomplished this rescuing and transferring through the work of Christ that vv. 15–20 describe. At the same time, however, this accomplished work is actualized in the life of each person as one is baptized. The writer emphasizes that believers already possess these blessings of a new position and identity. This emphasis supplies the writer with the tools he needs to reject the visionaries' teaching by assuring the recipients that they already possess the blessings the visionaries offer.

As the verb "rescued" echoes the experience of the exodus as a pattern of God's acts for God's people, so "transferred" recalls language used to speak of the forced exile of conquered peoples (e.g., Josephus, *Ant.* 9.11.1). The writer is not implying that God forces people into the kingdom; rather, he emphasizes the power over other cosmic forces that God exercises in the rescue of believers. This thought also completes the image of rescue by signifying what believers are rescued *to*, that is, "into the kingdom of [God's] beloved Son," a realm diametrically opposed to the realm of darkness.

The expression "the Son of his love" is probably a Semiticism for "his beloved Son" (so most commentators, but contra Lightfoot 142) and thus an echo of the language the Gospels use when relating Jesus' baptism and transfiguration. Second Peter 1:17 is the closest New Testament parallel to this way of referring to Jesus, and it is an explicit citation of the words spoken at Jesus' baptism (even though the writer puts it "on the holy mountain" and so at the Transfiguration). So speaking of Christ as "his beloved Son" confirms that vv. 13–14 draw on baptismal language, with the focus remaining on the acts of God that give baptism meaning. Verses 14–20 take up the reference to the "Son of his love" and explicate its significance for the situation the recipients face.

New Testament writers seldom speak of the kingdom of the *Son*; instead, they nearly always use the language of the kingdom of *God*.[72] We probably should not overinterpret this unusual way of referring to the kingdom. After all, calling it the kingdom of the Son does not indicate that God no longer rules; in Colossians, if Christ rules, God rules through him. Moreover, when Paul speaks of the Parousia in 1 Cor 15:20–28, he asserts that Christ hands the kingdom over to God at the second coming, thus returning rule to the one who granted it to him. Perhaps, then, if any difference is to be found between the two, the kingdom of the Son is best understood as the kingdom of God as it is manifest during the interim between the resurrection of Christ and the Parousia. God, then, has made the recipients members of the kingdom in which God's blessings are now located. Again, this is an accomplished fact, not something they must strive to attain.

---

72. This is the only place in the New Testament where the expression "kingdom of his Son" appears. However, Eph 5:5 speaks of "the kingdom of Christ" and 2 Tim 4:1 also seems to refer to the "kingdom" of Christ. Cf. Luke 23:42, where the penitent criminal on the cross speaks of "your kingdom."

The language of v. 13 has a distinctly political ring, with its talk of rescue from one ruler and transfer into the dominion of a different king. If this language does draw on formulas recited at baptisms, as seems likely, it indicates that becoming a member of the church has political meanings. One's allegiance must shift to the king of a new realm. This requires the believer to relativize all other allegiances and commitments. Allegiances to family, city, nation, empire, and all aspects of life must now be evaluated through the values of the kingdom in which that believer has now been made a citizen. This is a dramatic shift in identity, a shift that brings blessings and that grounds the responsibilities to live worthily. The emphasis in vv. 13–14 is on the blessings that believers receive because of this rescue from the structures that dominate the world and this transfer into the kingdom ruled by Christ.

The readers have now been shown that the manner of life that is worthy of the Lord does not come to them through their own struggle. Rather, vv. 12–13 demonstrate that their new identity and relationship with God have been given them; they are heirs, they have been rescued, they have been given a new citizenship. Their living of lives pleasing to God (v. 10) is part of the reception of these gifts. In contrast to the other teaching, which places in doubt the salvation of those who do not experience visions, the writer proclaims that the recipients are already in the kingdom. Thus they should live as citizens of this kingdom and as heirs of God. They must recognize that it is not just that their behavior is to be different, but that they have changed realms of existence: they have a new Lord. But thus changing realms of being is not a simple once-for-all change; it must be renewed constantly with every decision they make (see the comments of Schweizer 54).

By calling the kingdom the kingdom of the Son, the author shifts the readers' attention to focus on the Son rather than on the acts of the Father. This change prepares for the focus on the work of Christ in v. 14 and on the person and work of Christ in the poetic material of vv. 15–20. Since this turn serves the flow of the argument so well and the wording is unusual, the author of Colossians probably brought together various traditions when composing vv. 13–14.[73]

[14] Beginning in v. 14, the writer maintains a sustained focus on Christ for the first time in Colossians. Furthermore, the broad assertions about the status of believers and blessings they possess in vv. 12–13 are narrowed in v. 14 so that the issue at hand is the forgiveness of sins. The introductory "in whom" (*en hō*) may indicate that this is again preformed, liturgical material, because such a use of pronouns sometimes signals the presence of liturgical material. The phrase

---

73. Rudolf Hoppe (166–68) also thinks it more probable that the Colossian writer put various preexisting pieces together than that vv. 12–14 were composed as we have them before the letter was written. Lindemann (23–24) is uncertain about whether v. 13 belongs in a baptismal context but observes that the reference to the Son is the keyword that allows the movement into v. 14, which does employ baptismal material.

"in whom" both defines the realm within which believers ("we") receive redemption and sets out the means by which their redemption is accomplished.[74]

In common Hellenistic usage the word "redemption" (*apolytrōsis*) means primarily the ransoming of a captive or prisoner. Verse 13 has already implied that before the readers came to believe in Christ, they were captives of evil powers. There the image is one of rescue, while in v. 14 it is the purchasing of freedom. The primary point, and the point the images share, is that the readers—and all believers—have been emancipated. The redemption metaphor, however, includes the paying of a price. Both the following poetic material and the prepositional phrase with which v. 14 begins ("in whom") show that the work of Christ comprises the ransom.[75] This image for understanding the function of Christ's death and resurrection had wide currency in the early church: within the New Testament, it is found in Paul (Rom 3:24; 8:23; 1 Cor 1:30), the Gospels (Matt 20:28; Mark 10:45), Hebrews (9:15), 1 Peter (1:18), and Revelation (5:9).[76]

Once again in v. 14, the writer asserts that believers (who make up the "we" of this verse) have already been redeemed, that they exist in this condition in the present. This is important as the writer specifies the nuance of redemption he wants to emphasize: forgiveness of sins.

Colossians defines the redemption that believers now possess by placing "forgiveness of sins" in apposition to it. The connection between forgiveness of sins and the metaphor of redemption goes back as far as Ps 130:7–8 (129:7–8 LXX). While forgiveness of sins was a regular part of the early Christian proclamation, Paul uses the plural "sins" with statements about forgiveness only in the tradition he quotes in 1 Cor 15:3 ("Christ died for our sins"). Paul usually speaks of sin in the singular, as a force or realm in which one may be imprisoned. The writer of Colossians draws on that understanding of the human plight apart from Christ when he speaks of the "ruling power of darkness" (v. 13). Use of the plural ("sins") in v. 14 does not run counter to Paul's understanding of the death of Jesus, but neither is it the way he usually speaks. Perhaps the difference is more terminological than conceptual (Hübner 54). By adopting the common usage of the early proclamation (as seen by its presence in the tradition Paul quotes in 1 Cor 15:3), the writer advances his persuasive strategy at this point.[77] While the other teachers evidently cast doubt on whether the readers

---

74. Thus "in whom" is both local and instrumental.

75. Barth and Blanke (191) assert that redemption is not related to paying a ransom here but rather to the sacrifice of the Servant of God in Isa 53:10. While there may well be a connection with Isa 53 here, the imagery of ransom is explicit in the text.

76. The ideas of adoption as heirs and redemption are found together in Rom 8:32, as they are in Col 1:12, 14. While the noun *apolytrōsis* is uncommon in both the New Testament (only appearing 10 times) and general usage, other words that convey similar meanings are used throughout the New Testament (e.g., *lytroō, lytrōsis, agorazō*).

77. If Colossians is still quoting a tradition here, that would also account for the plural.

possess forgiveness and prescribe a way they may attain it, the plural "sins" in Colossians suggests that the readers have been forgiven of whatever sins they had committed. Therefore, they do not need what the other teachers offer.

The basic assertions of the entire first section of Colossians are found in vv. 12–14: through the preaching of the gospel and the Colossians' acceptance of it, God has made them heirs, rescued them from darkness, moved them into the kingdom, redeemed them, and forgiven their sins.[78] These metaphors speak of salvation and relationship with God; the writer presents these acts of God as accomplished, already completed. It is clear, therefore, that the readers do not need to accept any new regulations or have special religious or visionary experiences to gain a place with God. Verses 12–14 give the initial statement of the points made in expanded form in 1:21–23, the verses that set out the thesis of the whole letter. It is the forgiveness of sins that the readers have been led to doubt most, so assurance of forgiveness comes as the crowning clarification of what it means to have been adopted by God and to have been awarded citizenship in God's kingdom. The hymnic material in vv. 15–20 now supports these claims.

1:15–20 Poetic Confession of the Place of Christ

The style and vocabulary of vv. 15–20 set them apart from the surrounding verses.[79] The composition becomes rhythmic, and there are unmistakable parallels between the first and second halves of the section (see below). Many New Testament interpreters identify these verses as an early Christian hymn, often seeing it as an adaptation of an earlier pagan or Jewish hymn (e.g., Käsemann; Robinson; Deichgräber 146–54; Standhartinger 1999, 205–12). When it is understood as a hymn, many then identify the elements that have been added to it, whether by its first Christian adapter or by the writer of Colossians or both.

Though a long interpretive tradition identifies vv. 15–20 as a hymn, that classification is too specific. In this period, hymns and poems were composed strictly according to rhythm and meter. To make the material in these verses fit into any recognized metrical scheme requires radical surgery.[80] Still, the material pos-

78. Similarly, though working with different divisions of the text, Hoppe (164) finds the assertions in 1:13 to be the basic assertions of 1:12–2:7.

79. Lohmeyer (39–41) and Löwe (301–9) expand the hymnic section to include vv. 13–14 and vv. 12–14 respectively. Though vv. 12–14 do begin to use more poetic language and employ some widely recognized elements of confessional material, it remains more probable that those verses serve as transition and introduction to the more-formal material in vv. 15–20 (see the above discussion of 1:12–14).

80. How difficult it is to find the meter may be reflected in the way the Nestle-Aland[26] sets the text of this material. In that edition, vv. 15–18a are set as poetry, but vv. 18b–20 are set as prose. This seems to indicate that the editors did not find sufficient characteristics of poetry to set the verses in that form. On the other hand, the Nestle-Aland[27] sets all of vv. 15–20 as poetry. Still, differently, the UBS[4] sets none of it as poetry.

sesses a more exalted style than regular prose and bears the marks of parallelism in its parts, as well as other features indicating that it is poetic. Perhaps we can speak of it, with Lohse, as possessing the "free rhythm of hymnic prose" (44). Its repetitive structure (cf. v. 15 with v. 18b and v. 16 with v. 19) suggests that it is preformed and perhaps liturgical material. Yet it does not fully possess the formal characteristics necessary to call it a hymn. Perhaps this is because the person (or church) who composed it did not have the skills to produce a formally correct hymn. After all, the early church included few members who would have possessed the level of education usually associated with writing according to such formal criteria. Furthermore, since we have so little evidence about early Christian hymns, we can claim little certainty about their form. Perhaps many or most did not fully conform to the usual standards of composition that we know from extant poets. So we remain on firmer ground if we think of this material as poetic and liturgical, without identifying its genre more specifically. After all, the characteristics it lacks would not necessarily keep it from being used in the antiphonal recitation that probably characterized early Christian worship. The piece would best fulfill its function in Colossians of supporting the assertions in vv. 12–14 and vv. 21–23 if it was already known to the readers (so also Lohse 46). So the writer is probably citing a piece the recipients know.

The poetic material's lack of precise metrical structures has allowed a proliferation of theories about its structure. Interpreters have found 2, 3, 4, or 5 strophes, depending on what they omit as editorial additions by the writer of Colossians (see the list in Balchin 78–79). The hypothesis that best suits the poetic material standing in the text is that it consists of two stanzas, with the second stanza beginning at v. 18b. This structure recognizes the parallels between these two beginnings (*hos estin*, "who is"), the following *hoti* ("because") clause in vv. 16 and 19, and then a *di' autou* ("through him") phrase in vv. 16 and 20. However, vv. 17–18a disrupt the balance between the two stanzas. The two clauses that comprise vv. 17–18a function as a transitional interlude between the stanzas, which moves the reader from speaking of Christ as participant in creation to Christ as the Savior of the church and the world.[81]

This poetic material supports the assertions of vv. 12–14, especially the claim that believers receive redemption and forgiveness of sins in Christ (Lohse 46). It also supplies the basis for the reconciliation with God and standing of holiness that vv. 21–23 attribute to the readers. Thus vv. 15–20 undergird the writer's assertions about the secure place that believers possess with God because they are in Christ. While vv. 15–20 have sometimes been identified as the heart of the letter and as the place its major theological points appear, this mislocates the poetic material in the flow of the letter's argument. Verses 15–20

81. See the analysis of Wright (444–68) and the earlier but somewhat similar view of Lightfoot (143).

obviously contain many important christological statements, but these assertions about the nature and work of Christ are not in dispute. If they were a matter of contention, the author would present arguments for them, giving reasons the readers should believe these things about Christ. But these understandings of Christ are simply stated, apparently with the expectation that they will be accepted by the readers with no supporting argument. So the author and readers agree about them.

The dispute that Colossians engages involves the implications that these statements about Christ have for the recipients' relationship with God and the value of the practices the other teachers advocate. The recipients have not sufficiently considered the implications these confessions have in relation to that other teaching. The writer must convince the readers that their place with God is sure without adopting the things the visionaries teach. Since this is his goal, in vv. 15–20 he supports the claims that they are rescued, transferred into the kingdom, redeemed, and forgiven (vv. 13–14) because of Christ's nature and work. Then, in vv. 21–23, he builds on these confessional statements about Jesus to say that they are reconciled and holy because of who Christ is and because this exalted and powerful Christ has brought them salvation.

1:15 He is the image of the unseen God,
Firstborn of all creation,
16 Because in him were created all things:
Those in the heavens and upon the earth,
Those seeable and unseeable,
Whether thrones,
or lordships,
or rulers,
or authorities.
All things were created through him and for him.

17 And he is before all things,
And all things are sustained in him,
18 And he is the head of the body,
That is, the church.

He is the beginning,
Firstborn from among the dead,
So that he might be preeminent over all,
19 Because in him all the fullness was pleased to dwell
20 And to reconcile all things through him and for him,
Having made peace through the blood of his cross
[through him]:[a]

> Whether things on the earth
> Or things in the heavens.

a. There is strong textual support for the phrase *di'autou* ("through him"), including P⁴⁶ and ℵ, but it is absent from B. See the commentary on this verse.

[15–16] The poetic material opens with the assertion that Christ is the "image of the unseen God." Nearly every statement in vv. 15–20 is fraught with difficulties, not least because of the weight the church has put on this passage in its formulations of christological doctrines. The opening clause contains two puzzles: the meanings of "image" (*eikōn*) and "unseen" (*aoratos*). We must think about these together, because the meaning assigned to either affects what the other connotes.

In the early christological controversies, some seized upon the word "image" to make far-reaching theological claims. Some argued that it means that Christ was of the same substance as the Father (e.g., Gregory of Nazianzus, *Or.* 30.20; Theodoret, *Interp. Colossians*). Others said this designation for Christ meant that Christ was invisible, just as God was (Origen, *Princ.* 1.2.6; Chrysostom, *Hom. Col.* 3), while yet others contended that the reason the Bible could say that God appeared to people was that Christ, as the image of God, was visible while God remained invisible (Novatian, *Trin.* 18.1–3). All such claims over-read this word. By itself, *eikōn* can mean something as simple as the image of the emperor on a coin (Matt 22:20; Mark 12:16; Luke 20:24) or an idol crafted in the likeness of a person (Rom 1:23) or even of the beast of Revelation (see 13:14–15). On the other hand, outside the New Testament, "Wisdom" and the Logos are described as the image of God (e.g., Wis 7:26; Philo, *Leg.* 1.22, 43; 7.1; *Conf.* 146–47). Within the Pauline corpus, *eikōn* also enjoys some more exalted uses: believers are conformed to the image of Christ (Rom 8:29; 2 Cor 3:18), and Christ is again the image of God in 2 Cor 4:4.

Such wide diversity of usage precludes establishing any technical elements of a Christology on this term's use here. If one reads *eikōn* within its literary context, Christ is proclaimed the "image of the unseen God." *Aoratos* ("unseen") may mean "invisible" or "unseen."[82] Within the Old Testament, God appears to and is seen by a number of people. Perhaps most notably, Moses sees God's back because no human can bear to look directly at the glory of God (Exod 33:17–23). God is clearly visible in this story. But Ezekiel speaks of likenesses and is unable to see clearly the presence of God on the chariot-throne (1:26–28). In the New Testament, some statements indicate that humans cannot

---

82. *Aoratos* seldom appears in the New Testament: it is used in only four other verses: Rom 1:20; Col 1:16; 1 Tim 1:17; Heb 11:27. The usage is varied enough that these few appearances do little to clarify its meaning in Col 1:15.

bear to look at God (1 Tim 6:16), but Jesus has seen God (John 6:46). On the other hand, *aoratos* in 1 Tim 1:17 assigns "invisible" to God as an attribute, though one could praise God for being "unseen" or "unseeable" (in the sense that humans are unable to see God), or invisible. Even the repetition of the adjective in v. 16 does little to clarify the meaning of *aoratos* in v. 15 because the beings Christ creates could be either unseen or invisible. However we render *aoratos*, its purpose is to emphasize the transcendence and otherness of God.[83]

While *aoratos* could describe an aspect of the being of God, and so be rendered "invisible," that seems more speculative and is unnecessary to the context. Furthermore, claiming that God by nature is invisible sets this passage in significant tension with a number of statements in the Old Testament. The central point this clause makes is that Christ is the means by which God reveals Godself to the world.

Christ, as God's image, is the knowable and approachable manifestation of God in creation. The word *eikōn* by itself does not imply equality or "complete likeness" (contra MacDonald 58). Rather, *eikōn* identifies Christ as God's means of revelation and the representation of God in the world. Christ is the one through whom the transcendent, unseen God is made present and active in the world. As the rest of the hymn proclaims, it is through Christ that God both created and now redeems the world.

Affirmations about the exalted place of Christ quickly follow this assertion about the revelatory character of Christ and are consistent with calling Christ to be God's image, but the language of "image" by itself does not convey that meaning in the ways it has often been claimed. This is especially clear in light of Col 3:10, where the new life of believers is renewed "in accord with the image [*eikōn*] of the one who created" it. Still, this poetic statement has more in mind than what the phrase "image of God" means in Gen 1:26 (where the LXX uses *eikōn*). In Genesis, being created in the image of God conveys dignity and value;[84] in Colossians, Christ existing *as* the image of God serves to make God known to the whole created realm in a clearer and more exalted way. As God's image, Christ is the representation of God, the manifestation of God's character and power, in and to the world.

After describing Christ as God's image, the poet proclaims that Christ is the "firstborn of all creation." This passage, too, has provoked, or at least allowed, significant discussion about the nature of Christ. While some have read such passages to indicate that Christ is a created being (e.g., the Arians), others contend that it designates only status, not chronology. "Firstborn" is a

---

83. Perhaps Origen's interpretation points in this direction. He says that *aoratos* here means incorporeal (*Princ.* 4.3.15).

84. However, Pokorný (74) contends that there is an allusion to Gen 1:26 here because he understands the mention of the "image of God" in Genesis to indicate that humanity represents God to the rest of creation.

more ambiguous expression than it seems to modern readers. It can certainly speak of chronological priority (see its use in 1:18) and of rank, but not necessarily of an actual birth or coming into being. The use of the title "firstborn" in Judaism demonstrates its range. On several occasions, Israel is called God's firstborn (e.g., Exod 4:22; Jer 31:9; Sir 36:17 [36:11 LXX]), and in Ps 89:27 (88:28 LXX) the king is God's firstborn. Clearly, the word designates rank and preference rather than chronology or anything about literal birth in these passages. Similarly, designating Christ as God's firstborn sets him above all others. It also signals that he is the one who has the right to the blessings of God. So Christ is the one who may distribute those blessings to others.

The genitive phrase "of all creation" (*pasēs ktiseōs*) is comparative rather than partitive: it does not distinguish Christ from various individual created things but compares him to all created things as a group (Meyer 225). Syntactically, it could be partitive, but the poetic material does not seem interested in making an assertion about whether or not Christ is a created being.[85] Rather, it seeks to set Christ in the highest rank in relation to all created beings—which includes all beings except God.

These poetic statements about Christ and his role in creation echo what other writers say about God's hypostatic Wisdom. Among Jewish authors, Wisdom is a manifestation of God and a means through which God created the world (Prov 8:22; Wis 7:17–24; 9:9; Philo, *QG* 4.97; *Cher.* 125), and even God's "firstborn" (Philo, *Conf.* 62). In many ways, the poetic material in Colossians has Christ fulfilling the functions others had Wisdom perform.[86] Such understandings of personified Wisdom would have given the recipients a background against which to hear these assertions about Christ. Jewish authors who assign such functions of creation and revelation to Wisdom do not seem to think such attributions violate their commitment to worship only God. Similarly, neither the author of this material nor the readers of Colossians seem to have seen significant conflict between their worship of one God and what they confess about Christ in this passage.

Verse 16 is bounded by an *inclusio*: it begins and ends by speaking of "all things" being created "in him" (*en,* then *eis*). The verse is probably not formally structured as a chiasmus (contra Pokorný 77; MacDonald 60) because the material that lies between these parallel statements does not manifest the consistent parallels needed for a chiasm.

---

85. Barth and Blanke (246–48) comment that the references to Christ as "firstborn" in Colossians do not support the idea that Christ is a created being or that he is eternal.

86. After noting the parallels between what is said about Christ in this poetic material and what other writers say about Wisdom, *logos*, and *anthrōpos* in Hellenistic Judaism, Robinson (277–78) asserts that this cluster of ideas has been adopted "*en bloc*" by the author of the hymn before it was incorporated into Colossians.

Christ holds the rank of "firstborn" in v. 16 because the whole creation came into existence "in him." At the beginning of v. 16, the phrase "in him" (*en autō*) could mean either that creation came into existence "by means of his actions" or that it exists "within him" (i.e., envisioning the creation residing within the cosmic body of Christ). The end of v. 16 may indicate that the writer of the pre-formed piece had both of these ideas in mind because there all things come into existence both "through" (*dia*) and "in" (*eis*) Christ (see below the discussion of *eis*). The context suggests, however, that the primary meaning of *en* is instrumental: Christ is God's means of creating the world.

Verse 16 expands on its assertion that Christ created all things by adding two pairs of kinds of created things. These pairs each include all created realms and beings. These expansions celebrate and make more emphatic the claim that *all things* were created through Christ. The first pair, "in the heavens and upon the earth," designates those beings and powers that exist in this world and in the realm above. This may help us understand what the author refers to when he names various beings later in the verse. The poem uses the plural of the word "heaven" here. Use of the "heaven*s*" is common in the first century because most people envisioned the cosmos as a series of layers, with varying numbers of layers in the higher reaches called heavens. The New Testament commonly uses the plural to speak of the realm where God and angelic beings reside; the plural is even used in the expression "kingdom of heaven" (e.g., Matt 13:45, 47, 49; Mark 11:25; Luke 11:2). Paul speaks of the third heaven in 2 Cor 12:2, but uses the plural only three times in the undisputed letters, seeming to prefer the singular (e.g., Rom 1:18; 10:6; 1 Cor 8:5; 15:47). When Colossians uses the plural in this poetic material, the writer includes all the heavens that the readers may envision and so all the beings in all those realms. As the following pair ("seeable and unseeable") indicates, all beings are included even though those of the underworld are not explicitly named. Perhaps they are not mentioned to maintain the balanced opposites within these pairs—after all, this is poetic material, not an all-inclusive technical mapping of the cosmos.

The second descriptive pair, "seeable and unseeable," again sets out all-inclusive categories; all things are either seen or unseen. This contrastive duo renews the question of the meaning of *aoratos*. It could point to beings that, by their nature, are not visible to the human eye, or simply to beings in another realm that are not seen because they reside in the heavens (or the underworld). Either way, in the context of Colossians the beings mentioned include those beings that the visionaries who have been teaching in Colossae see and imitate in their visions.

To this point, the poetic material has proclaimed the superior place of Christ in relation to all beings in all realms of creation and the dependence of all creation on Christ's work in creation. The poet made this proclamation with general designations for all other beings, but he becomes more explicit in the last part of v. 16, specifying particular types of beings included among those created through and dependent upon Christ. These names of the angelic powers are not unique to Colossians. The same names for these beings appear in Jewish literature (*2 En.* 20.1; 61.10; *T. Levi* 3.8; *T. Abr.* 14.12). There is no reason to think that the author of Colossians inserted this list into a preformed liturgical piece to include the beings that the visionaries claim to see. The only basis for such an assumption is unsupported mirror-reading, an insufficient basis for such a claim.[87]

Although it seems strange to twenty-first-century readers, early Christians, along with everyone else in the ancient world (both Jews and Gentiles), believed in realms populated by numerous beings, some very powerful. Even Paul believes that there are genuine powers, actual beings, involved in the cults at which most people worshiped. In 1 Cor 8:5–6, Paul acknowledges the existence of those other beings, but denies them the name and rank of God. For him, only God may be worshiped and served, even though those other beings exist and may harm people who refuse to worship them. For the composer of this poetic material and the readers of Colossians, these titles belong to real beings who reside in various parts of the cosmos. Their names suggest that they belong among the most powerful beings; they are "thrones," "lordships," "rulers," and "authorities."

While these titles clearly designate heavenly beings, they probably have an additional point of reference. These names also designate visible social and political offices, structures, and realities. This is the only place in the New Testament where "thrones" refers to a power beyond the natural realm (Hay 58), so it seems unlikely that it does not include human rulers here. Other Christians, notably the author of Revelation, see direct connections between the supernatural powers that oppose Christians and the powers that literally rule the earth.[88] This is the case in this poetic material in Colossians as well. The poet includes the powers of the world among the named rulers and authorities. This understanding takes seriously the two opposing pairs that precede this list of powers. Those pairs mention things on the earth and in the heavens, things both seen and unseen. Since the list of beings that follows the contrasting pairs designates more specifically the beings contained within those named realms, the powers include earthly thrones and visible rulers as well as nonearthly and unseen

---

87. Mirror-reading is a technique some have used in trying to identify situations that the Pauline Letters address. This technique involves the assumption that anything an author says must be responding directly to something the opposition is asserting. For example, if an author tells a church not to steal, the opposed teachers must be saying that stealing is a good Christian thing to do. For discussion of the problems with this method, see Samuel Sandmel, "Parallelomania," *JBL* 81 (1962): 1–13; John M. G. Barclay, "Mirror-Reading a Polemical Letter: Galatians as a Test Case," *JSNT* 31 (1987): 73–93.

88. Furthermore, it is relatively unusual for some of these terms, particularly *archē*, to refer to spiritual powers rather than political rulers (see LSJM 252).

powers. To sever the connection between these realms is to remove the letter from its first-century context, a setting in which those realms were always seen as intimately connected.

The claim that these powers are subordinate to Christ sets the church at odds with the rest of the first-century world. People outside the church see the beings they worshiped in various cults as more powerful than Christ: that is why they worship them rather than joining with the worshipers of Christ in the church. The claim of Christ's superiority also sets the church against the claims of the empire. Rome's propaganda included claims that the Romans ruled the world because the gods willed it. The poet and the church that recites this piece in worship reject such claims by asserting the subordination of all powers to Christ. Therefore, the church possesses an allegiance that supersedes the claims of the empire. They belong to the power that truly rules the cosmos, though that reign is not yet realized. This alternative allegiance will require them to live in ways that people around them see as disruptive and perhaps subversive or even illegal (see comments on limits for associations' meetings in *Excursus: Reading the Household Codes* after 3:17). In other parts of Colossians, the various instructions about how to live will explicate further the meaning of that different allegiance.

Verse 16 declares the superiority of Christ over all created beings in the cosmos, whether in the earthly realm or in realms beyond. The writer bases this superiority on Christ's priority and on his role in the creation of the whole cosmos. So Christ stands as far above all other beings in the cosmos as the creator stands in relation to the created. As if this were not a sufficient exaltation of Christ, the poem's writer goes on to assert that all the created cosmos was created not just *by* Christ, but also *in* or *for* (*eis*) Christ. The final clause of v. 16 begins with "all things."[89] By placing the subject of the clause's passive verb at the beginning, the writer makes the subject ("all things") emphatic: "*all things* are created by him." This is the second time in v. 16 that the writer claims that the whole cosmos was created by Christ; the first statement uses the instrumental *en*; here at the end the poet uses the preposition *dia* (through).

The poet expands this declaration with a second prepositional phrase, *eis auton*. The preposition *eis* has a broad range of meanings. It may mean simply "in" or "into," but it may also designate a goal toward which something or someone moves. A number of interpreters see this as its meaning here in Colossians, usually seeing an eschatological goal in view (e.g., Lightfoot 155;

---

89. Meyer argues that "all things" begins a new sentence. However, it seems better to keep together all of v. 16 since it fits together so closely in its line of thought. Starting a new sentence at the beginning of v. 17 is also preferable to allowing the whole poetic section to continue a single very long sentence. The UBS[4] punctuation begins the sentence with the words "with joy" in v. 11 and continues it through the end of v. 20. This creates an unnecessarily long and complex sentence, even for Colossians.

Pokorný 78–79; Aletti 102–3; MacDonald 60). The change in the verb's tense in this clause supports such a reading. In the initial clause of v. 16, the verb "created" (*ktizō*) appears in the aorist tense, pointing to the act of creation as something accomplished in the past. The end of v. 16 has the same verb, but now in the perfect tense. The perfect implies that something has been accomplished but that it also has an ongoing aspect or effect. Perhaps the use of the perfect tense shows the author thinking that Christ continues to work as creator not just of things that already exist, but also of the things God intends to bring about through Christ. In that case, the preposition *eis* designates Christ as the goal to which the creation is continually moving. The cosmos has Christ as its summative moment. MacDonald (160) notes that *1 En.* 49.1–4 speaks of Wisdom as a force that moves the world toward its final conclusion. If a similar thought lies behind this formulation in Col 1:16, the verse designates Christ as both the origin and the divinely intended goal of all creation.

Colossians 1:16 uses the prepositions *en* ("in"), *dia* ("through"), and *eis* ("for"), as 1 Cor 8:6 and Rom 11:36 use *dia* and *eis* to speak of the relationship between Christ and the world. Colossians 1:16 does not, however, use the preposition *ek* ("out of, from") to describe this relationship, though Paul does use it to speak of God's relationship with the world in 1 Cor 8:6. Lohse understands this selection of prepositions to indicate that the writers of these texts see God as the source of creation, with Christ always as mediator of this act of God (50 n. 125). This is certainly the theological stance that the Colossian poem advocates, whether or not the particular prepositions are chosen to express it. The assertions in 1 Corinthians and Romans that creation came into being through Christ demonstrate that this idea is not a late theological development. Already in the early 50s of the first century, Christians were thinking of Christ as a preexistent being through whom God created the cosmos.

Verse 16 concludes the first section of the poetic composition. In this verse the poet declares that Christ is the definitive revelation of God to the created realm and the agent through whom God created the cosmos. Even beyond this, Christ is the intended goal of creation. Perhaps this indicates that the cosmos should conform to his character. If so, the final line prepares well for both the interlude in vv. 17–18a and the second stanza of the poetic material in vv. 18b–20. For the church, those sections claim identification with Christ, and so conformity to his character, as well as reconciliation with God—God's intention for the world. They proclaim further that all of this is wrought by Christ.

[17–18a] Verses 17–18a form an intermediate section that both summarizes the first section (so also Pokorný 81) and prepares for the following section of the poem. Since vv. 17–18a stand apart from the two main stanzas that comprise this poetic section (see the analysis above), they may have been composed separately and specifically for insertion within the preformed material in Colossians to facilitate the shift from the first to the second stanza. Whether composed separately or as an original part of the preformed text, these verses use ideas from both stanzas that smooth the transition between the two parts, both of which contribute to the argument that Colossians is developing: vv. 15–16 vigorously assert Christ's superiority to all created beings, and vv. 18b–20 relate that superiority to ecclesiology and soteriology. So the transition is from a discussion of the nature of Christ and his work in creation to his work as Savior (Meyer 233). Colossians does not just make this a general claim about Christ being the Savior (indeed, does not use the language of salvation in this section); rather, the writer brings this claim into the lives of the readers by proclaiming Christ to be the Lord of the church, that community to which they belong (Aletti 106).

Verse 17 first reiterates that Christ is "before all things." In Greek, v. 17 begins with *kai autos* ("and he"). This placement of the pronoun *autos* makes it emphatic, so the focus of attention remains steadfastly on the position of Christ. The main verb of this first clause (*estin*, "is") returns to the present tense. Perhaps this verb signals a continuing stress on the preexistence of Christ and his timeless position of superiority in relation to creation (Meyer 231; Lindemann 27). To speak of Christ's preexistence, however, proclaims only that Christ existed before anything was created, without addressing questions about his eternal nature. This is a comparative statement: Christ is "before all things." Clearly this is not a position that Christ attained through conquest or any other means. He is before all created things chronologically and therefore also according to rank. Perhaps, as Lohse (52) says, this clause expresses the idea that Christ is "Lord over the universe."

The second clause in v. 17 again places "all things" (*ta panta*) in an emphatic position. With the verb *synistēmi*, the focus now shifts from the act of creation to sustaining the existence of the cosmos. Not only is Christ the mediator of initial creation; he also is the means by which God continues to hold the world in existence. Platonists and Stoics also used such language to speak of God holding the cosmos together (e.g., Ps. Aristotle, *Mund.* 6; see Lohse 52), and Philo adopted the idea as well (*Her.* 281, 311).[90] In line with this use, the Colossians hymnic piece attributes to Christ the function of sustaining the cosmos, thereby asserting that the whole cosmos and all the beings in it are continually dependent upon him for their very existence. This is yet another way that Christ's almost immeasurable superiority to all other powers is evident; they could not even continue their existence without the cohesion and stability with which Christ undergirds the whole cosmos; it is because of Christ that there is "a cosmos instead of a chaos" (Lightfoot 156).

At the beginning of v. 18 the focus narrows from the cosmos to the church. As at the beginning of v. 17, so also v. 18 begins with *kai autos* ("and he") and

90. This is another function attributed to Wisdom in some texts. See Wis 1:7; Sir 43:26; cited in Aletti 104 and Lohse 52.

thus keeps Christ at center stage. Many interpreters argue that the words "the church" (*tēs ekklēsias*) were added to the preformed text at this point, thus changing the emphasis from a cosmological statement to an ecclesial and eschatological statement (e.g., Lohse 55–56; Pokorný 81; Lindemann 27). Whether it was part of the original composition or added by the writer of Colossians makes little difference for its meaning in Colossians. Such hypotheses about additions to the original poem at this point, in any case, are "unnecessarily complicated and improbable" (Hay 60), because this phrase serves as a transition to the affirmations about the relationship between Christ and the church that follow. So this verse applies the implication of Christ's lordship over all things in the context of the church. The connection with the claims about Christ sustaining the whole world (v. 17b) implies that Christ is the one who sustains the church.

Verse 18 first proclaims that Christ is the "head of the body." Talk of a deity having the world as his body is not unknown in the ancient world (e.g., Plato, *Timaeus* 31b–32a, 47c–48b; Orphic frg. 168; see E. Schweizer, *TDNT* 7:1024–41). This imagery expressed both God's governance of the cosmos and God's relationship with it. The first stanza already gave voice to these ideas. Now the writer uses "body" language to introduce comments about Christ's relationship with the church. He identifies the church, not the cosmos, as the body of Christ.

This understanding of the church as the body of Christ differs from what we find in 1 Cor 12, where the *local congregation* is the body of Christ. In that setting, Paul uses body language to call for unity in a single community in the way it was often used in political settings. He uses it in that way because the problem he addresses in 1 Corinthians concerns strife within the congregation. In Colossians, the body of Christ is not the local assembly, but the church worldwide. Here the writer draws upon body language to make a rather different point from that in 1 Corinthians. In Col 1:18 the writer highlights the relationship between the church and God's agent of creation, who is superior to all other powers. This is not a direct development of Paul's use of body imagery in 1 Corinthians. The writers faced different problems and so employed the same image in different ways. In 1 Corinthians the issues centered on intracommunity relations, while in Colossians the questions concern the way believers have access to God and forgiveness of sins. So, to address a very different situation, the author of Colossians draws on resources other than those Paul used in 1 Corinthians.

When Colossians identifies the church as the body of Christ, it gives its readers significant status. The ecclesiology expressed here closely identifies the church with Christ, and indeed, connects them so closely that it is difficult to envision a more intimate relationship. As the body of the creator and sustainer of the cosmos, believers share in Christ's dignity and position. Other beings in the cosmos have nothing to offer those who are already the body of the one who supports the existence of the whole cosmos. At the same time that the image raises and secures their status, it also designates Christ as the one to whom they owe obedience since he is the head of the church. Chapters 2 and 3 will develop those related themes of the church's intimate relationship with Christ and the obedience its members owe him. Attention to both themes should lead the readers to reject the visionaries' teaching.

[**18b–c**] The second main stanza of this poetic material begins in v. 18b. Just as v. 15 began with "he is" (*hos estin*), so does v. 18b; and as v. 15 designates Jesus as the "firstborn," v. 18b again gives him this title. Verse 18, however, identifies Christ as "firstborn" (*prōtotokos*) over a different group, and thus signals a major shift of topic. In v. 15 Christ is the "firstborn" in relation to all creation, while in v. 18 he is "firstborn" in relation to the dead. For the latter, he is their word of hope, and so the topic of the hymnic piece shifts from protology to soteriology. Perhaps, since discussion of the resurrection places us in the realm of eschatology, the parallels with v. 15 indicate that the poetic material draws on ideas of the new creation. If so, it develops a conceptual connection between the two major sections and shows how the transition from creation to ecclesiology and soteriology transpires in vv. 17–18b.

The first assertion about Christ in v. 18b is that he is the "beginning" (*archē*). This term helps connect the themes of creation and soteriology because *archē* can mean the "origin" or "first cause" of creation. Philo calls Wisdom both the "beginning" and the "image" of God in the same passage (*Leg.* 1.43). So the ideas of priority in both time and originating power are present here.[91] *Archē* takes on an eschatological meaning in Col 1:18b. Here Christ is not primarily the source of the original creation, but of the new creation. Still, those two creations are linked, as they perhaps are in Rom 4:17 as well (Pokorný 83–84).

The term "beginning" not only conceptually links v. 18 with v. 15 but also takes up a title given one of the kinds of beings that Christ created (v. 16). In 1:16, I have translated the word *archē* (in the plural) as "rulers." The poem may intend to set Christ above all the beings listed in v. 16 by assigning to him this same designation and giving it in the singular. That is, rather than a plurality of beings in this classification, as there is for all those in v. 16, Christ is uniquely the Ruler and thus the one to whom all the others are subordinate. If this is intimated, it is nevertheless a minor point in comparison with the emphasis on Christ as the creator of the new life through the resurrection. The poet calls Christ the "beginning" primarily to identify him as the point of origination for the church and the source of its existence. This claim surely entails that he is its ruler.

The second claim about Christ in v. 18b is that he is "firstborn from among the dead." This claim is inseparable from and interprets, perhaps even defines,

---

91. Revelation 3:14 makes this sort of connection between "beginning" and "image" when it calls the risen Christ "the *archē* of all creation."

the assertion that Christ is the "beginning." As in v. 15, calling Jesus "firstborn" designates his priority and rank: he is above all others. It may also intimate that he is the founder of the group; in Gen 49:3 and Deut 21:17 (LXX), *archē* and "firstborn" (*prōtotokos*) appear together as designations of a group's founder. Revelation 1:5 also uses both "firstborn" and the cognate *archōn* as descriptors of Christ when he appears to John. The NRSV translates *archōn* as "ruler" in Rev 1:5, a rendering that emphasizes position rather than priority. Translations seldom voice the meaning of "ruler" for *archē* in Col 1:18, but it seems likely that the initial readers would have heard this nuance in *archē*, as well as "beginning." In the context of the poetic material in Colossians, an element of priority is also unmistakable. In 1:18, the combination of "firstborn" and "beginning" designates Christ as the one who opens the way to new life for others.

That he is "firstborn *from among the dead*" makes this a statement about eschatology, and thus, as we noted, "beginning" also has an eschatological orientation. It is through Christ that others may obtain life beyond death. Christ's resurrection initiates the new possibility for existence that is now available to persons in the church. This assertion provides yet more security about the recipients' relationship with God through Christ: in v. 18a they are his body; in v. 18b he is the originator of, and the means by which they attain, the resurrection.

The term *prōtotokos* ("firstborn") seldom appears in the New Testament. In two of its eight appearances, it refers literally to a firstborn child (Luke 2:7; Heb 11:28; a minority of manuscripts, including C and D, also have the word in Matt 1:25). The remaining six usages all refer to Christ, except Heb 12:23,[92] where the saved are called "the assembly of the firstborn." That title assigns them place and privilege rather than chronological priority. But Rom 8:29 clearly has priority in mind as well when it calls Christ the "firstborn among many" children (RSV). In Rom 8:29 believers are conformed to the image of Christ to fulfill God's will that Christ be the firstborn among many heirs. There Paul understands Christ, as firstborn, to be the pattern for and means by which others come to and live for God. This seems to be the sense of "firstborn" when it appears in Col 1:18.

The image of Christ as "firstborn" in this poetic material implies a relationship between Christ's resurrection and the believer's resurrection that coheres well with what Paul says in 1 Cor 15. There Paul argues that the believer's resurrection is posited and guaranteed in the resurrection of Christ.[93] In Col 1:18, "firstborn from among the dead" communicates that idea, as it implies that others will follow in the likeness of Christ's resurrection. So this statement draws on ideas and images known in Pauline circles to identify Christ and the place of believers in relation to Christ.

92. The other five are Rom 8:29; Col 1:15, 18; Heb 1:6; Rev 1:5.
93. Paul uses the imagery of "firstfruits" rather than firstborn in 1 Cor 15.

The final clause of verse 18 explains why the poem refers to Christ's place as "firstborn" and "beginning" or "ruler": so that Christ "might be preeminent in all things." These identifications of Christ give reasons for his position above all others in the cosmos. If it were standing in isolation, v. 18b–c might be understood to say that Christ becomes preeminent through the resurrection (MacDonald 62), but the context of the whole poetic statement renders this unlikely. The first stanza pictures Christ as God's means of creation, so he does not need to attain a place of preeminence. At the same time, identifying Christ as God's means of *reconciling* the world does maintain and even enhance that preeminence. The poet says that Christ is preeminent not just in the church, but also "in all things." So the resurrection confirms Christ's supremacy over everything in the cosmos (even death), not just things in the church (Meyer 235–36; Hay 62). Such a confession affirms the security of the believers' position as well, because they are Christ's body and the company that will participate in the resurrection of which Christ is the firstborn. Since Christ is over everything, believers cannot be wrested from that safe place by anything in creation.

[19–20] Verse 19 provides further support for the proclamation of Christ's preeminence. While v. 18 declares that Christ is the "beginning" (and "ruler") and "firstborn" so that he might be preeminent, v. 19 says he is supreme *because* "all the fullness" dwells in him. The expression "all the fullness" designates all the nature and character of God and so secures for Christ the highest possible position. There is little reason to think that "the fullness" (*plērōma*) refers to the later gnostic conception of the pleroma. Gnosticism was probably still developing when Colossians was written. And even though ideas such as the pleroma were present in the thought world of the time and region, this passage gives no indication that it draws from or reacts to this type of thought. This statement about the divine presence is emphatic. It does not merely affirm a presence of God in Christ; it also attributes to him the possession of *all* the fullness. It proclaims that all that God is dwells in Christ, so no one could be higher. This affirmation, then, emphasizes the majesty and superiority of Christ to all others.

The verb *eudokeō* can mean "to take pleasure in," but it also has the meaning "to determine, resolve."[94] We should retain both nuances of this verb in v. 19: God resolved to dwell in Christ *and* God took pleasure in residing in Christ. Interpreters have taken the aorist tense of *eudokēsen* ("was pleased") to refer to the incarnation generally (Meyer 239), to a specific event in Jesus' life such as his baptism (Hay, who sees this as a possibility [62]), to the whole salvific work of Christ (MacDonald 63), or to the resurrected Christ (Lindemann 28). The cosmic context of the whole poetic piece and the claim that Christ is the *archē* in v. 18 suggest that this verb indicates more than that God bestowed the full-

---

94. BDAG (404) puts Col 1:19 under the heading of "consent, determine, resolve" and renders the phrase "all the fullness willed to dwell in him."

ness at some moment in relation to the incarnation. Rather, it refers to God's decision before creation that Christ would be God's agent of presence, creation, and salvation (Aletti 110).[95]

God determined not only to dwell in Christ but also "to reconcile all things" through him. God remains the actor, with Christ as the agent of reconciliation. This statement in v. 20 assumes that there has been a disruption in the relationship between God and the world. This idea was not present in the preceding parts of the poetic section. But now it appears and, as it does, connects the poetic insertion more directly to the themes in vv. 13–14, with their comments about powers of darkness and redemption. While the proclamation of Christ as ruler and the presence of alienation in the cosmos seem to stand in tension, their juxtaposition reflects the experience of the early church. In their assemblies, those early believers experience the presence and power of God through Christ. This experience confirms their newly acquired relationship with the God who is above all others. Yet the reaction of the rest of the world to their newfound salvation is hostility. That hostility has real and harmful consequences, at least socially and economically, even if they suffer no state-sponsored physical persecution. While they proclaim that Christ is ruler, the forces of evil still hold power and oppose his rule and his people. So the recipients know both realities that this hymnic piece acknowledges. They experience both the alienation of the world from God and God's saving and reconciling power. In the midst of this life, they proclaim that full reconciliation is forthcoming because the exalted Christ is the agent of that reconciliation. The structure of this clause in v. 20 stresses the agency of Christ. The prepositional phrase "through him" (*di' autou*) comes before the infinitive "to reconcile" and so is emphatic.[96] Thus, the emphasis remains on the work of Christ as the agent of God's acts, now God's salvific acts.

As the infinitive "to dwell" (*katoikēsai*) is aorist, so is "to reconcile" (*apokatallaxai*). This could mean that reconciliation is a fully accomplished event, rather than something that waits for the last day (Lohse 58). But the aorist infinitive does not necessarily designate a past event; rather, it can refer to an act as a whole, with no indication about its timing or progress. Thus, when the author uses the aorist here, he is referring to the whole of God's work of indwelling Christ and reconciling the world. Furthermore, the experience of the recipients does not allow a fully realized reading. This statement operates within the framework of the partially realized eschatology that we find throughout the New Testament. The reconciliation has been accomplished at one level, but its full realization awaits a later time. The introduction of the poetic insertion in

95. Lightfoot (159) supports this view by arguing that in the LXX *paroikia* means a transitory dwelling, while *katoikia* means that something resides in a place permanently.

96. This mirrors the beginning of v. 19, which starts with the prepositional phrase *en autō* and so explicitly keeps attention on Christ.

vv. 12–14 recognizes that the rescue of believers is not accomplished all at once in a past time, but that it is realized at various times in the lives of the believers. Similarly, the following application of the hymnic material in vv. 21–23 also recognizes that the reconciliation has been accomplished in individuals at various times. Even if the poet had a fully realized eschatology, a supposition that is unlikely, the writer of Colossians does not. Perhaps the poet sees reconciliation as a continuing work just as he views the act of creation.[97]

The named object of God's reconciling work in Christ, "all things," indicates the cosmic scope of that work. The whole created order is affected, including all the beings listed in v. 16. Nothing is left out of Christ's reconciling activity. This is another sign that the poet does not advocate a fully realized eschatology, because it is clear to the readers that the powers of evil are still active in the world as forces that oppose the will of God. Yet the final destiny of all is reconciliation; God's creating will not be thwarted.

This is the language of praise and poetry, not systematic theology. This passage does not advocate a universalism that entails the salvation of all. Other passages in Colossians (e.g., 2:22) assume that some things perish, so the author cannot be advocating a blanket universalism. The affirmation of 1:20, however, does emphasize the power and range of God's reconciling will. Through Christ, reconciliation is accomplished, but it must be accepted to be realized in each person and being. If this is not the case, the warning to the readers in 1:22–23—to remain faithful to the gospel they have already received—loses its force (see below).

The first clause of v. 20 ends with the prepositional phrase "to him" (*eis auton*), just as it began with a prepositional phrase ("through him," *di' autou*). The "him" at the beginning of the phrase clearly refers to Christ, but the pronoun at the end of the phrase may refer to either Christ or God. If the preposition *eis* means "to," the pronoun refers to God, in which case the phrase means that "all things" are reconciled "to God." However, the pronoun *autos* is not usually reflexive (though it sometimes is in the New Testament); that is, it usually points to someone other than the subject of the action. If *eis* means "in" or "by," the "him" may still be Christ. The meaning would then be that the reconciliation is ordered by and conformed to the supremacy and lordship of Christ (Aletti 111). The use of the preposition *eis* in v. 20 parallels its use in v. 16, another verse that began with a prepositional phrase (*en autō*). If the meaning of *eis* in v. 20 conforms to its use in v. 16, it points toward the goal of the reconciliation. This parallel suggests that v. 20 asserts that all are reconciled to God, even though the meaning of a word used in a parallel can be different. Still, it may be less redundant for the poet to specify the one to whom all are reconciled than to repeat the

97. Though v. 20 does have the aorist *apokatallaxai*, v. 16 has the aorist *ektisthē* but then the perfect *ektistai* at the end of the verse. Thus, Christ's work of creation is both accomplished and ongoing. We should understand the aorist of v. 20 to allow the same range of thought.

idea that the reconciliation is through Christ, an assertion to which he has already given voice in this clause, and that he will reformulate in the next ("*through* the blood of his cross"). Paul makes God the object of reconciliation in 2 Cor 5:19, where Paul says that through Christ, God reconciled the world to Godself. So if the poet identifies God as the object (and agent) of reconciliation, he reflects a current of soteriological thought present in Pauline communities.

Verse 20b employs another metaphor to speak of the salvific work of Christ, "having made peace." Again, the poet uses an aorist participle and even specifies the time that this act was accomplished: at the crucifixion. But again, while the church celebrates the accomplishment of bringing peace, it is not fully present in the experience of the readers of Colossians or the churches that have recited this liturgical piece. They still experience opposition, but this affirmation assures them that the peace they desire is a certain possession, brought into being through the death of Christ. It may seem surprising to find a mention of making peace in the midst of a celebration of Christ's triumph (MacDonald 64). This is not, however, a strange combination to first-century recipients who are familiar with the claims that Rome makes about itself. Rome claims to bring peace to the world, yet does so through the defeat of others. Rome claims to "make peace" in its celebrations of triumph over enemies. Such claims form the backdrop for the poet's description of the work of Christ.

To this point in the hymnic material, the disruption of God's relationship with the cosmos has not explicitly involved hostility between God and the other powers. The image of making peace, however, draws the recipients back to that understanding. The hostility of ruling powers was already evident in 1:13, where the writer proclaimed that God has rescued them from evil powers. Those powers have not served as they were created through Christ to function, and so the work of Christ restores them to that original place. But that reconciliation is not yet fully accomplished; that is, the cosmos is not "in the eschatological state of salvation" (Pokorný 88). The final line of the poetic material probably also alludes to this hostility when it lists the things of both earth and the heavens as the things that have been granted peace and have been reconciled. The basic point of v. 20 is that Christ's saving work encompasses the whole cosmos, just as his creating work did.

Interpreters most often identify "blood of his cross" as a phrase added to the preformed piece by the writer of Colossians.[98] Given the roughness of the meter throughout this material, however, it is difficult to make such determinations. If the phrase is an insertion, it points to something that the writer of Colossians wants to emphasize.[99] Since in the undisputed letters Paul uses "blood" only

---

98. Including Deichgräber (150), who finds fewer additions than many interpreters.

99. It seems unlikely that the writer wants to balance the theology of Christ's glory evident in the hymnic material with his own theology of the cross, as Lohse contends (60).

once when not drawing on preformed material, either the poet or the author of Colossians draws on the wider church's tradition as well as on Paul for this formulation (Lindemann 30–31). "Blood of his cross" designates more specifically where the reconciling and peacemaking work of God in Christ takes place. The death of Jesus effects this change of relationship with God. The phrase evokes images of a sacrifice, an idea less troubling to first-century readers than to present-day readers. Such an understanding of the death of Jesus appears in Paul and in the tradition before Paul (see 1 Cor 15:1–3). But here in Colossians there is perhaps less emphasis on the notion of sacrifice than on identifying Christ as the one who gives himself (cf. MacDonald 113). This emphasis maintains the thrust of the whole poetic piece.

Given the understanding of "making peace" that is part of Roman propaganda, asserting that Christ makes peace through the cross is astonishing. Christ accomplishes this task in what appears to be a defeat rather than a victory. Including this reference to the cross signals how different the church's values are from those around them. To claim that God has acted in the crucifixion of Christ requires the adoption of a countercultural interpretation of the cosmos. It is a strange claim that the divine work of reconciliation is accomplished through the cross. The tradition that allowed the suffering of martyrs to atone for the nation's sin could prepare the way for it in some ways (e.g., 4 Macc. 6:26–30). But the church claims more than this. It proclaims that God acted through a death on the cross to defeat the powers of evil. This defies all cultural expectations.

This element of the hymnic material also addresses the teaching that Colossians opposes. By identifying the death of Jesus as the place where reconciliation is effected and peace achieved, Colossians turns the readers' attention away from any experiences that some might claim as necessary for forgiveness and a relationship with God. This single phrase, "through the blood of his cross," identifies the cross—not a visionary experience—as the means by which this change in relationship is accomplished, and thus also intimates that such visions are not the point at which one attains access to that relationship.

A number of important manuscripts have the prepositional phrase "through him" [or "it"] follow the reference to the cross (see the note with the translation above). Though it does not appear in Codex Vaticanus and other important early witnesses, it may be part of the original text. Whether original or added later, this prepositional phrase, by reiterating the point, emphasizes that it is through Christ or his cross that all things are brought to a state of peace with God. Whether it is original to Colossians or not makes little difference, because the connections it emphasizes are already firmly established.

The inserted poetic material ends by defining the "all things" that are reconciled in Christ. It specifies that "all things" includes things both on earth and in the heavens. This parallels, though with the elements transposed, the initial expression of the things Christ created in v. 16. Just as everything in existence was created through Christ, so all things in all realms will be returned to God through Christ.

The church fathers drew heavily on Col 1:15–20 as they developed the doctrine of the Trinity and their understanding of the nature of Christ. They often read this material as though it were a theology text. But it is not that sort of material; instead it is liturgical and poetic. Such genres are not well suited to enunciating intricate theological nuances; they are for praise and thanksgiving. Readers must, then, be cautious about basing details of theological doctrines on such material. In the exalted language about Christ, some more-current readers find a binitarian theology that moves away from Jewish monotheism (Hay 65). The point of this liturgical piece, however, is not to declare Christ's equality with God but to identify Christ as the mediator of all God's acts (Aletti 117). The early church's experience of God in worship was mediated through Christ; this is the reality to which this praise gives voice. This simple and yet theologically profound message is also what the writer of Colossians needs as he battles the visionaries' teaching.

It is also the exuberance of praise rather than sober, balanced theological expression that allows the liturgist to proclaim the accomplished reconciliation of all things. Given what Colossians has to say about judgment, its writer is not asserting universal salvation. The struggle with the false teachers and the descriptions of the readers' former lives (1:21–22; 2:13) assume that some will not be saved. The poetic expressions do declare that all life and all salvation come through Christ and that all other beings are inferior, and subject, to him. Thus, experiences with other angelic beings are irrelevant to the Colossians' relationship with God.

The insertion of the preformed poetic or liturgical material in vv. 15–20 bolsters the assertions in vv. 13–14. The preformed material supports the assertions that salvation resides in the kingdom of Christ and that the recipients already possess redemption and forgiveness in Christ. The liturgical material supports these assertions by identifying Christ as the agent of both all creation and all salvation. Furthermore, it establishes the church as the sphere in which salvation is found. This poetic piece also prepares for the statement of the central theses of the letter in 1:21–23 by identifying Christ as the one who accomplishes the reconciliation and provides the forgiveness the recipients need for a present relationship with God and guiltlessness in future judgment. Because of what God has accomplished through Christ, their salvation comes to them in the church and through the cross of Christ. This proclamation bears the implication that all other means to relationship with God and forgiveness before God are unnecessary and that to insist on reliance upon other means is unacceptable.

1:21–23 You Have Been Reconciled and Forgiven in Christ

The immediately preceding poetic material in 1:15–20 focused on Christology. The celebration of the person and work of Christ there supports the soteriological assertions of vv. 13–14. In vv. 21–23 the topic shifts back to soteriology. Thus, claims about the status and forgiveness of believers frame the liturgical material of vv. 15–20. Just as the poetic praise of Christ in vv. 15–20 supports the claims about salvation made in vv. 13–14, so that same praise supports the claims to salvation that vv. 21–23 make for the recipients. Verses 21–23, then, are connected to both vv. 15–20 and vv. 12–14. Furthermore, the themes and vocabulary of vv. 22–23 echo the language of 1:3–6 (e.g., both mention "faith," "hope," "saints/holy" [*hagious*], and "heaven," and both identify the gospel preached in Colossae as the same as that preached all over the world), so vv. 3–6 and vv. 21–23 form an *inclusio*. Thus, vv. 21–23 bring the extended thanksgiving prayer to an end.

Verses 21–23 apply some of the fundamental assertions of the preceding liturgical material (vv. 15–20) specifically to the letter's recipients. Verse 21 begins to address the readers directly, changing to the second-person plural (you) from the third person (they), and v. 22 renews the use of the image of reconciliation in v. 20. Verse 20 rejoiced in the reconciliation that comes to all through Christ's cross, then vv. 21–22 identify the letter's recipients as people in need of this reconciling work and as those who have, in fact, been reconciled.[100] Verses 21–23, however, do more than provide the local and individual application to the cosmic claims of the liturgical material (see MacDonald's characterization of the passage [77]). The author certainly wants the readers to recognize that reconciliation has come to them personally. But beyond this he sets reconciliation and forgiveness in an eschatological context with his use of "Then . . . but now" (vv. 21–22). This construction often signals an eschatological affirmation in the Pauline corpus. So while vv. 21–23 highlight a personalizing element to vv. 12–20, they do not focus exclusively on the experience of the readers (see below on v. 22).

Verses 21–23 both end the first major section of the letter and set out the themes of the major sections of the rest of the letter. In the language of rhetorical analysis, vv. 21–23 serve as the *partitio*, the part of the speech that announces the main themes (Aletti 39, 119–20; Sumney 2002a, 343–44). The letter's themes appear in an order that inverts their sequence in the rest of the letter: (1) the holiness of the saints, spoken of in 1:21–22, is developed in 3:1–4:6; (2) the readers' faithfulness to the received gospel, spoken of in v. 23a, is developed in 2:6–23; and (3) the presentation of Paul as the bearer of the true gospel in v. 23b is expanded in 1:24–2:5. This reversal in sequence creates a

---

100. The mention of the "body of his flesh" in v. 22 may also echo the language of v. 18, where the body of Christ is the church (Hay 67).

smooth transition to the immediately following discussion of Paul's ministry in 1:24–2:5.

The central point of 1:21–23 and of the whole letter is that the readers, and by extension all believers, have been reconciled to God and so are guiltless in God's judgment. God reconciles them through the death of Christ, if they adhere to the gospel they have received from Epaphras. Verses 21–22 restate powerfully the soteriological affirmations that vv. 12–14 have already announced. In the face of teachers who say that the recipients' salvation is in doubt because they do not have visionary experiences, Colossians proclaims vigorously that their acceptance of the work of Christ through the gospel they have already believed provides forgiveness and a gracious relationship with God. The writer proclaims the good news that God has taken the steps necessary to reconcile those who are purposefully hostile toward God and God's purposes, and God does this in an act that changes the way God is present in the world.

1:21 But then you were alienated and hostile in your inner being and with your evil works, 22 but now you have been reconciled[a] through his fleshly body, through his death, so that he might present you holy and spotless and blameless before [God],[b] 23 if you remain faithful, founded and steadfast and not movable from the hope proclaimed in the gospel which you heard. This is the gospel that has been preached to every creature under heaven and of which I, Paul, have become a servant.

a. *Apokatēllaxen* ("he reconciled") is found in ℵ, A, and C; *apokatēllagēte* ("you were reconciled") appears in B and (with a slight spelling variation) P[46]. So there is good textual support for each. Barth and Blanke (220) opt for *apokatēllaxen* because this third-person singular can account for more of the alternative readings found in other manuscripts. However, Lightfoot (161–62) selects the other reading on syntactical bases. I have rendered the verb in the aorist passive second-person plural here ("you have been reconciled"); see my comment on v. 22 below for the explanation for this decision. Note also Metzger's (621–22) dissent from the decision of the editorial committee of UBS[4] to adopt the third-person singular.

b. The text has the pronoun *autou*, which I render "God." See the comment on v. 22 for support of this reading.

[21–22] After the poetic section (vv. 15–20) ends with its proclamation of the reconciliation of all things in Christ, v. 21 reminds the readers that they were once outside that sphere of reconciliation. Verse 22 sharpens the contrast between the ideal conditions described in v. 20 and the actual situation of the readers before their conversion. So vv. 21–22 highlight both the dreadful state of the readers before their conversion and the gloriousness of their current place in Christ. Finally, v. 23 makes possession of these blessings dependent on the recipients remaining true to the gospel they have received from Paul's emissary.

When v. 21 recalls the time when the recipients were alienated from God, the author does not focus their attention solely on their own spiritual biographies, even though much early preaching in the context of baptism used this motif (Dahl 33–34; Hay 66). Nor does the emphasis lie on the distinction between Gentiles and Jews (contra Barth and Blanke 219), though some hint of this distinction may be present. Rather, this statement sets their reconciliation in an eschatological context (cf. Lightfoot 161; Dunn 106). The former time of v. 21 is contrasted to the "now" of v. 22. Within the hymnic piece, vv. 18–20 introduced the eschatological frame of reference taken up in vv. 21–22. Verses 18–20 declare that Christ is the "firstborn from the dead" and the one through whom God acts anew to offer and engender peace by means of the cross. Elsewhere in the Pauline corpus, the "then . . . now" paradigm points to this eschatological watershed. In 2 Cor 5:16–19 Paul describes a new way of viewing all things, even Christ, because of the believers' participation in the new creation that is in Christ.[101] There, as here in Colossians, reconciliation with God is a central element of the new life made possible through the death and resurrection of Christ. So the "then . . . now" statement in Col 1:21–22 conveys two ideas: there has been a radical change in the lives of the readers, and this radical change is part of the eschatological change in the cosmos wrought by the work of Christ.

The primary metaphors these verses employ to speak of the status of believers are relational. They were alienated, but now are reconciled. The word Colossians uses for "alienated" (*apallotrioomai*) appears in the New Testament only here and in Eph 2:12; 4:18, but the metaphor of alienation and reconciliation serves elsewhere as a way to understand the work of Christ (e.g., Rom 5:10–11; 2 Cor 5:18–20). Here in Colossians, people need reconciliation because of the enmity that has existed on their part toward God, not because of God's hostility toward humanity. The word *echthros* may be translated as either a noun or an adjective; that is, the text may describe the readers as "enemies of God" or as "hostile toward God." Since the word is paired with "alienated," it seems better to understand it as the adjective "hostile." The point is that the basic orientation of the readers' lives was formerly one of opposition to God and God's purposes for the world.

Two elements of the sentence give clear expression to the extent of this hostility toward God. First, this alienation and hostility are "with respect to your inner being [*dianoia*]."[102] *Dianoia*, often translated "mind," refers to the whole of one's being, viewed in one aspect of it. The LXX translators often used it for "heart" (*lēb*; e.g., in Exod 36:1; Deut 29:17 [29:18E]), and Heb 8:10 uses it as a parallel to "heart" (*kardia*). Colossians uses *dianoia* to paint hostility toward

---

101. An eschatological nuance may also be present in Rom 11:30; Eph 2:13; Titus 3:3–4.
102. Pokorný (91) identifies *tē dianoia* as a dative of relationship.

God as the overriding disposition of the readers' whole direction of life and thought before their conversion; it was a central part of who they were. As Calvin (314) says it, all of the person was "wholly at variance with God." Their hostility toward God and God's will dominated their entire existence.

This inward direction and disposition comes to expression in "evil deeds," the second element of their hostility v. 21 mentions. The inner alienation and hostility led those who possessed them to commit acts that violate God's will. Such acts made the recipients transgressors in need of forgiveness. The writer lists no specific acts that belong within the category of "evil deeds" (though such a list would include those found in 3:5), and probably has no specific sins in mind. Rather, he envisions a life that is oriented completely by its hostility toward God, an alienation that manifests itself in both inner life and outward acts, acts that are the natural outgrowth of the inner disposition.

Verse 21, then, paints a bleak picture of the state of the readers before the salvific work of Christ and their acceptance of it. This state of existence is not peculiar to the Colossians; it is the state of all Gentiles, if not indeed of all people. Verse 21 is less a biographical depiction of these particular readers than a general description of the way humanity has turned away from God and God's will for the world. As a whole, humanity has alienated itself from and been hostile toward God. God is not the one who harbors hostility. People may have sinned against God, but in this context, God is not the one who needs to be appeased. All of the alienation and hostility are on the side of humanity; nevertheless, God is the one who acts to ameliorate the hostility.

After sketching the dismal situation of humanity in v. 21, the author lets v. 22 announce its end with the phrase "but now." The parallel structures in vv. 21 and 22 show that v. 22 is a direct response to the problem described in v. 21.[103] "But now" refers to both the personal situation of the readers and the new eschatological situation present in the whole world, because it refers to the "moment of divine reversal" (Dunn 107). In the New Testament, and particularly in the Pauline corpus, the ministry, death, and resurrection of Christ mark the pivotal point in God's dealings with the world by initiating the eschatological era. These acts begin a new era of God's relatedness to the world. In Rom 3:21 Paul uses "but now" (*nyni de*) to introduce his discussion of the way Christ's work radically changes the relationship between God and humanity. Paul also uses this expression to speak of the change of the ages in Rom 7:6; 11:30; and 1 Cor 15:20 (perhaps also in Rom 6:22). This act of God creates a new reality in the

---

103. O'Brien (65) sets out the parallels in this way:

pote ontas	*apēllotriōmenous*	"Being then . . . alienated"
	en tois ergois	"in the works"
nyni de	*apokatēllaxen*	"but now . . . reconciled"
	en tō sōmati	"in the body"

world, one in which God invites all to participate. Similarly, in Col 1:22, the phrase "but now" designates the eschatological "order of things" (Lightfoot 161). This is the new reality that the recipients of Colossians have joined through their acceptance of the gospel.

While vv. 18–20 articulated the cosmic ramifications of the eschatological acts of God, v. 22 applies that cosmic, eschatological work to the readers.[104] The cosmic and the local become nearly indistinguishable as the cosmic is replicated in the individual (MacDonald 77). Through their participation in Christ, the "first-born from among the dead" (v. 18), the readers have been incorporated into "the Easter time" (Pokorný 91), into the state of the reconciliation of all things.

The manuscript evidence is divided over whether the first verb in v. 22 should be "he reconciled [*apokatēllaxen*] you" or "you were reconciled" (*apokatēllagēte*). The former states that Christ (or God) accomplished the reconciliation; the latter identifies the recipients as those who have been reconciled. The shift in focus in this section to the effect of Christ's work on the readers suggests that the passive reading fits the context better, and so it has been adopted here. This decision does not affect the primary assertions of this verse. The question involves only whether this verb emphasizes the divine act or its consequence.

The eschatological act of God described in v. 22 directly addresses the desperate situation described in v. 21. In the face of alienation and hostility, the readers have been reconciled to God. Whether the passive second-person plural ("you were reconciled") or the active third-person singular ("he reconciled") is the better reading, the central affirmation is that the alienation and hostility were overcome by divine initiative, not by those who were hostile. The writer may envision either Christ or God as the one who does the reconciling. In vv. 19–20, "the fullness" reconciles all things in Christ. Verse 22 may carry that subject forward so that God reconciles humanity through the death of Christ. On the other hand, the rest of v. 22 has Christ as the actor, which leads the reader to envision him as the actor in reconciliation. The writer probably has Christ most immediately in view because Christ serves as God's agent and representative throughout this part of Colossians. But perhaps the author purposefully left this statement ambiguous, finding both God and Christ appropriate in this role and not wanting to limit the statement's meaning. What remains clear is that the reconciliation comes from God.

---

104. If the UBS[4] and NA[26] are correct that the text reads *apokatēllaxen* (i.e., the active third-person singular rather than the passive second-person plural), then perhaps the author's desire to keep their reconciliation in the context of cosmic and eschatological reconciliation shows itself in the absence of the personal pronoun "you" in the first half of v. 22. Only after "to present [that he might present]" (*parastēsai*) does the pronoun appear, and here it is primarily the object of that preceding infinitive and only secondarily (if at all) serves as the object of "[he] reconciled" (*apokatēllaxen*).

The relational metaphor of reconciliation points primarily to the establishment of good relations between parties. Where enmity and hostility have characterized humanity's attitude toward God, now God has acted in a manner that changes the people's outlook. Through Christ, God has shown love, goodness, goodwill, and a willingness to forgive to such an extent that it overcomes the hostility that existed in the minds and actions of the readers.

God accomplishes this reconciliation through the death of Christ. The writer expresses this with the unusual phrase "through his fleshly body [in the body of his flesh], through his death." There is significant evidence that "body of flesh" is a Hebraism (see 1QpHab 9.2; *1 En.* 102.5; Sir 23:17 [23:16E]) that simply refers to bodily existence (Barth and Blanke 221; Horgan 880; O'Brien 68).[105] The writer may use this expression to distinguish the body of Christ on the cross from the glorious body of Christ mentioned in v. 18 (Lightfoot 162; Schweizer 91; Hay 68). The preposition *en* ("through," "in") that precedes "body of his flesh" is instrumental; that is, it designates the means by which the reconciliation is accomplished: the physical body of Christ on the cross. While the writer maintains the distinction between the two bodies of Christ, an essential connection remains. The recipients' reconciliation is accomplished through Christ's physical body, but they experience that reconciliation in Christ's cosmic body, the church. So their relationship with God (and one another) depends completely on Christ.

The prepositional phrase "through his death" specifies further the means by which reconciliation to God is accomplished. It is not only the incarnation of Christ but also his willingness to die for others that removes the hostility from the hearts of those who allow his death to reveal God's character to them. In the cross God identifies with those who suffer estrangement and hostility, and through the resurrection (presupposed from vv. 18–20) God demonstrates that God also overcomes these conditions and offers a relationship to those who are estranged.

Verse 22 specifies that the result of the death of Christ is to "present you holy and spotless and blameless before [God]." The adjectives "holy" and "spotless" are used in sacrificial contexts to describe the required characteristics of things sacrificed. But the sacrificial cult is not the primary setting for this metaphor. The verb "present" (though also used in cultic contexts) and the adjective "blameless" indicate that the writer is thinking primarily in judicial rather than cultic terms; he now has the final judgment in view.[106] Though there is significant ambiguity about who does the presenting and to whom, the context

105. It seems unlikely that Dunn (108–9), O'Brien (68), and Lincoln (606) are correct that "body of flesh" counters a false teaching either questioning the reality of Christ's death or denigrating physical existence. There is insufficient evidence that such teachings were present in this church. The primary evidence for this hypothesis is mirror-reading, an insufficient basis for such a claim.

106. See further the discussion of Sappington 187–88, 227; cf. Abbott 227.

recommends Christ as the one who presents believers to God. This allusion to
judgment expands the ways the author wants his readers to think about the
effects of Christ's death. He intimates that one of the ways God enacts reconciliation is by providing forgiveness and so guiltlessness at the judgment.
Though the writer does not explain the connection between reconciliation and
forgiveness, perhaps he thinks of guilt as one of the things that contributes to
the alienation and hostility that humanity has toward God. He may envision forgiveness as a *consequence* of reconciliation, so that it is one of the benefits that
accrue to those who are rightly related to God. Alternatively, he may view forgiveness as a *corollary* of reconciliation so that it is an aspect of God's reconciling act.

The adjectives "holy," "spotless," and "blameless" may refer to the current
life of believers, as well as to final judgment (so Calvin 315; Lightfoot 162;
Aletti 125). But while Colossians devotes much energy in what follows, especially in chapters 3 and 4, to exhorting the readers to live lives that are appropriate to their new life in Christ, that element remains in the background in v. 22.
The verb "present" suggests an emphasis on the judgment. The writer uses the
same verb in 1:28, where he clearly has the final judgment in view. The conditional clause that begins v. 23 confirms that v. 22 has the judgment rather than
current ethical living in view because it indicates that the readers will be blameless only if they fulfill the conditions set out in v. 23.

With the mention of guiltlessness in judgment, the writer returns to the topic
set out in v. 14 and addresses a primary concern of the readers: how they obtain
forgiveness and a place with God. In the face of teachers who argue that the
Colossians must attain visionary experiences to receive forgiveness, Colossians
declares that they already have forgiveness through the death of Christ, who is
God's agent of creation and the bearer of reconciliation to the whole of creation.
Since this Christ is the purveyor of their forgiveness, they can possess full confidence about their relationship with God.

[23] Verse 23 begins with the emphatic conditional particles *ei ge*, "if
indeed." The writer designates a single condition on which the readers' blamelessness at judgment and their reconciliation depend: they must remain faithful
to the gospel they have already accepted. This implies that they must reject the
visionaries' teaching. The conditional particles do not express doubt that the
readers will remain faithful. They may be translated "assuming that" (Abbott
227), and thus denote as much confidence as doubt (Dunn 110). This conditional phrase indicates that the readers have a choice about whether to live in
the reconciled state described in v. 22. Since living in the reconciled state
requires a choice on their part, being reconciled to God includes an element of
human responsibility. So the announcement of the good news of God's acting
to reconcile becomes a summons to adhere to the faith, even to faithfulness to
the Pauline gospel.

The readers must remain *tē pistei*. This could mean they must remain in "the faith" that was delivered to them, or that they must remain "faithful" to that message; that is, it can refer to the message (O'Brien 69) or the disposition of the readers (Dunn 110; Hay 68–69). The verb *epimenō* (to remain) often takes a dative that designates a disposition (e.g., Rom 6:1; 11:22, 23). Since *tē pistei* is a dative, it probably refers to the disposition of faithfulness here: "if you remain faithful." This seems to imply that the Colossians have already expressed faithfulness in some ways and must now express that manner of life in their rejection of false teaching.

The writer's pleonastic tendency exerts itself as he uses three words to depict the faithfulness the readers need if they are to retain their state of reconciliation with God. They must (1) remain firmly upon the foundation (*tethemeliōmenoi*) that was already laid, (2) remain there "steadfast" or "immovable," and (3) "not be moved." The repetition of the injunction with the three relatively synonymous ideas makes the statement emphatic. The readers must not shift in the least from the teaching they have already received from Epaphras, or they risk losing the reconciliation and forgiveness they enjoy through that gospel.

Colossians calls the object the readers must continue to hold the "hope of the gospel." The context suggests that the expression means "the hope that comes from the gospel."[107] The recipients do not yet fully possess this hope, even though they have already been reconciled to God. The allusion to judgment in v. 22 and the demand that they maintain their faithfulness to the gospel both indicate that this hope has a future aspect. The previous mention of the "hope stored up for you in the heavens" (1:5) and the need for "patience and long-suffering" (1:11) have prepared the readers for this intimation of the future aspect of salvation. The references to future eschatological events and hopes throughout chapter 1, and particularly in the theme-setting section 1:21–23, demonstrate that the eschatology of Colossians is not as fully realized as many interpreters contend. This letter certainly emphasizes the current possession of God's gifts (e.g., reconciliation) as one of its strategies to lead the readers to reject the visionaries' teachings. But its references to hope and endurance demonstrate that Colossians looks forward to a fuller consummation of God's blessings in the future.

The reference to hope in v. 23 reminds readers of the future aspect of the gospel and makes their participation in that future contingent on their adherence to the gospel they have already received. This brings the readers to a central point of the letter: they must continue to adhere to the gospel that Epaphras brought to them; it is the gospel that brings reconciliation and blamelessness at judgment. The development of this theme in 2:6–23 makes abundantly clear

---

107. This seems more likely than the possibility that the writer sets the gospel in apposition to "hope," as Horgan (880) suggests.

that adhering to this gospel means rejecting the teaching the visionaries advocate. The admonition of 1:23 only intimates what the later section will state forcefully: the gospel that brings the gifts of God is incompatible with the visionaries' teaching. Furthermore, adopting the other teaching amounts to abandoning the gospel and so losing that good relationship with God and guiltlessness in judgment. Thus, adopting that new teaching has an effect precisely the opposite of what its proponents claim.

The final two clauses of v. 23 enhance the previously received gospel's standing by speaking of its universality and its attachment to Paul. The hyperbole evident in the earlier assertion that the same gospel the readers have accepted was preached all over the world (1:6) is now exaggerated yet more. Now the gospel has been preached to "every creature under heaven." This universal preaching of the gospel implies its universal validity (see the comment on 1:6). Furthermore, this hyperbole is a typical way Greco-Roman speakers secured their reputations (MacDonald 76–77). Thus it provides a good lead into the discussion of Paul's ministry in 1:24–2:5, as well as confirming the validity of the gospel that he preaches and they received from Epaphras, Paul's emissary.

The final clause of v. 23 has Paul claim that the gospel the letter's recipients have accepted from Epaphras is the gospel of which he is a servant (*diakonos*). This statement both claims apostolic status for the previously received gospel (by implication, in opposition to the other teaching) and begins to shape the image of Paul that Colossians emphasizes. The absence of the title "apostle" does not indicate that the writer wants the recipients to see Paul on the same level as Epaphras or Tychicus (contra O'Brien 71; Barth and Blanke 224). Such an understanding misreads the literary and historical contexts. There is no need to reassert Paul's apostolic status if no one is questioning it (Lightfoot 163–64), particularly since the writer attributes this title to Paul in the greeting (1:1).[108]

Paul (and much of the rest of the New Testament) commonly uses "servant" (*diakonos*) to speak of those whose vocation is ministry, including himself. This designation expresses a theology of ministry that was central to Paul's self-understanding and to the understanding of the church's leadership found in the Gospels (Matt 20:20–28; Mark 9:30–37; 10:32–35; Luke 22:24–30; John 13:1–20). It reveals a perspective that requires leaders to possess a willingness to perform lowly tasks for the good of the church and the advance of the gospel. The contrast between Paul's understanding of leadership and apostleship, on the one hand, and Hellenistic culture's understandings of leadership, on the other, is particularly clear in the Corinthian correspondence (1 Cor 1–4; 9 [particularly v. 19]; 2 Cor 4:7–12). There he forcefully argues that leadership in the

---

108. The copyist of Codex P and the original hand of ℵ may have felt a need to incorporate some claim to apostolic status here because those manuscripts have "preacher and apostle" (*kēryx kai apostolos*). Codex A has "preacher and apostle and servant" (*kēryx kai apostolos kai diakonos*).

church must not include claims to superiority or demands for deference. Rather, Christian leadership expresses itself in accepting voluntary humility and putting the good of the church before one's own advantage.[109] In similar fashion, Colossians adopts servant language to speak of Paul and his position in relation to the gospel and the readers.

Colossians also adapts the meaning of *diakonos* ("servant" or "minister") to fit the circumstances it addresses. This is the first time in the New Testament that Paul is identified as a servant of the gospel, rather than a servant of God, Christ, or the new covenant. In the context of Colossians, this is important because the content of the gospel is at issue. Paul is a servant of the gospel to which Colossians urges the readers to remain faithful. It is to this universal gospel, the gospel that brings reconciliation and forgiveness, that Paul is committed.

When the writer calls Paul a "servant," he introduces an image of Paul that 1:24–2:5 develops. According to 1:24–2:5, Paul suffers and works hard for the readers and for all believers who do not know him. Colossians again designates Paul a *diakonos* in 1:25 in connection with both his suffering and his relationship to the Word of God. As will become evident in 1:24–2:5, the writer encourages readers to accept the letter's instructions by identifying Paul as one who struggles and suffers on their behalf. Here Paul garners authority from his suffering for their sake rather than primarily from his apostolic status. Calling him a *diakonos* in 1:23 does not diminish his standing or make him like Epaphras and others; rather, it prepares readers for the imagery of Paul's service to them and his trustworthiness. Instead of lowering his status, this use of *diakonos* readies the ground for a different basis of authority, while not rejecting apostolic authority.

Calvin (316) comments that it is "no ordinary confirmation" to hear that the whole church and the apostle teach the same gospel Epaphras has preached to the recipients. Clearly these descriptions of the previously received gospel serve to establish it as the true gospel to which the readers must adhere. This affirmation of the gospel already accepted lays the groundwork for the polemic against the other teaching that begins in earnest at 2:8. The final words of v. 23 also make a smooth transition to the extensive discussion of Paul's ethos in 1:24–2:5.

Overall, 1:21–23 sets out the basic theses that will be discussed at length in the rest of Colossians: the holiness required of believers (v. 22), the necessity of adhering to the received gospel (v. 23), and the identification of Paul as the bearer of the authentic gospel (v. 23). This section has proclaimed that the readers' reconciliation with and forgiveness before God depends on the death of Christ yet also remains contingent upon their adherence to that original gospel.

---

109. For more extensive discussion of ministry in the New Testament, see Sumney 2002b, 27–42.

Since vv. 15–20 are framed by statements about forgiveness, one of the main functions of that liturgical material is to support the claim that the readers have indeed been forgiven in Christ. Verses 21–23, then, assert that the cosmic work of Christ is effective for the readers and put their relationship with God into the context of the liturgical affirmations of vv. 15–20. So the letter's recipients have a place in God's eschatological reclaiming of the world through Christ. This affirmation of the readers and the gospel they have originally received serves well as preparation for the letter's more direct arguments, which begin in 1:24.

Excursus 1: Metaphors for the Work of Christ in Colossians 1:12–23

Colossians 1:12–23 employs a wide range of images to speak of the way God has expressed love for humanity. These metaphors include adoption (v. 12), rescue (v. 13), granting of citizenship (v. 13), redemption (i.e., making a ransom payment, v. 14), forgiveness of sins (v. 14), and reconciliation (vv. 20, 22). Each of these contributes nuances for understanding God's acts on behalf of humanity that the others do not. The adoption metaphor implies an intimacy and sharing of resources, drawing on the image of God as a generous father who distributes the inheritance. Talk of rescuing them addresses feelings of helplessness in a world that has overwhelmed and oppressed those not among the empire's elites. This metaphor designates God as the one who has freed them from the powers—both spiritual and earthly—that oppress them. At the same time, it intimates that readers cannot accomplish this on their own, perhaps as a counter to the other teachers' demands that they accomplish certain visionary feats.

The metaphor of transfer into the kingdom speaks of the change in allegiance that must accompany these gifts from God. If Colossians envisions God granting believers full citizenship, then they are granted privileges but also given new responsibilities to fulfill. The language of redemption directs attention to the world of commerce or perhaps recalls the image of rescue. All the Colossians were familiar with the redemption of slaves, including those who were enslaved by being captured in war. Enslaved prisoners of war were sometimes purchased from their captors and thus regained their freedom and returned to their family.

The language of forgiveness points to the legal sphere, where transgression, determination of guilt, and a just response are paramount. Finally, reconciliation is primarily a relational metaphor, but it operates in two ways in Colossians. In the poetic material of 1:15–20, the *Christus Victor* idea dominates. Here Christ, through the cross, imposes a peace on the cosmic powers (v. 20). But in v. 22, reconciliation, again accomplished by means of Christ's death, takes place through a change in the hearts of those who were once hostile to God. Each of the foregoing metaphors provides a different means for thinking about Christ's work. None of these metaphors is sufficient by itself to fully describe the astonishing act of God's love that Christ's work accomplishes. The needs of the recipients and the tendencies of the author (including cultural inclinations) determine, to a significant extent, which metaphors predominate.

Forgiveness and reconciliation are the two metaphors to which Colossians gives the most attention and emphasis in 1:12–23. Since the other teachers claim that a person must receive visionary experiences to possess forgiveness from God, the writer's assurances about guiltlessness in judgment counter one of the most damaging aspects of that teaching. This assertion of forgiveness is a central affirmation of the letter. The recipients' new relationship with God is a corollary of their right status in judgment. The death of Christ draws believers to accept this new relationship with God, a relationship that also enables them to stand guiltless before God in judgment. The reconciliation of believers is a part of the cosmic reconciliation of all things in Christ. Though this new relationship of peace involves coercion and defeat of hostile cosmic powers, the readers' continuing experience of the world demonstrates that the reign of God has not completely taken control of the world. Some, perhaps most, of those powers have not relinquished their hold on the world. Thus, believers still face hostility from outsiders, false teachings in the church, and temptations to sin. So Colossians' statements about the current peace do not express a fully realized eschatology. After all, even the recipients' place in judgment is contingent on their remaining faithful to the gospel (v. 23).

The motifs and metaphors that appear in Col 1:21–23 exhibit remarkable parallels with 2 Cor 5:14–21. When Paul wrote 2 Corinthians, he was estranged from that church because of the powerful influence of other teachers who were attempting to lead the Corinthians to reject Paul's apostolic status. In that context, too, Paul emphasizes reconciliation, that between God and the Corinthians, as well as that between the Corinthians and himself. In 2 Cor 5:14–21 Paul draws together the imagery of reconciliation and an eschatological theme, using "now" (*nyn*), just as Colossians does. The love that Christ exhibited in his death enables the reconciliation that Paul seeks with the Corinthians by incorporating the whole church into the reality that Christ's death creates. In addition, God reconciles the world to Godself in conjunction with granting forgiveness in judgment. So the same two primary metaphors are related in ways similar to what we find in Colossians. Finally, the affirmations of Christ's role in creation in Col 1:15–20 parallel Paul's declaration of a new creation in 2 Cor 5. Thus both Col 1:12–23 and 2 Cor 5:14–21 bring together the motifs of (1) reconciliation, which is (2) accomplished through Christ's death and also (3) provides forgiveness of sins and so blamelessness in judgment, and (4) all of this is viewed as participation in the eschatological era. Though these similarities do not prove that the author of Colossians had this 2 Corinthians passage in mind as he wrote, they do demonstrate the ways early Christians saw these particular metaphors and motifs as complementary and interrelated.

Forgiveness and reconciliation feature most prominently as the ways Col 1:12–23 interprets the work of Christ because they provide the most effective counter to the teaching the letter rejects. The readers need assurance about their place with God and an explication of the means by which it was attained, a means that excludes the need for visionary experiences. Since Christ is the agent of creation, firstborn from the dead, head of the church, and reconciler of the whole cosmos, believers can be certain that his death is fully sufficient to grant them forgiveness and the relationship with God that makes them heirs of God's gifts.

Argument 1

Accept This Letter's Teaching and Instruction Because Paul Is the Trustworthy Bearer of the True Gospel

Colossians 1:24–2:5

PAUL IS THE TRUSTWORTHY BEARER OF THE TRUE GOSPEL

This is the first section of the body of this letter's argument. The previous section, 1:21–23, set out the thesis and the three main proofs the writer would use to demonstrate that the readers should remain in the apostolic teaching they have received from Epaphras and so reject the visionaries. These three proofs that the readers have been reconciled to God and have the proper relationship with God are (1) that they are already forgiven and holy, (2) that they must remain faithful to the gospel they have already received to maintain their relationship with God, and (3) that Paul is the reliable preacher of this authentic gospel. Colossians takes up these proofs in reverse order. Verse 23 introduces the third proof of the letter's thesis when it identifies Paul as a servant of the genuine and universal gospel. Thus, it introduces the topic of 1:24–2:5: Paul's ministry and his love and concern for the Colossians and all believers he does not know, a concern that he manifests by his willingness to suffer for their benefit. Thus, this section establishes Paul as a person to whom they should listen.

While it may seem odd to twenty-first-century readers to count the character of the person and one's goodwill toward the hearers as evidence that one's point of view is correct, ancient rhetoricians recognized that such appeals were effective tools.[1] Aristotle even said that it was sometimes the most effective form of proof one could offer (*Rhet.* 1.4). Many ancient rhetoricians devoted significant effort to discussing *ethos*, the character of the speaker. They agreed that it was important to develop an image of yourself that showed what kind of person you were and that you had the best interest of the audience in mind. Even in criminal cases, the character of the person was sometimes a central piece of evidence showing that the person was either guilty or innocent.[2] *Ethos* is so

---

1. Dunn (113) notes that Paul often writes of his own work and his personal involvement with the recipients immediately after the thanksgiving. If it is correct that the thanksgiving of Colossians extends through 1:23, then this writer is following that practice as well. (Such details may count in favor of Pauline authorship.) This observation is interesting because it highlights the importance that Paul gives to establishing his ethos in his letters.

2. For particularly clear examples, see the *Major Declamations* of Quintilian. For further discussion of ethos, see the essays on ethos in *Rhetoric, Ethic, and Moral Persuasion in Biblical Discourse: Essays from the 2002 Heidelberg Conference*, ed. T. H. Olbricht and A. Eriksson, Emory Studies in Early Christianity (New York: T&T Clark, 2005): esp. Manfred Krause, "Ethos as a Technical Means of Persuasion in Ancient Rhetorical Theory," 73–87; and Sumney 2005, 301–15.

effective because audiences listen more receptively to people of good character. So Colossians uses this tool to keep the readers in the apostolic faith.[3]

The image that a speaker develops of oneself is always a fiction, which is not to say untrue. Rather, the image that one constructs of oneself is always a partial image, an image that emphasizes some aspects of one's total self and minimizes or excludes other aspects, because they are either irrelevant (or at least less helpful) or detrimental to the speaker's cause. If Colossians is pseudonymous, this is an especially important task. The image the writer constructs of Paul must cohere with what the readers know of Paul and must project an ethos that will move the readers both to perceive him as someone who has their good at heart and to consider him an authority they should obey. This is the primary task of 1:24–2:5.

This larger section, 1:24–2:5, is composed of two subsections: 1:24–29 and 2:1–5. The disclosure formula ("I want you to know . . .") in 2:1 signals a minor shift in the argument, as does a slight change of focus from Paul's identity as a minister of the gospel (1:24–29) to his relationship to the readers (2:1–5).[4] The first-person singular, "I," also substantiates the connection of 2:1–5 with 1:23 and 1:24–29, where the author also has Paul speak in the first-person singular.

1:24–29 Paul Suffers for the Benefit of the Church

1:24 Now I rejoice in my sufferings[a] for you, and I fill up what is lacking in the afflictions of Christ in my flesh, for his body, which is the church, 25 of which I became a minister according to the commission of God, which he gave me, to fulfill the word of God among you.[b] 26 This word of God[c] is the mystery that was hidden from ages and from generations, but now it has been revealed to his saints, 27 to whom God wanted to make known among the Gentiles the great richness of the glory of this mystery,[d] which is Christ in you, the hope of glory.[e] 28 We proclaim this mystery,[f] admonishing every person and teaching every person with all wisdom, so that we might present every person complete in Christ; 29 for this[g] I work strenuously according to God's working, which works in me powerfully.[h]

a. The pronoun "my" is not in the text. This leaves open the possibility that the sufferings Paul rejoices in are the sufferings of Christ. But since these sufferings are "for *you*" rather than "for *us*," they refer to the sufferings of Paul. See MacDonald (78) for other grammatical arguments that favor this rendering.

3. Pokorný (95) identifies 1:24–2:5 as a digression because 2:6 connects well with 1:23. But this underestimates the importance of ethos in the context of the ancient world. Furthermore, if 1:21–23 outlines the arguments to follow, we should expect 2:6 to connect well with 1:23.

4. It seems unlikely that 1:24–29 is arranged as a chiasm, as Aletti proposes (134), but this suggestion does reflect the strong connections among the themes of the section.

b. The prepositional phrase *eis hymas* ("among you") could be taken with what precedes it, Paul's being commissioned by God, or with what follows, fulfilling the word of God. The meaning assigned the preposition *eis* affects this decision. If it is rendered "for, with respect to," then it may attach to the commissioning of Paul. But if we render it "among," then it attaches better to what follows. Since the flow of thought is moving toward Paul's proclamation of the gospel among the Gentiles, the latter option is preferable.

c. The words "This word of God" do not appear in the Greek text but are added for the sake of clarity so that a new English sentence can begin here. Since all of 1:24–29 is a single sentence in Greek, some breaks for the sake of English syntax are necessary. It is clear in Greek that the "mystery" is the "word of God."

d. The interrogative pronoun *ti* serves as a comparative (how great, how much), which is the subject of the understood verb *estin* ("is"). The noun *ploutos* ("riches") is a predicate nominative. Thus literally these words might be translated "how great is the wealth [or riches]." The following genitive noun, *doxēs* ("glory"), may be a genitive of quality that provides an attribute of "wealth" and thus be rendered "wealth of the glory"; or it may be a Semiticism (so Barth and Blanke 265) and thus be read "glorious wealth." The translation adopted here takes *doxēs* as a qualitative genitive. While there is no significant difference in the meaning of this phrase, seeing a Semiticism here may influence the translation of "hope of glory" at the end of the verse. The translation of that phrase is more important because viewing it as a Semiticism ("glorious hope") might dim its eschatological hue by diminishing the likelihood that it refers to end-time blessings (for my interpretation, see the comment on v. 27 below).

e. Here I render *doxēs* as an objective gentive rather than as a Semiticism ("glorious hope").

f. "This mystery" is the rendering given the masculine relative pronoun *hon* that begins v. 28. Its antecedent may be Christ, but it may also be "Christ in you," or perhaps it reaches as far back as *mystēriou* ("mystery"). In many ways the latter two options are synonymous. This broader meaning is accepted here because it seems to fit better with the end of the verse, where we see that Paul wants to present "every person . . . in Christ." That is, the thought flows more smoothly if he proclaims "Christ in you" as a means to present every person "in Christ." Whichever option is preferred, however, there is no substantive difference in the meaning.

g. Again the antecedent of the pronoun *ho* is not clear. It is understood here to refer to the presenting of "every person complete" since that maintains the line of thought, which has Paul laboring for the benefit of the readers.

h. "Powerfully" translates the prepositional phrase *en dynamei* ("in power"). This phrase functions adverbially, modifying the participle *energoumenēn* ("which works").

These verses focus on the ministry of Paul and several functions of that ministry, including suffering, "fulfilling" the word of God, and proclaiming the mystery through teaching and admonishing. At the same time, the readers are drawn into that mystery because their reception of Christ is at least part of the "mystery" that has now been revealed. Thus, they are drawn into Paul's ministry.

The adverb "now" (*nyn*) begins this paragraph (actually, all of vv. 24–29 are a single sentence). *Nyn* often signals a transition, but it may do more here. If so, it seems unlikely that it refers simply to the circumstances of Paul's life as they are described in the letter. *If* it has a fuller significance, *nyn* may have an eschatological nuance, as it often does in the Pauline corpus. When *nyn* and its emphatic form *nyni* appear in the Pauline corpus, they sometimes highlight the change of eras that the coming of Christ initiates. *Nyn* and *nyni* draw a contrast between the old age and the new in Rom 3:21, 26; 5:11; 7:6; 2 Cor 5:16; and Eph 3:5, 10 (cf. the use of *nyn* in Col 1:26b). This contrast stands in the background of the use of these adverbs in Rom 5:9; 6:22; 2 Cor 6:2; Gal 4:9; and Eph 5:8. *Nyn* and *nyni* also appear in the Pauline Letters with the simple non-theological meaning of "now," "at this time" (e.g., 1 Cor 5:11; Phil 1:5). The references to the sufferings of Christ and Paul in Col 1:24 open the possibility that in v. 24 *nyn* draws the readers' attention to the eschatological context, to their living in the new time of God's activity in Christ, in Paul, and in Christ's body, that is, the church. If this eschatological nuance stands in the background of *nyn* in v. 24, this may be another indicator that Colossians' eschatology is less realized than many interpreters view it to be. After all, suffering remains in the present, but it will not continue after the final consummation.

[24] At first blush, verse 24 startles and indeed shocks the reader. It contains some astonishing assertions. The first is that Paul rejoices in his sufferings, sufferings that are "for you." It seems strange that anyone would derive joy from suffering, but this is a theme found in the Pauline corpus (2 Cor 7:4; 8:2; 1 Thess 1:6; cf. Rom 5:3; 12:12). When the author writes that Paul rejoices "in suffering," the preposition "in" (*en*) may mean either that Paul rejoices in the midst of his sufferings (i.e., while he is enduring them) or that he rejoices because of them. The latter meaning seems more likely here because of the role that suffering plays in what follows. Paul does not exult in his sufferings because he is a masochist, but because of their function: they are "for you." In the undisputed letters, Paul makes suffering for the good of his churches a significant part of his apostolic ministry. This is a special emphasis of 2 Corinthians (see, e.g., 1:3–11; 4:1–15, esp. vv. 10–12) but appears in other letters as well (e.g., 1 Cor 9:12; Gal 6:17; Phil 3:10). In Colossians, however, Paul's sufferings play a more central role than in most other Pauline Letters. Throughout the letter there are references to suffering for the readers, as early as 1:24, 26–27 and as late as its penultimate sentence (4:18). These sufferings define both Paul's apostolic ministry and his relationship with the readers. Thus the hardships help establish his authority; he is an apostle who has authority over Gentile churches, but he exercises that authority by taking on suffering for them. This use of authority creates a willingness on the part of the letter's recipients to listen to his advice, because he works for their good in other settings and so must have their good at heart in this situation. This claim to suffer for them seems strange in a letter to a church Paul has never visited, but it is a claim that the writer finds important and even expands so that he presents Paul as someone who works

hard for all believers who have not met him (2:1). Such assertions reveal something about the way the author of Colossians views Paul and Paul's authority (see 2:1–5). Colossians claims authority for Paul over all Gentile churches.[5] The writer does not base this authority solely on Paul's call, but also on his suffering for the benefit of those churches.

The most arresting claim in v. 24 is that Paul's sufferings fill up what is lacking in the afflictions of Christ. Interpreters have devoted a great deal of attention to this statement. Protestant scholars have been particularly concerned to reject interpretations that allow for practices such as the veneration of saints. Both Catholic and Protestant scholars have felt the need to defend the full sufficiency of Christ's sacrifice for the salvation of humanity. Indeed, if this statement encroaches on that full sufficiency, it contradicts what the writer has said in 1:20, 22–23 and will say in chapter 2. Furthermore, such a limitation on the meaning of Christ's death would play into the hands of the visionaries, who are claiming that something more than Christ is needed to receive God's blessings. Thus it would work against much of the letter's argument. Moreover, the word used for suffering or tribulation (*thlipsis*) is never used elsewhere in the New Testament to refer to the sufferings of Christ. Thus it seems less likely that it refers to the expiatory suffering that Jesus endured on the cross.

To avoid these problems, some interpreters focus attention on the rare verb *antanapleroō*, "to fill up." This verb appears only here in the New Testament, occurs nowhere in the LXX, and is rare in other extant materials. The word is formed in an unusual way; it has *two* prepositions (*anti* and *ana*) prefixed to a verb (*pleroō*), instead of the more-common single preposition. Earlier commentators (e.g., Lightfoot 164–66) argued that this anomaly shows that the writer clearly distinguishes Paul's sufferings from those of Jesus. But such arguments are contrived. The addition of the second prefix probably adds nothing to the meaning of the verb. There was a tendency in Koine Greek (a tendency that is exaggerated in Colossians) to prefer compounds, even when they add nothing to the meaning. Examples of this in Colossians include *epi-ginōskō*, "to know" (1:6), *epi-menō*, "to remain" (1:23), and the doubly prefixed *apo-kat-allassō*, "to reconcile" (1:20; see the discussion in Barth and Blanke 256).

Other than the notion that Christ's redemptive sufferings are deficient, interpreters' understandings of Paul filling up "what is lacking in the afflictions of Christ" fall into three types.[6] (1) Paul's sufferings serve as edification but do not supplement the expiatory work of Christ's death (e.g., Lightfoot 165–66; Lindemann 33–34).[7] Such sufferings build up the church by giving an example

---

5. While the writer probably has in mind the churches of Turkey and southern Europe, he does not limit his statement to them; he says Paul suffers for the whole body of Christ.

6. For a fuller summary, see Roy Yates 1970, 88–92.

7. Hübner (69) describes these sufferings as signs of "cross-existence" that the preacher is to supply and asserts that the understanding of suffering in Colossians is comparable to that in 2 Cor 4.

and, since they occur in the present, fulfill a function that the past death of Christ does not. (2) Others argue that Paul's sufferings can be the "sufferings of Christ" because of the mystical union believers have with Christ (e.g., Calvin 318–19; MacDonald 79). (3) The most common view among commentators at present is that these sufferings are something like the messianic woes pictured in much apocalyptic literature. In this scheme the righteous must endure a certain amount of suffering before the end comes. The more suffering a particular righteous person endures, the fewer sufferings remain for others. Thus Paul's suffering can be "for the church" in the sense that he bears more sufferings so that others will not have to endure them (e.g., O'Brien 78–80; Dunn 114–17).

Colossians' assertion about Paul's sufferings is best understood in the light of descriptions of the noble death in Greco-Roman literature.[8] Two different understandings of the ways a noble person's suffering and death function as vicarious suffering appear in this literature. Sometimes this vicarious suffering has an expiatory role. Such a notion appears in 4 Maccabees when the old Eleazar prays that God will count his sufferings as punishment for the sins of the people (6:28–29). The author of 4 Maccabees believes that the sufferings of the righteous can atone for the sins of others (17:21–22; see also 12:17). But more often the sufferings and death of the just or righteous are understood as examples for others to follow. Such suffering is also understood to be vicarious suffering, even though not expiatory. Again, 4 Maccabees demonstrates this sense of vicarious suffering. The text repeatedly says that the sufferings of Eleazar and the seven brothers and their mother, who are tortured to death by Antiochus IV, provide examples that the readers should follow (e.g., 7:9; 9:23; 12:16). But their example teaches a lesson much broader than we might expect. As 4 Maccabees applies the example, it does not call the reader to martyrdom, but to recognize that reason is stronger than emotion (e.g., 16:1–2; 18:1–2). This knowledge enables a person to obey the law in any circumstance.

Similarly, Seneca says that the afflictions and hardships of the good are given by providence so "that they may teach others to endure them; they were born to be a pattern" (*Prov.* 6.6). In *Epistle* 24 Seneca encourages a certain Lucilius not to be troubled by the suit filed against him, but to recall the deaths of noble philosophers. Seneca expects the reminder of their suffering in extreme circumstances to help Lucilius maintain his philosophical outlook amid his smaller problems. He significantly reveals that this is not unusual advice: "Those stories have been droned to death in all the schools" (24.6). So the idea that a death has a vicarious function, vicarious in the sense that it calls forth imitation and so helps others maintain the proper life and avoid pain, is fairly

8. The following treatment is informed by David Seeley, *The Noble Death: Graeco-Roman Martyrology and Paul's Concept of Salvation*, JSNTSup 28 (Sheffield: Sheffield Academic Press, 1990). See also Sumney 2006, 664–80.

common in first-century culture. These examples do not simply aid those who hear of these sufferings when they endure similar troubles. They also are broad exhortations in the face of the vicissitudes of life, intended to help others maintain the philosophical or religious life.

Since Paul's sufferings are central to Colossians, it is important to understand their functions. Viewed in light of the meaning assigned the noble death in contemporaneous Jewish and philosophical literature, Paul's sufferings are indeed vicarious, but not expiatory. The death of Jesus alone remains expiatory, but Paul's sufferings can truly benefit others.[9] Both understandings of vicarious suffering appear in close proximity in Colossians: Christ's expiatory suffering is the theme of 1:18–23 and Paul's mimetic (imitative) suffering appears in 1:24. Such a juxtaposition is not a difficulty for readers accustomed to thinking in these categories. After all, the death of Eleazar has both purposes in the space of just a few verses in 4 Maccabees.

If mention of Paul's tribulations implicitly exhorts readers to imitate them,[10] it may seem strange that we find no explicit indication that the readers are suffering persecution. But "witnessing" such suffering had relevance for occasions other than those in which a person finds oneself in the same sort of extreme circumstance. That is, the examples apply not only to people faced with violent persecution or a martyr's death, but also to anyone encountering any difficulty that tempts one to draw back from the beliefs for which the martyr suffered. Thus in Colossians, Paul's sufferings implicitly exhort the readers to maintain the teaching that the letter advocates because his sufferings call them to adhere to his teaching, just as the suffering of the martyrs in 4 Maccabees summoned its readers to obey the law. The imitation Colossians implicitly calls for is obedience to the gospel that Paul proclaims and the commands he gives.[11] Paul's sufferings, then, are vicarious in the sense that they provide an example demonstrating the value of his gospel and so helping the readers adhere to that gospel in the face of a different teaching.

The last part of v. 24 contains a play on words that both specifies the location of Paul's sufferings and identifies the persons on whose account he endures them: his sufferings are "in my *flesh*" (their location), "for the sake of his *body*" (those whom his suffering benefits). Echoing 1:18, the writer then defines

9. Barth and Blanke (295) give the meaning "for the benefit of" for the preposition *hyper* in 1:24, so that Paul suffers for the benefit of the church, but not "for it" in the sense of substituting for it.

10. Hay (74) rejects the notion that Paul's sufferings are given as a model to imitate, but he has not taken into account the frame of thought described above.

11. This brings us close to Lightfoot's understanding of Paul's sufferings, though now with first-century categories for understanding such a reading. Lindemann (33–34) also asserts that Paul's sufferings are vicarious without supplementing the saving work of Christ. See further Sumney 2005.

Christ's body as the church. At the beginning of v. 24, Paul's sufferings benefit the readers of this letter, but now the recipients of the blessings that flow from
Paul's suffering include the whole church.

Both the expansion of the beneficiaries of Paul's sufferings to encompass the
whole church and the statement that those sufferings supplement the tribulations of Christ go beyond the claims Paul makes for his sufferings in the undisputed letters. But both assertions play an important role in Colossians. Since
Paul has probably already suffered a martyr's death, comments about his suffering are even more powerful than if he were still alive. Furthermore, since he
endured those pains for the whole church, the scope of his mission includes the
actual readers of the letter, as well as the implied readers (see the introduction
for discussion of the recipients of the letter). Paul suffered for the benefit of all
believing readers, whoever they may be. Thus, since he has shown goodwill
toward them, they should heed his instructions contained in this letter.

[25] The beginning of this verse identifies Paul as a minister (*diakonos*) of
the church. This is a new designation for him,[12] just as "minister/servant
[*diakonos*] of the gospel" was a new designation in 1:23. In the undisputed letters Paul calls himself a minister of God (2 Cor 6:4), of the new covenant (2
Cor 3:6), of righteousness (2 Cor 11:15), and of Christ (2 Cor 11:23). The idea
that one might be a minister of the church, however, is not foreign to Paul. In
Rom 16:1 he calls Phoebe a minister or deacon (*diakonos*) of the church in
Cenchreae, and he mentions the deacons (*diakonoi*) of the Philippian church
(Phil 1:1). In each case *diakonos* refers to a local church position, though the
precise nature of those positions remains unclear. These passages show that
calling a person a *diakonos* of the church is not strange language in Pauline
communities. Yet the meaning that Colossians attaches to *diakonos* differs from
that in Rom 16:1 and Phil 1:1. Paul does not hold a position within a local congregation; rather, he is a minister of the whole church. Since his commission
extends to all churches, so does his authority. There is no tension between the
roles of "minister of the gospel" and "minister of the church"; they are one and
the same vocation. As the following verses show, being a minister of the church
means that Paul is engaged in proclaiming the gospel. This meaning becomes
more emphatic as the discussion proceeds through v. 29 until it is clear that the
work of an apostle includes the work of preaching as a central element. This
view coheres well with the understanding of apostleship found in the undisputed letters (so Hübner 69; see 1 Cor 1:17).

Paul has become a minister of the church according to the *oikonomia* of God.
The noun *oikonomia* has a wide range of meanings, including "management,
plan, commission, training." The more probable meanings in this context are
"plan" and "commission." Since the meaning "plan" appears mostly in litera-

---

12. Paul does, however, refer to himself and his associates as "your slave" in 2 Cor 4:5.

ture later than Colossians, "commission" is the better rendering here (though the nuance of plan may be included, so that the use of this term intimates that Paul's commissioning fulfills or leads to the fulfillment of a part of God's plan). Paul is a minister of the church who has been commissioned by God. This statement balances the assertions of v. 24: Paul's sufferings do not benefit the church because Paul is superior, but because God has given him a task to perform. This nuance is even clearer if the backgrounds of the terms "minister" (*diakonos*) and "commission" (*oikonomia*) remain visible to the readers. Within the New Testament, *diakonos* refers to the roles of minister and deacon. But outside the New Testament, it designates a servant, often a slave. Similarly, a cognate of *oikonomia*, the word *oikonomos*, identifies the manager of an estate. Such managers usually came from lowly backgrounds and were often slaves. Colossians' use of *diakonos* and *oikonomia* in v. 25, then, may keep ideas about Paul and his ministry from becoming too inflated.

Attributing Paul's commission to God is also an effective strategy for avoiding resentment about the powerful claims made about him in v. 24. To be sure, Paul lives an extraordinary life that benefits the readers and even the whole church, but he holds this place only because God has commissioned him to fulfill this function.[13]

Paul's divine commission is to "fulfill the word of God among you." This ambiguous expression could point to the *goal* of Paul's proclamation, to "present every person complete in Christ" (v. 28; so Aletti 138). But the expression is better understood as a statement about Paul's preaching among Gentiles. Romans 15:19 uses the verb "fulfill" (*plēroō*) to speak of the geographical progress of the gospel through Paul's preaching. In Colossians, rather than supplying particular regions, Paul is fulfilling the word by preaching everywhere among the Gentiles. Such expressions indicate that the gospel is not complete until it has been proclaimed. The word of God is not fulfilled, has not accomplished its purpose, until it has been made known through preaching.

Verse 25 does not claim that the work of evangelism is completed, only that God has commissioned Paul to engage the task. The language of fulfillment probably also has an eschatological orientation. Not only did the section begin with the adverb "now," but what follows is clearly eschatological (v. 26). Thus, Paul's commission is a part of the eschatological acts of God, and his proclamation to Gentiles facilitates the advancement of God's plan for the world.

When Colossians calls Paul's message the "word of God," the writer could mean either that it is a message from God (genitive of origin) or a message about God (objective genitive or genitive of content). The writer would probably

---

13. This attributing of one's accomplishment to the divine squares with the advice Plutarch gives when describing how to avoid resentment when telling of one's accomplishments. See Plutarch, *On Inoffensive Self-Praise*, in *Mor.* 542E; cf. 541C.

affirm both meanings here. Just above, Paul's commission is "of God," with the meaning that it is from God; immediately following v. 25, the focus shifts to the content of the message. The expression probably possesses a multivalence broad enough to encompass both meanings.

[26] Verse 26 begins to explicate the content of the "word of God" that Paul has been commissioned to preach. So the focus shifts from Paul's commission and qualifications to the content of the message. This verse draws heavily upon the language and concepts of apocalyptic eschatology. It identifies a time when the message that Paul proclaims was hidden and then characterizes the present as the time in which that secret has been revealed.

The "word of God" is "the mystery that was hidden." The word *mystērion* was used widely in religious communities of the Hellenistic world. It denoted a rite in classical times and later the meaning behind the rite. By the first century it was used by mystery religions (*OGIS* 528, 331; *Socratic Ep.* 27.3; Athenagoras, *Leg.* 32.1), by apocalypticists (*1 En.* 63.3; *2 Ezra* 14:26), and even by the Qumran community for the teachings revealed to the Teacher of Righteousness (1QpHab 7; see also Moule 80–81; MacDonald 81). In such contexts the term could refer to a rite and its meaning or to a divine secret. In Colossians it points to the divine secret that has now been revealed. The schema of a mystery that was hidden but is revealed at the end often appears in apocalyptic literature. Paul draws on this scheme in 1 Cor 2:7–10 and Rom 16:25–27, and it was then developed by others in Pauline churches, including the authors of the Deutero-Pauline Letters (see Schweizer 107).

This great mystery has remained hidden "from ages" and "from generations." The preposition "from" (*apo*) may designate those from whom the mystery was hidden. If so, then the "ages" are spiritual powers and the "generations" are the people from whom the divine word has been concealed. But in this context, *apo* probably has a temporal meaning because the statement about ages and generations is followed immediately by the clearly temporal expression "but now." So it distinguishes the time of the church's existence from all previous eras.

"But now" that mystery has been revealed. The eschatological moment has come. In many apocalyptic texts, the mystery is often not revealed (except to the few who receive a special revelation) until the end (e.g., *1 En.* 104.11–13). For the early church the coming of Christ has initiated the end. All of the New Testament writings participate in such an eschatological understanding of the ministry, death, and resurrection of Christ. Paul expresses this idea in Rom 3:21: "But now . . . the righteousness of God has been disclosed." In Paul's theology, an element of this eschatological scheme always remains in the future so that believers do not yet possess the fullness of God's blessings. The claim in Colossians that the mystery has been revealed has led some to assert that this letter lacks such a future element because believers now have access to the mystery (e.g., MacDonald 81). Verse 28, however, manifests a future expectation when the writer admonishes the readers so that he might "present every person complete in Christ." Rather than being evidence of a fully realized eschatology, the assertion that the mystery of God's word has been revealed "now" counters the visionaries' claims that the readers need experiences beyond merely being "in Christ" if they are to be fully the people of God (Pokorný 103). Countering such teachers is reason enough to emphasize the present blessings that believers possess in Christ. The future element has not been lost or rejected, only muted because of the letter's purpose (cf. Aletti 139).

The mystery has been revealed "to his saints" (see the discussion of "saints" at 1:12 above). The repeated mention that believers are God's holy ones reminds the readers of the status that God has granted them. Such designations help the readers continue to reject the visionaries' teaching by reminding them of the blessings and standing they already possess in Christ. At the same time, they implicitly call the readers to live in ways that are appropriate for holy people.

The acclamation that this mystery is revealed to the saints distinguishes Colossians from Ephesians. In Ephesians, the mystery is revealed to the "holy apostles and prophets" (Eph 3:5), but in Colossians to "the saints," to all believers. Perhaps the author of Ephesians understands differently the place the apostles hold in the revelation of the gospel. The particular occasions of the letters, however, may account for much of the difference. Colossians is silent about *how* the church received the mystery and so does not directly contradict Ephesians. After all, the gospel could be revealed to the saints through apostles. Indeed, Paul's importance in delivering the gospel can hardly be doubted in this paragraph of Colossians, which affirms that he suffers for them and fulfills the word of God among them. Thus he has been, in some ways, the mode by which they learned the mystery. But Colossians throughout emphasizes that the revelation has been given to all believers in order to counter those who say that only those with visions can know God's will fully.

[27] The style of Colossians again becomes elaborate in v. 27, particularly with its piling up of genitives. Perhaps this style emphasizes the richness of the hope that believers possess (Pokorný 104). It may also have a liturgical ring to underline the wondrous character of God's acts for believers (Dunn 121). The mention of "riches" and "glory" echoes Rom 9:23–24 and 11:33, and Col 1:26–27 also parallels the thought of Rom 16:25–26, with the mention of the mystery once hidden but now revealed. All three of these Romans passages comment on the inclusion of Gentiles among the people of God. Since the same matter is a central point in Col 1:26–27, the writer may well be reflecting the thought found in those Romans passages.

Verse 27 identifies God as the one who acts to save "the saints." Thus the verbs of v. 26 as divine passive verbs have their subject named. The claim that believers have already received divine revelation through the exercise of God's will counters the visionaries' claims that the revelation necessary for a relationship

with God comes in visionary experiences. According to this verse, God's will—
not human striving—grants this revelation.

The glory that God makes known is not directly the glory of God but the
glory of the "mystery," a mystery that the writer immediately identifies as
"Christ in you." Focus thus remains on the ways that God has acted on the
Colossians' behalf. In the context, an important element in this mystery is the
inclusion of Gentiles among the people of God. It is the mystery "among
the *ethnē*." The word *ethnē* literally means "nations," but throughout the New
Testament it is the word for non-Jews. That also seems to be its meaning here
(contra Hay 76). But the central theme in Colossians is not the unification of
Jews and Gentiles in Christ; rather, the main point remains more narrow. This
text proclaims that God has acted specifically for the letter's recipients, not just
non-Jews in general. Still, the writer says first that the glory of this mystery has
been revealed to the Gentiles.

Once the elaborate writing style has captured the reader's attention, the
writer begins to disclose the content of the mystery now revealed to "the saints"
(v. 26), and more particularly to Gentile believers. The content of the mystery
is "Christ in you." The mystery is not just Christ, but Christ *in you*. This phrase
may mean either that Christ dwells within the believer—and so be a reference
to the indwelling of the Spirit (e.g., O'Brien 87; Dunn 122–23)—or that Christ
is among the Gentiles (e.g., Pokorný 103; Aletti 141–42). The context and the
language can support either meaning. Which view one takes depends, in large
part, on whether the phrase's meaning is determined by the immediately preceding "among the Gentiles," a phrase that is certainly parallel with "Christ in
you," or by the immediately following "hope of glory." The expression "hope
of glory" points to a future consummation in which believers will take part
through their participation "in Christ." The content of the hope is future glory.
Verse 28's reference to the judgment confirms that this expression looks to the
Parousia. Since "hope of glory" points to the Parousia, it casts an eschatological hue on the context, increasing the likelihood that "Christ in you" refers to
possession of the Spirit, because the coming of the Spirit is an eschatological
phenomenon. Yet so is the entrance of Gentiles into the people of God. Perhaps
it is best, therefore, to allow some multivalence to the expression "Christ in
you." Since the acclamation of the inclusion of the Gentiles (the recipients
among them) leads to comments about receiving "glory" when one comes
before God, the phrase both echoes the language of inclusion of the Gentiles
and points to God's presence with each person (cf. Hay 76).

Christ's presence among the Gentiles is not the full and final content of the
mystery; there is an element yet to come. Though some interpreters see no
future aspect to the eschatology of Colossians, the phrase "hope of glory" points
inescapably to a future fulfillment. Mention of this still unfulfilled element of
the mystery does not help the writer show that the visionaries are wrong, but

neither does it significantly weaken the case against them. When the writer speaks of future hope, he immediately indicates that it is realized when one comes before God at judgment (v. 28). Thus this hope is fulfilled only then, not in any visionary experience in the present. Visions cannot offer more than what the readers already possess: knowledge of and participation in God's mystery, a mystery that includes a sure hope for the future.

The phrase "in you" assigns the letter's readers a position of astonishingly high status. Not only are they the recipients of God's revelation; they also are a significant part of the mystery itself, part of God's plan for the whole world. Nothing the visionaries offer them can possibly compete. A higher status or greater blessing can hardly be envisioned, yet this is the status that Colossians claims for all believers. God values humanity to such an extent that having people, particularly Gentiles, come to faith in Christ plays a part in God's plan for the entire cosmos. This passage intimates that the gospel is not truly the gospel until the presence of Christ is experienced among and in those who accept the message. This suggests that the love God has for the world requires acceptance and embodiment of that love in believers' lives.

[28] The writer shifts from first-person singular ("I") to first-person plural ("we") at the beginning of v. 28. "We" refers to Paul and his coworkers, perhaps especially Epaphras, Tychicus, and Onesimus. Paul, however, is still in the forefront, even though the horizon has been widened. Not since v. 14, where "we" meant all believers, has Colossians used the first-person plural, and it has not designated Paul and his coworkers since 1:9. The first-person plural will not appear again until 2:14, where again it refers to all believers, and Colossians will not again refer to Paul's coworkers or any group other than all believers with the first-person plural. So this is an unusual statement for Colossians. In the setting of Colossians, the change to "we" enables those in positions of leadership, particularly anyone known to have connections to the apostolic mission, to claim authority to engage in the admonishing and teaching that this verse subsumes under the proclamation of "Christ in you," the mystery that was hidden but is now revealed.

The verb *katangellō* ("proclaim") is rare in the Pauline corpus (used only six times), but outside the New Testament it is sometimes used in connection with proclamations in sacred festivals. The New Testament and other early Christian literature associate this verb with missionary proclamation (J. Schniewind, *TDNT* 1:70–72). This nuance of the term, combined with what follows in v. 28, suggests that the writer expects proclamation to include admonishing and teaching. This implies that bringing people to merely acknowledge the facts of the gospel does not complete the task of proclamation. Preaching must lead to something more, to changes in people's lives.

The author of Colossians is not the first to bring together admonishing and teaching (see, e.g., Plato, *Pro.* 323D; Plutarch, *Mor.* 46; other examples in

Lightfoot 170). Admonishing (*noutheteō*) encompasses both warning and the summons to ethical living, as well as offering correction, and is intended to lead to change or repentance.[14] In the Pauline corpus (the only place this word appears in the New Testament), *noutheteō* is associated with the work of a pastor (J. Behm, *TDNT* 4:1021–22). It probably refers to more than just repentance at the beginning of the Christian life, though that is not excluded. Such admonition continues throughout the believer's life, as the content of this letter demonstrates. When the writer includes admonition within proclamation here, it may authorize the correction of some members by leaders—hinting that some need to repent, while others need to hear the warning that may keep them from needing to repent, particularly if they are considering the visionaries' teaching.

The broader term "teaching" includes whatever is necessary to strengthen faith. Such instruction is no less important than admonition, even though it is not necessarily directed at a particular problem. "Teach" is a milder word than "admonish" and is not immediately associated with ethical matters. But the distinctions between "admonishing" and "teaching" should not be overdrawn because of the frequency of hendiadys in Colossians.[15]

Admonishing and teaching are to be done "with all wisdom." This phrase designates the manner of the proclamation rather than its content. The writer is not claiming that this message contains all wisdom—though he says that elsewhere (e.g., 2:2–3 and the exalted Christology in 1:15–20)—and so it probably does not directly counter the teaching of the visionaries. Rather, this phrase affirms that Paul and his coworkers conduct their ministry in a way that is wise and thus effective. Their teaching increases the hearers' faith; their admonitions lead to ethical living and, where needed, repentance.

Verse 28 repeats "every person" three times to emphasize the universality of the gospel that Paul preaches and to indicate that no one is excluded. This repetition may be a veiled rejection of the visionaries' exclusiveness (so Lightfoot 170), since they claim that only those with experiences like theirs are truly God's people. Perhaps "every person" refers specifically to all who come to Christian faith through Paul, whether directly, through his letters, or through his coworkers (cf. Hay 77). In its third use, "every person" includes only those who respond with faith, because only believers are "in Christ." But perhaps the nuance is not precisely the same in all three instances, so that "every person" could refer to a broader group in its initial uses and a more limited group at the end of the verse. After all, the repetition is present for rhetorical effect, not to

14. Lightfoot (170) cites Plutarch's *Mor.* 68, 452 to demonstrate the connection of admonition with repentance. See also J. Behm, *TDNT* 4:1019–22.

15. MacDonald (83), however, sees significant distinctions, to the point that these three terms plot the outline of Col 1:1–2:5 as proclamation; 2:6–23 as warning; and 3:1–4:6 as teaching on Christian living.

designate precisely the people whom the writer has in view. (Furthermore, Paul's proclamation did not always achieve its goal, so not everyone he preached to joined those "in Christ.") The important conclusion for readers to draw is that this teaching of Paul and his associates is intended for them, as well as for the implied readers, that is, the Colossians.

The last clause of the verse supplies the goal of the admonishing and teaching, to "present every person complete in Christ." Though some interpreters think that this phrase refers solely to the present existence of believers (e.g., Barth and Blanke 267), the verb "present" points to eschatological judgment. The phrase "in Christ" does not count against seeing a reference to the final judgment because God has been the actor throughout this section, and Christ has been the one through whom God acts. Here God is judge, and those who come before God are "in Christ." In some way, the writer also envisions Paul being present for and having a role in the judgment proceedings of those in his churches, because he presents them at judgment. This again increases his stature and helps to create an image of him that will lead the readers to obey his instructions that follow in 2:6–23.

While the divine mystery is "Christ in you" (v. 27), the readers are also "in Christ." "In Christ" designates the sphere in which God perceives believers at judgment. It is also the sphere in which they conduct their lives now. Thus the goal of Paul's preaching is to encourage all believers to live their identity fully as persons who are "in Christ" so that at God's accounting they will be found complete.

The word translated "complete" (*teleion*) has a wide range of uses in the first century. It can mean "mature," "fully developed," or "perfect." In addition, it was used within mystery religions to designate initiates. It seems unlikely that the writer has in view a mystical relationship with God related to the meaning found among the mystery religions (contra MacDonald 83). After all, a principal purpose of Colossians is to assure its recipients that they need no experiences beyond baptism to be counted among the people of God. The basic idea is that those who adhere to Paul's teaching will be fully prepared for judgment. By implication, the readers do not need the visionaries' teaching because Paul's teaching has all they need for completion. Thus their completeness may have both a present and a future aspect: they already possess all the knowledge and blessings of God available in the present, and they are living in ways that acknowledge their coming accountability to God.

[29] After vv. 26–28 define the "word of God," the focus returns to Paul's suffering, thus picking up the theme sounded in v. 24, but now with a different nuance. The suffering of Paul is still for the Colossians, but the remarks are more specific; he struggles to help them prepare for God's judgment, as the opening prepositional phrase, "for this," indicates. The first-person singular ("I") reemerges at the beginning of v. 29, when the topic returns to suffering for the church. In this way, Colossians reserves for Paul the role of apostle who suffers for the readers (and the whole church), while Paul's coworkers share the task of proclaiming the message in v. 28. Colossians does not completely set the apostle's suffering apart from all other suffering that leaders endure for the church, but Paul is the exemplary case. Throughout the Pauline corpus, others suffer for the good of the church (e.g., Rom 16:3–4; 1 Cor 16:15–16; Phil 2:25–30), and in Colossians, Epaphras is a fellow slave who is faithful "for you" (1:7; 4:12–13). Similarly, Tychicus is a faithful servant (or minister: the word is *diakonos*) and fellow slave (4:7). Thus, others accept positions of service and so accept difficulties for the good of the church, but Paul's suffering is particularly efficacious. Therefore, Paul is the one to whom the readers should listen, the one they should obey.

Still, the distinctiveness of Paul's suffering for them must not be exaggerated. The verb that describes Paul's experience (*kopiaō*, "work") appears in many contexts. It refers to strenuous labor, exhaustion from battle, and simply weariness from working.[16] Within the Pauline corpus it often refers to work on behalf of the community, and Paul uses a form of the word to speak of missionary and pastoral work, whether his own or that of others (e.g., 1 Thess 5:12; 2 Cor 10:15). Since the verb and its cognate noun can both be used for common manual labor, the writer's use of *kopiaō* suggests that he has not exalted Paul's sufferings and work to the degree that they are in a completely different category from the suffering and work of other leaders. By the second century, Christian writers use *kopiaō* with decreasing frequency in connection with the work of church officers, arguably because its association with manual labor made it seem inappropriate for esteemed leaders (F. Hauck, *TDNT* 3:829–30). Perhaps Colossians' use of this verb within v. 29 helps readers refrain from overestimating the distance the writer puts between the sufferings of Paul and those of other believers.

Paul undertakes his pastoral ministry vigorously, working "strenuously" for the Colossians. The verb *agōnizomai* ("to struggle, strive") originally was associated with contests in the stadium, but by the first century it designated any contest, fight, or struggle. Especially suggestive are the word's metaphorical uses. Fourth Maccabees employs it to describe the endurance of martyrs (e.g., 17:3–14), and philosophers and moralists use it to speak of the difficult pursuit of virtue (Plutarch, *Gen. Socr.* 593D–594A; idem, *Phoc.* 37; Philo, *Somn.* 2.145). Colossians uses *agōnizomai* in the general sense of striving to emphasize the intensity of Paul's devotion to his ministry and to the readers. This devotion is a cause of his suffering and martyrdom.

Paul does not fulfill his ministry and endure his suffering by his own power; he labors instead "according to God's working." The text has the pronoun "his,"

---

16. E.g., Lam 5:5; 4 Macc 9:12; Josephus, *J.W.* 3.19; 6.142. See Spicq, *TLNT* 2:322–29; F. Hauck, *TDNT* 3:827–30.

not the word "God." The other option for the source of this working is Christ, whose name appears in closer proximity. God is the primary actor in vv. 24–28, however, so it seems likely that this is the case here as well. Either way, the basic point is that Paul does not perform these tasks on his own, but through divine power.[17]

The author adds emphasis to his identification of the divine source of Paul's strength by using both the noun *energeia* ("work, strength") and its cognate verb *energeō* ("working"). Perhaps this way of showing emphasis is a Semiticism (so Dunn 127); it is also another example of the writing style of Colossians. The accumulation of words that express the same idea continues as the verse ends with *en dynamei* ("powerfully").

This verse's most important point is that God empowers Paul's work for the Colossians, and for the whole church. Paul's successes and his apostleship are not of his own doing. While he does labor strenuously, he remains completely dependent upon the power of God. His sufferings are part of this strenuous work, and he is able to endure tribulation for the sake of the church only because the working of God enables him. Verse 29 echoes Phil 2:12–18, where Paul tells the Philippians to live out their salvation because God enables them to live as they should. Paul even admonishes his readers to proper living and mentions future judgment in the Philippians pericope, just as the author of Colossians does in 1:28. These sections of Philippians and Colossians address the same basic point: the power of God dwelling in the believer is what enables Christian existence. In Colossians, however, the focus narrows to apostles or ministers. Still, the power of God enables the ministry of the apostle in the same way that it enables all Christian obedience and life.

The subsection 1:24–29 forms an *inclusio*, ending as it began, with reflection on the work of Paul and the benefits that work confers on the Colossians, as well as on the whole church. Notably, Colossians does not mention that Paul is an apostle in this section. The notion that this is particularly apostolic suffering must be drawn from the larger context, from the writer's use of first-person (particularly singular) pronouns, or from the idea that God issued Paul's commission. This section speaks of Paul not as an apostle but as a servant or minister (*diakonos*), even if one commissioned directly by God. Perhaps identifying him as a *diakonos* allows some of the authority he accumulates in this section to spill over onto the leaders of the church addressed by the letter. If they work hard and suffer for that church, they too will be in a position to claim the attention of the church when they admonish and teach, especially when they call the church to reject the visionaries' teaching. Unlike Paul, such

---

17. In the New Testament the noun *energeia* appears only eight times, all in Eph 1:19; 3:7; 4:16; Phil 3:21; Col 1:29; 2:12; 2 Thess 2:9, 11. In each of its New Testament occurrences, it refers to divine activity, except for 2 Thessalonians, where it refers to the working of Satan.

church leaders do not have the whole world as their charge, and though they were not commissioned directly by God, the church they serve will be inclined to listen to them as it sees the ways their lives mirror Paul's life and ministry.

Throughout 1:24–29 the Colossians are the recipients of blessings from others, whether Paul or God. Later in the letter they will be called to act, but as this section develops its image of Paul and prepares them for the instruction and exhortation to come, it enumerates all that Paul and God have done for them. Once they recognize these gifts, they will more readily listen to and obey Paul. Beyond his suffering and God's enabling of Paul in his struggles, another significant element of the apostolic (and more broadly ministerial) office appears: proclamation includes teaching and admonishing. The preaching of the church should educate in the faith and encourage proper living. Such encouragement includes giving correction when it is needed. Proclamation has the goal of transforming lives so that Christians may stand aright at God's judgment. This section, then, sketches an important aspect of the role of preachers, teachers, and others with a pastoral charge. Their job is not completed when they have led people to conversion or even when they have given them good theological categories. Rather, the work of such leaders is to bring their churches to "maturity in Christ in anticipation of God's final assessment" (Hay 77).

2:1–5 Paul Toils to Help the Church Remain Faithful to the True Gospel

2:1 For I want you to know how great my struggles are for you and for those in Laodicea and for all those who have never met me in person.[a] 2 I struggle so that their hearts might be encouraged[b] as they are united in love and so[c] possess all the riches of fully assured understanding and[d] knowledge of the mystery of God, that is, Christ, 3 in whom all the treasures of wisdom and knowledge are hidden. 4 I say these things[e] so that no one may deceive you with plausible-sounding arguments. 5 For even though I am physically absent, I am present with you in spirit, rejoicing because I see your order and the firmness of your faith in Christ.

a. Literally, "have not seen my face in the flesh."

b. The verb *parakaleō* had a broad semantic range that included "extending an invitation, acting in a friendly manner, comforting, warning, imploring." I render it "encourage" here because that meaning brings with it elements of both comfort and exhortation.

c. I have translated the preposition *eis* as "so possess." In this construction it probably expresses the result of the encouragement the readers (and others) may draw from Paul's struggles on their behalf.

d. The conjunction "and" does not appear in the text, which begins a second prepositional phrase with *eis*, but has no connective particle.

e. Literally, "I say this."

The previous section (1:24–29) and this section (2:1–5) are intimately related; together they comprise a single larger unit. They possess continuity in theme, vocabulary, and style. But 2:1–5 more directly prepares for the admonition and polemic of 2:6–23. The disclosure formula in 2:1 ("I want you to know") signals a new start. Like other writers of the first century, Paul often uses such formulas (e.g., Rom 1:13; 11:25; 1 Cor 10:1; 2 Cor 1:8; 1 Thess 4:13) to begin a new unit of thought. Verses 4–5 belong in this section because they continue to address the relationship between Paul and the readers, particularly giving attention to the authority Paul has even though he is not present—a matter of special interest for a pseudonymous letter.

[2:1] Like the previous section, 2:1–5 begins with comments on Paul's suffering for the benefit of the Colossians. In 2:1 the writer of the letter has Paul tell them how great his struggles for them are. The intensity of that struggle contributes to Colossians' construction of an image of Paul as the one who cares so deeply for the readers that he is willing to suffer for them. The mention of struggles in 2:1 echoes the use of the cognate *agōnizomenos* ("strenuously") in 1:29 and so probably includes the struggles Paul engages as he strives to present "every person complete in Christ."[18] This suggests that at least one aspect of his struggling is responding to problems in his churches. But the parallels with 1:24 also suggest a broader understanding that includes the suffering inflicted on him as well as his inner anguish about the church (see 2 Cor 11:28). Paul's struggling thus refers to the engagement of his whole being in the service of the church. Since this section leads directly into the polemic against the visionaries, the matter of responding to problems within Paul's church may be emerging as an element of his struggles and suffering, though that is by no means their full extent.

Perhaps the writer recognizes the strangeness of having Paul say that he suffers and works laboriously for the Colossians, people he has never met; he therefore addresses that issue in 2:1–3, where Paul suffers not only for the Colossians but also for the Laodiceans and all who have never met Paul. Why mention Laodicea rather than Hieropolis or some other city? Perhaps the Pauline mission had been more successful in Laodicea, or there were close relations between these two churches (Dunn 129). Or perhaps communication links were closer between the churches in these two cities (Barth and Blanke 272). The mention of Laodicea here and in 4:16 may indicate that the church in that city faces the same problem that Colossians addresses (cf. Schweizer 115). If the letter is pseudonymous, this verse supports the conjecture that the letter's actual intended recipient is the church in Laodicea (Lindemann 36). While this is by no means certain, it is a reasonable conjecture.

---

18. While *agōn* ("struggle") sometimes refers to the sufferings of martyrs, it is unlikely that Paul's martyrdom is directly in view here (contra Lohmeyer 92).

Paul does not suffer for the Colossians and Laodiceans alone; he struggles for all believers he has not met. This assertion universalizes Paul's place in the church, just as did his suffering for the whole body of Christ (1:24) and his proclaiming to "every person" (1:28). He has a ministry to the whole world.[19] Suffering for a group of people confers trustworthiness because it shows that the sufferer attaches significant value to the good of the group addressed. Paul's suffering at least identifies him as a person to whom they should listen, and since that suffering is for the whole church, it extends his authority so that it encompasses all readers.

In a manner typical of this letter, Colossians makes the point emphatically through repetition. Instead of simply saying that Paul suffers for the good of those who have never met him, it adds "in the flesh." This last phrase is unnecessary (Dunn 129), but it is consistent with the style of Colossians.

[2] The goal of Paul's struggles for those who have never met him is that "their hearts might be encouraged." In v. 1 Paul's struggles are for "you," but in v. 2 for "*their* hearts." This change of pronouns emphasizes that the scope of Paul's mission encompasses all believers and so explicitly includes any actual, as well as the implied, readers. This "encouragement" includes both comfort and exhortation. They need to be comforted in their perplexity at the visionaries' teaching (cf. Hübner 73), and they need to be exhorted to hold to the apostolic teaching and reject any other teaching. These two aspects of encouragement are interrelated. The need for encouragement is not limited to concerns about false teaching. People in the early church regularly encountered social and economic persecution because of their faith. Such persecution might range from ridicule to physical danger or people refusing to engage in business dealings with church members. Subordinates who lived in households in which the head of the household was not a believer faced particularly difficult circumstances as they navigated their way through expectations that stood in tension with their faith. Some, perhaps most, may have faced reprisals or been forced to engage in activities that violated their faith (see the comments on 3:18–4:1). Persons in such circumstances would be encouraged to know that they were not alone in their struggles; Paul struggles with and for them. Furthermore, they have his example to encourage them on this path (see the comment above on 1:24).

The heart, as the center of the will and mind as well as of the emotions, needs admonition along with comfort, as the rest of the verse shows. The love, understanding, and knowledge mentioned in this verse are elements that comprise this encouragement. It is probably overly specific to assert that "their hearts" refers either to the heart of each individual or to the hearts of the people as a community. The primary emphasis seems to be on the latter understanding

---

19. Hay (78) notes the claim in *1 Clem.* 5.6–7 that Paul taught the whole world.

because their hearts are "held together," but Paul's suffering can also encourage the heart of an individual.

Their hearts are encouraged not only by Paul's struggles but also by being "united" or "knit together." This verb, *symbibazomai*, is used to speak of the function that ligaments have in holding the body together (e.g., Eph 4:16), but it can also mean "to draw a conclusion" or "to instruct." It means "instruct" in all its appearances in the LXX, and such a meaning fits the context in Colossians, where the author counters false teaching (O'Brien 93). In this verse, however, the dominant idea that the verb conveys is "being united," because this meaning fits better with the following prepositional phrase, which specifies what holds them together. Still, since the letter's recipients gain knowledge through this unity, as the next two prepositional phrases indicate, the nuance of instruction is not absent.

The readers are held together by love. Since this is a means by which the Colossians' hearts are knit together, it is closely related to the encouragement that flows from Paul's ministry. Love here designates the sphere within which believers live and has its source in God. Since the phrase "in love" depends on the participle "united," this love involves relations within the church and so concerns the attitude one takes toward fellow believers. First Corinthians 13 develops the same sort of understanding of love. In 1 Corinthians, love guides the use of spiritual gifts to produce unity by setting the good of the church above what is advantageous for the individual. Paul's service to the community, though not explicitly called love, gives content to this concept in Colossians. Paul's struggles for their sake may be the primary example that gives content to the idea of love in this verse.

As a result of being "united in love," the readers possess "fully assured understanding." The writer of Colossians expresses this thought with considerable flair, through a pleonastic style that captures the greatness, the superabundance, of this understanding. In opposition to teaching claiming that the readers need to know what they can experience and learn only in visions, Colossians asserts that they already possess completely certain understanding and that it flows from their unity in love. The distinction between those with visions and those without visions surely creates divisions, which the visionaries apparently claim have soteriological significance. By implied contrast, the community's unity, a widely recognized social value in the ancient world, assures them that they have already committed themselves to the correct teaching.

The third prepositional phrase that relates to "being united" also concerns the content of the readers' faith; they possess "knowledge of the mystery of God." This phrase gives sharper definition to the "understanding" that the previous phrase says believers enjoy. The language of mystery echoes 1:26–27, suggesting that the author is continuing to think in apocalyptic categories. In apocalyptic literature, knowledge of the divine mysteries was often obtained through visions and heavenly journeys. Colossians, however, claims that the readers already possess that knowledge and therefore have no need of visionary journeys. In fact, knowledge of the divine mystery is what makes them the church. Lest anyone begin to claim that only some possess knowledge of this mystery, the author immediately states its content: Christ! The insertion of "Christ" at this point in the construction of the Greek is awkward (Hay 79). The abruptness is not the result of careless writing; rather, this is an emphatic way of directing the readers back to Christ as the sum of Christian knowledge and existence. This statement parallels 1:27, where the divine mystery is "Christ in you." As 2:3 states explicitly, knowledge of Christ includes all divine wisdom and knowledge. Once again there is an implicit contrast to the other teachers' claims to possess knowledge through visionary experiences that supposedly provide salvation and forgiveness.

The style of v. 2 is extravagant; the pleonasm characteristic of Colossians is in full bloom. Readers should not look for nuances of difference between "understanding" and "knowledge" or in the precise emphasis of each preposition. Rather, readers are to experience the fullness of what they possess in Christ through the ministry of Paul. Thus, the style contributes to the argument and helps to establish some of the basic points that make it possible not only to reject the other teachers' views, but also to embrace a joyful life of faith, because of the richness of the blessings that believers possess in Christ.

[3] The prepositional phrase "in whom" builds on the author's identification of Christ as the mystery of God. This phrase prepares the reader for the constant use of "in whom" and "in him" throughout 2:6–15, where such phrases locate the divine blessings in Christ. Verse 3 repeats much of the content of v. 2: both verses speak of knowledge and understanding (or wisdom) in connection with Christ, and both use language of wealth. This repetition makes the claims in these verses emphatic, as do the use of the adjective "all" and the mention of both wisdom and knowledge. These assertions assure the readers that they can know with certainty that Christ is the sphere in which the highest knowledge of God resides.

If "*all* the treasures of wisdom and knowledge" are in Christ, it is useless to seek them elsewhere. Since the next sentence speaks directly of the teaching that the writer opposes, v. 3 intimates that the way the other teachers seek knowledge of God yields nothing; everything they seek through visions is in Christ instead. Moreover, since the Colossians are already in Christ, they already possess this wisdom and knowledge.

The imagery of "treasures of wisdom and knowledge" found in Christ echoes the doxology in Rom 11:33 and the praise to wisdom in Isa 45:3 and Prov 2:3–6. Knowledge and wisdom sometimes appear together as generally equivalent in Jewish literature (e.g., Sir 21:18; Wis 1:6–7; 1QS 4.3, 22; 1QH 1.18–19; CD 2.3; further, Sir 1:25 refers to the "treasuries of wisdom" that contain "sayings of truth" [*epistolēs*] cf. O'Brien 95–97), though the extant evidence does not support the claim that it was common to speak in this way. Given the tendency of Colossians to accumulate synonyms, the writer is probably not drawing a distinction between knowledge and wisdom. Instead, the repetition creates an impression of the fullness that is found in Christ.

While this imagery draws on the Wisdom literature, in the context of 1:24–2:5 it should also be read through the lens of apocalyptic (Dunn 132). In apocalyptic writings, those swept up on a heavenly journey sometimes saw or heard discussions of the "hidden treasures" of God (e.g., *1 En.* 18.1; 46.3, cited by Dunn 132). The earlier mention of a mystery that was hidden and then revealed (1:26) supports reading the language in 2:3 within an apocalyptic framework.

The presence of apocalyptic thought here raises two issues. The first involves the extent to which Colossians contains a realized eschatology. Clearly, this letter emphasizes what the readers have already received. They already have access to "all the riches of fully assured understanding" (v. 2) and "all the treasures of wisdom and knowledge" (v. 3). But since the writer still looks forward to the future act of God's judgment (1:28), a significant future dimension remains in the letter's eschatology. Emphasis falls on the eschatological blessings that the readers already possess because of the problem addressed by Colossians. Since the visionaries contend that others in the church lack the knowledge and experiences necessary for redemption and forgiveness, Colossians responds by asserting that they already possess all such things in Christ. The writer must make this claim about the present to address directly the debate in which the readers are engaged. So Colossians may not fully disclose the author's eschatological perspective, but only represents his polemical development of some of its elements. The writer's eschatology retains a significant future aspect.

The second issue raised by the influence of apocalyptic thought is the meaning of the adjective "hidden" (*apokryphoi*) in v. 3. Especially since Colossians' eschatology accents present fulfillment, the notion that the divine treasury is now hidden seems out of place. As a way to lessen this difficulty, O'Brien (95) asserts that *apokryphos* means "stored up" rather than "concealed." But the term does not carry that meaning elsewhere. In the New Testament it refers to what is hidden or not revealed (e.g., Mark 4:22). In other literature, it is even used to speak of hidden treasure (e.g., 1 Macc 1:23; Josephus, *Ant.* 12.250) and figuratively of secret wisdom (e.g., Philo, *Sacr.* 62). If the word carries its usual meaning, readers encounter the paradox that the mystery has been revealed, but the treasures of wisdom and knowledge are hidden. Yet perhaps this seeming paradox is not as strange as it first appears. The mystery is revealed "to the saints," not to the whole world (1:26). If the treasures are hidden in Christ (2:3), from whom are they hidden? They are not hidden from the letter's recipients, who are held together by the knowledge of Christ, but these treasures are hidden from others. Those it is hidden from certainly include nonbelievers and perhaps also the powers that Christ must defeat to bring reconciliation and forgiveness to the church. This affirmation of the hiddenness of wisdom and knowledge also lends additional support to those who have held steadfastly to the gospel that they received earlier and who reject the claims of the visionaries. If the visionaries suppose that they have gained knowledge of heavenly things through other means, Colossians asserts that all heavenly knowledge and wisdom are in Christ and are hidden from those who do not belong to Christ through adherence to the letter's understanding of the gospel. Thus, in some ways, the affirmation that the treasures are hidden creates a boundary marker. Indeed, it amounts to a direct refutation of the visionaries' teaching. If they claim a relationship with God through what they learn in their visions and, further, claim that this knowledge is only available to those who have such experiences, Colossians counters by saying, "No, we have the true knowledge and it is hidden from you."

This veiled counterclaim sets up the direct address about the visionaries that follows. Though 2:1–3 deals with Paul's relationship with the readers and what they possess through his suffering and their knowledge of Christ, vv. 4–5 begin urging the readers to reject the other teachers and thus take up the theme of the next section, which is also the primary purpose of the letter. The warnings about the other teachers in v. 4 are repeated in v. 8, so that 2:1–5 and 2:6–19 overlap. This kind of transition is not unusual for Colossians (Hay 79). Verses 4–5 belong with 2:1–3, and with all of 1:24–2:3, because v. 5 continues the topic of Paul's relationship with the Colossians, particularly his presence with them even though he is not physically present, a theme already broached in 2:1.

[4] When Paul uses the words "I say these things" (*touto legō*; more literally rendered, "I say this"), the words that begin v. 4, he sometimes means that he is ready to put things in his own words or give the recipients his interpretation (e.g., 1 Cor 3:4). Elsewhere it simply indicates that he is about to give an important reason why he has raised the matter under consideration. This second meaning is primary here as the *touto* ("these things") looks back, but what follows is certainly a polemical description that gives the writer's evaluation of the other teaching.

"These things" could refer to what comes after the expression rather than to what comes before it. Here, however, the phrase probably points to what came before because it is followed by *hina*, "so that." When *hina* follows this expression in the New Testament, "I say these things" (*touto legō*) always refers to what has come before. Therefore, it is more natural to read it in that way here (O'Brien 97). "These things" brings all that has been said since at least 2:1, and probably since 1:24, directly to bear on the visionaries' teaching. All that Paul has said about himself and the acts of God in Christ have the purpose of helping the readers to reject the other teaching.

The letter takes an abrupt turn to polemics in v. 4, as the writer speaks directly about that other teaching. He says he does not want anyone to deceive the readers. The other teachers do not understand themselves to be deceivers; rather, this is the writer's polemical evaluation.[20] He offers a second evaluation with a play on words (*paralogizomai*, "to deceive," followed by *pithanologia*, "plausible-sounding arguments"); the other teaching comes to them in "plausible-sounding arguments." The nuance of *pithanologia* is difficult to capture. It may simply mean arguments that are probable as opposed to being demonstrable according to the laws of logic (Plato, *Theaet.* 162e). On the other hand, it may have a more unfriendly cast and so mean something like "specious argument" (Dunn 133) or "gross rhetoric" (Schweizer 118). Understanding the word in this way, Dunn suggests, indicates that the teachers are reworking arguments from Paul to make their own points. It is reasonable to envision these teachers reworking Paul's arguments when they advocate having visionary experiences, because Paul, after all, is known to be a visionary himself (cf. 2 Cor 12:7). Still, *pithanologia* may not have quite such a polemical tone; vocabulary was available to make the point more clearly (e.g., *pithanologikē* means the art of using specious arguments; on the other hand, *pithanologos* denotes persuasive speech without necessarily connoting that the speaker is deceptive [see LSJM 1403]). The writer may grant that these arguments *sound* plausible or reasonable, because they cite Paul. But these persuasive-sounding arguments turn the Colossians away from the genuine apostolic gospel. In one sense, that makes the arguments specious. *Pithanologia* allows that less polemical nuance that does not insult the people who are giving serious consideration to those arguments—which do, after all, *sound* plausible. This statement gives the impression that the readers' decision about the other teaching has not yet been made. They have not yet adopted it, but it is attractive enough that the writer must provide convincing reasons for them to maintain the faith as they had accepted it earlier.

[5] Having launched the first direct strike against the other teaching, the writer now returns to the topic of Paul's relationship with the Colossians. This frames 2:1–5 with an *inclusio*; the passage both begins and ends with references to Paul's relationship with those he does not know or with whom he is not present. The mention of rejoicing in v. 5 also recalls 1:24 and so ties together all of 1:24–2:5.

Verse 5 concedes that Paul is absent but minimizes the significance of his absence by granting him a presence among them nonetheless. This simultaneous acknowledgement of physical absence and spiritual presence echoes 1 Cor 5:3, a passage in which Paul claims a genuine presence among the Corinthians, even though he is not physically present. In the Corinthian setting, Paul exerts

---

20. This is another occasion when Paul is shown to be trustworthy because he has the welfare of the Colossians in mind (MacDonald 87).

his authority within the congregation through his nonphysical presence in a more direct way than in Colossians. But just as Paul claimed authority in Corinth, the author of Colossians intends the readers to recognize the absent Paul as an authority to whom they should defer.

For the fourth time since 1:22, the writer uses the word *sarx* ("flesh"). In none of these instances does the word have the negative connotations it often has in Paul (Dunn 134). In fact, presence "in the flesh" is superior to presence "in spirit" (just as it was in 1 Cor 5:3). So "flesh" bears no moral connotations in this context.

While Paul is absent "in the flesh," he is present with the readers "in spirit." It is difficult to discern what the word "spirit" connotes here. Perhaps the author sees Paul bound to the community by the Holy Spirit because it is the Spirit that binds the community together (Pokorný 108; O'Brien 98). But if he intended to refer to this function of the Spirit, he would probably have mentioned it as one of the ways the readers' hearts are bound together (v. 2). Furthermore, Colossians seldom mentions the Spirit and has not spoken of it directly since 1:8. So it seems unlikely that this is what the author intends, even if that was what Paul had in mind in 1 Cor 5. Yet Colossians claims more for Paul than what we mean when we say we will "be there in spirit." The writer probably means that Paul is present *by means of this letter*, which conveys his words, authority, and presence (Hay 80).[21] Yet more may be involved because, through this presence, Paul can observe the community and its faith. Somehow, he can participate in their life, even when absent and even when he does not know them (Schweizer 120).

One of the results of being "present in spirit" is that Paul is pleased with the Colossians' adherence to the faith. His pleasure with them is expressed with the participles "rejoicing" (*chairōn*) and "seeing" (*blepōn*), in that order. As we observed of the participles "bearing fruit and growing" in 1:6 and 1:10, the order of these two participles seems inverted. Perhaps the relationship of the two participles helps explain their order in 2:5: together they mean "rejoicing because I see" (cf. O'Brien 98–99; MacDonald 87). Even though Colossians tends to use multiple words to express an idea, both participles here convey an important idea. "Rejoicing" brings this section on the relationship between Paul and the readers to a close with a compliment to the readers. Such compliments prepare the readers to accept what the writer recommends. Furthermore, by returning to the language of 1:24, the author binds the section together through mention of Paul's rejoicing about them and his work for them.

Paul's "seeing" the Colossians probably claims more than that he can simply observe them. It suggests that he can oversee them even though he did not

---

21. Perhaps Dunn (134) underestimates the power of Paul's presence through the letter when he comments that "in the spirit" "implies a more effective presence than simply the letter itself." The purpose of 1:24–2:5 is to establish just such an effective presence.

found the community and even though he has not known them. Throughout 1:24–2:5, the writer only implies that Paul possesses this authority. There are no strident claims about Paul's authority, but by now it has been established and in v. 5 it is exerted: he examines the faith of the community.

Paul's examination determines that the Colossians' faith remains intact; he discerns its "order" (*taxis*) and "firmness" (*stereōma*). Both words were used in military contexts, *taxis* to speak of an orderly formation (e.g., Zenophon, *Anab.* 1.2.18) and *stereōma* to speak of fortifications or center of strength (1 Macc 9:14). If such martial nuances remain, which is doubtful, it would prepare the readers for the harsh words about the other teachers in 2:6–23. Whether or not the readers heard these as military metaphors, the statement's purpose is to congratulate the Colossians for rejecting the other teaching, at least until now. At the same time it signals that these other teachers are a real threat to the community's faith. It is difficult to tell whether these words of affirmation are simply compliments to gain the readers' goodwill or whether the Colossians have, as a church, managed to reject the other teaching, with only a few drawn into its ranks. The tenor of the letter suggests that most of the church has not yet accepted the visionaries' teaching (Olbricht 308–28). This evaluation, therefore, while perhaps somewhat exaggerated, represents the author's basic assessment of the readers' situation in relation to the teaching he opposes.

The implied readers (i.e., the Colossians) remain firm in their "faith in Christ." This is the only time in the Pauline corpus where the noun "faith" (*pistis*) appears with this preposition for "in" (*eis*), though the cognate verb *pisteuō* does appear with *eis*. (Dunn [135] also notes that this noun construction occurs in Acts 20:21; 24:24; 26:18.) This phrase indicates that the Colossians' trust and belief is in Christ. It is "in Christ" that one responds to the acts of God that have been discussed since 1:24, and in the poetic material in 1:15–20. This is one of the passages in the New Testament that assert the necessity of believing *in* Christ, not just *with* Jesus. That is, Christian identity is not determined solely by believing the things Jesus believed, but also and necessarily by believing things about the identity and work of Christ. Such an affirmation does not suggest a late date for Colossians. Already in the undisputed Pauline Letters (the earliest Christian writings we possess), believing things about who Jesus was— especially what his life, death, and resurrection mean for one's relationship with God—is central to Christian identity.[22] So Colossians remains within that

---

22. In Gal 2:16, for example, Paul speaks of Christians as those who have come to believe in Christ; the meaning of this statement changes little regardless of whether *pistis christou* means "the faithfulness of Christ" or "faith in Christ." Another example is 1 Cor 15:1–4, where Paul identifies the confession that Christ's death was "for our sins" as a tradition handed down to him and representing a part of the central affirmation of the church. So from its earliest days, the church's identity was formed by believing this about Christ and his death.

stream, without, on this score, plowing new ground or extending any tendencies that are not already developed.

Colossians 2:1–5 reiterates, personalizes, and expands some points made in 1:24–29. The struggles and suffering of Paul are not just for the church generally; they are also for the Colossians, the Laodiceans (possibly the actual recipients of the letter), and for all believers who never met Paul. This certainly means the whole church, but the idea is expressed in a way that the first readers and then successive readers of Colossians are claimed by the mission of Paul. In 2:1–5, Paul's struggles benefit the readers, particularly as they strive to maintain their faith in the face of false teaching. Not only are Paul's sufferings for the readers; he also is present among them even though physically absent. This presence of Paul both enables a feeling of relatedness and extends the reach of his authority to the readers.

In addition to securing the place of Paul, 2:1–5 reaffirms that all possible spiritual wisdom and understanding reside in Christ. Then, for the first time, the writer directly juxtaposes this fullness to the "plausible-sounding arguments" of the visionaries.

The whole of 1:24–2:5 establishes an ethos, an image or characterization, of Paul that creates a relationship with the readers, whether they are the Colossians, the Laodiceans, those who have never met him, or the whole body of Christ. Paul suffers for them all. Thus he is someone who has their good at heart and can be trusted to offer good advice. But he is even more than a trustworthy friend; he is also an exemplar. His sufferings benefit believers everywhere because those sufferings teach the value of adherence to the gospel message and thereby encourage others to recognize the gifts they possess because of their place in Christ. Strengthened in this way, the readers can reject the other teaching being proffered.[23]

The writer claims a place of authority for Paul by stating that Paul is a servant or minister (*diakonos*) commissioned by God to proclaim the eschatological acts of God in Christ. Moreover, Paul has a role in the presentation of these Gentile believers at judgment. Together, the commission by God and Paul's sacrificial suffering for the readers give him a place of authority that can be rivaled by few, if any. This establishment of authority inclines the readers to do as they are instructed in the rest of the letter and most immediately to reject the visionaries' teaching. Now that Paul's right to speak with authority has been established from many angles, the writer can proceed to direct confrontation with the other teaching.

---

23. Hay (81) asserts that in this section Paul's work and suffering are "a model of appropriate Christian self-denial" in contrast to the asceticism of the other teachers. Paul's sufferings are a model in only a limited sense, however; they serve as an example of the value of the teaching the readers have received from the original preaching in their community.

Argument 2

Accept This Letter's Teaching and Instruction Because Only This Message Is Consistent with the Faith You Have Already Received

Colossians 2:6–23

REMAIN FAITHFUL TO THE GOSPEL YOU RECEIVED

Colossians 2:6–23 comprises the second major section in the argument of the letter and contains the letter's central polemical statements. It forcefully exhorts the readers to reject the visionaries' teaching and provides theological rationales for doing so. This section gives further expression to some teachings introduced in early parts of the letter that the author sees as indispensable for a relationship with God and for Christian identity. This section's more direct judgments about the other teaching and its exhortation not to accept that teaching carry more weight now that the previous section (1:24–2:5) has presented Paul as one who is trustworthy and willing to suffer for the readers—and this in addition to being an apostle (1:1).

Verses 6–23 consist of three distinct sections: an introductory and transitional section (vv. 6–7), an explicit rejection of the visionaries' teachings that provides further theological bases for the readers' relationship with God (vv. 8–15), and a more direct rejection of specific elements of the other teaching (vv. 16–23). The introductory section draws together many themes from previous parts of the letter as it prepares the readers to see why these theological truths require them to reject the visionaries' teaching. The theological elements that vv. 8–15 bring to the foreground highlight the person and work of Christ to show how the place of believers with God is determined by who Christ is and what he has done for them. For the writer, a correct understanding of who Christ is and what he has accomplished for believers necessarily precludes accepting the other teaching. Once he sets these theological matters in relief, in vv. 16–23 he turns to deal directly with commands and instructions that the visionaries advocate. These verses contain both general warnings and specific prohibitions, along with characterizations of the other teaching calculated to turn the readers from it.

As in 1:21–23, so also 2:6–23 employs a wide range of metaphors to describe what the work of Christ has accomplished for believers. In various ways these metaphors express that believers already possess everything the visionaries promise with their new regimen and visions. Among the images the writer uses to speak of the gifts that believers have received are that they have been given fullness (v. 10), have been circumcised (v. 11), have been given life (v. 13), have been forgiven their trespasses (vv. 13–14), have been freed from the grasp of cosmic powers (v. 15), and above all, are "in him" (vv. 6, 7, 10, 11, 15; additionally v. 13 has "with [*syn*] him"). All these images declare that the readers already have the full relationship with God that the visionaries claim one can attain only through their commands and the resultant visions.

This section's main goal is clearly to enable the readers to reject the visionaries' teaching, but much else remains unclear. The section contains obscure and unusual metaphors, uncommon vocabulary, and sentences that are nearly unintelligible. Moreover, in several places the letter's pleonastic redundancy (e.g., "circumcised with the circumcision," v. 11; "grow with the growth," v. 19; "commands and teachings," v. 22) makes achieving clarity difficult. In spite of these and other difficulties, the section's main point remains clear: the readers must adhere to the apostolic gospel that they have heard from Epaphras. That gospel contains the authentic understanding of Christ, an understanding that recognizes Christ and him alone as the one who provides access to God.

2:6–7 Hold On to the Faith

2:6 Therefore, just as you received Jesus as Christ and Lord,[a] live in him, 7 rooted and founded in him and secured by the faith, just as you were taught it, and abounding in thanksgiving.

a. This rendering of the names for Jesus reflects the unusual way they are given. More literally, the text has "the Christ, Jesus the Lord." See the comment on vv. 6–7 for discussion of the significance of this unique way of referring to Jesus.

[6–7] The "therefore" (*oun*) of v. 6 marks the beginning of a new section. The appearance of the letter's first imperative also marks a new beginning here. Verses 6–7 summarize much of what has gone before and have a direct connection to v. 5, but the argument takes a significant turn at v. 6. The previous section, which presents Paul as the authoritative and reliable teacher, closes in v. 5 with a compliment to the readers (perhaps a *captatio benevolentiae*, a bid for the audience's goodwill), observing that they remain firm in the faith and warning them about those who present specious arguments. Then in v. 6, that affirmation of their faithfulness becomes an exhortation to remain faithful. This is a good example of the Pauline indicative-imperative paradigm. The command rests on and is a coordinate of whom God has made believers and what God has given them.

When the writer says that they "received" Christ, he designates the teaching they had originally accepted as the authentic teaching of the church. The verb "receive" (*paralambanō*) is a common way New Testament writers, particularly Paul, speak of passing on received tradition (e.g., 1 Cor 15:1). If the writer drew on rabbinic ideas about passing on tradition, his Gentile readers probably missed that nuance. Still, this statement affirms that they already possess the gospel that the whole church believes.

The tradition passed on to the readers contains the apostolic teaching about Christ and its meaning for their relationship with God. The writer expresses this idea succinctly, constructing an unusual arrangement of titles and names for Jesus. He places the name "Jesus" between "the Christ" (*ton christon*) and "the Lord" (*ton kyrion*). Both the order of the words and the repetition of the article before Christ and Lord are unusual. This expression, however, allows the writer to claim more clearly that Jesus is both Christ and Lord. What these titles entail for him remains less than obvious. Still, both give Jesus a cosmic identity in this context.[1] The proclamation of his role in the creation and reconciliation of all things in 1:15–20 clearly establishes his lordship over all. Furthermore, Colossians uses "Christ" to identify Jesus with the mystery of God and the repository of all divine wisdom and knowledge (2:2–3), the presence of God in their lives (1:27), and the one in whom they have placed their faith (2:5). Colossians ties these cosmic elements to the human Jesus in 2:6. Thus the crucified Jesus—his sufferings have been mentioned in 1:24 and his crucifixion will be of greater importance in 2:14–15—is also the cosmic Lord and Christ. This way of referring to Jesus alludes to the whole complex of the teachings about the person and work of Christ that Epaphras had first brought them.

The imperative that necessarily flows from accepting the tradition about Christ is that they live in accordance with that teaching. Literally, they are commanded to "walk in him." The New Testament commonly uses the verb *peripateō* ("to walk [around]") to speak of a person's manner of life (e.g., Mark 7:5; 1 Cor 7:17; Eph 4:17; 2 John 4). The received message about the person and work of Christ contains within it a demand to live in a particular way; the gospel includes ethics. This statement again utilizes the Pauline indicative-imperative paradigm. But as in the undisputed Paulines, this statement of the relationship between what God had done for and made the readers, on the one hand, and what is required of them, on the other, does not simply suggest that the gift demands a response. Rather, the Christian manner of life is part of the gospel; thus, receiving the tradition entails living the Christian life. Colossians is about to embark upon a pointed rejection of the visionaries' regulations. But both immediately before (2:6–7) and after (3:1–4) rejecting those regulations, the writer indicates that accepting the gospel does include adopting a particular manner of life. Indeed, the believer must live the gospel.

Colossians exhorts believers to live "in him" (*en autō*). This is the first of five times "in him" appears in vv. 6–15. In addition, "in whom" (*en hō*) and "with him" (*syn autō*) appear in these verses. These prepositional phrases and yet other associations with Christ made through prepositions that are embedded as prefixes of compound verbs emphasize the intimate relationship that

---

1. It is unlikely that calling Jesus "the Christ" reminds the readers that he is the Jewish Messiah (contra Dunn 140).

believers share with Christ. In this first appearance of "in him," Christ is more than the guide and standard for proper living; he constitutes the sphere in which believers live their lives. Christ defines their identity and their way of life. Verses 8–15 will provide various reasons why Christ must be the sphere in which believers live.

Verse 7 contains four participles that describe the manner in which believers "live in him."[2] The first two participles draw on agricultural and construction metaphors to describe believers' state of existence: they have been "rooted and founded in him." The use of the perfect tense in the verb "rooted" (*errizōmenoi*) indicates that their previous implanting in Christ continues to sustain them. "Founded" appears in the present tense. So they began their Christian existence by being rooted in Christ, and their lives continue to be built on being "in him."[3]

The third participle, "secured," also relates back to the imperative "live" rather than describing how believers are rooted and founded. Believers' lives "in him" are secured by "the faith." Faith here refers to the content of their faith, not to the believer's disposition of trust or faithfulness. While the phrase "secured by the faith" may mean that they are secured within the realm of the faith or that they are helped to retain their faith, it probably means that they are secured in their lives in Christ by the faith (i.e., *tē pistei* functions as an instrumental dative). The faith that secures believers "in him" is the faith that they had already been taught. Thus holding to the faith that Epaphras had delivered to them forms a part of the way the Colossians live in Christ. The rest of chapter 2 will argue that this being "secured by the faith" includes rejecting the visionaries' teaching.

Living in Christ also entails "abounding in thanksgiving." This participle echoes 1:10–12, which also defined living in Christ by using four participles, the last of which was giving thanks. Perhaps the writer returns to this element of Christian existence because it flows from the assurance that believers possess because they are secure "in him." Thus, rather than striving to attain visions, they may rejoice that they have been *given* their relationship with God through Christ.

2:8–15 Reject the Visionaries' Teaching Because You Already Possess God's Blessings

2:8 Watch out, so that no one may take you captive with their empty and deceitful philosophy, which is based on human traditions, on the elements of the world, and not on Christ. 9 Because in him all the fullness of deity

---

2. These four participles are perhaps parallel with the four participles that follow *peripateō* in 1:10–12 (Wilson 241–42). The two sets of four have several commonalities, including these: in each set the last of the four is "giving thanks," and in both passages the first two involve agricultural metaphors of growing.

3. This awkwardness in the prepositions is present in the text: they "are founded-on in him."

lives bodily, and you have been made full in him, 10 who is the head of all principalities and powers.[a] 11 In whom you were also circumcised with a circumcision not performed with human hands, but by putting off the body of the flesh with the circumcision of Christ; 12 you have been buried with him in baptism, in whom also you were raised through the faithful working of the God who raised him from the dead. 13 Though you were formerly dead because of[b] your trespasses and the uncircumcision of your flesh, [God] made you[c] alive together with him, forgiving all our[d] trespasses. 14 He canceled the written account that was against us, with its decrees against us; he has taken it away,[e] nailing it to the cross. 15 Thereby [God] disarmed the principalities and powers and shamed them publicly, triumphing over them in [Christ].[f]

a. Literally, "every principality and power."

b. The manuscripts P[46] and A insert the preposition "in" (*en*) before "trespasses." This makes the instrumental nature of the trespasses clearer. But even if that preposition is not the original reading, the following datives serve as instrumental datives, so that the meaning remains essentially the same.

c. The manuscripts א, A, and some later ones have "you" (*hymas*), the reading given here. Though P[46] and B have "us" (*hēmas*) and a second corrector of א omits the pronoun altogether, the reading given in the text is preferable. This reading preserves the distinction between Jews and Gentiles, making the Gentiles the ones who were both dead and made alive. A copyist might have changed the pronoun to "us" to make it conform to the following pronoun.

d. A second corrector of א changed this pronoun to "your" (*hymin*), but P[46] and B both have "our" (*hēmin*).

e. Literally, "he took it out of the middle."

f. At the beginning of v. 15 I have supplied the understood subject "God" and at the end clarified the pronoun *autō* with its referent, "Christ."

[2:8] After the general exhortation to hold on to and thankfully live out the gospel the readers have received at the beginning of their life in Christ (2:6–7), v. 8 speaks more directly of the immediate challenge to faithfully maintain that gospel. This new exhortation (*blepete mē*) takes the form of a warning. Colossians urges the readers to exercise vigilance lest someone carry them off as booty or take them prisoner. This rather drastic image emphasizes the threat that the writer sees in the other teaching. Becoming a captive in a war often meant becoming a slave. So beyond the violent snatching that the verb implies, it also suggests enslavement by those who advocate seeking visions.

Use of the singular "[no] one" (*tis*) in this warning does not indicate that the author has just one person in mind. In first-century polemics, antagonists commonly avoided directly naming those who caused a problem. This denigrated the opponent by refusing to grant them enough status even to be named. Of course, if Colossians is written after Paul's death, the author cannot name the real teachers because that would render the pseudonymous nature of the letter too obvious. So the teachers that Colossians opposes remain the anonymous "anyone."

From the perspective of Colossians, the visionaries try to ensnare the readers with "empty and deceitful philosophy"—rendered more woodenly, "philosophy and empty deceit." In this phrase, "and" (*kai*) is epexegetical, so that "empty deceit" describes the "philosophy." This represents the writer's polemical description of the teaching and certainly does not reflect the way the other teachers understand their own teaching. To call the teaching "philosophy" is not, in itself, a derogatory appellation. Many teachings called themselves a philosophy, including groups we would call religions. Philo (*Legat.* 156; *Mut.* 223), Josephus (*C. Ap.* 2.47; *Ant.* 18.11), and 4 Maccabees (7:7–9) call Judaism, or a particular group within Judaism (e.g., Pharisees), a "philosophy." Without the addition of "empty deceit," calling the teaching a philosophy might even constitute a compliment. Colossians' use of the term "philosophy" does not indicate that the visionaries themselves described their teaching with this term (contra T. Martin 1996, 29–30). Only excessive use of mirror exegesis leads to this conclusion. Even if they did use this word, it tells us nothing about what they taught or how they thought about themselves, because "philosophy" had such a broad range of meanings. By branding the visionaries' teaching an "empty and deceitful philosophy," the author simply pronounces it devoid of value.

The next three phrases of v. 8 are parallel, each giving the author's evaluation of the source of the "empty and deceitful philosophy." The sentence's structure demonstrates the parallel nature of these phrases: each begins with the preposition *kata*, which means here "based on" (see my translation). These are all derogatory descriptions, not quotations of what the visionaries claim *for* their teaching (contra T. Martin 1996, 30–33). Verses 7 and 8 give contrasting descriptions to the two teachings under consideration. In v. 7 the writer accumulates complimentary descriptors for the authentic gospel, and conversely in v. 8 he multiplies derogatory accusations to describe the other teaching. His portrayal of the visionaries as those who violently capture the readers and his depiction of their teaching as empty and deceitful demonstrate the polemical nature of these comments; thus, this characterization of their teaching does not provide an accurate description of what they teach or claim.

First, the writer charges that this teaching is "based on human tradition."[4] This description of the visionaries' teaching contrasts it with the tradition

---

4. The dangers of mirror-reading such a statement are illustrated well by the contrasting views of T. Martin and Bieder. T. Martin (1996, 30) reads this expression to mean that the opponents of Colossians borrow from a standing philosophical tradition, while Bieder (14) asserts that "tradition of humans" opposes the opponents' claim to a superhuman source.

alluded to in vv. 6–7, the tradition that gave the readers their place in Christ. The writer repeats this accusation about the other teaching's origin in v. 22, where he labels their views "human commands and teachings." The expression "based on human tradition" also appears in the saying of Jesus reported in Mark 7:7–8 and Matt 15:3, 6, 9 (with the quotation of Isa 29:13). These Gospel passages contrast human tradition with the genuine will of God. Colossians intends to make that same contrast in 2:8. The author implies that since this teaching has a human origin, it is not from God. Conversely, it implies a divine origin for the gospel that the readers have originally received.

Colossians next characterizes the visionaries' message as teaching based "on the elements of the world" (*ta stoicheia tou kosmou*). This phrase has been the subject of extensive debate among scholars. Modern interpreters most often identify the *stoicheia* as angelic beings, believed by many in the ancient world to rule various parts of the cosmos. There are, however, no extant first-century uses of this word that refer to such beings. First-century writers do use *stoicheia* for the "elementary things," sometimes the letters or sounds that make up parts of a word (e.g., Philo, *Her.* 210; *Agr.* 136; *Congr.* 150). Its other common first-century use is for the elements from which many Hellenistic philosophers thought the world was made (earth, air, fire, water). Either of these latter meanings is preferable to finding a reference to the spiritual powers that rule the cosmos, because these meanings represent the ways first-century writers used the word. Whatever meaning we assign to "elements of the world," this statement does not indicate that the visionaries claim their teaching comes from the *stoicheia* or that the *stoicheia* play any role in their teaching. Rather, the author gives another polemical evaluation, denigrating their teaching by associating it with the *stoicheia*.[5] This depiction again implies that their teaching has a worldly source instead of a divine one. Naming the *stoicheia* as the source of the opposed teaching also accuses it of having come from the elementary (indeed, simplistic by comparison) and unenlightened ideas of the world, which lack the knowledge and life that Christ brings when the authentic gospel is preached.[6]

The third accusation about the visionaries' teaching in v. 8 asserts that it is "not [based] on Christ." This characterization exposes the basic problem with the other teaching: it does not accord with the authentic gospel the Colossians have already received. The phrase suggests something broader than that they have the wrong Christology; it means that the source and content (inseparable

---

5. T. Martin (1996, 31) is correct when he asserts that relating their teaching to the *stoicheia* would not have been automatically seen as derogatory. But in this case, the context and the structure of the passage (the three parallel phrases) show that relating it to the *stoicheia* devalues the visionaries' teaching.

6. Even if the *stoicheia* are spiritual beings, v. 8 would only say that the visionaries received their teachings and regulations from them, not that they were being worshiped.

here) of the visionaries' teaching is other than and inferior to Christ. Thus, if the readers follow the other teaching, they accept a message that has an inferior ultimate source. Furthermore, it turns them away from Christ.

These evaluations of the visionaries' teaching no doubt surprise the readers. The visionaries have claimed a heavenly origin for their teaching and have argued that their regulations and the resulting visions enhance one's relationship with God. Colossians not only denies those claims but also asserts that this teaching distances believers from God and violates what God has given them in Christ. The teaching the visionaries proffer, then, endangers the relationship with God that the writer accorded believers in v. 7; their lives in Christ have been secured by the faith, but the new teaching violates that faith.

[9–10] Verses 9–10 support the claims that the visionaries' teaching is worthless and incompatible with Christ. These verses assert that God's presence in Christ brings the blessings that believers possess through the gospel and demonstrates that the opposed teaching is false. A clearer understanding of the access to God that believers receive in Christ shows the other teaching to be false and damaging. The focus on Christ does not indicate that those teachers promote a different Christology; rather, the previously received Christology contains within it affirmations that demonstrate the new teaching's faults.

Though some interpreters find quotations of preformed, often hymnic material in 2:9–15 (e.g., Cannon 48–49), the evidence does not support that hypothesis. The author does use poetic language here, and he borrows from known metaphors and traditions. He also employs an elevated style. But these features do not demonstrate that he inserts an extended quotation here. Rather, he draws on and alludes to themes and language from the poetic material in 1:15–20 and other church traditions to address the problem at hand.

Verse 9 explains why the readers must not allow the other teaching to ensnare them (the *hoti* ["because"] is causal). The writer places "in him" (*en autō*) at the very beginning of the sentence to make it emphatic. This is the third appearance of "in him" since v. 6, and the phrase appears again at the beginning of v. 10. These words express a central theme of the section: Christ constitutes the sphere in which believers receive God's blessings of forgiveness and life. But in v. 9 the meaning of the phrase "in him" shifts from its previous uses. Rather than emphasizing the place of believers in Christ, this statement clarifies *why* Christ is the sphere in which believers find salvation. The foundational assertion about Christ in v. 9 explains what makes being "in him" so valuable.

Verse 9 echoes and expands 1:19, specifying explicitly that the "fullness" that resides in Christ is "all the fullness of deity." With characteristic pleonasm, Colossians makes its point more emphatic by adding "all" (*pan*) to "fullness." The choice of the word *theotētos* over *theiotēs* also indicates that the writer employs the most exalted language available to speak of the fullness that dwells in Christ. *Theiotēs* could refer to many kinds of beings and powers in the spirit world, but *theotētos*, the word Colossians uses here, could apply only to those recognized as gods. The distinction is particularly clear in Plutarch (*Mor.* 415c), who says that few *daimones* (spiritual powers) ever attain to deity (*theotētos*). *Theotētos* refers to the divine nature itself or to the essence of divinity (Lightfoot 181–82; Abbott 248; and many more recent interpreters). It is not merely godlikeness that dwells in Christ, but actually the divine nature itself.

Use of the present tense "lives" (*katoikei*) may connote something about the continual state of Christ's existence. Thus, Lightfoot translates this verb "has its fixed abode" (181). While this reading may place too much weight on the tense of this verb, the point of the passage demands that the fullness remain in Christ, otherwise the advantage of being in Christ would be lost.

Verse 9 defines this continual dwelling of deity in Christ in one further and surprising way; it resides in him *sōmatikōs*, "bodily." The present tense verb "lives" makes the straightforward rendering "bodily" difficult for many interpreters because the passage appears to affirm a continuing bodily existence for the risen Christ.[7] As early as Augustine (*Ep.* 187.39), interpreters have seen this expression as a metaphor for the church, just as the church is called Christ's body in 1:18 (so also Hay 89). Others have argued that "bodily" has the sense of "in reality," in an implied opposition between shadow and substance (Calvin 182–83; Aletti 169; Pokorný 122).[8] But the text does not support these metaphorical readings of the word. Neither does this statement specify one particular moment of Christ's existence; it refers to both the incarnation and the present, risen existence of Christ (Barth and Blanke 314). In its affirmation of the bodily nature of Christ's resurrection existence, it agrees with 1 Cor 15:20–48, where Paul argues that the resurrected Christ continues to live an embodied existence.

Perhaps Colossians also inserts "bodily" here to reject the visionaries' ascetic tendencies by affirming bodily existence, going so far as to say that the fullness of deity is embodied. Or more likely, this affirmation of embodied existence counters the visionaries' high assessment of visions in which one has out-of-body experiences. At the very least, the whole of v. 9 sets things related to Christ apart from and above teachings and experiences that have any other source. And since the fullness of deity continues to dwell in Christ bodily, Christ and therefore the fullness of deity maintain contact with the bodily lives of believers. This implication becomes explicit in v. 10.

7. The present tense may not absolutely require this reading. Lightfoot (182) asserts that it refers to the incarnation. On the other hand, Lindemann (41) contends that the present tense indicates that only the resurrected Christ is in view.

8. See the more complete listing of renderings of this word in Barth and Blanke (312–14). Hay (89), though not taking this view, acknowledges that *sōmatikōs* can mean "in reality," citing Philo, *Her.* 84. But this passage can be read straightforwardly, though the meaning may expand so that it is also metaphorical. Yet even this is insufficient to support the meaning of "in reality."

The phrase "in him" again appears in an emphatic position at the beginning of v. 10. What is "in him" has again changed; while the fullness of deity dwells "in him" in v. 9, in v. 10 believers live "in him." This returns to the nuance of "in him" found in vv. 6 and 7. The author asserts in v. 10 that believers "have been made full" because they are in Christ. This affirmation expresses the goal toward which v. 9 has pointed. The perfect tense of the verb indicates that believers received fullness in the past and that they continue to possess it. The author makes both the current possession and the location of this fullness important. The visionaries do not necessarily employ the language of "fullness" (contra Lohse 100–101), but its use here responds to their contention that believers need to supplement what they now possess in Christ. In the face of teaching that says believers need experiences of God beyond incorporation into Christ to attain forgiveness and to have a proper relationship with God, Colossians asserts that believers have already received everything *in him*. Believers can be certain of these blessings because "all the fullness of deity" dwells in Christ and they reside in him. By virtue of their being incorporated into Christ, God grants them access to all God's blessings.

Verse 10 demonstrates that the basic issue in Colossians is soteriological, not christological. The letter's christological affirmations serve as the basis for the soteriological acclamation that believers have salvation because they are in Christ. A sufficient response to the visionaries' faulty soteriology, however, necessarily includes both a proper Christology and a proper understanding of how one gains access to Christ. Verse 10 asserts that the "fullness" of forgiveness and relationship with God are "in him;" vv. 11–12 then take up the question of how one attains access to those blessings. But before the writer shifts to discussing the means of access to God's blessings, he returns to another aspect of Christ's supremacy.

The final clause of v. 10 asserts that Christ, the one in whom believers have received fullness, is the "head of all principalities and powers." These "principalities and powers" include both the beings of the spirit world, which most in the first century believed exercised significant power over the material world, and the cultural, social, and political structures of the world. In the New Testament, these spiritual beings and power structures are usually hostile forces, and here they are envisioned as hostile. When the writer states that Christ is the head of these powers, he means something rather different from his meaning when he says Christ is the head of the church, which is his body (1:18). Verse 10 does not say that the powers are Christ's body, only that he is their head. Colossians uses the imagery of the head and body in different ways. In 1:18, where Christ is the head of the body, Christ supplies its life and strength and is intimately related to the church, as well as being the one the church must obey. This use of the image denotes relationship. But "head" (*kephalē*) may also convey the meaning of ruling or exercising sovereignty, as it does in several passages in the LXX.[9] When Colossians describes Christ as the head of the powers, *kephalē* means "ruler."[10] Since Christ rules over them, believers need nothing from them and need have no ultimate fear of them. The Christ who wields power over every other force in the cosmos guarantees believers' relationship with God.

Since the visionaries see such powers in their visions and imitate those powers in their practices, the writer puts these celestial powers in their place in relation to Christ; they are Christ's inferiors. The teachers may well have claimed such beings as the source of their teaching. By making them inferiors of Christ, the author gives his readers one more reason not to listen to the visionaries' instructions. After all, believers already participate in the fullness that comes through Christ, the ruler of such beings. Given the status of Christ in relation to the powers, the readers gain nothing by adhering to teaching that comes from them. Furthermore, the relationship that believers have with Christ determines their relationship with God. Christ's status, then, renders irrelevant any teaching or experience that might come from other powers.

[11–12] Verses 11–12 begin a subsection (vv. 11–15) that articulates the means by which believers have come to possess the fullness that v. 10 asserts they have in Christ. Verse 11 uses the metaphor of circumcision, the first in a series of metaphors, to describe their entrance into Christ. Verse 12 identifies this circumcision with baptism. Therefore, the author uses circumcision to refer to the readers' initiation into the church. He makes baptism the moment at which believers enter the realm "in Christ," the place where the blessings of God are found.

Verse 11 begins by directing attention to Christ in much the same way that vv. 9 and 10 did. Verses 9 and 10 began with "in him" (*en autō*); v. 11 begins with "in whom" (*en hō*). The variation in pronoun does not change the meaning. The writer continues to emphasize that the readers live in the presence and blessings of God because they reside "in Christ." Since they have come to enjoy this status "in him," and since they maintain it only through steadfastness to the gospel they have already received, they must reject the new teaching. Whatever the visionaries offer, it pales in the light of all that believers already have "in Christ." The visionaries can offer the readers nothing of true significance that Christ has not already secured for them and given to them.

Verses 11–13 indicate clearly that the author of Colossians is Jewish and the readers are Gentile. Verse 13 distinguishes between the "you" who were uncircumcised and the "we" who have been forgiven. While a pseudonymous author

9. Isaiah 9:13 LXX uses the image of *kephalē* (head), and then v. 14 explains that it means *archē* (ruler). See also Deut 28:13; Isa 7:9; 1 Kgs 21:12 [20:12 LXX]; manuscript A of the LXX has *kephalē* (head) in Judg 10:18; 11:8, 9, 11, while manuscript B has *archōn* (ruler). See Fitzmyer 503–11; Arnold 1994, 346–66.

10. Colossians expresses similar ideas in 1:20 and 2:15. In those passages, Christ defeats and subdues the powers.

might be astute enough to remember to portray himself as Jewish, since Paul was Jewish, a non-Jew would probably not select circumcision as a favorable metaphor through which to express the idea of incorporation into Christ. Circumcision was viewed unfavorably by the majority culture in the first century, and some Jews even had surgery to reverse their circumcision (1 Macc 1:15; Josephus, *Ant.* 12.241). It was even seen as a sign of sexual impropriety, particularly of constant arousal. Few in the Greco-Roman world other than Jews saw circumcision favorably, and many thought of it as mutilation.[11] A converted Gentile, then, would probably not offer circumcision as a metaphor for entry into the fullness of God's blessings.

Circumcision is a useful metaphor in the context of Colossians because of its associations with entering and possessing a covenant relationship with God. For Jews, it was a sign of distinction from those around them and of their identity as the people of God. From its introduction in Gen 17, it served as a sign of the covenant bond between God and Israel. Those who bear this sign are God's people, while those who do not are outside the covenant. The church's similar associations of baptism with covenant relationship and identity as God's people make circumcision a good choice for a metaphor—at least among Jews. These associations also indicate that the metaphor of circumcision does not suggest here that the visionaries required it for membership in the Christian community.

In some ways, identifying circumcision with baptism may seem to open the way for women to possess equal standing with men among the people of God, because while circumcision was only for males, baptism is the way that all enter the covenant with God in the church. Thus, women pass through the same ritual and bear the same sign as men. But this was probably not on the writer's mind when he penned this passage, because extant Jewish literature seldom, if ever, suggests that women were not fully within the covenant.

This is the first place where circumcision appears as a symbol for baptism in extant early Christian writings (MacDonald 99).[12] Colossians presents this metaphorical circumcision as an accomplished fact; since the readers have been circumcised, they already enjoy God's forgiveness and fullness. Colossians delineates three characteristics of this circumcision they have received: it is "not with hands," it is "putting off the body of the flesh," and it is "of Christ" (cf. Lightfoot 183). A circumcision not performed by human hands is a spiritual cir-

11. See the comments of Dio Cassius, *Rom. Hist.* 80.11; Strabo, *Geogr.* 16.2.37; Herodotus, *Hist.* 2.36–37; Philo, *Spec.* 1.1.2. For discussion of views of circumcision in the ancient world, see Frederick M. Hodges, "The Ideal Prepuce in Ancient Greece and Rome: Male Genital Aesthetics and Their Relation to *Lipodermos*, Circumcision, Foreskin Restoration, and the *Kynodesmē*," *Bulletin of the History of Medicine* 75 (2001): 375–405.

12. However, Cannon (41–43) contends that it is an obvious connection and, based on 1 Pet 3:21, a common one in the early church.

cumcision, one that involves the heart and so commits one to faithfulness to the covenant with God. This figurative sense of circumcision appears in Deut 10:16; Jer 4:4; Ezek 44:7; and 1QS 5.5. These passages call on the people to circumcise their hearts, that is, to turn from their unfaithfulness and serve God. Deuteronomy 30:6 promises that after the exile God will circumcise the hearts of the Israelites so that they will love and serve God as they should. This is the kind of circumcision that Colossians says has been accomplished among its readers; since their circumcision was not done by hands, it was an act of God. Furthermore, this spiritual circumcision—including the relationship with God and the internal reorientation it symbolizes—constitutes an *eschatological* act of God, as the following connection to the death and resurrection of Christ indicates.

This spiritual circumcision is accomplished "by [with an instrumental *en*] putting off the body of the flesh." While it is possible to see this "putting off of the body" as a reference to death, and more particularly to the death of Jesus (Dunn 157–58), the context indicates that it refers to something that has happened to the believers. Thus, "putting off the body of the flesh" is the immediate means of access to the fullness.

The noun "putting off" or "stripping off" (*apekdysis*), which has two prefixes, is very uncommon.[13] Perhaps the combination of two prefixes adds intensity to the expression, so the baptized have determinably put off this "body of flesh." The question that remains is, What have they so vehemently put off?

The expression "body of the flesh" is also rather unusual. The multiple ways Colossians uses "flesh" (*sarx*) complicate our discernment of the phrase's meaning. In some places *sarx* denotes sinfulness (e.g., 2:18, 23), while in other places it simply refers to earthly life (e.g., 1:22, 24; 2:1; see Hay 90–91). In 2:11 "flesh" represents evil, even while Colossians affirms the goodness of bodily existence. Rejection of "the flesh" does not constitute a judgment against material existence or embodiment as a mode of existence. Rather, here *sarx* refers to that element of our humanity that is dominated by evil. So "body of the flesh" is not a redundant expression but refers to that aspect of one's person that has been corrupted by sin or, to draw on the images of 1:13–14, that evil has taken captive. The "body of the flesh" expresses the same idea found in Rom 6:6, where Paul speaks of the "body of sin" (Tannehill 49). The appearance of the verb "strip off" (*apekdyomai*)[14] in 3:9 supports this understanding of "body of flesh." *Apekdyomai* is a cognate of the noun "putting off" (stripping, *apekdysis*), used in 2:11. In 3:9 *apekdyomai* speaks of stripping off "the old person with its deeds" and coordinates this act with putting on the "new person," which

13. This is the first time *apekdysis* appears in extant literature; it is not found independent of Pauline usage, and does not appear again until about the 12th century (see BDAG 100).

14. This verb appears only twice in the New Testament, both in Colossians. See the discussion of it in the comment below on 2:14–15.

signifies life in Christ. In chapter 3, the thing stripped off is one's preconversion life, envisioned as the sinful manner of life that characterizes all life outside of Christ. Believers have put off that old way of living in their spiritual circumcision. Thus, when the writer uses the expression "body of the flesh," he is working within eschatological categories. This eschatological frame of thought becomes more dominant in the following verses.

All the action in this verse has God as its subject (whether expressed or implied). Just as believers do not perform their own circumcision (not even their spiritual circumcision takes place as the result of their own effort: the verb "circumcised" is in the passive voice), so they do not put off their sinful selves by their own power. This is an act of God. And just as circumcision entails a faithful response, so God's removal of believers' old nature entails their effort to live according to the new nature, as much of the rest of Colossians makes evident.

The phrase "with the circumcision of Christ" renames the circumcision not done by hands. It does not speak of the circumcision of the child Jesus nor of his death (contra Tannehill 49; Dunn 158). If it were about Christ's death, the possessive "his" would probably accompany the noun "circumcision" (MacDonald 100). The whole of v. 11 has the spiritual circumcision of believers in view. The expression "the circumcision of Christ" continues that line of thought. The circumcision of Christ, then, brings one into the covenant established in Christ and marks one for membership "in him." The beginning of v. 12 identifies this spiritual circumcision with baptism. This identification with baptism makes "the circumcision of Christ" the entrance into Christ, by which God grants forgiveness and the power to live for God.

Verse 12 continues the discussion of the means of access by which believers have come to possess fullness in Christ, but now the writer explicitly names baptism as that means. Believers received "the circumcision of Christ" when they were "buried with him in baptism." This affirmation continues the "in Christ" theme begun in v. 6, though now using "*with* him." The change in prepositions fits this description of baptism. Baptism enacts a central part of the gospel story. But it is more than a reenactment, because the baptized not merely observe but also participate in the action; in baptism they are buried and raised with Christ. They become a part of the gospel narrative as they are brought into Christ and are made to share in central elements of its story.

This verse shares so many things with Rom 6, particularly vv. 3–4, that Abbott (251) says it reads nearly like a commentary on that passage. Whether Colossians draws directly on Rom 6 or just on the same traditions (Lohse 103) makes little difference. Either way, the common elements in these passages demonstrate that the early church understood baptism as an act in which the believer identifies with Christ, particularly with Christ's death, burial, and resurrection, and in this act receives forgiveness and relationship with God. Baptism represents the "foundational structure" (Pokorný 126) of the gospel and serves as the point of access to the blessings that the gospel supplies.[15] Baptism provides the entrance into the "fullness" that believers have "in him." Since the readers have been baptized, they have been identified with the gospel story, possess its blessings, and so, by implication, do not need the new regulations and experiences that the visionaries urge on them.

The prepositional phrase that follows "in baptism" may be translated "in whom" (referring to Christ) or "in which" (referring to baptism). In its immediate place in the sentence, the syntax suggests that the pronoun has the immediately preceding word "baptism" for its antecedent. Moreover, inserting "in him" at this point makes the sentence a bit rough. The context, however, suggests understanding the phrase as a reference to Christ because the motif of being "in Christ" dominates the whole section. Furthermore, these words form a syntactical parallel with the beginning of v. 11, where *en hō* clearly means "in whom/him."[16] Finally, the parallel in thought with the beginning of v. 11 (receiving spiritual circumcision bears much the same meaning as being raised with Christ) also makes it preferable to render the phrase "in whom." But the decision about its antecedent changes little in the substance of the passage's meaning, except that choosing "in which" allows the emphasis to shift a bit more to baptism. With either rendering, though, believers are raised with Christ in baptism and through this rite begin to exist in the realm of Christ.

"In him" (or "in baptism"), believers not only die; they are also "raised with" and "in" him. Many commentators see a monumental difference between the ways Rom 6 and Col 2 speak of the result of baptism. In Rom 6, believers receive "newness of life," but in Colossians they "are raised with" Christ. In the undisputed letters, Paul never uses the term "resurrection" for the current experience of believers. But Colossians and Romans do not differ as radically as some have thought. The resurrection that the believers possess in Colossians bears no resemblance to the overrealized eschatology that 2 Thessalonians and 2 Timothy reject (Lohse 105). And Paul's partially realized eschatology does assert that believers participate in the "new age" and possess new life in Christ. While Rom 6 does not use the term "resurrection" for existence in the present, vv. 4 and 11 assert that believers have died with Christ and live a new life to God. This is new life that believers possess now. Paul understood the indwelling of the Spirit as a gift of the end times that anticipated the fuller gifts of the Parousia. His eschatology was complex enough to encompass the idea that the new age has broken in and that believers possess some of the blessings of God's reign now, while at the same time they look forward to the complete consummation of the kingdom of God. The same is true for Colossians. This writer

---

15. The same basic elements and structure are also found in 1 Cor 15:3–4: Christ died for our sins and was buried and raised.

16. Both have *en hō kai* followed by a passive verb.

speaks of participating in the resurrection of Christ, but still waits expectantly for the Parousia (see 3:4, 6). The future element could hardly be forgotten since one of the primary issues the letter addresses is whether the readers have been forgiven and so are prepared to come before God in judgment. The emphases and vocabulary in Colossians and Romans differ, but there is little difference in their theological assumptions or systems (so also Pokorný 129–32). The apparent differences arise because of the different circumstances the two letters address: Rom 6 deals with the place of ethics in the believer's life, Colossians with whether its readers securely possess God's blessings or need something beyond their incorporation into Christ at baptism. Colossians' emphasis on the present possession of God's gifts, including being raised with Christ, responds to the needs of its readers.

This resurrection of believers with Christ comes about "through the faithful working of the God who raised" Jesus. This phrase specifies what, really *who*, makes baptism effective: the God who acted so powerfully in raising Jesus continues to act by joining believers to the gospel story and incorporating them into Christ at baptism. Nearly all translations and commentators understand the *pistis* that appears in v. 12 as a reference to the faith that the baptized possess, that is, their faith *in* the working of God. But the context suggests a different meaning for *pistis*. Among its several meanings, *pistis* can mean "faithfulness" or "trustworthiness." All of vv. 10–12 focuses on God's acts on behalf of believers. That emphasis continues in this affirmation about being raised with Christ. So rather than being raised with Christ because they have faith, believers are raised with Christ because the power of God continues to act faithfully ("through the faithful [working]," *dia tēs pisteōs*) on their behalf. This does not mean that the baptized do not need faith; vv. 6–8 declare the importance of adhering firmly to the proper beliefs. But in vv. 10–12 the accent falls on the acts of God. Believers can be confident about their place before God because God, in God's faithfulness, grants it to them in Christ. This affirmation of God's faithfulness reminds them of the secure basis of their relationship with God; just as God acted to raise Christ, so God faithfully acts for them.

Throughout Colossians, God is made known in Christ and works through Christ. The writer gives renewed expression to that understanding of God's presence by identifying God as the "God who raised him [Christ] from the dead." Thus, he links the nature and character of God to the Christ event, most particularly to the resurrection. The God who raised Christ now exercises that extraordinary power on behalf of believers, to raise them to life with God. Whatever the visionaries say separates the readers from God pales in comparison with the power that God has exerted and continues to exert on their behalf through Christ. God's faithful exertion of this overwhelming power grants believers the forgiveness that the visionaries deny them and raises them to new life in the fullness of God that resides only in Christ.

[13] Verse 13 restates and reframes the reality that v. 12 proclaims. At the same time, it succinctly restates the basic point of this section and of the whole letter: God has forgiven the sins of believers and has given them life with God in Christ. Verse 13 takes up some of the metaphors from vv. 11–12, but gives them different shades of meaning.

The first image that v. 13 reuses with a different nuance is death. In v. 12, the old existence is put to death when the believer receives baptism; in v. 13, that prefaith existence is a form of being dead. New Testament writers use this metaphor in both senses (for existence as death before baptism, see Luke 15:24–32; John 5:25; Eph 5:14; Jas 1:15; Rev 3:1; perhaps also Rom 6:13; for death in baptism, see Col 2:12 and Rom 6:2–4). Colossians can use these rather different meanings of death in such close proximity because its primary concern is to proclaim the scope of the new life that believers now possess in Christ (Schweizer 147).

In v. 13 the believers' prebaptismal existence as a state of death has their relationship with God in sharpest focus (as the following reference to trespasses indicates), but it carries a broader meaning as well. This existence as dead includes their subjection under other powers, both terrestrial and celestial. It also includes the absence of the meaning and goodness in their lives that life in relationship with God affords. This is the life of hostility to God (1:21), from which God has rescued believers (1:13).

The cause[17] of their deadness to God and lack of meaningful existence is, first of all, their "trespasses." These trespasses are not violations of the Mosaic law, because Colossians addresses Gentiles. Moreover, Paul uses "trespasses" to speak of the disobedience of Adam, a person not under the law (Rom 5:15–18, 20). The word "trespasses" (*paraptōmata*) conveys the same idea as the plural "sins" (*hamartiai*). Paul's use of the singular "sin" usually points to a power that captures and rules over humans; the plural designates acts that violate God's will or law. Since the readers of Colossians are Gentiles, the trespasses in view consist of violations of the innate moral nature of humans, violations their own consciences condemn others for, yet they commit themselves (as in Rom 2:14–16). These transgressions are the practical manifestations of the unbeliever's hostile stance toward God (1:21). These acts not only demonstrate one's hostility toward God by violating God's character; they also diminish life as God intends it. These transgressions diminish life to such an extent that Colossians can properly describe that existence as death.

The second cause of the readers' former existence in death is "the uncircumcision of your flesh." This phrase clearly identifies the readers as Gentiles.

---

17. Taking *en* (in) primarily as instrumental, though it may also convey a local sense, that they were within the sphere of transgressions. Even if the preposition *en* is a later addition to the text (it is absent from B and א, though it appears in P^{46}), the datives that follow it would still be instrumental.

While it refers to literal, physical circumcision, it was not the absence of the physical act of circumcision itself that imposed death, as the connection with trespasses demonstrates. Rather, circumcision symbolizes membership in a covenant relationship with God. Therefore, lack of circumcision expresses estrangement from God. This mention of circumcision probably echoes v. 11, where spiritual circumcision removes the sinful nature (Pokorný 134–35; contra Harris 106). Ezekiel 44:7 provides a precedent for using circumcision as both physical and metaphorical in the same context. That passage speaks of Gentiles as uncircumcised in both flesh and heart. Similarly, Col 2:13 identifies its readers not only as Gentiles who lived outside a covenant relationship with God but also as those who lived lives directed by the aspect of their being that is dominated by sin.

That state of living in death is now past for believers. Though they were dead, God (the unexpressed subject) has brought them to life with Christ. Contemporary Judaism sometimes identified God as the one who gives life (*Jos. Asen.* 8.2; 12.2), even gives life to the dead (Wis 16:13; 2 Macc 7:9, 22–23; cf. *Jos. Asen.* 8.10; see Dunn 163). Colossians 2:13 may draw on this tradition, even though it does not have the restoration of physical life in mind. Instead, the writer proclaims that believers receive new life with Christ in the present. That is, God has rescued them from spiritual death and has given them fullness (v. 10). They now possess the life for which God has claimed them and in which God grants them a favorable relationship. Their pre-Christian lives of meaninglessness, hostility toward God, and domination by sin amounted to death. But now God has acted to reverse all those things and has given them life. This contrast between the former manner of existence and what believers possess now is a recurring and important theme in Colossians (1:12–21; 2:8–15, 20; 3:5; see Dahl 33–34). The writer uses it to reassure the readers of their place with God and to encourage them to live in ways that manifest the new life that God has given them. In 2:13, the focus remains steadily upon what God has given them in this new life.

Connection to Jesus distinguishes Colossians' statements about God giving life from similar statements in non-Christian Jewish works. Believers in Christ are not just made alive; they are also "made alive *together with him.*" The new life they possess comes to them through God's act of raising Christ from the dead and their connection to it. This intimate link between God's acts in Christ and those for believers furthers this section's emphatic assertion that those who are "in him" possess all of God's blessings that one can possess before the Parousia. This affirmation about the sphere of salvation lays the groundwork for the writer's contention that the Colossians do not need the visionaries' regulations or experiences to supplement what they already have in Christ.

Colossians highlights forgiveness of trespasses as a central element of God's gift of new life. Receiving life entails release from guilt, hostility, and subjection to sin. Those trespasses that expressed hostility toward God and diminished the lives of the persons who committed them have all been forgiven (see 3:13 for discussion of *charizomai*, the verb used for "forgiving"). The emphatic "*all* our trespasses" indicates that every impediment to relationship and life with God has been removed. God has not simply taken away a particular number of transgressions but removed the whole category from consideration.[18] Transgressions and sins no longer define the lives of believers because they have been raised to new life with and in Christ.

An important change in pronoun occurs in this last phrase of v. 13. Since v. 6, all statements about the readers' current status, warnings about other teaching, and comments about the working of God have employed the second-person plural ("you"). The writer has clearly distinguished himself from the readers, especially in his comments about circumcision. Those who were "dead" and "made alive" are "you." But in the last phrase of v. 13, those who receive forgiveness suddenly become "us." To this point in vv. 6–13, the writer had in view the situation of Gentile believers in particular. But when he speaks of the forgiveness that God grants, he includes himself and all believers. Having used images that distinguish Jews from Gentiles, Colossians now makes clear that God grants life and forgiveness to all people, Jews and Gentiles, on the same basis. All believers receive forgiveness through their death and resurrection with Christ; all have a relationship with God because they are "in him."

These comments about forgiveness and the gift of new life in v. 13 give expression to one of Colossians' central assertions: God grants forgiveness and all blessings to everyone who has been baptized into Christ. Believers need no other regulations, rites, or experiences to attain these gifts. Verses 14–15 provide support for this assertion of forgiveness by identifying the crucifixion as the means of forgiveness and of release from the powers that formerly held them captive.

[14–15] These verses support the preceding assertions of forgiveness and fullness of life with God by using images and language unusual for the Pauline corpus and, indeed, for the whole New Testament. In the space of these two verses, we find three words that appear nowhere else in the New Testament (*cheirographon, prosēloun, apekdyesthai* [here and in Col 3:9]), three more that appear nowhere else in the Pauline corpus (*exaleiphein, hypenantion, deigmatizein*), and one that appears in only one other place (*thriambeuō*). This collection of unusual vocabulary, along with the poetic style, accumulation of participles, and portrayal of the divine drama of cosmic redemption, leads some to postulate that these verses contain quotations of a preformed hymn (Lohse 106; Cannon 44–45). But the stylistic tendencies of Colossians include

18. Similarly, Hübner (84) identifies "all our sins" as a qualitative rather than a quantitative statement.

a penchant for accumulating participles, and the passage mixes metaphors that are radically different (Hay [93] says they are intentionally clashing). Therefore, it seems better to treat these verses as the composition of the author. While he clearly drew on traditional material and imagery, he gave this shape to those materials as he wrote the letter (Sappington 206–7; Hübner 84–85).

Verse 14 begins to explicate the forgiveness that believers enjoy by proclaiming that God has "canceled the written account that was against us." This first image of forgiveness refers to erasing or canceling the record of believers' sins. This is the only time in the New Testament this metaphor for forgiveness appears. In first-century nonreligious usage, the *cheirographon* (the word commonly translated in v. 14 as "handwriting") often designated a record of a debt (Polybius, *Hist.* 30.8.4; Tob 5:3; 9:5; see Barth and Blanke 369–71). In their visions of the judgment, apocalyptic texts sometimes include a book in which angels have recorded the deeds of humans (e.g., *1 En.* 89.61–64, 70–71; *2 En.* 53.2–3). The *Apocalypse of Zephaniah* (3.6–9) and the *Vision* [or *Apocalypse*] *of Paul* (17) call this book of records a *cheirographon*, the same word that appears in Col 2:14. Moreover, the *Apocalypse of Zephaniah* is concerned with guilt and wiping this book clean, as well as with triumphing over the accuser (Sappington 164, 214–17; Dunn 164–65). In Colossians, the *cheirographon* represents the record of sins that is kept in heaven.[19] This understanding coheres with the word's usage in other texts and fits the immediate context, where the subject is how sins are forgiven. Furthermore, many early interpreters also understood the *cheirographon* as a reference to a certificate of debt that has been expunged, hence as a wiped-clean record of sins.[20]

The next phrase, "with its decrees [*dogmasin*]," may be understood in many ways. Some interpreters see a reference to the Mosaic law. Thus, when the text says that "the written document with its dogmas was taken away," it means that believers are freed from the law. But this meaning does not fit the context because Colossians has no discussion of the place of the Mosaic law in the life of the believer. Among the earliest interpretations was the idea that these decrees were not a bad thing but were the commands of the gospel, by which believers are freed from sin.[21] This reading fits the grammar but runs counter to the immediate context's emphasis on freedom from sin as a gift accomplished through the work of Christ. More recent interpreters find the writer eliminating the regulations that the other teachers impose (Schweizer 150–51; Pokorný

---

19. Carr (1981, 54–57) points to the penitential *stelae* of Asia Minor as the origin of this metaphor. While the context mentioned above seems closer to Colossians' meaning, Carr's view would see the point of the image in the same way.

20. E.g., *Const. ap.* 8.8; Augustine, *Pecc. merit.* 2.49 (probably also *Tract. ep. Jo.* 1.5); Ambrose, *Ep.* 41.8; Ephraim Syrus, *Hymns on the Nativity* 4; John Cassian, *Inst.* 3.3.

21. E.g., Chrysostom, *Hom. Col.* 6 (on 2:6–7); Basil, *Ep.* 265; *Spir.* 28; see the additional references in Lightfoot 188.

138; Dunn 165–66). This meaning fits both the grammar of the sentence and the context, particularly because Colossians uses *dogma*'s cognate verb to speak of the visionaries' regulations in 2:20. There is, however, another possibility. The interpretations cited above all understand the term *dogma* in the way the NRSV does, as "legal demands." But *dogma* commonly designates an official or judicial proclamation. For example, Luke 2:1 uses this term for the imperial decree calling for the census that sends Mary and Joseph to Bethlehem, and Codex A reading of Heb 11:23 uses it for Pharaoh's decree ordering the execution of Hebrew babies. These uses of *dogma* show that it has a broader range of meanings than "regulations." Since the problem that Colossians battles centers on the status of believers in judgment, in this context *dogma* refers to the decree of condemnation based on the heavenly record of sins.[22] The first part of v. 14, then, declares that the record of the believers' sinful deeds and the corresponding decree of condemnation have been erased. Thus, they are free from condemnation.

This reading of *dogma* makes the following phrase, "that was against us," easier to understand. The neuter nominative "that" (*ho*) does not agree with the plural "decrees" but does agree in number and gender with the singular neuter "record" (*cheirographon*). Thus, the phrase modifies the "account," not the "decrees."[23] Colossians, then, identifies the record of sins that generated the condemnation as the thing that stood "against us." But, since this "account" of deeds produces the "decrees" of condemnation, they were also "against us."

Not content to simply assert that the record of believers' deeds and its corresponding condemnation have been erased, the writer elaborates by saying that it has been taken away. The instrument that destroyed the record of these deeds (the neuter-singular pronoun agrees with *cheirographon*) is the cross of Christ. Graphically the author says that this record was nailed to the cross. This image may draw on the practice of posting a placard on a cross that publicizes the crucified person's crime. Alternatively, it may envision Christ embodying that record of their sin (Dunn 166). If this language comes from preformed or traditional material, as many think, that usage adds weight to the assertion. This declaration affirms unquestionably that the cross is the means by which God forgives sins, without advocating a specific theory of atonement.

The perfect tense "has taken away" indicates that the record of sin was removed in the past and that its removal continues in force. In the face of a teaching that denies believers forgiveness without further regulations and experiences, Colossians asserts that God has forgiven their past offenses and that

22. Both *Jub.* 39.6 and *1 En.* 100.10 mention such a decree in judgment scenes, but since these works are extant in Ethiopic rather than Greek, we can confirm only that this idea is at home in a judgment scene, not that *dogma* was used for it (see Sappington 218–19).

23. This understanding of the antecedent for *ho* is particularly important when interpreters identify the "decrees" as laws, or more particularly, as the law of Moses.

their record remains clean because of the cross. Such an affirmation leaves no place for the visionaries' regulations, experiences, or judgments. The forgiveness and new life that believers receive at baptism has its basis in the cross, the means by which God expunges the record of sin and removes it from interfering with their relationship with God.

Verse 15 employs the image of a cosmic battle in which God or God's agent defeats other celestial powers. While such imagery is not uncommon, it is quite anomalous to find that this defeat of the enemy comes in a crucifixion. Crucifixion almost universally signaled defeat and humiliation. But the early church radically reinterpreted it so that it came to symbolize the way God relates to the world. In the midst of difficulty and apparent defeat, God's ultimate goodwill for God's people is accomplished. In the cross, thus, God not only forgives sins but also defeats all forces of evil that oppose God by trying to separate God from God's people.

As it has been since at least v. 11, God remains the primary actor in v. 15. Thus, God (rather than Christ) subdues the powers, even as God acts *in* Christ.[24] Christ remains God's agent in this defeat of the powers that frees God's people.

The verb that begins v. 15, *apekdyō*, has the basic meaning "to strip off." In this context, it may allude to candidates removing their clothes in preparation for baptism or to Christ being stripped at his crucifixion (Hay 94). If the metaphor is as direct as this last possibility, then Colossians asserts that when the powers thought they were stripping Jesus at the crucifixion, they are the ones who really were exposed and shamed (Lohse 112). Another meaning of *apekdyō*, however, is "to disarm," stripping one's foe on a battlefield. The context suggests this meaning here (Pokorný 141), particularly since images from the Roman triumphal procession immediately follow. The parallels between 2:13–15 and 1:12–14 also suggest that "disarm" better captures the meaning here, because in 1:12–14 believers are rescued from the grip of hostile powers, whom Christ must defeat to effect their rescue (Sappington 211–12). Whether or not the primary meaning of *apekdyō* is "to disarm," v. 15 asserts forcefully that the cosmic powers have been shamed and humiliated, and thus they have no power to pronounce judgment on believers.

The "rulers and authorities" whose defeat v. 15 proclaims are the same spiritual powers mentioned in v. 10. There Colossians names Christ as their head, their ruler. Verse 15 indicates that establishing Christ's rule required force, because God overcame and disarmed (or stripped) them at the cross. There is some tension between portraying Christ as the creator of these powers in 1:16 and God needing to conquer them in 2:15. But the tension is no greater than in

---

24. This reading excludes interpretations of the participle *apekdysamenos* that have Christ strip himself of the powers (e.g., Lightfoot 190–91; note also the early interpreters he cites who held this view).

any scheme in which some created beings rebel against their creator. Many apocalyptic works envision similar scenarios. In Col 2:15 these beings play a role in the judgment, perhaps as the angelic beings in charge of punishment (Pokorný 189) or, better in this context, as the accusers of those who appear in judgment. Such beings function in these ways in various apocalyptic works (e.g., Zech 3:1; *Apocalypse of Zephaniah* B; 3:7–9; Rev 12:10; see Sappington 208–12) when they accuse God's people at judgment. In so doing, they are no longer simply working at God's behest; they have become hostile forces that use the account of people's sins to evoke condemnation. In Colossians, the cross erases the record of evil deeds that these powers could use to condemn others. Thus, the cross disarms them; they no longer pose a threat to believers at judgment.

Not only does the cross nullify the weapon that the powers wield against God's people; God also defeats and humiliates the principalities and powers themselves in a public display. They are completely overwhelmed: stripped, disarmed, and publicly shamed. There is no thought of appeasing these powers, as one would find in the mystery cults; instead, God defeats them in Christ and his cross (Thurston 45). These statements emphasize the overwhelming power and efficacy of the cross. Furthermore, if these powerful celestial beings pose no threat to those who are "in Christ," the demands of the other teachers in Colossae manifestly bear no importance.

The final description of God's overwhelming defeat of these powers proclaims that God "triumphs over them." This statement employs the image of the Roman triumphal procession. A triumphal procession was a victory parade in Rome that included the display of those who had been defeated. This act purposefully humiliated the vanquished and sometimes ended in their execution. Colossians envisions such a demonstration of God's victory over the principalities and powers; they are shamed and must endure a public demonstration of their defeat and powerlessness. The resurrection constitutes this public element of their defeat as their apparent victory over Christ at the cross becomes the proclamation of his lordship over all creation.

Colossians uses this radical and violent imagery to assure its readers that they have nothing to fear in judgment. The visionaries' regulations and judgments against them are irrelevant to their relationship with God and standing before God. For persons incorporated into Christ, even the powerful and celestial beings who accuse people before God have been swept away and rendered powerless.

Verse 15 contains two paradoxical statements about the way God has acted: (1) God subdues created beings through God's agent Christ, and (2) God gains this victory over them through the cross. Such paradoxes are inherent in the cross, that sign of defeat and humiliation shown by the resurrection to be a *locus* of God's power and God's acts in the world. Throughout his letters, Paul emphasizes the paradoxical nature of seeing the cross as the means through which God acts to save humanity and as the paradigm for Christian existence.

This comes to expression with particular force in 1 Cor 1:18–2:8 (see also 1 Thess 2:1–14, which emphasizes the paradox of experiencing persecution because one is a believer in Christ). In highlighting the paradox of the cross, then, Colossians is fully Pauline.

The final phrase in v. 15 may mean "in it [i.e., the cross]" or "in him [i.e., Christ]." Even though the cross would be the closer antecedent, the whole of vv. 6–15 has focused on the benefits of being "in him." Therefore, it is preferable to understand the phrase with reference to Christ. These last words of the section thus form an *inclusio* with 2:6. Christ is the means by which God accomplishes all these acts that secure believers' forgiveness and relationship with God. In vv. 6–15, Christ is the means by which God works; the one in whom the fullness of deity resides; the one in whom believers receive forgiveness of sins, new life, and fullness; and the one in whom the readers live and are rooted and founded. Since God grants access to this sphere of life through baptism, believers need no additional regulations or experiences to attain standing before God and fullness of life with God. Such a definition of being "in Christ" excludes anything that the visionaries might require, offer, or threaten, because the baptized already possess God's favor and blessings. Verses 6–15 leave this application to the other teaching mostly implicit; vv. 16–23 make these connections with the visionaries' teaching explicit.

2:16–23 Reject the Visionaries' Practices and Judgments against You

To this point, Colossians has given the readers overwhelming reasons not to acquiesce to the visionaries' judgments. Now, in 2:16–23, the writer directly counters their specific demands. He enumerates and evaluates their unacceptable regulations. All of this description and evaluation is polemical. He gives no "objective" account of what the visionaries teach or require of others; rather, he describes them in ways that make these practices unacceptable. In addition to presenting only evaluative statements about the visionaries' practices and beliefs, significant portions of these verses are very difficult to translate because of their syntax and vocabulary. That may be because the author draws on the visionaries' vocabulary, or because he makes his evaluations so dominant that they obscure his meaning for later readers.[25] This would not cause the letter's original recipients any difficulty because they already knew what the visionaries taught. This section alternates between rejecting specific demands that the teachers make on the Colossians and giving reasons for rejecting them.[26] The

---

25. It seems unlikely that the syntax is difficult because the author has lost his composure, as Hay suggests (101).

26. Hay (101) outlines this alternation in this way: vv. 16, 18a–c, and 20–21 reject demands, while vv. 17, 18d–19, 20, 22, and 23 give warrants.

writer wants the Colossians to see the important theological issues at stake in what the visionaries advocate. Then they will understand why they must not adopt those teachings and practices.

2:16–19 Reject the Visionaries' Judgments

2:16 Therefore, do not let anyone condemn you on the basis of food or drink or the observance of festivals or new moons or Sabbaths. 17 These things are a shadow of the things to come, but the body of Christ [already] exists.[a] 18 Do not let anyone willfully disqualify you through the humility and worship of angels,[b] which things he has seen when entering [the heavens]. He is puffed up for no reason by his fleshly mind and by not holding fast to the head, 19 from whom the whole body, being supplied and held together by [its] joints and ligaments, grows with the growth from God.

a. There is considerable debate about how this last phrase relates to the previous phrase because it does not fit well with what comes before it no matter what reading one adopts. My translation inserts "already" to recognize the eschatological inference introduced by the preceding "things to come" (see the comment on v. 17).

b. The prepositional phrase "of angels" may go with either "worship" alone or with both "humility" and "worship," as it is understood here. It could be rendered "angelic humility and worship."

[16] With "therefore" (*oun*) the writer links his instructions to reject the visionaries' demands directly to his interpretation of the death of Jesus as the means of expunging any account of sin and as the defeat of any powers that might try to keep account of sin (2:13–15). The Colossians must not allow anyone to pass judgment on them in these matters of diet or religious festivals because Jesus' death has freed them of such judgments.

Though the pronoun "anyone" (*tis*) is singular in v. 16, and pronouns referring to the visionaries remain in the singular throughout vv. 16–19, the writer probably does not have one particular person (e.g., the leader of the visionaries) in mind when he uses the singular. Perhaps the singular makes his rejection of the visionaries' judgments emphatic: *no one* is permitted to judge the readers on the basis of these kinds of regulations and practices.

Once again, what stands out about the visionaries is that they pass judgment against their fellow believers on illegitimate bases. This illegitimate passing of judgment constitutes the primary reason that Colossians rejects the visionaries. Their ascents into heavenly realms and even their admiration for what they see there are not particularly problematic. Many members of the early church, including Paul, had such experiences. The problem is that these teachers make such experiences mandatory for all. They make these experiences the evidence that one has been forgiven by God and is truly "of Christ." They may even claim that such experiences are the occasion when people receive God's forgiveness. These kinds of claims explain why Colossians moves from the affirmations about forgiveness and its source (Christ's crucifixion) in 2:13–15 directly into this extended rejection of the bases for judgments that the visionaries levy against other church members. For Colossians, the work of Christ alone, not exalted and exciting spiritual experiences, brings forgiveness and relationship with God.

Colossians exhorts the readers not to let anyone judge them on the basis of regulations about food and drink. No further details surface about what these dietary regulations might be, but the following reference to feasts includes the Sabbath and thus suggests that they are related to Judaism. There are, however, few drink regulations in the Old Testament or in first-century Judaism. Of course, the Pauline communities did have regulations about food sacrificed to other gods (1 Cor 8–10), and the letters to the churches in Revelation demonstrate that arguments about proper eating habits continued, as some church leaders whom the writer of Revelation opposes allowed or encouraged Christians to eat food offered to other gods (see 2:14, 20). Colossians does not, however, have these rules in view (contra Barth and Blanke 338). Nor does the writer of Colossians worry about the consciences of individual believers (as in Rom 14). Rather, these rules about food and drink comprise a part of the visionaries' preparation for receiving visions.

Food and drink restrictions commonly played a part in religious practices of the Hellenistic world that supposedly led to mystical contact with the gods. Preparation for the mystical experience of initiation into the mystery at Eleusis in Greece and those of Cybele and Attis in nearby Phrygia (Sallust, *De deis et mundo* 4) included fasting. Similarly, initiation into the Isis cult involved a ten-day preparation period in which there were food and drink regulations (Apuleius, *Metam.* 9.23, 28, 30).[27] Apocalyptic writers also fasted as a prelude to visionary experiences (e.g., *2 Esdr* 5.13, 19; 6.31, 35; *2 Bar.* 9.2; 12.5; 20.5–6; *Apoc. Ab.* 12.1–2).[28] Some of these fasts included drink regulations, others only food regulations. The New Testament also associates visionary experiences and fasting in the accounts of Jesus' baptism and temptation (Matt 4:2; Luke 4:2; [perhaps implied by the angels' activity in Mark 1:13]) and Paul's vision of the risen Christ (Acts 9:9) though his fasting occurs after his vision. So the kind of regimen that the Colossian visionaries have taken up and now want to impose on others was well known in antiquity as a way to induce mystical and visionary experiences (similarly Lincoln 631).

---

27. For these and further references to such fasting, see J. Behm, *TDNT* 4:926–31.

28. For these and further references to fasting in apocalyptic Judaism, see Behm, *TDNT* 4:926–31; Sappington 65–66.

The regulations that the visionaries advocate also involve the observance of festivals drawn from Judaism, as the mention of the Sabbath indicates. The vocabulary chosen and the order in which the holy days appear also suggest a connection with Jewish feasts. "Festivals," "new moons," and "Sabbaths" appear together as a summary of all religious days within Judaism in 1 Chr 23:31; 2 Chr 2:3 (2:4E); 31:3; and Isa 1:13–14; and these terms appear in this order in Hos 2:13 (2:11E) and Ezek 45:17. So it seems certain that Colossians has Jewish festivals in mind. Even though he probably has no specific passage in view, the writer draws on a recognizable way of referring to Jewish calendrical observances.[29]

But the goal of these regulations is not observance of the Torah or conversion to Judaism. The combination of holy days and dietary regulations in this single clause of v. 16 suggests that the two types of rules belong together in the visionaries' teaching. The visionaries call for observance of certain food and drink prohibitions on these holy days. Perhaps, as Lohse suggests (115–16), they coordinate the keeping of these holy days with astrological speculation.[30] In any case, the visionaries may see these holy days as the most opportune times to attain visionary experiences. Since they understand these observances as the path to the visions that are the sign of salvation, or perhaps the place where salvation is attained or experienced, Colossians accuses them of improperly judging those who refuse this regimen. Therefore, Colossians rejects both (1) the interpretation of these experiences that sees them as a requirement, or sign, of forgiveness and salvation and (2) the means the visionaries use to attain those visions. Those "in Christ" need no such regimens or experiences to secure their relationship with God, because Christ has already brought them the fullness of forgiveness and reconciliation.

[17] Verse 17 supports the preceding rejection of the visionaries' observances (v. 16) by offering an evaluation of those rules, saying that they are a shadow of something that the readers already possess. This verse is one of the most difficult to translate in the letter. Rendered most woodenly, it says: "These things are a shadow of the things to come, but [or 'and'] the body of Christ." To complete this sentece, translators must insert some verb in the second clause; and depending on how they understand the term "body," they have chosen various verbs, which give the verse different meanings. Interpreters almost universally interpret the conjunction *de* ("but") in the middle of v. 17 as an adversative that sets out opposites,[31] and then they identify those opposites as

29. However, Thornton (97–100) has shown that "new moons" could also refer to pagan festivals. See also Hay 104.

30. Elchasai and his followers are an example of people who conflated Jewish feasts and astrological speculations. See the description in Hippolytus, *Haer.* 9.16.2–3.

31. The exception to this interpretation is Barth and Blanke (340–41), though their reading of the verse differs from that offered here.

"shadow" and "body." This understanding rests on an assumed Platonic or broadly Hellenistic topos in which the body is real and the shadow is illusory.[32] But such a reading creates significant interpretive problems. For example, if the "body of Christ" refers to the earthly existence of Jesus as the reality that is to come, it is hard to see how his life gives reality to the regulations alluded to in v. 16, particularly since drink regulations were not a significant part of Torah observance. If, on the other hand, the "body of Christ" refers to a reality that will come into being at the Parousia (Hay 105), the writer's argument is fairly weak, because that reality has not come (cf. Abbott 265). Alternatively, others who identify "body" as a metaphor for reality take the verse as asserting that Christ possesses the reality, not just the shadow or illusion (Harris 117, 120). This reading, however, implies that Sabbath observance was illusory in the time before Christ, a harsher evaluation of the Mosaic covenant than we find in the rest of the letter.

Beyond these problems in Colossians itself, the contrast between *skia* ("shadow") and *sōma* ("body") is not a common topos in the first century, as many interpreters assume. The more usual contrast is between *skia* and *eikōn* ("figure" or "image") or *eidos* ("form"). When ancient writers do use *sōma* in a contrast with *skia*, the difference is usually more comparative than oppositional. For example, Philo argues that external goods are a shadow of the true good that a person should seek (*Post.* 112.4). Here, Philo asserts that both external goods and the true good are things that make life more meaningful; one is better than the other, but both are beneficial. In other places in Philo, the "shadow" represents a reflection that provides access to the higher realm (*Conf.* 190; see Lincoln 631–32). While there are places where the shadow/body contrast (using *sōma*) compares the illusory with the real (e.g., Josephus, *J.W.* 2.28.3), they are too few to consider the contrast a commonplace that automatically conveys this dramatic opposition.

A better way to understand the expression "body of Christ" lies closer to hand: the "body of Christ" is the church (so also Aletti 194). Colossians has already used this language for the church in 1:18 and 1:24, will use it again in 3:15, and expands the image significantly in the immediately following sentence (2:19). Thus, Colossians employs "body" with a double sense here; it refers to the church and serves as a contrast to "shadow." While no translation of this part of v. 17 is certain, its sense is to contrast the spiritual blessings in the church with the other teachers' regulations.[33]

Since "body of Christ" refers to the church, the conjunction *de* is more contrastive than directly adversative; that is, it contrasts the value of the blessings

---

32. With this understanding, the NRSV translates the last part of the verse "but the substance belongs to Christ."

33. See T. Martin's discussion (1995, 249–55) of the translation of this verse, along with his suggested emendations.

believers possess in the church with the regulations of the other teachers, yet does not set them in complete opposition. This reading allows that those regulations may have had some value before the arrival of the fullness of blessings available in Christ; they are not illusory or completely without value, only less valuable than what is available in the church. Therefore, Colossians does not assert that observance of regulations from the Mosaic covenant has always been illusory.

This contrast also recognizes the eschatological nuance of the passage. The first half of v. 17 ends with a reference to "the things to come" as a way to designate what comes to believers because of their participation in the eschatological age (Lincoln 632).[34] Though the contrast may include some reference to the blessings to come at the Parousia, the main emphasis rests on what believers enjoy now by being in the church. Thus, they already possess something superior to what the other teachers' regulations offer.

[18–19] Verse 18 renews the exhortation not to accept the visionaries' judgments. Now the writer uses the verb *katabrabeuō* ("to disqualify"), a New Testament *hapax legomenon*, to press his admonition. *Katabrabeuō* is an even stronger term than *krinō* ("to judge, condemn"), the verb v. 16 used to characterize the visionaries' assessments of those not in their group (Abbott 266). *Katabrabeuō* originally referred to an umpire or judge ruling against an athlete. In other usage it sometimes implied that the person has been deprived of justice or defrauded (see LSJM 885; *PGL* 705–6, with uses in Chrysostom, *Hom.* 7.1 [on Colossians]; and Theodotius). If the Colossians hear this latter nuance, it suggests that the judgments the visionaries render against them are fraudulent or at least unjust. This accusation about the visionaries' judgments begins a series of yet more forceful appraisals of their behavior and teaching.

Colossians next evaluates either the way these teachers experience their visions or the way they judge the readers. Most commentators and nearly all translations understand the participle *thelōn* to say that the teachers "take delight in" (or some similar expression) "humility and worship of angels." "Take delight in" is not a common meaning for the verb *thelō*, though the LXX does occasionally use it with this meaning (e.g., 1 Sam 18:22; Ps 112 [111 LXX]:1; and a few other places).[35] If *thelōn* belongs with the following phrase, it bears this unusual meaning and denigrates the visionaries' practices by commenting on their manner of participating in them. It suggests that their experiences have made them arrogant. The text does not, however, demand the

---

34. Both Rom 5:14 and Heb 10:1 use participles of *mellō* ("to come") to speak of realities that are present for the church, but that people of previous times had only been able to look forward to as blessings to come in the eschatological era. Colossians 2:17 uses a participle of the same verb to name "the things to come."

35. However, MM do not list this as a usage in the papyri.

adoption of this unusual meaning of *thelōn*. Participles such as *thelōn* can serve an adverbial function; thus it heightens the level of the polemic against the other teachers by accusing them not merely of judging unfairly but also of doing it "willfully."[36] This reading fits a context in which the major problem is that people are being condemned for illegitimate reasons. If *thelōn* modifies "disqualify," then it further denigrates the visionaries' judgment by saying not only that it is unjust but also that the injustice has ill will as its source.

Whether *thelōn* attaches to the description of the teachers' visions or to their illegitimate judging, its purpose remains the same, to give a bad impression of these teachers. The contrast with Paul could hardly be more stark. In 1:24–2:5, Paul suffers for the readers and assures them of their place in God's plan and their possession of God's blessings. He rejoices about them as he sees their faithfulness. Paul is the loving and trustworthy friend. The visionaries, on the other hand, try to deceive and entrap the readers (2:4, 8). They not only unjustly condemn the readers but even do so willfully. Given these alternatives, the choice to listen to Paul should be an easy one. Whatever the visionaries may claim, Colossians paints them as people who do not have the readers' good at heart. These characterizations incline the Colossians to listen to Paul and the instructions in this letter, because they come from a reliable and loving source, and to reject the other teaching, because it comes from an unreliable source.

The rest of v. 18 shows that the visionaries use the visions they see and the practices they adopt to condemn others. In those visions they see the "humility and worship of angels." The words "of angels" (*tōn angelōn*) seem to modify both the worship and the humility, because both are governed by a single preposition (*en*). Furthermore, the following phrase begins with a plural pronoun, which seems to include both the humility and the worship as things seen in these visions.

One of the central interpretive issues of Colossians is whether these teachers worshiped angels or worshiped with angels. The genitive "of angels" (*angelōn*) can be either subjective (angels doing the worshiping) or objective (angels are the thing worshiped). Only context determines which meaning is correct. Since Colossians contains no other indication that anyone advocates worshiping beings other than God, it seems more likely that the problem concerns worshiping with angels. The connection between "humility" and "worship" makes this understanding more probable, particularly if "of angels" modifies both terms. If the phrase does modify both, the genitive probably relates in the same way to both nouns. Since the genitive is almost certainly subjective in relation to "humility," it is probably also subjective in relation to "worship."[37] These teachers do not worship angels, but worship with angels in

36. Abbott (266–67) adopts this reading, arguing that Paul does not use the kind of Hebraism that "take delight in" would involve.

37. See further the arguments in Sappington 159–60; Aletti 195–96; Barth and Blanke 345–46; Sumney 1999, 199–201.

their visions. They subsequently want to impose those worship practices in the church's services. Those unwilling to adopt these practices fall under condemnation. Colossians does not condemn participation in the worship that these people see in their visions, only the judgment that they render against those who do not have these experiences. Colossians also rejects the visionaries' interpretation of their experiences, an interpretation claiming that believers must have such experiences to be truly forgiven and have a saving relationship with God.

In Col 2:18, "humility" is not a general attitude or disposition of the self. Hellenistic and Roman culture did not count humility a virtue. It was a characteristic of those without social or economic position, a kind of servility. In the LXX and the New Testament, however, humility is a virtue, particularly when it defines a person's attitude toward God. In Col 2:18, humility refers to what the visionaries see in their experiences, the practices of angels in the presence of God. They find this "humility" desirable because it is the humility "of angels." Apocalyptic writings have no shortage of passages in which the recipient of a vision observes angelic worship (e.g., *2 En.* 20.3–21.1; 22.2–7; *Apoc. Ab.* 17.1–21 [presenting a song taught by an angel to Abraham, which they sing together]; *Apocalypse of Zephaniah* [cited by Clement, *Strom.* 5.11.77]; 4QShir [which has an extensive angelic liturgy]). In these contexts the angels sometimes kneel or bow before God, thus expressing humility. The heavenly beings in the opening worship scenes of Revelation engage in similar acts of submission (4:10). Thus worship and expressions of humility are intimately associated in this literature.

Apocalyptic writings also commonly associate "humility" with heavenly ascents. The humility that such writings commend is a necessary precondition for their visions (e.g., *Gk. Apoc. Ezra* 1.3–5; *Apoc. Ab.* 9 [has Abraham abstain from meat and wine], 12 [from all food and drink]; *Ascen. Isa.* 2.7–11).[38] As we have seen (in the comment above on 2:16), a wide range of groups in the cultural context, including particularly mystery cults, used fasts of various sorts to prepare for (we might say, induce) mystical experiences. "Humility" is certainly broader than fasting, and in Tertullian it can involve several practices associated with attaining heavenly ascents (*Fasting* 6, 7, 9, 12).[39] Clearly, some who sought visions understood regulations about food and drink as preparation for visions and also as expressions of humility. Lohse (118) helpfully understands *tapeinophrosynē* ("humility") as "the fulfillment of specific cultic regulations." This understanding allows the word to function well within the contexts of both the angelic worship and the practices that prepare for experiences in which that worship is seen.

38. Francis 1973, 168–70. See there Francis's references to such practices in Philo.
39. See also Herm. *Vis.* 3.10.6 for use of "humility" in connection with receiving visionary experiences.

These parallels between the practices and experiences of apocalyptic writers and the visionaries of Colossians fit well with the latter's insistence on observances of holy days from Judaism (v. 16). For these teachers, observing the holy days and the food and drink regulations enables ascent to a heavenly vision. They do not view full observance of the law as a requirement for Gentile salvation. For the Colossian visionaries, mystical experiences, not Torah observance, are necessary for salvation, or at least serve as a minimal or initiatory sign that one has indeed received God's forgiveness.

The next phrase of v. 18 is no less difficult to translate or interpret. Literally it reads "which [things] he has seen entering in." The phrase's plural relative pronoun, "which things [*ha*]," suggests that the teachers see both angelic humility and angelic worship in their visions. The verb *embateuō* (another New Testament *hapax legomenon*) has the general meaning of entering into a place (e.g., a room or country), but there are also more specific uses relevant for understanding its appearance in Colossians.[40] Dibelius (1973, 85–88) observed that mystery cults used *embateuō* to refer to their initiation experience. At Claros its meaning even seems to narrow to attaining a second level of initiation, though the earliest extant appearance of this meaning comes from 132 C.E. (Arnold 1996, 106–9, 120–21). Other writers, however, employed the term more broadly to speak of consulting an oracle.[41] Furthermore, when apocalyptic texts speak of "entering" the heavenly sphere, they do not describe the experience with the verb *embateuō* (e.g., *3 Bar.* 2.2; 3.1–2; *T. Levi* 2.6–8). Thus, this verb probably has its more general meaning of entering rather than some technical meaning in the visionaries' teaching.

Since the Colossian visionaries drew on elements of both Judaism (e.g., Sabbath) and the mysticism of the broader culture,[42] they may have borrowed *embateuō* from one of those settings, as many interpreters argue. Even if they do adopt the term, however, its use tells us little about the content of their teachings, practices, or experiences beyond what we already know: they have visionary experiences that play an important part in their teaching.

Verse 18 contains one more derogatory evaluation of the visionaries (still using the singular to refer to them): each is "puffed up for no reason by his fleshly mind and by not holding fast to the head." Colossians asserts that they

40. Barth and Blanke (348–49) follow Abbott by assigning the meaning of "scrutinize thoroughly" to *embateuōn*. While this may be a meaning within the semantic range of this verb, it does not seem to fit the context in Col 2.

41. See the inscriptions from Claros that use the term in this way that are cited by Francis ("The Background of *EMBATEUEIN* (Col 2:18) in Legal Papyri and Oracle Inscriptions," in Francis and Meeks 1973, 200–201).

42. Arnold (1996, 104–6) also thinks that the teachers were influenced by both mystery cults and apocalyptic Judaism, but finds participation in the veneration of other beings part of what they have brought in from the surrounding religious environment.

are full of false pride. Their baseless arrogance springs, he charges, from an unspiritual mind, a mind that belongs to the unredeemed reality. This statement deliberately contrasts their adoption of practices of humility and their possession of false pride. Their practices have produced the opposite of what they claim. The visionaries' "fleshly minds" have produced excessive pride.

In 2 Cor 12, Paul comments on the way extraordinary visions can lead to pride. He says that God refused to remove his "thorn in the flesh" so that he would not become proud in the wake of his visionary experiences (vv. 6–9). Perhaps, then, the pride that visions have engendered in the teachers at Colossae is not so surprising, because such exalted experiences of God have presented Paul with the same temptation. While Paul's thorn redirected his inclination, pride has overtaken the "fleshly minds" of the Colossian visionaries.

Within the Pauline corpus, "flesh" (*sarx*) almost always represents the sphere of sin.[43] While Colossians uses *sarx* in a neutral way elsewhere (1:24; 2:1), here the term clearly makes the accusation that their minds are sinful because they are detached from Christ, the allegation he adds in v. 19. The visionaries, then, have no basis for their pride. In fact, once the writer reveals the true source of their teaching and practice (their "fleshly mind"), they should feel shame. Rather than spiritual superiority, their visions have brought them shame and degradation. Surely the visionaries would vigorously dispute this accusation and characterization. Still, the author of Colossians urges his readers to adopt these assessments of the visionaries' character and claims.

Verse 19 reinforces the charge that the visionaries' teaching and judgments are unspiritual by asserting that they have detached themselves from Christ, the source of all real spiritual blessings and growth. The visionaries' diligent striving for mystical experiences has actually separated them from Christ rather than brought them closer to him and the heavenly realities found in him. This verse sets the practices and experiences of the visionaries in opposition to participation in the blessings believers have in Christ. The writer constructed the same sort of opposition in 2:8, where he contrasts "based on Christ" to "empty and deceitful philosophy," "human traditions," and "the elements of the world." Both verses mark the visionaries' teaching as incompatible with a connection to Christ. These two passages also demonstrate that the teachers opposed by Colossians claim a connection with Christ, and so are within the church (contra T. Martin 1996, 28–34); otherwise, asserting that they have no connection to Christ would carry no argumentative weight.

Though the word "Christ" does not appear in v. 19, the references to "the body" (vv. 17, 19) indicate that Christ is the "head" to whom the visionaries are

---

43. This should not be confused with "body" (*sōma*), which is not understood to be the realm of evil or sin. Furthermore, Colossians uses *sarx* without this nuance of belonging to the sphere of evil in 1:24 and 2:1. There it is a neutral term (see the commentary on those passages).

not holding fast. In addition to the sense of the passage, the writer's use of the masculine pronoun, rather than the feminine pronoun that should follow the feminine noun "head" (*kephalē*), also suggests that he has Christ in view (Schweizer 164).

The head imagery has a different shade of meaning in v. 19 than it had earlier in Colossians. In 1:18, "head" designates Christ as the one who rules in the sphere of the church (cf. this function of head in 2:10),[44] while in 2:19 the head gives life, vitality, and strength to the body. According to 2:19, the visionaries have cut themselves off from the true source of salvation and spiritual blessings. The way the writer speaks of the connections within the body and to the head implies that the connection to the head must inform relationships within the body. All parts are connected and growing together as one "whole body." The writer may further intimate that the visionaries' condemnation of fellow believers and prideful stance in relation to them indicate that they are separated from the head. "One's attitude to the body, the church, is indicative of one's relation to its head" (Lincoln 632).

Colossians emphasizes the unity of the church by speaking of "the whole body" being supplied and held together. The "joints and ligaments" perform these tasks. These signify respectively the places where the limbs are joined and what holds the body together.[45] Here they serve as the channels through which the life that comes from Christ flows. They function as the conduits that enable growth. This consideration of the workings within the body focuses attention on the importance of relations within that body, particularly on the care that the various parts have for one another; they deliver nourishment to one another and hold the whole together with what they receive from the head, Christ. Thus they nurture one another in a way that strengthens each and the whole. This sort of interdependence and service to one another stands in sharp contrast to the visionaries' willful judging.

The internal unity of the body, seen in the images of joints and ligaments, enables "the whole body" to "grow with the growth from God." This growth occurs because of the body's connection with Christ, its head. The body's growth depends on its firm connection to its head—a clear enough physiological fact, even if the readers need it spelled out for them in this analogy. Christ supplies the life and growth that the church possesses.

The growth experienced by those connected to Christ comes "*from God.*" This phrase may define the growth's origin or its quality. In either case, it is the type of growth that the church needs to exist. This growth, which members experience in the context of the church's community, is wholly distinct from

---

44. However, in 2:10 the "rulers and authorities" are not the body of Christ.

45. See the discussion of the use of these terms in Aristotle and other ancient authors in Lightfoot 198–200.

the mere swelling of the visionaries' heads (v. 18: they are "puffed up"). This genuine growth in depth of experience with God comes to believers without the visionaries' rules and experiences. Those experiences pale in comparison with the growth that God provides for all who remain connected properly to Christ. Rather than momentary heights of mystical experiences, the faithful have a lasting, genuine, and deepening experience of God through the life of the church, which is firmly holding to Christ. While such growth manifests itself in various ways, those ways all outshine what the visionaries offer because they flow from the proper head, Christ.

In vv. 16–19, Colossians provides a series of reasons why its readers should not accept the condemnatory judgments that the visionaries render about them. The writer charges that these teachers' regulations offer less than what believers already possess; their illegitimate judgments spring from bad motives; they are arrogant because of their unspiritual minds; and they have cut themselves off from Christ and so separated themselves from real growth in relationship to God. Such teachers have nothing to offer members of the body of Christ.

2:20–23 The Visionaries' Teachings Have No Value

Verses 20–23 continue the attack against the visionaries' teaching, but the focus shifts from evaluating their motives and results to direct rejection of their regulations and practices. As will be clear in chapter 3, the writer is not against rules for behavior, even strict rules. What he opposes is the regimen that the visionaries advocate as the means to attain the visions they require for forgiveness and salvation. Believers must reject such demands because they are already members of the body of Christ. The regimen that these teachers advocate is at best useless and perhaps even harmful (depending on the interpretation of v. 23).

While vv. 20–23 clearly continue the polemic begun in v. 16, they also introduce the shift toward ethical instruction that begins in 3:1. In v. 20, the writer introduces the image of dying with Christ, the image on which he builds to open the following section. The exhortations of 3:1–4 begin with "Therefore, if you have been raised." This parallels the opening of v. 20: "If you died." The same imagery ("put to death") appears again in 3:5. Despite this link with the imagery that follows, the connections with 2:16–19 are even closer. The polemical recitation, evaluation, and rejection of the visionaries' demands make that connection unmistakable. These links to what precedes and what follows demonstrate that chapters 3–4 relate closely to chapters 1–2. The ethical instructions that appear in chapters 3–4 have an important connection to the argument that chapters 1–2 give against the visionaries' teachings and practices.

> **2:20** If you died with Christ, why do you accept any[a] commandments from the elements of the world, as though you were living in the world? **21** They

give regulations such as Do not handle, Do not taste, and Do not touch.
22 These [prohibited things] are all destined for destruction by consumption [and such prohibitions] derive from human commands and teachings. 23 These regulations,[b] though they have a reputation for wisdom with their self-chosen worship and humility that includes[c] severity to the body, are of no value; they lead to gratification of the flesh.

a. This translation identifies *ti* as an indefinite pronoun rather than an interrogative pronoun. The only difference in the appearance of these types of pronouns is the accent mark on the interrogative. Since the earliest manuscripts do not have accent marks on any words, the insertion of an accent is a matter of interpretation. In this case, the addition of the accent would require some terms in this verse to be read in unusual ways. See the arguments for understanding *ti* as an indefinite pronoun in v. 20 in the comment below and in T. Martin 1996, 37–42.

b. This translation identifies the antecedent of the pronoun *hatina* ("these things") as the specific regulations cited in v. 21. Alternatively, the antecedent of *hatina* could be more general "human commands and teachings." The choice of antecedents makes little difference in the meaning of the sentence.

c. Though ℵ and A insert *kai* ("and") between "humility" and "severity to the body," other important manuscripts do not. Among those that lack the *kai* are P[46] and B. If the *kai* is the correct reading, then Colossians lists three characteristics of the visionaries' teaching. If it is absent, then "severity to the body" *defines* "humility," as it is rendered here.

[20] Verse 20 reminds the readers of their place in Christ (Lincoln 633) and the implications that status has for their assessment of the visionaries' teachings. The writer first says that believers have been united with Christ in his death. This assertion relates vv. 20–23 to the interpretation that Colossians gives the death of Jesus in 2:9–15. The reference to Christ's death reminds the readers that through Christ's death they have received forgiveness and life with God, and that Christ has subdued all accusing powers. These assurances prepare the letter's recipients to hear the exhortations that follow.

Translators usually understand v. 20 to assert that believers have died *with* Christ and *away from* the "elements of the world." But this rendering requires the preposition *apo* preceding "elements" to function in a very unusual way.[46] When *apo* appears with *apothnēskō* (to die), it usually designates the cause of death, not something from which the person has escaped. So it is better to connect the prepositional phrase "from the elements of the world" with the following verb *dogmatizesthe* ("dogmatize," "accept commandments"). The author brings this prepositional phrase forward in the sentence to set it in direct

46. But see the explanations of the use of *apo* here in Abbott 272 and Harris 127. The following discussion of the translation of v. 20 follows T. Martin 1996, 37–43. See translation note a (above) on taking *ti* as an indefinite pronoun rather than an interrogative.

opposition to the phrase "with Christ." Thus he juxtaposes two options from opposing realms of existence, asking how, if you died with Christ, you can still accept commandments based in your former realm of existence (T. Martin 1996, 37–43; O'Brien 151).

The image of dying with Christ renews Colossians' attention to baptism. In 2:12–13, the writer has described baptism as being "buried with" and "raised with" Christ, bringing new life and forgiveness. The connection between new life and forgiveness should not be lost in this context because dying with Christ frees one of any obligation to the rules that the visionaries use to pass judgment against others. Believers enter the new life through baptism; it is the act that unites believers with Christ in his death and resurrection. Participation in this rite, then, grants them admission into a new realm of existence, indeed, into the eschatological reality initiated by Christ. Life in that reality has no use for the regimen the visionaries offer. In fact, it excludes such rules because they belong to the former existence. What the other teachers offer through their rules, believers already possess by virtue of their dying and being raised with Christ in baptism.

The success of the polemical evaluations that follow depends on this reminder that through baptism the readers have entered a new realm of existence. Colossians has expended considerable effort in assuring its readers that God has granted them entrance into this realm and expounding the benefits they possess by virtue of their participation in it. From within this new life, they can recognize that the visionaries' regimen is of no consequence. The blessings of God have come to the baptized through their union with Christ; they need no other regulations for spiritual well-being or for genuine experience of the presence of God. And while this new life includes mandates, as the writer will elaborate beginning in chapter 3, those demands are manifestations of the new life, not attempts to gain access to God or God's forgiveness.

After reminding the readers of their union with Christ, the author asks incredulously how they could accept teaching from the "elements of the world." The incongruous nature of these two things seems painfully obvious to him, and he thinks it will be to the readers as well, when they see the matter couched in these terms. The way he phrases the question allows that the readers have not yet adopted these rules (contra Harris 128) and that the rules are being imposed on them. Though the readers have not yet acquiesced to the other teaching, they are moving closer to accepting it. Colossians' sharp response to that teaching indicates that it is indeed attractive.

The first denigrating evaluation of the visionaries' rules in v. 20 relates them to the "elements [*stoicheia*] of the world." The writer intimates that by submitting to commands from the *stoicheia* (see the discussion of the *stoicheia* at 2:8), believers take a step backward into an inferior sphere of existence. Since they have already been transferred into the higher realm through being united with Christ, they need no instruction or guidance from the former and lower existence.

This evaluation implies that the visionaries inhabit the lower realm, rather than the higher place, as they claim.

The phrase "as though you were living in the world" confirms that the author conceives of dying with Christ as a transfer from one realm of existence to another. This phrase nearly chides the readers for even considering the visionaries' regimen without thinking about its implications and the meaning of their baptism. The author reminds them that they no longer inhabit the world of which they once were a part, the world ordered by the *stoicheia*. God has freed them from that existence to live a new life in Christ. If they accept the visionaries' rules, however, they reenter the old existence and again submit themselves to its standards and values. They have nothing to gain and much to lose if they remove themselves from the realm of God's blessings by accepting the way of life based on the *stoicheia*. This interpretation of what the visionaries offer makes their teaching wholly unacceptable.

[21] Verse 21 caricatures the regimen that the visionaries impose (Lincoln 633; cf. Pokorný 153) rather than actually quoting their rules (as suggested by Lightfoot 202; O'Brien 137; T. Martin 1996, 96). The absolute nature of these demands[47] seems exaggerated in comparison with the statement of their regulations in v. 16. As given here, the prohibitions are somewhat repetitious: the first proscribes handling and the third touching. There may be a slight escalation from handling to touching, but nothing else distinguishes them in this context. Between these commands about touching comes the proscription against tasting. So at least some of the prohibitions that lie behind these caricatures pertain to dietary regulations. This fits the account of the regulations in 2:16, but extends them into a wider range of life. Proscriptions that involved various aspects of life, including sexual abstinence, often appear among the preparations for mystical or visionary experiences (or coming into the presence of a god at a temple).[48] Whether the visionaries seek to impose a wide range of regulations remains uncertain. The only hint that these regulations might extend beyond food is the comment about "gratification of the flesh" at the end of v. 23.

Whether the statements in v. 21 refer to food only or to other areas of life, the regulations that lie behind them are part of the other teachers' means of attaining visions. They may not advocate constant adherence to these prohibitions. If we infer from v. 16 that these prohibitions applied only on holy days, those times deemed most opportune to attain visions, then these calls for abstinence from food and drink (and perhaps other things) do not provide evidence that the visionaries require a rigorous asceticism. The regulations do not function as discipline of the body but as preparation for a heavenly ascent.

---

47. Harris (128–29) notes that *mē* with the subjunctive points to a categorical rejection.

48. Lightfoot observes that in 2:21 both *thinganō* and *haptō* can be used for sexual relations (203–4). He further reasons that the context excludes those meanings here.

[22–23] Verses 22–23 contain a series of evaluations of the visionaries' prohibitions, and though no certain translation of v. 23 is possible, it clearly supplies further reasons to reject the opposed teaching. The beginning of v. 22 does not constitute a parenthetical aside, as some propose (e.g., Lightfoot 204; Abbott 274), because it contains the first element in this series of evaluations. Yet it poses a translation difficulty because it begins with a plural pronoun ("these things," *ha*) that syntactically has the prohibitions of v. 21 as its antecedent. Verse 22 asserts that "these things" are destroyed through use or consumption. It is difficult to see how prohibitions are destroyed through use or are consumed. The expression "these things," then, probably refers to the things prohibited rather than the commands, even though "human commands and teachings" stands closer to the pronoun in the sentence. Our reading increases the probability that all three proscriptions of v. 22 refer to food, because they are "destined for destruction by consumption."[49] If "these things" does refer back to the things prohibited, then Colossians says that the things regulated by the visionaries' prohibitions have no lasting significance—indeed, they are things that God intended for people to use and consume (Lohse 124). While this may not be the most powerful point the author has to make, the language he chooses ("all," "destruction") paints the visionaries' teaching with unappealing tones.

The second evaluation of the other teaching's prohibitions identifies their origin as human rather than divine. This assessment directly opposes the visionaries' claims to receive their teaching, worship practices, and method of attaining visions from a heavenly source, that is, from observations in their visions.

This repudiation of their teaching echoes Isa 29:13, where God accuses the people of worshiping in vain and of imparting human commandments and teachings. The Isaiah passage associates unacceptable worship with human commands. The worship practices that the visionaries have adopted form a significant part of the problem that Colossians addresses; not only has the writer talked about angelic worship in 2:18, but again in v. 23 he singles out worship practices as problematic. Thus, the nature of the problem at Colossae may have reminded the writer of this Isaiah passage. However, the same Isaiah passage also appears in the mouth of Jesus in parallel stories in Mark 7:1–8 and Matt 15:1–12. When the Pharisees and scribes question Jesus about why his disciples do not follow the Pharisees' tradition concerning ritual washing before meals, he responds by calling them hypocrites and citing nearly the whole of Isa 29:13. So the early Jesus tradition known to Mark contains a citation of this Isaiah passage. Both Mark and Matthew quote this passage in the context of a dispute about food. Given that food prohibitions are an issue in

---

49. The noun *apochrēsis* ("consumption") is another New Testament *hapax legomenon* in this section.

Colossians, the nature of the problem may also have reminded the author of this Jesus tradition.

Isaiah 29:13, then, has two associations (worship practices and food regulations) that could bring it to the author's mind. Whether or not the Jesus tradition mediates this passage, the author intentionally alludes to Isaiah. Among the reasons for identifying this as an intentional citation of Isaiah (even though the wording is not exact)[50] is that both "commandments" (*entalmata*) and "teachings" (*didaskaliai*) are rare words in the LXX, each appearing only four times, and they appear together only in Isa 29:13.[51] An allusion such as this, which the writer apparently expects his readers to recognize, adds power to his polemical evaluation of the visionaries' teaching. He implicitly identifies it as the sort of teaching that God condemns in Isaiah and perhaps as the kind of teaching that Jesus condemns when he quotes this same passage. This identification of the visionaries' practices with earlier teachings that provoke God's condemnation leaves the readers no choice but to reject the visionaries' teachings. These echoes of Isaiah produce an evaluation of the opposed teaching that is as devastating as the assertion in v. 19 that the visionaries are no longer connected to Christ.

[23] To this point the writer has set out many powerful reasons for the readers to reject the visionaries' teaching. In v. 23 he gives two more, intertwined and polemical evaluations of that teaching. Verse 23 is one of the most difficult verses in the New Testament to translate, and every proposal has significant problems. Among the many difficulties with understanding its vocabulary and syntax, the most difficult problem structurally is how the last phrase fits into the sentence, and how to understand it. The two basic options for the meaning of the last phrase are that the visionaries' demands (1) lead to gratification of the flesh or (2) are of no value for restraining the flesh.[52] While the latter reading requires an unusual meaning for the preposition *pros*, the former must allow for the insertion of a long independent clause or parenthesis between the parts of the sentence that belong together. The reading adopted here understands the subject and verb of the main clause to be separated from the concluding prepo-

50. Matthew and Mark have precisely the same wording throughout the entire quotation, which is an exact quotation of the LXX until the last line, that to which Colossians alludes here. While both Colossians and the two Gospels have changed this line of the Isaiah passage, they have changed it in different ways. Still, it retains the same basic meaning.

51. *Entalma* appears in Job 23:11, 12; Isa 29:13; 55:11. *Didaskalia* appears in Prov 2:17; Sir 24:33; 39:8; Isa 29:13. *Didaskalia* also appears in Ps 10:3 (11:3E) in the A rescension of the LXX.

52. A third option for this phrase is that found in Theodore of Mopsuestia (*Epistulam Pauli ad Colossenses*, in PG 66:931) and other church fathers. They argue that *sarx* should be understood in a positive sense here so that the phrase means something like "gratification of natural desire." Thus the phrase is a rejection of ascetic practices that do not give proper attention to the body. But the meaning of *sarx* in Paul is usually negative, as it is here in Colossians; it signifies the realm outside of Christ; *sarx* is not a neutral or positive term in this passage. Thus, this attempt to overcome the problems of v. 23 is unsuccessful.

sitional phrase by a long independent clause (option 1).[53] This reading allows the heightened polemic to continue to the end of this paragraph, with the writer rejecting the visionaries' additional observances as actually harmful, not just ineffective.

Verse 23 begins with a reference to "these regulations," that is, the visionaries' rules caricatured in v. 21. The writer starts an evaluation of those prohibitions ("[They] lead to gratification of the flesh") when a second evaluation ("Though they have a reputation for wisdom,. . . [they] are of no value") diverts his attention before he completes the first thought. Only after offering the second evaluation does he return to complete the judgment he started at the beginning of the sentence. The intervening evaluation acknowledges that the observances and rituals that the visionaries call for seem to embody some wisdom. In the Hellenistic world, moderate asceticism was often seen as a sign of wisdom. But having conceded the appearance of wisdom, the writer asserts that the visionaries' practices actually have no value.

After acknowledging that such practices may give one a reputation for wisdom, the writer characterizes a few of them. He first mentions "self-chosen worship." This is the earliest appearance of this word (*ethelothrēskia*) in Greek. It was probably created for use in this context. It is possible that the visionaries coined the term for their practices (O'Brien 153), yet it is difficult to see what advantage they might gain by using it. Whether they or the author coined it, this context generates a new word. Possible nuances of the prefix *ethelo-* suggest that the author of Colossians coined it. This prefix probably implies some affectation or pretense (Lightfoot 206; Francis 1973, 181). If that is the case, he disparages their observances as "pseudo-religion" (Hay 111). Even the word the writer chooses for worship (*thrēskia*) conveys this impression because it ends with *skia*, the word used for "shadow" in v. 17. While the word for worship is commonly spelled *thrēskeia*, the form combined with *ethelo-* here is *thrēskia*, a very uncommon word in this period.[54] So this newly coined word may well echo the author's evaluation of the visionaries' teaching as a mere shadow of what the Colossians now already possess in Christ (2:17). The writer may have chosen this unusual word to imply that these practices belong to the realm outside of Christ and are performed only for show.

It is significant that Colossians characterizes the visionaries' practices as worship. This characterization and the connections to holy days in 2:16 indicate that their observances include worship practices. The extra burden of

---

53. For an excellent discussion of the structure of v. 23 and an argument for the view adopted here, see Hollenbach 254–61.

54. LSJM (806) does not cite an example of this latter spelling until the third century C.E. The word appears in *Orientis Graeci Inscriptiones Selectae* (*OGIS*) 210.9, in an inscription from Nubia. This is the only instance of its use that LSJM cites.

worship that they have adopted derives from what they observe in their visions. They see and perhaps participate with angels in worship of God and then insist that those who are truly saved will adopt these same worship practices. By bringing these practices into the church, the visionaries believe that they are elevating current practice or even enabling angels to worship with them. If they had observed these rituals without imposing them on the whole church or claiming superiority, the writer would probably not have been troubled by them. But the visionaries want to impose these practices on the whole church, arguing that they are necessary for forgiveness and a proper relationship with God.

By describing their practices as "self-chosen worship," the author implies that the visionaries' food and drink regulations are ritual observances. The combination of dietary regulations and holy days in 2:16 and this description of their practices as worship suggest that the visionaries do understand their dietary regulations as ritual observances. So they call for some forms of dietary abstinence on holy days as a form of ritual preparation for visionary experiences.[55]

The second characteristic that gains the visionaries a reputation for wisdom is "humility" (*tapeinophrosynē*). As observed in connection with v. 18, Hellenistic culture did not consider humility a virtue, though biblical texts do count it a virtue when it designates an attitude of approach to God. But even in the New Testament *tapeinophrosynē* appears only rarely. Of the seven times it appears, three are in Colossians (2:18, 23; 3:12).[56] In Col 2, it has a more particular meaning than it has in the other New Testament uses, including that in Col 3. Verse 18 identifies angelic humility as one of the things the visionaries see in their heavenly ascents. Imitation of that humility before God comprises at least a part of the extra measure of worship that the visionaries have adopted.

Furthermore, in the context of visionary ascent, humility can refer to dietary regulations and other practices of abstinence (see the comment above on 2:18). "Humility" probably refers to such practices of abstinence here, particularly since the following words speak of "severity to the body." So the "humility" that the visionaries practice and advocate includes both practices they see in liturgical settings in their visions and practices that enable visionary experiences. They infuse their dietary abstinence with cultic significance, at least identifying it as a means of fostering mystical experience in the context of worship. The ancient world highly prized mystical experiences. Therefore, entering such a state in a worship setting or on a holy day after having observed the prescribed dietary rules would lend credibility to the visionaries' teaching and accrue honor for its adherents.

55. Harold Attridge (483–98) cites *2* and *3 Enoch* along with *Zostrianos* (NHC 8.1) as texts in which people are transformed into an angelic state after following particular rituals. While these examples are later than Colossians, they show that such ideas were current in the wider culture.

56. The other four appearances of the term are in Acts 20:19; Eph 4:2; Phil 2:3; 1 Pet 5:5. Similarly, the simpler form *tapeinos* appears only eight times.

Although many manuscripts include "and" (*kai*) after "humility," other important manuscripts do not (e.g., P[46] and B). On the whole, it seems more likely that it was not originally in the text (so also T. Martin 1996, 50–51; O'Brien 135; Dunn 188; Lincoln 634). If the "and" is present, then "severity[57] to the body" is a third characteristic of the visionaries' practice. If it is absent, however, "severity to the body" modifies "humility"; their expression of *tapeinophrosynē* thus includes practices that the writer characterizes as ascetic. The visionaries' dietary regulations are the only practices that could be characterized as ascetic. "Severity to the body" is Colossians' polemical, exaggerated characterization of their "humility." The ascetic regimen that the visionaries adopt seems to be related only to their desire to attain visions. Thus, they only commend such abstinence for short periods of preparation; they are not rules by which they live at other times.

After mentioning some practices that give the visionaries a reputation for having wisdom, the writer provides his own evaluation of them. He says emphatically that they lack any value at all. The indefinite pronoun "any" (*tini*) increases the intensity of this appraisal. Although the visionaries contend that their abstinence regulations and worship practices draw one closer to God and the divine presence, Colossians declares that they have no value. Such practices may lead to a reputation for wisdom, but they have no significance for persons who are "in Christ." They do not lead to a better relationship with God, to forgiveness, or to superior spiritual status. Seen from the perspective of one who has "died with Christ" and remains within the body that is nourished by Christ, its head, these practices offer no advance in spirituality.

The final explicit appraisal of the visionaries' teaching and practices gives an even sharper judgment than the immediately preceding comment that they are completely worthless. The final phrase in the verse resumes the thought begun with the initial words of v. 23, "These regulations." Completing this train of thought, the author says that these abstinence regulations actually "lead to gratification of the flesh." That is, rather than controlling untoward desires, they actually inflame them. Of course, the other teachers would deny this vigorously.

The term "gratification" (*plēsmonē*), the third New Testament *hapax legomenon* in this verse, is an interesting choice. It can signify either "satisfaction" in a good sense (e.g., of thirst) or excess. Both meanings appear in the LXX (examples of the nuance of satisfaction include Exod 16:3; Lev 25:19; Isa 30:23, while Isa 1:14; Ezek 39:19; Hos 13:6 have the nuance of excess). The word is regularly used in connection with food. Thus, in the context of a dispute about dietary regulations, the author chooses a word typically related to the consumption of food. Whether its association with food has influenced his choice of words, in this context *plēsmonē* clearly means excessive indulgence because it is satisfaction of "the flesh."

---

57. *Apheidia* ("severity") is another New Testament *hapax legomenon*.

In keeping with Paul's characteristic usage, "flesh" (*sarx*) is not a neutral term here in Colossians. It does not stand for the body or material existence, each of which possesses value as something created by God, and "body" is, after all, the image Colossians uses for the church. Colossians uses "flesh" in a neutral sense in 2:1 to speak of personal encounters. But in 2:23 it carries its more-common Pauline meaning; it designates the realm that runs counter to God's will, as in 2:18–19, where the "mind of the flesh" directly opposes connection to Christ. In v. 23, the phrase "gratification of the flesh" indicates that these regulations lead people who observe them to capitulate to their sinful nature or to the realm where sin reigns.

This assessment of the visionaries' regulations, then, closes with rhetorical flair.[58] The appraisal does not necessarily mean the writer believes that the proposed dietary regulations regularly lead people to the sin of excess. This is a polemical evaluation that puts the other teaching in the worst possible light and so makes it as unappealing as possible. Here is the climax of the evaluations the author has given throughout vv. 20–23. He has said that the visionaries' commands and practices come from the "elements" (v. 20), are from a human rather than a divine source (v. 22), are completely without value (v. 23), and finally, lead to sin (v. 23). The author has been building up to this final accusation as the capstone of his complete rejection of the opposed teaching. Such a conclusion intends to make it impossible for the readers to consider adopting what the visionaries offer.

All the evaluations of the visionaries' teaching and practices depend on theological assertions already made in Colossians, particularly its interpretation of the death of Christ—and believers' incorporation into that death and into the resurrection—as the way to forgiveness, reconciliation, and relationship with God. The current section begins by rejecting the visionaries' condemnation of the readers for failing to conform to their dietary and calendrical regulations (2:16). Colossians bases this rejection directly (note "therefore" in v. 16) on the forgiveness that believers receive through the death of Christ and God's subduing of the powers in Christ. Then in v. 19, believers' participation in the body of Christ assumes that their baptism identifies them with Christ, as the image of being buried and raised with him intimates in 2:12–13. Finally, their death with Christ and through it entrance into a new realm of existence, which identification with him entails, undergirds the exhortations and evaluations made in vv. 20–23. Verses 20–23, then, begin with the reminder that believers have died with Christ as they again explicate the meaning of that death in relation to the other teaching. The central theological affirmations of the letter, then, support the writer's direct critique of the visionaries' program in 2:16–23.

---

58. This verse closes the discussion so polemically that Pokorný (154) calls v. 23 "slightly demagogical," and Lightfoot (208) argues that the writer cannot mean that those rules lead to evil because such a claim is too extravagant to be effective.

One of the underlying problems that Colossians addresses in its rejection of the visionaries' teaching and outlook is their individualism. As was true for mystery religion initiates, the experience that these teachers seek primarily benefits the individual who has the experience. Defining spirituality as something that benefits only, or primarily, the individual rather than the community was common in the ancient world. Paul combats this outlook throughout 1 Corinthians, where he must constantly call that church to seek the good of the community. Colossians 2:19 implies that the visionaries care more about their own fulfilling experiences than they do about the health and vitality of the community, the "body." Perhaps even by defining the "things to come" in v. 17 as the "body of Christ," the church, the author points to the need to focus on the community's experience rather than that of the individual. Moreover, the extensive attention to Paul's willingness to suffer for them emphasizes the centrality of the community, particularly when seen in contrast to the visionaries' attention to their own experiences in their personal visions.

For Colossians, genuine and full experiences of God are found in Christ and in the context of the community understood as the body of Christ. Requiring other spiritual experiences or visions underestimates the way the presence of God is mediated in Christ. To seek such experiences in ways that minimize or ignore one's identity with Christ is to reveal a lack of understanding about the meaning of baptism and the realities it brings to the life of the believer. The letter will continue to expound the meaning of baptism as it explores how those realities must come to expression in the ways believers live. Colossians calls its readers to recognize that they have entered a new reality in Christ through baptism. This reality renders other means to spiritual experience of little value and also demands that the letter's recipients adopt a particular manner of life.

Argument 3

Accept the Letter's Teaching and Instruction Because You Have Been Granted Holiness in Baptism

Colossians 3:1–4:6

GRANTED HOLINESS IN BAPTISM, LIVE HOLY LIVES

The theologically laden remarks in 3:1–4 form a sort of hinge in Colossians that serves as a center point of the letter (Lindemann 52). While most interpreters see this unit as the introduction to the letter's section on ethics, others identify it as the conclusion of the theological section, with the hortatory portion beginning at 3:5 (Bruce 263; Moule 110, 113; Lincoln 637). Interpreters often divide Pauline Letters into two parts, one that expresses the theological points and one that provides ethical instructions. Though there are some reasons to make such a division, the contrast, when stated so starkly, is overdrawn—particularly for Colossians. Many interpreters have also contended that the ethical sections of Pauline Letters have little connection with the theological points made or with the situation the letter addresses, a view especially associated with Martin Dibelius.[1] Such a view of Colossians, however, is untenable.

The contacts between the material in chapters 3–4 and that of chapters 1–2, especially 2:6–23, make such airtight divisions between parts of the letter unsuitable for Colossians. First, chapter 2 contains many exhortations (vv. 6, 8, 16, 18). Therefore, instruction about the proper manner of life for believers does not begin at some point in chapter 3. Second, and more important, chapter 3 repeats and develops prominent imagery from the preceding chapters. The images of being raised with Christ (3:1), dying (3:3), and putting to death (3:5) all echo imagery from chapter 2, and Christ's exalted position in 3:1 recalls the proclamations made about him in 1:15–20. The images of dying and being raised clearly relate to baptism, and so the metaphors of "putting off" (3:9) and "putting on" (3:12) develop a central theological claim of chapter 2. Throughout chapter 3 the writer employs the language of baptism and conversion that has played such a key role in the argument of chapter 2. Furthermore, the language he uses to describe the believer's orientation of life plays on the other teachers' quest for visions as the Colossians are exhorted to "seek the things above" (3:1). There may even be a passing glance at the visionaries' teaching when the writer urges the readers to be humble (3:12).

Colossians does not separate doctrine and ethics so that chapters 3 and 4 simply explicate the ethical consequences of the work of Christ or the believer's incorporation into Christ. Rather, these chapters draw the controversy with the

---

1. Martin Dibelius, *From Tradition to Gospel* (New York: Scribners, 1935), 237–40.

visionaries *into* the instructions about manner of life. Together, the exhortations to reject the visionaries' teaching and the ethical exhortations form an important part of the writer's argument against that teaching. The continuing references to baptism throughout chapter 3 show that these ethical instructions continue the letter's interpretation of baptism. This explication of the meaning of baptism holds a central place in the strategy that Colossians develops to criticize the other teachers. So chapter 3 continues the topic taken up in 2:6 and made explicit in 2:12: through baptism, believers have been incorporated into Christ in a way that already grants them all of God's blessings—far more than the visionaries can offer.

Therefore, 3:1–4 does not merely summarize what came before or introduce a section that gives ethical instruction. These verses recapitulate and refocus the topic at hand (i.e., the way a proper understanding of baptism shows that the visionaries' teachings are unnecessary and inferior) by opening a new aspect of the meaning of the believers' initiation into the church. While 3:1–4 opposes the visionaries less directly, it still serves as a counterpoint to 2:20–23 and thus contributes to the debate with those teachers. The ethic proposed in 3:1–4:6 redefines what it means to "seek the things above." Instead of living by the regulations that the visionaries urge as their way to attain visions, Colossians proposes a manner of life that grows out of the believers' identification with Christ in baptism. This way of living has elements of both personal and corporate morality.

3:1–4 Seek the Things Above

Colossians 3:1–4, then, signals a turn in the argument of the letter. At this point the writer no longer directly opposes the visionaries. Rather, he develops an alternative piety that grows out of his interpretation of baptism. In this explication he lays out consequences of baptism, as he incorporates this particular ethic into the meaning of baptism for believers' lives and place with God.

> 3:1 Since, therefore, you were raised with Christ, seek the things above, where Christ is, seated [there] at the right hand of God. 2 Focus your intent on things above, not the things on the earth! 3 For you died and your[a] life has been hidden with Christ in God. 4 When Christ, who is your life, is revealed, then you also will be revealed with him in glory.

a. While P[46] and א (among other witnesses) have the second-person plural here, other manuscripts, including B, have the first person, "our." It seems more likely that a copyist would change the reading to "our" to confirm the broader participation of all believers in Christ than that it would be changed to the second plural ("your") in order to fit the literary context of the passage. So the reading "your" is preferable because it better fits the context and also because of its strong external attestation.

[3:1–2] The new and theme-orienting paragraph of 3:1–4 begins with the assertion that believers have been "raised with Christ." Verse 1 begins with the Greek particle *ei*, which may be translated "if" (RSV, NRSV) or "since" (NIV, NJB). The better sense of the particle here is "since" because Colossians does not intend to express doubt about whether believers have been raised, but rather to assert their resurrection with Christ as a fact that serves as the foundation for what follows. This "since" is followed by "therefore" (*oun*), which connects 3:1–4 to what precedes it. Grammatically, and most immediately, "therefore" connects 3:1–4 to 2:20–23 and its evaluation of the visionaries' regulations. The direct conceptual link to 2:20–23 is the metaphor of "dying with Christ" (2:20); as believers have died with Christ, they have been "raised with" him (3:1). The connection also reaches back beyond 2:20 to the earlier affirmation of the believer's resurrection with Christ in 2:12. So this opening statement takes up a theme that has been a consistent part of the argument against the visionaries since the writer began to address them directly in 2:8.

In 2:12, burial and resurrection with Christ occur at baptism. In both 2:12 and 3:1, Colossians uses the aorist tense, "you were raised with" (*synēgerthēte*), to point to the past event of baptism as the moment at which this resurrection with Christ took place. So believers not only died with Christ to their old manner of living (2:20; cf. 2:11–12); they were also raised with Christ to a new way of life.[2]

In the undisputed letters, Paul says that Christians have died with Christ so that they might live a new life, just as Christ was raised from the dead (e.g., Rom 6:4). Here in Colossians, believers are raised with Christ and participate in Christ's resurrection. To assert that believers participate in the resurrection of Christ makes a somewhat more dramatic claim than saying that believers are raised to new life. But such an assertion does not imply a fully realized eschatology (see 3:4), though it does emphasize the present possession of eschatological blessings more strongly than Rom 6. This present resurrection does not mean that believers have received complete moral regeneration or immediate access to all end-time blessings, but that God has granted them a new sort of existence. The substance of this claim is therefore compatible with what Paul says in Rom 6 about the new life that believers have in the present, even though Paul does not use "resurrection" to describe it. This new life has moral implications; indeed, participation in it provides the ground of ethics. For Colossians, ethics is not built only on seeing Jesus as a model or example. Rather, believers live as they do because they participate in the resurrection life with Christ.

The recipients of Colossians must have been startled at the next phrase in 3:1. After spending half of this letter telling them not to seek visions of

---

2. The verb *synergeirō* appears in only one place in the New Testament beyond these two passages in Colossians: Eph 2:6, a passage that is probably dependent on these uses in Colossians.

heavenly places, the writer exhorts them to "Seek the things above [*ta anō*]!" An exhortation to "seek the things above" is rare in early Christian literature, and the expression *ta anō* appears only here in an exhortation within the New Testament (see Hay 116; Leppä 157). With this statement, Colossians begins to redefine seeking "the things above." The visionaries "seek the things above" by pursuing visions as a way to participate in the heavenly reality. Colossians affirms that seeking "things above" is appropriate for believers. In fact, it constitutes an aspect of participating in the resurrection life. But Colossians radically redefines this pursuit. Seeking "the things above" is an ethical mandate that embodies being "raised with" Christ, not following regulations that try to attain superior spiritual experiences or spiritual superiority. Colossians completely reorients the meaning of seeking "the things above" by basing the exhortation on the believers' *already-received* participation in Christ's resurrection.

In 3:1, the recipients' resurrection is a past event; the command to "seek the things above" is in the present tense, implying that this seeking is an ongoing process rather than a completed event. So there is no moral perfectionism here. Still, talk of present participation in the resurrection radicalizes the tension in Pauline ethics between the indicative and the imperative (Grässer 148). Not only have believers been given new life; in Colossians they also have been *resurrected with Christ*. Now they must struggle to live as resurrected people, to live in ways that conform to the new life that God has given them. Their orientation of life must flow from their participation in this new life.[3] The juxtaposition of this proclamation of the believer's resurrection with the imperative implies that how one lives comprises an important part of the new resurrection life. The Colossians must live out the resurrection by orienting their lives according to the instructions that follow.

If resurrection with Christ in 3:1 means that the eschatological reservation always present in Paul's thought has collapsed, as some interpreters think (e.g., Lindemann 53), there would be no need for the exhortations that follow. The language is radical, to be sure, pressing beyond anything that appears in the undisputed letters; nevertheless, some eschatological reservation remains. Both the presence of the imperatives and the direct mention of the Parousia in this paragraph (3:4) demonstrate that the writer of Colossians retains a substantive future aspect of eschatology. When read in context—both its place in the letter and the situation the letter addresses—Colossians' emphasis on possession of resurrection life may well reveal nothing different from the eschatology that we find in the undisputed Pauline Letters. The context necessitates a different emphasis, but one that does not necessarily entail a different stance on eschatology.

---

3. Barth and Blanke (393) assert that the verb *zēteō* (to seek) is used to express orientation to life, as it does in Matt 6:31–33.

The second half of v. 1 may make one assertion about Christ or two. It may make the single assertion that "Christ is seated above at God's right hand" (KJV, NIV) or the dual assertion that "Christ is above" and that he is "seated at God's right hand." The word order of the sentence (with the participle *kathēmenos* ["seated"] at the end of the clause, separated from the word that would make it a paraphrastic, *estin* ["is"]) makes the latter translation more likely (so most commentators since at least Lightfoot 209).[4] Thus the clause emphatically asserts not only that Christ is "above" but also that even in that extraordinary setting he holds the place of honor and power (MacDonald 127).[5]

Colossians exhorts its readers to seek the "things above" because that is where Christ is. As Colossians defines it, seeking "the things above" consists of living out one's connectedness to Christ. The exhortation to "seek the things above" is the broadest, most comprehensive command in the letter. Seeking the things above includes rejecting the visionaries' teaching and living according to the instruction given in the rest of the letter, which amounts to orienting one's entire existence toward new life in Christ.

With nearly all people of his day, the writer of Colossians envisions the cosmos as a series of horizontal layers, with the heavenly realms in which gods and other powerful spiritual beings live in the upper strata and humans in one of the lower layers. The higher one goes, the more refined the material of which the beings are made and the more powerful the beings are who live there. This view is prevalent among apocalyptic writers (e.g., *Testament of Levi*; *2 Enoch*; *Apocalypse of Abraham*) and in the New Testament. Such an understanding is particularly evident in 2 Cor 12:2, where Paul speaks of "the third heaven."

Colossians envisions Christ residing in the highest of these layers, the highest heaven, where God is.[6] Whatever realms the visionaries claim to see or enter while on their heavenly journeys, Colossians asserts that believers' lives are already secured in the highest of realms because they have been "raised with Christ."

Christ not only inhabits that highest realm but also holds the highest place of honor there, "at God's right hand." In this position, Christ exercises God's power and authority. This expression of Christ's exaltation and sovereignty draws ultimately on Ps 110:1. But Colossians probably depends more directly on the early church's use of the psalm than on the psalm itself (Hay 116–17).

---

4. E. Delebecque (390), however, reads it as a perfect periphrastic: "where Christ is seated at the right hand."

5. The NEB, NJB, RSV, and NRSV seem to accept the gist of the translation given here, but perhaps less clearly, translating "where Christ is, seated at God's right hand" or "the right hand of God."

6. Some interpreters deny that Colossians has a genuinely spatial conception in mind (e.g., Bruce 258–59; Schweizer 174, 178; Barth and Blanke 393). But the historical setting of the first century is strong evidence that this is the writer's understanding. Yet that does not mean that he is unable to invest that "geography" with theological significance.

Given its numerous uses in the New Testament, this expression of Christ's position must have played a significant part in the early church's proclamation.[7] This powerful Christian adaptation of a messianic conception claims authority for Christ over all of life and creation. Colossians, then, reminds its recipients that the one with whom they have been raised and in whom they live holds this most exalted place and so can dispense the highest blessings.

Colossians' reliance on early church tradition for its use of Ps 110:1 does not necessarily indicate that the writer is directly quoting a preformed liturgical tradition. While some interpreters do identify this part of 3:1 as a liturgical piece (e.g., Lohse 133; Hay 116), Meyer (344) contends that the only basis for such a judgment is an assumed late date for the letter. Whether the writer has a particular liturgical piece in mind is less important than that he draws on a known and accepted understanding of the place of Christ. He does not mention Christ's exaltation to make a new or unexpected assertion about Christ, but to bring that understanding of Christ to bear on the Colossian situation, particularly to make it the basis for the ethical instructions that follow.

This claim about the place of Christ again returns readers to the contrast between the reign of Christ and that of Caesar. Claims about the divinization of emperors are dwarfed by this declaration that Christ holds the highest position in the heavens. What Colossians demands of the readers in the following exhortations will often set them at odds with the values of the world around them. So the writer begins this section with a reminder that they adopt these values, attitudes, and behaviors because they are identified with Christ, the one who reigns over all realms of creation. And since Christ holds this most exalted position, believers can be certain of their relationship with God and the appropriateness of the manner of life to which Colossians calls them, even when that life brings disadvantage or even persecution.

Verse 2 restates the exhortation of v. 1 when it calls readers to "focus [their] intent on things above." The imperative verb *phroneō*, usually translated "set your mind on," has a broad range of nuances (even within the Pauline corpus), most having to do with how one thinks or evaluates things. More than "seek" in v. 1, *phroneō* may signal an inner attitude (so Lohse 133; Harris 137; MacDonald 127; Hay 117). But "seek" and "focus your intent" probably convey much the same point (Bratcher and Nida 74; cf. Pokorný [159], who comments that both verbs express "attitude of life"). Colossians uses *phroneō* here the way Paul does in Rom 8:5 and Phil 3:19. In those passages, it points to an orientation of life, designating the focus of one's attention and intentions.

---

7. Schweizer (174) asserts that Ps 110:1 is probably cited more often in the New Testament than any other verse from the Old Testament. O'Brien (162) lists the following passages as allusions to this psalm: Matt 26:64; Mark 12:36; Luke 20:41–44; Acts 2:33–35; 5:31; 7:55, 56; Rom 8:34; Heb 1:3, 13; 8:1; 10:12; 12:2; 1 Pet 3:22; Rev 3:21. Hay (1973, 15) finds 33 quotations from or allusions to this psalm in the New Testament.

Verse 2 puts "things above" in the emphatic position, just as in v. 1. The repetition of "things above" with a second-person imperative also makes the command emphatic. The injunction becomes even more forceful when the writer explicitly designates the opposite of "things above" as "the things on the earth." The form of this contrast is surprising. One would expect the contrast to be between things "above" and things "below," rather than "on the earth."[8] As vv. 3–4 will make clear, Colossians envisions the resurrection of believers with Christ as an event that has brought them into an existence that transcends their visible circumstances. Their participation in Christ's resurrection has transferred them into the kingdom of God's Son (1:13). Their new citizenship requires new perspectives and allegiances. Their attention must fasten, then, not on the transient and inferior realm of the visible structures of the earth, but on what belongs to the realm of Christ. In some ways, the writer bids them to look not back to their former lives, but forward to the consummation of the new life they possess in Christ.

The contrast between the "things on the earth" and the "things above" does not, however, betray a rejection of the material creation. This contrast concerns orientation of life, not the substance of which things are made. The author may even want the readers to hear faintly a rejection of the visionaries' regulations that involve food and drink, among other things.[9] But "earthly things" has a broader meaning here. It involves an assessment of the world's orientation, an orientation that fails to recognize Christ's defeat of the powers that control the world.

"Earth" here designates all that does not conform to the new life in Christ. In this context, the contrast between "above" and "earth" makes "earth" an eschatological category. "Earth" represents the things that do not recognize and participate in the new reality inaugurated in the life, death, and resurrection of Christ, that is, things that have not been "raised with Christ." The extensive discussion of eschatology in Rom 8 begins with Paul discussing the "already" of eschatology, that is, the blessings of the end times that believers possess in the present. That discussion contains one of the few instances where Paul uses *phroneō* as Colossians uses it in 3:2, 5. In Rom 8:5 (my trans.), Paul contrasts "those who are of the flesh" with "those who are of the Spirit." There he says that those of the flesh have their "minds set on" or are "oriented toward [*phroneō*] things of the flesh," while those of the Spirit are "oriented toward things of the Spirit" (my trans.). Although the specific imagery varies in the two

8. Grässer (154–55) suggests that "things above" and "things on the earth" take up the visionaries' categories. While this is possible, we do not have sufficient evidence to say that this is their vocabulary. Still, the writer may be influenced to use this language because of the way the visionaries frame their views.

9. Perhaps Barth and Blanke (395) are correct that "things on the earth" corresponds to the "elements of the earth" (the *stoicheia*) in 2:20.

passages, this is the very contrast Colossians makes in 3:1–2, a contrast that expresses an eschatological reality with implications for the way believers understand the present time and their current circumstances. The choice to "focus [their] intent on things above" also includes implications for ethics, as the rest of chapters 3 and 4 demonstrates.

[3–4] After exhorting readers to seek the things above, the writer returns to giving grounds for that demand in vv. 3–4. The *gar* ("for," "because") that connects vv. 1–2 to vv. 3–4 indicates that the latter verses provide reasons that support the exhortations in vv. 1–2.

Colossians begins grounding its exhortation to seek the things above by renewing its use of the metaphor of death. This metaphor functions in several ways in chapters 2 and 3. In 2:20–23, believers have died with Christ and so have been freed from the constraints of the world. Then in 3:1 they have been raised with Christ; the death of believers in 3:3 thus entails resurrection to life with Christ. This death and resurrection take place in the same act, baptism (2:12). So while death and resurrection appear in reverse order, with resurrection (3:1) mentioned before death (3:3), their order presents no conceptual problem because they occur simultaneously in baptism. In 2:20, however, the death metaphor functions in a different way. Believers remain dead (rather than being raised) because they die to the world's regulations. On the other hand, the comments about being buried and raised in 2:12 fit the thought of 3:1–3. Yet another use of the image of death appears at 2:13: instead of baptism bringing the death of the old way of life, death is the mode of existence for those outside of Christ. We should not homogenize these various uses of the metaphor of death. Each has an important point to make. The author's use of the same metaphor in multiple ways requires careful reading, but in these diverse ways this radical image dramatically emphasizes the importance of the change that has come to believers as a result of their belief in Christ.

Baptism not only signals the death of believers at some moment in the past but also has ongoing effects. The writer says that their lives "[have] been hidden with Christ." He uses the perfect tense (*kekryptai*, "have been hidden") to indicate that the past event of their death in baptism has continuing consequences. Though they possess this new life in the present, its reality remains hidden from most observers. The hiddenness of this life again speaks of an eschatological reality. This description of the believers' circumstances builds on the framework of a partially realized eschatology that looks forward to a later consummation. The full reality of the life they have is hidden for the moment, even to the believers themselves (Hay 117). The combination of a present hidden reality with a future full revelation is common in apocalyptic literature. Writings bearing an apocalyptic influence, including Revelation and the undisputed Pauline Letters, speak of hidden realities that await full realization. The description of believers' existence in Col 3:3 reflects this eschatological outlook. The eschatological reservation that is not explicit in vv. 1–2 surfaces both in this statement of the hiddenness of believers' lives and in the glance toward the Parousia in v. 4.

The hidden nature of this new life requires believers to continue struggling in the present, because this life is visible only through the eyes of faith. The way imperatives surround this assertion of the present possession of life indicates that believers must actuate this new life by seeking the things above, as Colossians defines that seeking with the instructions that follow. The gift of life and the demand to conform one's manner of living to it are inseparable.

Believers' lives are not just hidden; they are hidden "in God."[10] This affirmation makes the new life secure, even if hidden. Believers have been brought into the sphere of God's divine power and being. They inhabit a place where no power can condemn them and from which no power can wrest them. Life "in God" involves more than adopting a particular perspective on life (as Dunn defines it [207]); believers have been "caught up with the divine power that shapes the universe" (MacDonald 128).

The life "in God" is "with Christ." Believers' lives "in God" are intimately and inextricably related to their connection "with Christ." Through this connection to Christ, believers enter the sphere of God's eschatological blessings. Throughout Colossians, God's blessings and gifts are mediated to the world (even in creation) and to the church through Christ. In 3:3, life in God is mediated through Christ because believers receive this life through their association with Christ. This assertion of the place of believers returns attention to their close identification with Christ: believers have died with him (2:20), they have been raised with him (2:12; 3:1), and their continuing new life in God is found in intimate association with Christ. Verse 4 makes this connection to Christ even closer; here Christ *is* the believer's life.

Verse 4 contrasts the present time with the Parousia, "when Christ is revealed." There is a phase of revelation yet to come. Verse 4 looks forward to a future eschatological moment that will reveal the hidden aspects of Christ's reign and believers' union with him. Though this is the most direct reference to the not-yet of eschatological expectation in Colossians, it is by no means the only intimation of this future aspect of its eschatology. The references to the "hope of glory" in 1:27 and the coming "wrath of God" in 3:6 indicate that a future act of God remains an important element in the eschatology of Colossians. Hay (117) may be correct that v. 4 lacks eschatological excitement or worry about the eschaton's delay, but the tension between the assertions that Colossians makes about what believers have received and the readers' experience of the world (or

10. Schweizer (176) asserts that the expression "in God" does not appear in Paul. However, he acknowledges that "in God" appears without the article in 1 Thess 1:1 among the undisputed letters, and it appears again in 2 Thess 1:1.

even of their church, with its turmoil over the visionaries' claims) demands this completion of the work of God. As is true with most New Testament eschatology, the central issue is not the timing of the Parousia, but its certainty. Verse 4 provides that assurance of the completion and manifestation of the eschatological blessings of God.

The word Paul ordinarily employs to speak of Christ's appearance at the second coming is *apokalyptō*. But in 3:4, Colossians uses *phaneroō*, a word the undisputed letters do not use to refer to the Parousia.[11] Colossians may use this verb to echo 1:26, where the writer spoke of the revelation of Paul's gospel (Aletti 220).[12] If so, 3:4 indicates that the fullness of that revelation comes only at the second coming. Closer to hand, *phaneroō* also expresses in a "more natural" way than the verb *apokalyptō* the contrast between what is currently hidden and what will be "revealed" (MacDonald 129).

Colossians' combination of spatial and temporal imagery to speak of eschatological realities is unusual in the Pauline writings. In the undisputed letters, temporal imagery is much more common, although Paul does refer to eschatological blessings already existing in the heavens (e.g., 2 Cor 3:18; 4:16–5:3). By contrast, spatial imagery dominates Colossians' discussion of the eschatological blessings. In 3:1–4, Christ sits enthroned "above" at God's right hand, and believers' lives are already hidden in that heavenly realm in Christ. The problem that Colossians addresses leads its writer to employ this spatial imagery. In response to the visionaries' offer of immediate experiences of heavenly realms, the letter asserts that believers already possess more than such experiences can give them. This emphasis on present possession and the use of spatial imagery do not indicate that the writer has no, or only muted, future eschatological expectations. The apocalyptic work *2 Baruch* shows how writers could combine spatial and temporal language without compromising the importance of future fulfillment. Thus *2 Bar.* 48:42–50, tells of the things hidden in the heavenly realms, things that will be revealed only at the eschatological consummation (see Levison 93–100). The same juxtaposition of a present hidden reality and future revelation again appears in *2 Bar.* 4.2–7 (cf. Bevere 153–61). For many modern readers, the assertion that the eschatological reality already exists in heaven—and that believers participate in it, at least in some covert way—clashes with proclamation of a future consummation. But at least some first-century apocalypticists evidently found these assertions fully compatible. Thus, even though Colossians does not express the eschatological reservation as often as it appears in the undisputed letters, this does not neces-

11. Paul does use *phaneroō* in 2 Cor 5:10 to speak of everyone being "revealed" before the judgment bar of Christ, but he does not use it to refer to Christ being revealed.
12. This same verb is used again in 4:4.

sarily indicate that the eschatological scheme envisioned by Colossians differs significantly from that of Paul.

Colossians constantly reminds its readers that their relationship with and reconciliation to God—their forgiveness, their access to the blessings of heaven, and their freedom from striving to attain new spiritual experiences—all depend on their connection to Christ. Still, God remains the primary actor. This emphasis on God's acts continues as the writer uses the passive verb "is revealed" (*phanerōthē*) to speak of the revelation of Christ at the last day. This passive verb indicates that God initiates and consummates the eschatological time. Just as God raised Christ (2:12), so God will reveal Christ at the end. As central a role as association with Christ plays in the argument of Colossians, God remains the ultimate source of all the blessings that believers have in Christ and of all acts on their behalf.

Colossians does not diminish Christ's importance by identifying God as the ultimate actor. In fact, 3:1–4 makes the necessity of association with Christ particularly emphatic. In these verses, believers have been raised with Christ (v. 1), have their lives hidden with Christ (v. 3), and Christ even becomes their life (v. 4). In v. 4 identification with Christ is more complete than in v. 3 because their lives are not just *with* Christ, but Christ *is* their life.[13] A genuine, perhaps even ontological (so Wilson 130–31; Hay 119), change has been effected for believers; they now possess a new primary identity. Believers' lives are so closely bound up with Christ that "Christ is the source, center, and goal of the individual and corporate lives of believers" (Harris 140). Here Colossians in a more radical way expresses the identification with Christ that Paul articulates in Gal 2:20: "I no longer live, but Christ lives in me" (NIV). Christ does more than indwell and empower, for Colossians says that believers are taken up into the life of Christ. No more complete identification with Christ is possible. Such an affirmation definitively counters any claims that one needs more or better spiritual experiences. At the same time, identity with Christ implies that the life led by believers should manifest their identity with Christ. This assertion of union with Christ, then, also prepares for the ethical instruction that follows.

One of the indicators of the importance of Christ in 3:1–4 is its repetition of the word "Christ." In the space of these four verses, the word appears four times. In v. 4 and in v. 1, when "Christ" appears a second time, one might have expected the pronoun "he" or perhaps simply the verb with its subject implied, as often happens in Greek. The repetition of "Christ" leaves no doubt about the centrality of Christ for the believers' reception of eschatological blessings. Furthermore, in each of the four instances that the word "Christ" appears, it has the

---

13. See the translation note a (above) on the text-critical preference of "your" to "our" life in 3:4.

article "the" attached to it. While it is difficult to know what significance the article has in this context, it may, in opposition to the visionaries, identify Christ as *the* way to God and to eschatological blessings. It may also indicate that Christ is not just a name but also a designation for the position Christ holds. This would be consistent with the allusion to Ps 110 in Col 3:1. Whatever its significance (if it has any at all), the article appears with "Christ" with much greater regularity in Colossians than it does in the undisputed letters.[14]

Colossians' emphasis on the centrality of Christ is not an end unto itself. The combination of the position of Christ and believers' identification with him takes us to the working center of the letter. The readers need the confidence that they securely possess the fullness of God's blessings. Verse 4 provides further assurance of the readers' participation in these blessings by including them in God's revelation of Christ at the Parousia: when Christ is revealed for who he is, believers will be revealed with him. Believers are both identified with Christ (he is "your life") and revealed with him. Just as Christ's true identity and position on high is at least partially hidden in the present, so is their identity and their possession of eschatological realities. But that season of hiddenness ends for both Christ and believers when God makes them known. Only at that future moment will believers come to fully possess this reality. Notably, this all takes place as an act of God, not through the readers' conformity to regulations designed to attain something beyond incorporation into Christ. At the same time, however, these verses introduce a series of ethical exhortations. So ethical living plays an important part in the writer's understanding of identification with Christ.

A final assurance of the extraordinary quality of the eschatological reality that believers will experience comes in the final words of v. 4. Believers will be revealed with Christ "in glory." In 1:27, Colossians uses "glory" to designate the eschatological blessings of the Parousia. The writer again connects "glory" and the eschaton in 3:4. The basic meaning of *doxa* involves "honor" and "reputation" (LSJM 444). Drawing on its use in the LXX, the New Testament sometimes employs it to refer to the radiance of God (see, e.g., 2 Thess 1:9; cf. BDAG 256–58; G. Kittel, *TDNT* 2:242–49). When Paul uses *doxa* with reference to God, he sometimes utilizes it in praise of God, acknowledging God's identity and greatness (e.g., Rom 4:20; 11:36; 16:27; Gal 1:5; Phil 2:11; 4:20). In other places, the word refers to the overwhelming power and majesty of God's character (e.g., Rom 6:4; 9:23; 2 Cor 4:6). Paul also uses *doxa* to refer to the escha-

14. "Christ" appears with the article 13 times in Colossians and only 10 times in Galatians, Philippians, and 1 Thessalonians (letters of fairly comparable length) combined. The article appears with "Christ" predominantly in formulas such as "cross of the Christ" (Gal 6:12; Phil 3:18), "gospel of the Christ" (Gal 1:7; Phil 1:27; 1 Thess 3:2), "law of the Christ" (Gal 6:2), and perhaps "those of the Christ" (Gal 5:24). In these letters the only exceptions to formulaic use of the article are Phil 1:15, 17; 3:7.

tological blessings that believers receive at the eschaton (e.g., Rom 5:2; 8:18; 9:23; 2 Cor 4:17). When Colossians says its readers will be revealed in glory (*doxa*), it draws on the understanding of "glory" as both a divine attribute and an element of what they receive at the Parousia. Because Christ is their life and because they are revealed with him, God brings them into God's own majesty with Christ at the second coming.[15] Thus, believers will share in Christ's glory, which is itself the reflection of God's glory.

As a pivotal section in the center of Colossians, 3:1–4 both summarizes the arguments that have preceded and prepares for what follows by refocusing previous affirmations about Christ and the readers' place with Christ. This section turns the letter's argument in a new direction. In much of chapters 1 and 2, Colossians has argued that the readers must not adopt the visionaries' practices and teachings. Now it must provide the necessary counterpart to that rejection, an explication of the appropriate ways to manifest the life that they have been granted in Christ. The remaining parts of Colossians take up this task.

As the writer veers in this new direction, he affirms that believers already reside within the sphere of God's blessings. Their place is with and in Christ in the highest heaven. Indeed, they are even "in God." Thus, their relationship with God is secure. Nothing anyone might offer them could surpass this place with God and this access to the things "above." Since the Colossians must not seek the things above in the ways the visionaries propose, they need instruction about how to orient their lives to fit their existence "with Christ in God." It is not that Colossians has finished its doctrinal exposition and now turns to ethics. Rather, explication of this way of life describes a part of what it means to be raised with Christ. What follows in 3:6–4:6 fills out the meaning of the exhortation to "seek the things above."

3:5–11 Put Away the Old Life

After affirming that believers are raised with Christ and calling them to conduct their lives in accord with that new existence in 3:1–4, the writer begins to spell out more specifically how this new life must manifest itself. He also sets their conduct in the context of Christ's coming judgment (cf. Barth and Blanke 402). Notably, living the resurrection life, as Colossians describes it, does not include soaring visions or superiority to life's troubles. Rather, it is a life devoted to a holiness that encompasses both personal and communal morality. Most religions of the first century included few expectations about moral living. But

15. Perhaps it is drawing too fine a distinction to limit the phrase "in glory" to either an instrumental or a locative sense (Harris [141] notes these along with accompanying circumstance as alternatives). The language of the passage has been broad enough and diverse enough that this expression seems to include both these senses. That is, "in glory" denotes that believers are revealed "by [God's or Christ's] glory" and "in the sphere of [God's] glory."

Colossians does not just give the instructions that appear in 3:5–4:6 because of the bad moral condition of Gentiles. Something more fundamental is happening; Colossians is describing what the life identified with Christ must be. This is even more than filling out the consequences of a life determined by faith in Christ. Conducting one's life in accord with the instructions contained in 3:5–4:6 is a facet of what it means to have new life. It is the way one authenticates genuine possession of that new life and so genuine Christian identity (cf. Lohse 135).

The connecting particle "therefore" (*oun*) and the change in metaphor from "being revealed" (v. 4) to "put[ting] to death" signal the beginning of a new paragraph at 3:5. There is also a turn from more-general exhortations and descriptions of the new reality in Christ to the specifics of vice lists. The paragraph ends at v. 11, where the writer reminds readers of their oneness in the Christ, who is sovereign over all. The beginning of a new paragraph in v. 12 is signaled by another use of "therefore" (*oun*) and a new turn in the explication of the new life: while vv. 5–11 give instruction primarily about what to *avoid*, vv. 12–17 detail some things believers must *adopt* as God's chosen and beloved people. But all of 3:5–4:6 is tightly bound together as the delineation of the contours of life in Christ. So the paragraphs within 3:5–4:6 should not be separated from one another or from the metaphors they echo from chapters 1–2.

3:5 Therefore, put to death the members that are upon the earth: fornication, uncleanness, passion, evil desire, and covetousness, which is idolatry. 6 It is because of these things that the wrath of God is coming upon the children[a] of disobedience.[b] 7 You previously walked as one of them, when you lived according to these vices. 8 But now, put away all these things: wrath, anger, wickedness, slander, and abusive speech from your mouths. 9 Do not lie to one another, because you have taken off the old self with its practices 10 and have put on the new [self], which is continually being renewed in knowledge [and] in accord with the image of the one who created it. 11 In this new creation,[c] there is no Greek and Jew, circumcised and uncircumcised, barbarian, Scythian, slave, free, but Christ is all and is in all.

a. Literally "sons."

b. Both ℵ and A have the phrase "upon the children of disobedience," but it is absent in P[46] and B. That it makes the flow of the sentence smoother counts both for and against its original presence in the text because it may indicate that a copyist felt the need to amend the text or that the original author built the next prepositional phrase on this one. See the further remarks in favor of its inclusion in the comment below on 3:5–6.

c. Literally, only the word "where" (*hopou*) appears in the text. This connective adverbial particle designates the "new self" in its corporate aspect; therefore, I have rendered it in a way that makes explicit what the ellipsis implies.

[5–6] The new stage of the exhortation begins with an expression that connects it directly to many elements in the preceding parts of the letter; it calls them to "put to death the members that are upon the earth." The introductory "therefore" signals that the following instructions flow from what has come before; then the echoes of other statements about the readers' place with Christ draw those connections more securely.

The exhortation to "put to death," which could be translated more graphically as "kill,"[16] ties this statement to 3:4 most immediately but also to 2:20 ("You died with Christ") and 2:12 ("You have been buried with him").[17] The previous references to the believer's death in baptism all presume that this is a past event, something accomplished by God in that moment of identifying with Christ. But now in 3:5 it is an exhortation; their turning to God must include an actual change in their manner of life, a change so radical that it can be described as killing the former way of life. The lives of believers must undergo a complete shift in orientation and bearing, and this shift grows from, and indeed is part of, the change that takes place in the merging of their lives with Christ.

Colossians urges its readers to put to death "the members that are upon the earth." This phrase deliberately echoes 3:2, which exhorts them not to focus on the "things on the earth." In Greek the wording of the phrase "things on the earth" in v. 2 is precisely the same as "that are upon the earth" in v. 5. Both verses contrast "things on the earth" to "things above." When the writer says readers are to kill "the members" or "the limbs" "that are upon the earth," he is not rejecting material existence in favor of some kind of spiritual existence above the material world. Rather, the "things upon the earth" has become a moral—and eschatological—category, one that he defines more specifically with the vice lists that follow.

The bodily limbs stand for the sins committed through them (cf. Moule 115; Bruce 268; Aletti 224).[18] The same use of "limbs" or "parts" of the body is evident in Matt 5:29–30, where Jesus says it is better to pluck out one's eye and so lose that "member" than to use it for lust, which leads to the condemnation of the whole self at judgment. In *2 Bar.* 49.1–3, Baruch wonders about the nature of human existence in the future and asks whether we will have these

---

16. R. Bultmann gives "kill" as a meaning of this verb as it appears in broader usage (*TDNT* 4:894).

17. For discussion of the various ways that Colossians uses the metaphor of death, see the comment on 3:3 above. Colossians 3:5 develops the metaphor of death with the verb *nekroō* (to kill) rather than with *apothnēskō* (to die). Use of *nekroō* in 3:5 draws attention to the active role that readers must take.

18. If the vices that follow stand in apposition to *melē* ("members"), as some think (e.g., Cannon 53), it is even clearer that these "members" are parts of the person that are used for sinful purposes. Lightfoot (211), however, rejects this construal of the grammar.

"members" that are chained to sin. The *Testament of Reuben* identifies particular parts of the body with various sins: insatiability in the stomach, strife in the liver and gall (3.1–4).[19] These writings envision sins working through, and even residing in, parts of the body without assuming that bodily existence is evil in itself. *Second Baruch* can at least conceive of the idea that the limbs that now serve sin can be redeemed by God. Therefore, when Colossians begins its specific instructions about manner of life with such a forceful statement as "Kill the members that are upon the earth" (a more forceful translation than given above), it emphasizes the radical nature of the commitment required of believers; the whole of their existence must be determined by their identification with Christ.

Colossians initially gives substance to the exhortation to kill the members through which evil works by providing a vice list. Vice lists are attested in Iranian religions, Hellenistic schools of philosophy (especially among Stoics), and in Judaism (whether Hellenistic Judaism, the Qumran community, or some parts of the Hebrew Bible [e.g., the Decalogue: so Hartman 1987, 183–84; Lev 18–19: so Yates 1991, 243]). Furthermore, exhortations that use the two-ways motif (e.g., 1QS 1.1; 2.2–28, *Didache*; *Epistle of Barnabas*) also employ such lists. Various interpreters have argued that the vice lists in Colossians draw on earlier lists or have been influenced by Iranian traditions (e.g., Lohse 137; Lindemann 55). Nothing, however, ties the lists in Colossians to those from Iran except that both have a list of five things (see Bevere 183). Likewise, the similarities between the Colossians lists and other nonbiblical materials suggest only an awareness of the form, not formal dependence for content (Bevere 184–88). The vice list in Colossians is also distinctive, though not unique, in that it is directly hortatory, whereas most vice lists leave the exhortation to virtue less explicit. The few New Testament vice lists that are directly hortatory (see also Eph 4:31; 5:3–5; 1 Pet 2:1, 11) are all associated with baptism, just as Col 3:5 and 3:8 are.

Given the lack of evidence for direct dependence, it is best to see Colossians' vice lists as the products of the author bringing together a known form and a developing Christian tradition, a tradition that was shaped by the moral teaching of Judaism (see Cannon 54–79). This relatively independent production of the vice lists does not necessarily indicate that the Colossians had a particular need for the specific exhortations found in those lists. The Colossians probably did not have unusual problems with the specific sins mentioned in these lists (so, e.g., Lohse, 137–38; Hay 121).[20] Augustine comments that it is unthinkable that these vices would be present among people whose lives have been

---

19. For other and later uses of this imagery, see Schweizer 1963, 437–39; and Strack-Billerbeck 1:302.

20. However, Yates (1991, 243) thinks there may be some connection to the situation.

taken into God, as v. 3 affirms. Therefore, the command to put such things to death instructs the readers to put away even the "intrusion" of the thought of them (*On Continence* 29; *NPNF*[1] 3:392). On the other hand, these lists are related to the situation in the sense that they delineate what readers must avoid for them to live in a way that conforms to their resurrection with Christ.

The primary focus of the vice list in v. 5 is sexual ethics; the first four of the five vices listed employ language that the Pauline corpus uses for sexual sin. The theme of the list is set by the first vice, fornication (*porneia*). The understanding of *porneia* as any sexual intercourse outside of marriage has been challenged with the view that in Scripture and Jewish literature this term does not include "pre-betrothal, non-commercial, non-cultic heterosexual intercourse" (Malina 10–17). The high value placed on virginity for marriage in Scripture and in at least some of the surrounding culture, however, counters such an understanding of *porneia* (see Jensen 161–84). Philo's writings demonstrate that it was first-century Jewish practice, or at least the ideal, for both men and women to be virgins at marriage (*Spec.* 3.64; *Jos.* 6.163). Within the Pauline corpus, the discussion of marriage in 1 Cor 7:8–16, 25–40 assumes that sexual abstinence and marriage are the only alternatives for Christians. Given that Colossians is within the Pauline tradition, it seems clear that *porneia* here refers to any sexual intercourse other than that with one's own spouse within marriage.

"Uncleanness," the second vice mentioned in v. 5, has the cultic meaning of being unprepared to enter the presence of God in much of the LXX and some New Testament texts. In these contexts, "uncleanness" does not always entail sin. Within Judaism, contact with a corpse brings uncleanness, but this contact may be the result of proper care and preparation of a parent for burial. In that case, obeying the command to honor one's parents may require the child to become unclean. But in the context of a vice list in which it follows "fornication," "uncleanness" does refer to sin, specifically to immoral sexual conduct. Within the Pauline corpus, this alternative meaning appears perhaps most clearly in Rom 1:24, but 2 Cor 12:21; Gal 5:19; Eph 4:19; and 1 Thess 4:7 also associate "fornication" with "uncleanness." Though the range of sexual conduct that the term includes here remains unclear, "uncleanness" provides an important angle from which to view sexual ethics. Since "uncleanness" commonly has a cultic meaning, its use suggests a connection between sexual ethics and religious ethics that was uncommon in first-century religions other than Judaism.

The association of ritual purity with sexual ethics may suggest that Colossians views the gathering of the church as the creation of a sacred space. Ancient worshipers thought the gods were more immediately present and accessible in temple precincts and similar sacred spaces. If Colossians sees the gathered church as a sacred space, those entering it must be "clean," ready to enter the presence of God. As the writer defines it here, improper sexual behavior disqualifies one from entering the presence of God. This use of language associated

with ritual purity also suggests that the church's holiness includes both its conduct and its identity as the place set apart where the presence of God resides.

"Passion" (*pathos*), the third vice of v. 5, is a broad term that designates
either healthy emotions and states of mind or harmful emotions. Aristotle structures his discussion of *pathos* by pairs, with one state of mind being good and
the other harmful (*Rhet.* 2.1–11). In the New Testament, however, this term
appears only two other times (Rom 1:26; 1 Thess 4:5), and in both it refers to
sinful sexual desire. Given that it appears in a vice list in which both preceding
elements concern sexual conduct, "passion" is another sexual vice. Its juxtaposition with the following sin on the list confirms this understanding. The
inclusion of "passion" suggests that believers must avoid not only acts of sexual immorality, but also illicit desire.

The fourth vice, "evil desire," also refers to sexual desire. While the noun
"desire" (*epithymia*) has a wide range of meanings, even in the New Testament,[21]
the context suggests this specific meaning. The addition of the modifier "evil"
shows that the more-neutral understandings of "desire" are not in view here. Furthermore, *epithymia* is combined with *pathos* (passion) in 1 Thess 4:5 to express
the idea of "passionate lust." *Epithymia* is also associated with "uncleanness" in
Rom 1:24, where the primary sins Paul has in mind are sexual. Perhaps the vices
in Col 3:5 are becoming broader as the list continues (Lightfoot 211), but there
is little distinction between passion (*pathos*) and desire (*epithymia*) in this passage. These terms are virtually synonymous in this context (Barth and Blanke
403–4); both point to illicit sexual thought and desire. The requirement that
believers banish evil desires parallels the demand that Jesus makes about sexual
conduct in the Sermon on the Mount, where he interprets the command against
adultery by saying that it includes lust (Matt 5:27–30).

After the first four vices have addressed sexual misconduct, the list seems to
take a sharp turn with the final sin, covetousness. But perhaps the turn is not a
radical break; after all, among the things one is commanded not to covet in the
Decalogue is the neighbor's wife (Exod 20:17). This connection perhaps suggests why this would have seemed to be a reasonable member of this vice list.
Furthermore, the two previous vices involved illegitimate desires, just as covetousness does. Still, there is a shift in attention to greediness. Greediness
encompasses a wider range of inordinate desires than those involving sex and
money. In Aristotle, one may be greedy for honor, for example, as well (*Eth.
Nic.* 9.8.1168b; cf. Barth and Blanke 404). *Pleonexia* denotes that insatiable
inner desire for more, a greediness that leads to committing evil deeds
(G. Delling, *TDNT* 6:272; cf. BDAG 824). While moralists outside Christian-

---

21. E.g., in Luke 22:15 *epithymia* is used to express Jesus' desire to eat the Passover with the
disciples and in John 8:44 to speak of the "will" of the Father. Broader meanings are also found
within the Pauline corpus (e.g., Rom 7:7, 8; Phil 1:23; 1 Thess 2:17).

ity and Judaism condemned greediness, Paul cites it as one of the damaging results of humans refusing to honor God (Rom 1:29).

Colossians defines greediness as idolatry. The term "idolatry" (*eidōlolatria*) appears almost exclusively within Jewish and Christian sources (Bevere 202; LSJM [483] cites only New Testament and early Christian occurrences in its entry for this word). Within Jewish and Christian writings, it is a derogatory term for the religious practices and beliefs of polytheism (see BDAG 280). It would make little sense for participants to call their own rites the worship of statues. Many, perhaps most, polytheists had a more sophisticated understanding of sacrifice and the presence of gods at sacrifices and in images and temples than Jewish and Christian sources attribute to them. For example, polytheists did not identify the god with the statue standing in a temple. The worshipers at these altars would have used language such as *hierothytos* ("sacrificed") to refer to their offerings to a god. Derogatory descriptions of pagan worship are rooted in the prophetic tradition of Israel, where the prophets parodied those practices with the aim of turning Israel away from them (e.g., 1 Kgs 18:25–29; Hab 2:18–19).[22] Paul and other Jews in the church retained this polemical and ironic term to refer to the worship of various beings that others deemed gods. Colossians adopts the term "idolatry" and thereby participates in this polemic.

Various Jewish texts relate greed and idolatry (e.g., *T. Jud.* 19.1; Philo, *Spec.* 1.23–27; 1QpHab 6.1; 8.11–12; see Bevere 202–3).[23] Colossians may equate avarice or greediness with idolatry because greed puts the object sought in the place of God; it gives the thing sought more priority in one's life than God has (Thurston 52). This metaphorical understanding ranks covetousness among the most serious sins. Since the writer defines it as idolatry, perhaps he sees covetousness as the source of the previously mentioned sins (so Aletti 225; Barth and Blanke 404), though that may overinterpret its placement at the end of the vice list. Still, by tying avarice to idolatry, Colossians makes it one of the deep causes of human sin.

After composing the vice list under the rubric of things one must kill in the "earthly members," Colossians adds a second reason for rejecting these practices (contra Barth and Blanke 405): God's judgment comes on those who practice such things. Within the Pauline corpus, statements about coming judgment often appear in conjunction with vice lists.[24] Just as Paul does in 1 Cor 6:9–10,

---

22. Revelation 9:20–21 takes up the same motif.

23. Some Jewish writings also relate sexual immorality, the theme of this Colossians vice list, to idolatry. See Gen 38:21; Exod 32:6; Deut 23:17; Wis 14:12; *T. Reu.* 4.6; *T. Jud.* 23.1. See the discussion of Lincoln (642), who cites these texts for such a connection.

24. Judgment is referred to explicitly in Rom 1; 1 Cor 6:9–10; Gal 5:19–21; Eph 4:31–5:5. There are also intimations of judgment in Rom 13:11–14; 1 Cor 5:9–13; Titus 3:3–7. No mention of judgment appears in conjunction with the vice lists of 2 Cor 12:20; 1 Tim 1:9–10; 6:4–5; 2 Tim 3:2–5.

so here Colossians reminds its readers that they were once such people themselves, but now they have adopted a quite different identity. If the gift of this new identity does not sufficiently motivate believers to ethical living, the threat of God's judgment adds a reason to conform one's life to the proper standard.

Colossians calls God's condemnation of those who practice the vices of v. 5 "wrath." First-century readers were certainly accustomed to thinking of gods as vengeful and dangerously capricious, but that is not what "wrath" means in this context. Although it is threatening, New Testament authors do not view God's condemnation as anything beyond what is just. Justice is an essential characteristic of God and one that must be evident in God's judgment even of those who practice vice. Outside of Romans, the Pauline corpus contains few references to the wrath of God: twelve of the fourteen occurrences of *orgē* ("wrath") in the undisputed letters are in Romans—and one of the other two appearances is in a passage that many consider an interpolation (1 Thess 2:16). Within Romans, *orgē* twice refers to human anger (Rom 2:8; 12:19) and twice to the government exercising judgment on behalf of God (13:4, 5). One of Paul's assumptions about divine wrath is made explicit in Rom 3:5, where he rejects out of hand the idea that God's "wrath" could be unjust. So Paul sees God's "wrath" as God's just condemnation of sin. That is the understanding of wrath in Col 3 as well; it is God's fitting reaction to the evils exemplified in the vice list. This judgment of God, then, is not capricious or unjust.

Colossians uses the present-tense verb "is coming" (*erchetai*) in relation to the wrath of God. The present tense may indicate that the author thinks the exercise of God's wrath has begun and is already active in the lives of persons who engage in these vices. This makes the degradation of one's self in performing the vice part of God's punishment for the sin. This is the kind of judgment of which Paul speaks in Rom 1:18–32. In Col 3:5–11, however, future judgment is the dominant idea (see BDF 323; New Testament examples of this use of the present tense include Matt 17:11 and John 4:21). Though Colossians has paid more attention to the present aspect of eschatology, with its explicit mention of the Parousia, 3:4 has shifted attention to the future aspect. Moreover, the surrounding verses do not allude to the ways God's wrath shows itself in the lives of the disobedient. Verse 6, then, seems to be a second reference to the eschatological future.

The phrase "upon the children of disobedience" may be an interpolation. The textual evidence for identifying this phrase as a later intrusion into the text is comparable to that for seeing it as original (see note b with the translation above). If it is original, its identification of nonbelievers as "children of disobedience" shows that the author is thinking in eschatological categories. This suggests that he has future judgment in mind in the first part of the verse as well. Yet even if it is an interpolation, an early reader understood the text to point to future judgment. This also supports reading the reference to coming wrath as a future event.

Retaining the phrase as an original part of the text seems to make v. 7 flow more smoothly (see the comment on v. 7 below), but this phrase is then the only place in Colossians where the writer puts unbelievers in such a category.[25] Still, this description of nonbelievers fits well within the dualism characteristic of apocalyptic thought and also fits well in a literary context in which images of dying to an old life and living a new one and distinctions between the old and new self and between things above and below have shaped the discussion.

If the phrase "children of disobedience" is original, it also helps the writer avoid a direct threat of judgment against the readers. Since a basic problem addressed by the letter is that the visionaries pass judgment on the readers, the writer may have wanted to avoid a straightforward threat of judgment, even while reminding them of accountability to God. He accomplishes this by making nonbelievers the immediate object of judgment.

[7] Verses 7–8 reintroduce the contrast already seen in 2:12–13 between the readers' former lives and their current life in Christ: formerly they belonged among those on whom God's judgment is coming, but now they have died to that life and have been raised with Christ. The metaphor shifts in vv. 8–11 from death and resurrection to the changing of clothes and the changing of identities. Again, the different identities entail different ways of living.

The two clauses of verse 7 are parallel and form a chiasm. I render the language of the verse more literally here than in my translation to make the structure of the chiasm clearer:

Among whom (*en hois*)
  you walked
    then[26]
    when
  you lived
in them (*en toutois*).

The first phrase describes the readers' former lives, saying that they belonged among those who act in these ways; the second says that they characteristically participated in the vices of v. 5. Both the structure of the verse and its repetition highlight the contrast between the readers' former lives and their new, resurrection existence. The central elements of the chiasm ("then"/"when") point to the distinction between their previous manner of life and the demands of their new identity in Christ.

---

25. Hay (125) sees the phrase as an interpolation in part because this is the only place in Colossians that includes such a separation from nonbelievers. Among others who see it as an interpolation are Pokorný (167) and Harris (148).

26. I render this term (*pote*) "previously" in my translation.

The writer uses *peripateō* (to walk) to speak of the conduct of the readers' lives. In the Pauline corpus this verb always denotes manner of life, sometimes described broadly (e.g., Rom 6:4, "walk [live] in newness of life"; 2 Cor 5:7, "we walk [live] by faith"), sometimes with a specific act in mind (e.g., 2 Cor 4:2, "not walking [living] in trickery" [my trans.]). In Col 3:7 the statement seems rather broad: they lived among, and as one of, those people whose lives are characterized by the vices of v. 5. Although this may seem exaggerated, it fits well with the dramatic language of death and resurrection that is so prominent in this section of the letter.

The adverbial particle "previously" (*pote*, more literally, "then") is the last word in the first half of v. 7. The first word of the second half of the verse is the temporal particle *hote*, "when." Putting these two temporal particles together at the center of this verse emphasizes that these sins were part of the former manner of life, which believers have left behind; it thereby sets up the contrast that v. 8 then makes more explicit. These sins were part of their former lives, but they no longer have a place in the life they now live in Christ. This affirmation demonstrates that rejecting the visionaries' regulations, regulations that do not restrain sin (2:23), does not mean that believers have no moral code by which they must live. Their dealings with sin must be over.

The second half of v. 7 makes much the same point as the first half but uses somewhat different language. In the second half, the readers "lived" (*ezēte*) in that old manner of life. It may be that *peripateō* (to walk/live) in the first part of the verse points to behavior or practice, while *zaō* (to live) in the second part designates the condition in which readers lived or the sphere they inhabited (Lightfoot 213; Harris 149; cf. Barth and Blanke 406). The different tenses of the verbs may suggest this distinction. *Periepatēsate* ("you walked") is an aorist that simply relates an event or, as in this case, a state of being at a certain moment; *ezēte* is in the imperfect tense, a tense that typically denotes ongoing action. So it may signal that these sins were "a sustained way of life" (Dunn 217). But since *peripateō* usually designates a manner of life rather than a series of individual acts in the Pauline corpus (see above), it probably does not signify less than a constant way of living here. Therefore, it probably has a meaning quite similar to that of *zaō* in this verse.

Despite the difference in the verbs' tenses, the two parts of v. 7 are basically a tautology. This is particularly the case if "children of disobedience" (v. 6) is an interpolation (Pokorný 167). Then the first pronoun (*hois*) of v. 7 has the vices of v. 5 as its antecedent, and the verse emphasizes the extent to which these vices were a part of the readers' lives. The sense would be, "These vices characterized your manner of life when such acts defined your existence." But if "children of disobedience" is an original part of the letter, the first pronoun (*hois*) probably refers to them rather than to the vices of v. 5. In this case, the first half of v. 7 says that the readers formerly belonged to the group on whom the judgment of God is coming, while the second part says that the named vices were a constant part of their lives in that former time. The verse's meaning would then be, "When you belonged among the children of disobedience, these vices defined your existence." In that state, their behavior was suited to their identity. Since it is somewhat more likely that "children of disobedience" is original (see the comment above on v. 6), the first phrase probably identifies the readers as former members of that group. This understanding makes the verse less redundant, but no less emphatic. Thus, by recalling that the readers were among those destined to receive God's wrath, Colossians reminds them that they have passed from their former state of existence into a different life, which requires different behavior.

[8–11] Verse 8 sets out a direct contrast with the state of existence described in v. 7 and continues the author's exposition of the ethical demands of new life in Christ. Verses 8–11 delineate further what the readers must leave behind and why those old ways of living are incompatible with their new identity in Christ. In Christ, God has granted believers a new self that demands a new way of living.

The contrast in v. 8 begins with the phrase "But now." These words introduce a broader contrast than the personal or individual change that happened to each person at baptism. In the context, "now" refers to the eschatological change that came into the world in Christ. As noted above (see 1:22), in the Pauline corpus "but now" and similar expressions commonly point to eschatological realities. In 3:8–11, the author asserts that the old vices must be left behind because Christ has opened a new reality. Believers live in this new reality and thus must conform their lives to it. This eschatological contrast appears in the theme-setting section of 1:21–23, where v. 22 connects reconciliation to God with guiltlessness in judgment and therefore with holy living. When 3:8 echoes that eschatological contrast, it focuses on rejecting the evil practices of the old life, but vv. 9–11 widen the contrast so that it is between spheres of life, between the "children of disobedience" and those who put on the eschatological "new self."

Verse 8 expresses the personal appropriation of this change in eschatological realms of existence in a surprising way: rather than speaking of the new life as a possession given the believer, as in 1:21–22, the author marks the new existence with an imperative, "Put away!" In the hortatory context of chapter 3, emphasis falls on what believers must do in this new life. The gift of this new existence includes the demand to rid oneself of behavior that is inappropriate to the new life in Christ. As part of the transfer from their place among those "children of disobedience" (the people whose lives are characterized by the vices of v. 5), believers must purge their lives of the behaviors that characterized that old life.

The presence of the pronoun "you" in vv. 7 and 8 emphasizes the readers' own participation in both the former vice-filled life and the new resurrection life. This pronoun's repetition in v. 8 makes it emphatic. Given the nature of the dispute in which the Colossians are engaged, exhortations about the specific vices mentioned in v. 8 may be particularly relevant. So the repetition of the pronouns ensures that the readers understand that these vices are unacceptable for them, even amidst a serious dispute within the church.

The immediate object of the imperative "put way" is "all these things." Though this "all" may include the vice lists of both vv. 5 and 8 (Lightfoot 214; Barth and Blanke 406), it probably refers specifically only to the list in v. 8 (Moule 118; O'Brien 187). Still, "all" intimates a wider scope than just the five vices of v. 8, because the next verse speaks more generally of the practices associated with the "old self."

The focus of the vice list in v. 8 is not as narrow as that of the list in v. 5. While all the vices in v. 5, with the possible exception of greediness, were associated with sexual behavior, those in v. 8 concern behavior within the context of the community (see the comment below on v. 9). There is a case to be made that the vices of v. 5 derive from common Jewish accusations about Gentiles, but no such case can be made for the list in v. 8 (contra Dunn 218, followed by Bevere 213–14). The vices in v. 8 include conduct that other moralists of the first century would also have condemned.

The first two vices mentioned in v. 8 are "wrath" (*orgē*) and "anger" (*thymos*). These two are virtually synonymous (Pokorný 168; Barth and Blanke 407), as their appearance together in the LXX to signify intense anger shows (e.g., Exod 32:12; Jer 32:37; cited in BDAG 461). If any distinction can be made, *orgē* may denote a more settled emotion, while *thymos* designates an outburst of anger. This distinction appears in Diogenes Laertius (7.114) and Seneca (*Ira* 2.36; cited by Lincoln 643; others who see this distinction include Lightfoot 214; O'Brien 187). *Orgē* can also, however, signify outbursts of anger (examples cited in BDAG 720–21 include 2 Macc 4:40; Ignatius, *Eph.* 10.2). Both terms are also used to speak of condemnation by God (see the comment above on v. 5; see also Exod 32:12; Lev 26:24; Jer 32:37; Rev 14:8, 10, 19; 15:1, 7; 16:1, 19; 19:15). Given how similar these words are, the writer has probably included both to make his rejection of such attitudes and actions emphatic.

While denying wrath a place in the lives of believers, Colossians has given the wrath of God a legitimate place in the preceding sentence. The difference between the wrath of God and that of humans is not in the words used to describe them. (Both verses use *orgē*.) Rather, human wrath refers to an inappropriate, hate-filled, and in some cases (though not necessarily) physically violent reaction to others in the community. The behaviors listed in the second half of the list flow from such an attitude and comportment. When Colossians and other New Testament writers speak of God's wrath, they do not envision this sort of overreaction but rather God's just condemnation of sin (see the comment above on v. 6). They envision God in personal-enough terms that God does become angry in the face of the persecution of believers. Yet this anger does not lead God to violate God's own justice and mercy.

The third vice listed in v. 8, *kakia*, is a broad term that has the general meaning of "wickedness." In the context of a list that has the life of the community of believers in view, perhaps it is best understood as malice toward others. "Spite" is probably too narrow a meaning here (contra Barth and Blanke 407); *kakia* signifies any evil intent toward others that wishes or works them harm. It appears in this list because such an attitude harms the church's fellowship. Given that two vices involving believers' manner of speaking to and about one another follow it, malice that expresses itself through speech may be the primary focus. But the meaning of *kakia* is broader than evil that manifests itself in matters of speech. Believers must root out all sorts of ill will that promotes harming others.

The fourth vice, "slander," is the first explicit reference to sins of speech in v. 8. When it appears in the New Testament, the term used here, *blasphēmia*, usually refers to blasphemy against God. But the context of this vice list and the exhortation that follows in v. 9 suggest that *blasphēmia* in this verse means speaking ill of other people. Slandering or speaking disrespectfully (BDAG 178) of others is an outward expression of the wrath, anger, and malice that come before it in the list. Such speech is clearly antithetical to living as a community that manifests the life of Christ.

The fifth and final vice of this list is obscene and "abusive speech" (*aischrologia*), a New Testament *hapax legomenon*. In other literature it refers to telling obscene stories and to using obscene and abusive language to denigrate others (LSJM 43; BDAG 29). Such language necessarily damages the life of the community because it shows a lack of proper valuing of others.

The writer appends "from your mouths" to "abusive speech." This prepositional phrase modifies this last vice, not all those in the list. It does not attach to the whole list in part because the first three vices are not primarily about speech (Harris 150) and in part because that would impose too narrow a limit on the meanings of those first three vices. Wrath, anger, and malice are destructive in ways that reach beyond speech. MacDonald (137) may be correct that the addition of "out of your mouths" relates the exhortation to the ancient Mediterranean concern about what goes in and out of one's mouth, because it is a boundary of the body. If so, then Colossians adds a culturally powerful sanction to support the prohibition against obscene and abusive language.

At the end of the vice list in v. 8, the attention to sins of speech leads to the opening exhortation of v. 9: "Do not lie to one another." This command is not simply a summary of the preceding vice list (contra Pokorný 168), because that would limit the reference of the first three vices too severely. This reference to lying may, however, be broader than it first appears. In Rev 22:15, lying includes a wider range of evils than simply telling someone a falsehood. There it means acting falsely in general (Schweizer 193–94). If Col 3:9 has in mind the more general idea of acting falsely, this command could well apply to the whole vice list.

This command about dealing falsely with others is given sharper focus in another way; it exhorts readers to be honest "with one another." This phrase makes the church the primary context of this command. This orientation toward relations within the church has probably also been the major bent of the preceding vice list. The internal problems the church is experiencing highlight the need for instruction about intrachurch relations. There would be more than a little opportunity for dissimulation in the small groups that composed a city's house churches when sharp differences were being argued and when some were claiming spiritual experiences to establish their place in the community. Such debates strain relationships and allegiances. So a command not to lie or be false with others in the church is particularly appropriate as a conclusion to the vice list of v. 8, a list including sins that damage both one's inner life and communal life (Thurston 52).

This specific reference of the command "do not lie to one another" does not explicitly assume that it is permissible to lie to nonbelievers, but it may permit a different stance toward nonbelievers. Given the social circumstances in which most church members find themselves, the focus on truthful relations *within the church* may allow for some dissimulation in dealings with outsiders. Social inferiors (e.g., wives, children, and slaves) might find it necessary to deceive, or at least not to be totally forthcoming, about their membership in the church and their participation in its activities. Concerns about negotiating one's life in such a hostile environment were present for the early church, as for anyone else who would worship only God. So the explicit directive not to be false "to one another" may allow some space for negotiation with the surrounding world, which was hostile to the church and its worship of the one God. (See further the discussion of 3:18–4:1.)

The second part of v. 9 gives a direct theological basis for the exhortations in vv. 8–9a. Believers must rid themselves of those sorts of behaviors and attitudes because they have "taken off the old self." Verse 10 expands on this theme and continues to supply the basis for the exhortations of vv. 8–9a; the following section (vv. 12–17) then delineates further what "putting on the new self" means. Verses 9 and 10 provide bases for the commands of vv. 8–9a with causal participles. Though one could construe these participles as imperatives (Lightfoot 214–15; Lohse 141; Pokorný 168–69), because they appear between imperatives (vv. 8 and 12) and have some similarities with the imperative participles in Eph 4:24, "taking off" (*apekdysamenoi*) and "putting on" (*endysamenoi*) are not imperatives in Col 3:9–10. In this section, Colossians alternates between exhortations and their grounds. This pattern is obvious in 3:1, 2–3, 5–7, 13, 15. In these places Colossians supports its ethical demands with reminders of what believers have become or received in Christ. As v. 7 intimates that believers now possess a life that no longer includes the vices in v. 5, so v. 9 says explicitly that they have taken off that old way of being. Furthermore, the assertion that believers have taken off the old person supplies the indicative that one expects after the "but now" at the beginning of v. 8, where we find an imperative instead (cf. Abbott 283–84; Harris 151; O'Brien 188–89; Aletti 229). In this way vv. 8–9 tie together the gift and demand of faith in a most intimate way; how believers act is part of who they have been made in Christ.

The affirmation that they have "taken off" the old self also provides the transition from the more general term "put away" (*apotithēmi*) in v. 8 to the imagery of clothing, which introduces the exhortations of vv. 12–17. The causal participles ("taking off . . . putting on"),[27] then, ground the preceding and following exhortations. So this clothing metaphor creates a direct connection between the exhortations of vv. 8–9a and the affirmation of the new life that believers have been granted, and simultaneously prepares for what follows. Again, this intertwining of sections is characteristic of Colossians (see the comments on 3:1–4).

Believers must rid themselves of sin because their old existence was stripped off in baptism. Colossians uses the imagery of changing clothes for the transformation that happens to believers in baptism. Though there is no evidence that the practice of nude baptism and the accompanying change into different clothes afterward began until the mid-second century C.E. (Lincoln 643), the imagery is sufficiently powerful that it became a part of the rite. The language of changing clothes may not sound as dramatic as that of dying and being raised, but it was a powerful image in the first century. By Roman law, people of different social classes were required to wear different sorts of clothing. For example, some types of tunics or ornamentation of tunics could be worn only by those in the senatorial class, and different clothing was prescribed for single and married people (references to such differences appear in Suetonius, *Aug.* 35.2; Appian, *Bel. civ.* 2.120; Livy, *Hist.* 27.8.9; Dio Cassius, *Rom. Hist.* 51.20.2; see Winter 42–49, 82–94, 99–102). Such regulations may not have been as clear or as strict everywhere in the empire, but some marks of distinction had spread eastward. So when the recipients of Colossians hear the language of taking off old clothing and putting on new, it is a powerful metaphor that symbolizes a change in *identities*.

There are no extra-Christian examples of this metaphor for changing identities through religious experience or adoption of a philosophy. Although some interpreters cite Pyrrho as one who uses this metaphor (e.g., Dunn 220), this is

---

27. My translation above reflects the causal function of these participles by rendering them "because you have taken off . . . and put on."

not a direct parallel because Pyrrho writes of how difficult it is to get rid of old practices rather than of coming into possession of a new life (Barth and Blanke 411 n. 66).[28] The image, then, seems to be a creation of the early church.

What believers have put off is "the old self," that is, the self that lived in and was characterized by, and even identified with, sin. This is the state of existence described in v. 7. It was an existence in which "the whole personality" was "ruled by sin" (O'Brien 190).

In this context it is difficult to translate the word *anthrōpos* in the phrase "old self." Many translations render it "man," but *anthrōpos* is not usually a gender-specific word in Greek. Though it can be used for a male, it is more commonly a reference to humans without reference to gender. It is rendered "self" here to emphasize the depth of the transformation that the image expresses. But the thought of personal, individual transformation must not overshadow the corporate element of this new identity. As v. 10 makes explicit, believers have been joined to a new humanity. In the context of the questions that the visionaries have raised about the salvation and forgiveness of some members of the church and in such close proximity to the preceding community-oriented vices (v. 8), the corporate implications of *anthrōpos* are important. Hay (126) expresses the dual nature of the meaning of this term by translating it "being." We retain "self" here to denote the personal nature of the transformation, a transformation that entails participation in that larger corporate and eschatological reality (see v. 10).

Stripping off the old self requires a change in the way the believer lives, for taking off that self includes taking off its practices. As in v. 7, the old way of being is identified with the practices and attitudes that characterized it. Again, the relationship between manner of living and acceptance of God's gift of new life could not be closer, since even the affirmation of the gift of new life includes a reminder of that connection.

Not only have believers stripped off what identified them with the sphere ruled by sin; they have also "put on the new self" (v. 10). Conversion implies more than putting away old ways of acting and speaking; it includes receiving a new identity. The language of changing clothing continues to express this reception of a new identity. Believers have put on a new identity and so have received a new life, with the privileges and expectations commensurate with that identity.

---

28. See, however, the uses of this metaphor in Kim 25–69. He finds precedents in the priestly vestments used at the temple, in God's clothing of Old Testament characters (e.g., Gideon clothed with the spirit of God, in Judg 6:34; the high priest Joshua exchanges filthy clothes for festal attire, in Zech 3:3–5), and similar usage in some apocalyptic works (e.g., *1 En.* 62.15–16; *2 En.* 22.8–10). These latter uses, however, describe the future eschatological mode of existence, not the taking on of a new identity.

The word "put on" (*endyō*) is probably not yet formally related to baptism in the tradition, but baptism is certainly the point of transition that the writer has in mind. One of the primary ways Colossians has assured its readers of their place with God has been its interpretation of baptism. *Endyō* is also related to baptism in Gal 3:27, where Paul asserts that believers have "put on Christ" in baptism. This verb is not common in the Pauline corpus, appearing only eleven times in the undisputed letters.[29] Of those uses of the verb, only Gal 3:27 affirms the present possession of new life as an accomplished fact. Notably, both Gal 3:27 and Col 3:10, the two passages that assert current possession of the new life, have baptism in view. Verse 10, then, gives further attention to the meaning of baptism, asserting that believers have already received their new existence.

Colossians 3:10 differs from Rom 13:14, an oft-cited parallel (e.g., Schweizer 195; Dunn 221), in that it assures the readers that they have received the new life, while Romans exhorts them to put on Christ by ethical living. The better parallel with Rom 13 is the imperative of Col 3:12, where readers are given a similar exhortation. But Col 3:10 is a reminder of what believers have been given in baptism; they have undergone a transformation in their nature. Baptism is the place where they appropriate the eschatological new life that was initiated by Christ and that entails being conformed to his image. In the context of this letter, the claim that believers possess the new self includes the expectation that their lives conform to the standards and practices of the writer's exhortations because they have already received a new identity that does and must determine their lives. They do not adopt these practices to attain forgiveness or visions, or any other gift, from God.

Believers have not only received a new identity and life; that new self is "continually being renewed." The present tense suggests that this renewal is a continual process. Furthermore, "being renewed" (*anakainoumenon*) is in the passive voice, so the renewal comes from outside the believer. God is the source of the renewal that maintains and strengthens the believer's new self.

The combination of possessing a new self and needing it to be renewed expresses the eschatological tension in which believers live. They possess a measure of the eschatological gifts but continue to wait for their consummation. This statement provides further evidence that the eschatology of Colossians is not fully realized. In the face of the other teachers' arguments that believers need further experiences to gain God's favor, the writer claims that believers already possess eschatological blessings. However, the recognition that believers continue to struggle and need renewal tempers those claims. The believer does possess the new self, but something still awaits the end time.

---

29. Of those occurrences, five refer to putting on the new body after death (and four of these are in 1 Cor 15:53–54, the other in 2 Cor 5:3) and two speak of putting on armor as a metaphor for struggling against the powers of evil (Rom 13:12; Eph 6:11).

Verse 10 proclaims that in the time of struggle between initiation into that new reality and possession of its fullness, God renews that life in believers and enables them to live that new life. Thus, God empowers the believer to refrain from the behavior of the old self and to adhere to the life described in more detail in vv. 12–17.

Verse 10 says this renewal of the new self takes place in two ways: "in knowledge" and "in accord with the image of the one who created it."[30] When the writer makes knowledge one of the things by which the new self is renewed, he is picking up a theme that has run throughout the letter. This theme was sounded as early as the mentions of the "truth" in the thanksgiving (1:5–6) and became explicit in 1:9, where the writer says knowledge is the first thing that Paul prays for the Colossians to receive. Perhaps this theme counters the claims that the visionaries are making about the knowledge of heavenly things that they attain in their visions (Lightfoot 215; Pokorný 169; Thurston 53). In v. 10 the writer does not specify the object of this knowledge. It may be Christ, God, God's will, or more broadly, heavenly things. If the reference to knowledge has the other teachers in view, then the broader meaning is more likely.

Just as the visionaries claim to have spiritual experiences that bring them renewal through knowledge of heavenly things and thereby a closer relationship with God, so Colossians says that God grants this renewal through knowledge—but this happens through the believers' participation in the new life received at baptism without those visions. The preposition *eis* (in) may indicate that the renewal brings believers into fuller knowledge (MacDonald 138). Thus the author claims that God continually grants heavenly knowledge and spiritual renewal to believers; they do not have to attain exalted spiritual experience to receive it.

The renewal of the new self is patterned after "the image of the one who created it."[31] As the new self comes into being through resurrection with Christ, so now life in that sphere is renewed in accord with the character and nature of Christ, the image of God. In language echoing 1:15, now 3:10 names Christ as the paradigm for believers' renewal (Harris 153). Thus they are always being brought into greater conformity to Christ. We might even say with Schweizer (198) that believers are "being assimilated" into Christ.

Throughout Colossians, God remains the primary actor and Christ the one through whom God acts. In the Pauline corpus, God is always the Creator. Even in the poetic material of Col 1:15–20, where Christ is clearly the agent of cre-

30. Meyer (354) understands the construction of the sentence differently. He argues that the latter phrase modifies "knowledge" so that it is knowledge of the image of God that renews the person. However, it seems more probable in this context, where identity with Christ has been prominent, that the author wants to assert that the new self is renewed in the image of God.

31. As Harris (153) notes, the *auton* ("him [it]") at the end of v. 10 refers to the new self, not to Christ or humanity.

ation, he remains the "image of God" through whom God acts. That understanding is also at work in 3:10; God is the actor in the creation of the new self just as God was the actor in the original creation. Still, God acts—and is known—through Christ.

The expression "image of the one who created it" echoes Gen 1:26, where God creates humanity in God's image. But this echo need not suggest that the primary thought of Colossians is that the new self, in its individual and corporate manifestations, is humanity restored to the nature intended in creation (contra Lincoln 644). Rather, Colossians refers to a new eschatological reality that goes beyond restoration of the original glory of humanity. The reality of which Colossians speaks includes participation in the resurrection of Christ and the new kind of life initiated with the acts of God in Christ.

In a similar vein, this passage (like others in Colossians) probably does not reflect a second-Adam Christology (contra Moule 119; Bruce 272–73). If this christological rubric functions at all in Colossians, it remains implicit. Colossians does have an important sense of the corporate nature of existence in Christ and does understand the new life as an existing reality into which believers are admitted. But there is no evidence that these affirmations are rooted in the notion of Christ as the second Adam who restores humanity. The focus of Colossians is on Christ as the means by which forgiveness is received and the one with whom believers identify, and therefore the one through whom they gain access to heavenly and eschatological realities.

The corporate nature of the new self comes to the fore again in v. 11, and does so forcefully. Colossians asserts the oneness of all believers by citing a baptismal tradition. Paul cites forms of this tradition in Gal 3:27–28 and 1 Cor 12:13. The lists of opposites differ in each citation. Galatians is the only place in which male and female are included among the matched pairs, and Colossians has the only opposition of Scythian and barbarian. The absence of the male-female element of the tradition does not necessarily indicate that the Pauline communities were experiencing problems with women seeking leadership and acting in other ways that violated cultural norms, particularly since this line of reasoning must assume that slaves did not create such problems because they are mentioned (MacDonald 146; Barth and Blanke 415; contra Lincoln 644). MacDonald (146) suggests that the male-female pair may be left out of Colossians because inclusion of language that appears to diminish the importance of these opposites might be heard as support for ascetic practices such as those the visionaries were advocating.[32] Moreover, the baptismal tradition may not be a completely fixed liturgical piece at this point (Dunn 223). In this case, writers may alter the tradition to best suit their letters' occasions.

---

32. See further her citation of H. Attridge's work on *Zostrianos* (NHC 8.1), a work in which visionary experiences lead to ascetic practices and are combined with a rejection of being female.

Alternatively, the differences may reflect the variety of ways in which such liturgies were known and used.

The insertion of this baptismal tradition is unexpected in this context. It interrupts the flow of thought, which revolves around the metaphor of changing clothes. Furthermore, ethnic and social distinctions have not been an issue to this point in the letter. The clothing metaphor's connection to baptism, however, may have suggested use of the tradition. Since clothing was so important in matters of social and economic status, its use as a metaphor for changing identities may have reminded the writer of this tradition, which makes all identities secondary to being in Christ. The image of the new creation could also call this tradition to mind because it envisions a world so different from the one in which believers currently live.

Verse 11 begins with "where" (*hopou*)[33] rather than with a relative pronoun, as in the phrase "in which" (cf. vv. 6, 7). This adverbial particle refers back to the new self that believers have put on (v. 10) and implies that believers have been brought into an existing reality. Such a way of speaking fits with the other spatial language that Colossians uses for eschatological realities. It indicates that the new self is a corporate and an eschatological realm. Believers have been incorporated into a reality in which the normal distinctions made in the world no longer have primary significance. This conception of the new self stands in tension with the metaphor of "putting on" clothes. The tension in the language reflects the dual emphases of vv. 8–11. In these verses, ethics is both an individual and a community matter, and both aspects must receive proper attention for the picture to be complete. Throughout these verses, attention shifts from one emphasis to the other: each person is to rid oneself of vices, but the vices named affect community life; each person is individually clothed with the new person, but that new person is a corporate entity. The paragraph ends with an emphasis on the corporate nature of the believers' life in Christ.

An emphatic "there is no" (*ouk eni*) precedes the list of four contrasting pairs in v. 11. These words apply to each of the following pairs, though they appear only at the beginning of the list. Even this emphatic way of stating the matter does not mean that the differences among believers cease to exist.[34] Such distinctions do not cease to exist, and their importance is not denied. The point here (and in Paul's use of this baptismal tradition in 1 Cor 12:13; Gal 3:27–28) is that such differences are all secondary to the primary identity that believers have taken on in Christ. The idea of oneness in Colossians is not sameness. Throughout the Pauline corpus the diversity of believers is celebrated, even

33. In my translation, I fill out the meaning of *hopou* ("where") by rendering it "in this new creation."

34. Many interpreters seem to understand this tradition to say that such differences have been destroyed (e.g., Lightfoot 216) or that they no longer matter (Hay 127). However, the Pauline corpus as a whole, including Colossians, seems to have a more nuanced view.

though it often caused problems. Even in Galatians, Paul does not call for all believers to be the same, but for all to recognize that being one in Christ must take precedence over all differences. It is this primacy of the believer's identity in Christ that comes to expression in Colossians as well, as the end of v. 11 shows (see below).

The first distinction whose significance has been relativized is that of "Greek and Jew." In this pair, "Greeks" stands for all non-Jews, as it does in various (mostly Jewish) writers (Acts 17:4; Rom 1:16; Josephus, *J.W.* 7.45). This is the only place in the Pauline corpus in which we find these two groups together in a formulaic statement that has Greeks mentioned before Jews. There is probably no deep theological reason behind this change (Barth and Blanke 415), yet it may represent a shift from the outlook of Romans, where Paul asserts that the gospel is for the Jews first. But the situation Romans addresses accounts, at least in part, for the emphasis the theme receives in that letter. Still, it seems less likely that Paul would have written the words in the order found in Col 3:11. On the other hand, if this word order has any significance, mention of "Greeks" first may reflect a setting in which the church (at least the one addressed) is predominantly Gentile (O'Brien 192; Hay 128). From the perspective of the early church, the distinction between Jews and Gentiles remained the most significant ethnic difference because it had such obvious implications for practice of the faith. Though that difference remains, in the eschatological reality of the "new self," neither has higher status or position.

The second division in v. 11, that between "circumcised and uncircumcised," renames the previous opposed pair. Since Colossians nowhere identifies circumcision as an issue, its mention here does not indicate that the visionaries advocate it or that the debate with them centers on whether to adopt Jewish identity markers (contra Dunn 224). The writer may see an ethnic contrast in "Greek and Jew" and a religious contrast in this second distinction (Barth and Blanke 416). The debate that Colossians addresses does involve the value of the visionaries' rituals as a means of attaining visions and securing forgiveness from God. This reference to circumcision, then, could allude to the ritual distinctions between Jews and Gentiles. If so, this contrast suggests that the visionaries' rituals offer no benefit because even such a fundamental ritual of religious and ethnic identity as circumcision is so radically relativized that it offers no advantage (MacDonald 147–48).

The third pair that Colossians gives as exemplars of the divisions overcome in Christ is "barbarians" and "Scythians." A standard interpretation of these terms has been that they are escalations of the category of the uncircumcised.[35] But this reading overlooks the list's pattern of opposing pairs. The pattern does

---

35. Lohse (144) comments that Scythians are a particularly odd sort of barbarian, and O'Brien (193) says that they are the lowest type of barbarian.

change at this point. The members of the first two pairs are separated by "and" (*kai*), while the next two pairs have their members listed with no intervening conjunctions. Since the fourth pair (slave and free), however, is obviously an opposing pair, the hearer's expectation is that barbarians and Scythians also form an opposing pair.

Various nonbiblical writers use "barbarian" and "Scythian" to refer to the most distant and strange lands and peoples, with Scythian being a broad term for those of the distant north and barbarian for those of the distant south, where there are locations which even have the name Barbaria (see *Excursus: The Scythians* below). So this pair contrasts the northern and southern reaches of the world. This contrast expands the readers' thought about how far the eschatological new person reaches. The realm into which believers have been brought by putting on the new self encompasses not only lived and experienced ethnic and ritual differences but also all people, even those at the ends of the earth. Thus the eschatological, creating act of God encompasses the whole world.

The final set of contrasting pairs is "slave" and "free." This pair draws on one of the most important social-status distinctions of the ancient world. Dio Chrysostom (15.24) described slavery as the right to use another person as a piece of property or as an animal. That right of use included making slaves sexually available to their masters. The conditions under which slaves lived depended largely on their owner's character and circumstances. While most first-century slaves could expect manumission at around thirty years of age, such matters were entirely within the owner's control. And even after manumission, owners could impose restrictions on where former slaves lived and what occupations they practiced. Perhaps the most significant thing about being freed was that it brought with it the status of being a human.[36] When the received baptismal tradition includes the categories "slave and free," it declares that not even this fundamental societal distinction has significance in Christ. Both slave and free participate equally in the new self that is made in the image of Christ.

The four pairs in the list of v. 11 include ethnic, ritual, cultural, and social differences. In the church, all the differences signaled by such distinctions have lost their significance as means of evaluating others, because believers have taken on a new identity, a new self that is constantly being formed, indeed created, to conform to the character and person of Christ.

Verse 11 concludes with a statement even more radical than the assertion that eschatological existence is patterned after Christ. In contrast to the divisions of the preceding list (the final clause is introduced with "but"), "Christ is all and is in all." Christ creates a unity that transcends all the categories in that list.

---

36. For discussion of slavery in the Greco-Roman world, see S. Scott Bartchy, "Slavery (Greco-Roman)," *ABD* 6:65–73; D. Martin 1990; Jennifer A. Glancy, *Slavery in Early Christianity* (New York: Oxford, 2002).

Christ's being and his presence in believers render all valuations that derive from the divisions just mentioned meaningless (Barth and Blanke 417; Lincoln 644); in fact, being in Christ means that believers renounce the values of the world, specifically of the Greco-Roman way of ordering the world, in favor of a different set of values (Lindemann 59).

Christ is the defining feature of the new reality, and even the syntax of the sentence puts Christ in an emphatic position: Christ is the sentence's last word. This powerful statement makes two assertions about Christ. The affirmation that Christ is all seems to claim more, and something different, from the assertion that he is sovereign over the whole of creation, the claim made so emphatically in 1:15–20. The whole created order is not in view here, but rather the new creation, the eschatological reality of the new self to which believers have been joined. It is not merely that Christ has power to rule over all things, something said of him earlier in Colossians, but that he is the "all-determining principle" of the eschatological order (Meyer 357). Christ is what makes up this new reality, and it is fully identified with him. Other identities lose their ultimacy because believers' selves, corporately and individually, are formed so deeply by Christ; all other identities and values are subsumed under that most fundamental reality.

The second claim made about Christ is that he is "in all." This assertion speaks of the presence of Christ in each person. This is the way Colossians, in which direct references to the Spirit are nearly absent (perhaps seen only in 1:8), speaks of the immediate presence of God in believers' lives. This assertion of Christ's indwelling presence adds another perspective on the believers' relationship with Christ. The first claim is that they have been brought into a realm determined by Christ; this second claim is that Christ dwells in them in the realities of their stations in the broader world. This presence of Christ in all believers makes them one and leads them to live out that reality within the church.

One of the most striking aspects of the assertion about Christ at the end of v. 11 is its similarity with 1 Cor 15:28. In that passage Paul asserts that Christ turns over sovereignty to God at the Parousia. Paul says that when this transfer takes place, God will be "all in all." So it is arresting that Colossians makes a similar assertion, but here about Christ. Yet there are important differences in the statements. The first is that Col 3:11 has the conjunction "and" (*kai*) between "all" and "in all." Thus, this verse makes two claims ("Christ is all and is in all") rather than a single more inclusive claim about reigning and filling the entire cosmos. Perhaps the most important difference between 1 Cor 15:28 and Col 3:11 is that 1 Corinthians speaks of the ultimate sovereignty and sustaining of the whole cosmos, while Col 3 concerns only the eschatological reality into which Christians have already been drawn (cf. Hay 129). Colossians 1 clearly identifies Christ as the one through whom God created and sustains the cosmos, but that is not the topic in chapter 3, where the corporate identity of the new person is the subject. So the claim made about Christ in 3:11 concerns the present rather than the end-time state of affairs. These differences, and others,[37] show that while the similar statements in these two letters seem to stand in tension with each other, they are not necessarily incompatible.

The central thrust of 3:5–11 is that believers must rid themselves of ways of living that are not compatible with their new identity. They have been put into, and have put on, a new identity that conforms to Christ. These gifts require believers to reject old ways of being, especially those that might damage the community of which they have become a part. God makes the task of rejecting those old ways possible because God constantly renews believers so that they conform more and more to Christ. Colossians reminds its readers of the significance of their new status by noting that in Christ, God has overcome social, ethnic, and ritual differences and so has included all people within this new creation. After explaining what putting on the new self requires them not to do, in the next paragraph the writer turns to describe the kind of life that is compatible with this new identity.

Excursus 2: The Scythians

A wide range of ancient writers uses the term "Scythian" to designate the most barbaric of barbarians (e.g., Philostratus, *Ep.* 5; Josephus, *C. Ap.* 2.269; 2 Macc 4:47; 3 Macc 7:5). But this is not the only use of "Scythian" that was current in the first century. Cynics used the word to speak of the noble savage who has not been corrupted by culture.[38] Scythian was also a term associated with slaves because so many slaves had been procured from the region of Scythia (north and east of the Black Sea). Pliny the Elder (*Nat.* 4.12.80–81) even says that Scythians are descended from slaves. But it is probably too much to say that this term would automatically be understood as one referring to slaves. Campbell (1996, 120–32) argues that in Col 3, "Scythian" refers to slaves and "barbarians" to free people, making the last two pairs of opposites in Col 3:11 parallel, just as the first two are. But the evidence that "Scythian" would automatically be understood as a reference to slaves is too thin to support this interpretation. Furthermore, there is no evidence that "barbarian" would be taken as a reference to free people, as Campbell argues. Moreover, it seems unlikely that slaveholders of Asia Minor would classify themselves as barbarians (contra Campbell 1996, 128–31). The most Campbell (1996, 131) can say for this reading of "barbarian" is that it is "not an implausible equation."

37. A further difference in the two passages is that in 1 Cor 15 the immediate context concerns overcoming the enemies of believers, Christ, and God, a concern that does not appear in the immediate context of Col 3. Although the overcoming of powers was important in Col 1–2, the more immediate context of 3:11 focuses on believers being given a new identity and exemplifying it in their lives.

38. See the argument and references in T. Martin, "The Scythian Perspective in Col 3:11," *NovT* 37 (1995): 249–61. See also D. Campbell's rejection of Martin's argument that this understanding of Scythians supports the view that the teachers Colossians opposes are non-Christian Cynics ("A Scythian Perspective in Col. 3:11: A Response to Troy Martin," *NovT* 39 [1997]: 81–84).

Greek writers sometimes used "Scythian" as a broad term that included all the remote peoples of the north (remote, at least, from the perspective of the Greeks). Among them were Germans, Goths, and Sarmatians (a people related to the ethnic Scythians and living on the eastern edge of the Scythian region proper; see Goldenberg 91).[39] Pliny's (*Nat.* 4.12.81) discussion of the Scythians speaks of the wide range of peoples included, commenting that in his time the word refers only to the most distant of peoples. Both Strabo (*Geogr.* 1.2.27) and Ptolemy (*Tetrabiblios* 2.2.56) call people from the remote north "Scythians" and those from the distant south "Ethiopians." Their culture and skin color made these peoples distinct enough from the Greco-Roman world's inhabitants that they came to stand for the extremes of the world. Goldenberg (88–91) cites rabbinic texts that call the southern region of the world Barbaria, and there were actually cities with that name in Africa in this period. Indeed, a number of these texts speak of the distant regions of the world by pairing Barbaria and Sarmatia (e.g., *Pesiq. Rab. Kah.* 5.7; see Goldenberg 90 for several examples). Although these rabbinic texts are later than Colossians, they indicate that this was a common-enough expression in their own era, and some claim to represent traditions from the second century. The Greek uses of such language show that the contrast was known in the first century.

Given the options for understanding the barbarian-Scythian pair in Col 3:11, the view that it refers to the far northern and far southern reaches of the world seems the best reading. This is a less-strained reading than Campbell's interpretation of barbarian and gives a known meaning for both Scythian and barbarian. At the same time, it maintains the literary flow of 3:11 by recognizing that they form a contrasting pair, a pair that works with a contrast known in the ancient context.

3:12–17 Put On the New Self (or, Since You Have Put On the New Self, Act Like It)

Verses 12–17 are intimately related to the two previous sections: 3:1–4, which sets the theme for all of 3:5–4:6; and 3:5–11. After vv. 5–11 delineate the ways of living that those who have been "raised with Christ" and are seeking "the things above" must reject, vv. 12–17 set out the manner of life that those who have put on the new self must embrace. The development of themes across these sections illustrates how closely related they are. As v. 5 expanded upon the imagery of death from the previous paragraph to clarify the meaning of life in Christ, so v. 12 takes up the imagery of changing clothes from v. 10 to elucidate the demands that this new identity entails. Verses 12–17 give particular attention to the way believers should live as a community. Thus, the corporate aspect of their new identity in Christ remains a central theme. Verses 12–17, then, are both the continuation and the obverse of vv. 5–11. At the same time, vv. 12–17 serve as the introduction to 3:18–4:1 by explicitly placing every aspect of life under the lordship of Christ (v. 17).

---

39. This paragraph's discussion is dependent on David Goldenberg 87–102.

The inferential particle *oun* ("therefore") and the new description of believers as "elect" signal that v. 12 begins a new section. The summarizing nature of the exhortation in v. 17 indicates that it concludes the section. While the instructions to specific members of the household in 3:18–4:1 form a separate unit because of the section's genre as well as its content, v. 17 introduces those instructions by announcing that everything one does belongs within the sphere of things affected by their life in Christ. Thus, the intertwined nature of the sections of Colossians continues.

> **3:12** Therefore, as God's chosen people, holy and beloved, put on heartfelt compassion, goodness, humility, gentleness, and patience. **13** Put up with one another and forgive one another if anyone has caused an offense. Just as the Lord[a] forgave you, you forgive one another. **14** Above all these, put on love, which is the bond of perfection.[b] **15** Let the peace of Christ rule in your hearts. It is into this peace that you were called in one body. And give thanks. **16** Let the word of Christ[c] live richly in and among you as you teach and admonish one another with all wisdom, through psalms, hymns, and spiritual songs, sung with gratitude to God in your hearts. **17** And everything you say and do, do it all in the name of the Lord Jesus, giving thanks to God the Father through him.

> a. The original hand of א substituted *theos* (God) for *kyrios* (Lord) here. A second corrector of א changed the reading to *christos*. *Kyrios* is the preferred reading; it appears in P[46] and B (among other manuscripts) and accounts better for the other readings because it admits ambiguity about who has forgiven believers (God or Christ). The other readings are attempts to clarify that original ambiguity.
> b. *Teleiotētos* can be translated as either "perfection" or "maturity."
> c. An original hand of א changed the text to *kyriou* (Lord). A few later manuscripts (A and C) read *theou* (God). But the stronger reading, *christou*, is found in P[46], B, and a corrector of א. Perhaps these variants were attempts to align this statement with v. 13, where similar variants appear.

[3:12–14] Verse 12 begins with "therefore." This term connects the affirmation that they have "put on the new" (v. 10) with the demands that identity entails. Verses 10–11 declare that God has placed believers in a new reality and given them a new identity; v. 12 begins to define what this identity requires of those who receive it. (For discussion of the metaphor "putting on," see the comment above on v. 10.) Before turning to specific demands of their new life in Christ, v. 12 expands the meaning of that new identity by granting the readers a new title and describing them in two additional ways: as "God's chosen people" and as "holy and beloved." The exhortations that follow, then, rest on these particular aspects of having put on the new self.

Having been clothed with Christ, they are now "God's chosen people." This designation echoes an important Old Testament designation for Israel. Though this framing of the believer's identity is not common in the New Testament and is especially uncommon in Paul,[40] the Old Testament often uses it for Israel. The title "chosen" (or "elect") points to God's gracious initiative in calling God's people and to the covenantal relationship between them and God. By calling believers in Christ "elect," Colossians confers on them a privileged and obligation-bearing status. Just as Israel's election entailed accepting particular demands on their conduct and a mission in the world, so Christ-believers are blessed by being chosen and also take on accompanying demands.

The election of which Colossians speaks, therefore, does not conflict with its demands on the conduct of believers' lives. God confers election on the church by granting new life in Christ, and this necessarily requires those elected to reject their former way of being. Election entails both God's gift of new life and the believer's taking up that new life. Just as in the undisputed letters of Paul, the gift and the demands of faith are inseparable. Failure to strive to live as God requires is evidence that the person does not possess what Paul calls faith. In this section of Colossians, the indicative that expresses what believers have received and the identity they have been granted (i.e., that they are the elect) is so tightly interwoven with the imperatives of the Christian life that they are two sides of a single coin.

The two other descriptions of believers ("holy and beloved") continue to set the stage for Colossians' specific demands upon their conduct within the church. The Old Testament also associated holiness with Israel's election (Exod 19:3–6; Deut 26:18–19). Paul and the Pauline writings often call believers "saints" (i.e., "holy ones"). Beginning in the opening greeting, Colossians refers to its readers as holy at least four times in chapter 1 (1:2, 4, 22, 26, and probably also in 1:12 [see the comment on that verse]). The writer returns to that description here in the context of moral exhortation. While the earlier designations affirm believers' salvation in Christ (esp. 1:22), this reminder of their identity prepares readers to receive instruction about how to live in a manner congruent with the holiness that God has granted them.

The designation "beloved" or "loved" with no further qualification appears only here in the Pauline corpus. The Pauline writings often refer to the love of God and in two places do designate believers as those who are loved (by God in 1 Thess 1:4 and by the Lord in 2 Thess 2:13). Pauline writers also speak of those who love God and exhort believers to love others. But the simple title

---

40. In the undisputed Paulines, *eklektos* appears only in Rom 8:33 and 16:13. However, it also appears once in each of the Pastorals (1 Tim 5:21 [where it refers to angels, not Christians]; 2 Tim 2:10; Titus 1:1).

"beloved" appears only in Col 3:12.[41] This description may echo 1:13, which counts Christ as God's beloved Son. If so, the word "beloved" strengthens believers' identification with Christ; they belong in the category of beloved because they are in Christ, who is the beloved Son. Calling the readers "beloved" also prepares for the exhortation to be loving in v. 14. Thus, the blessed status that they have received from God as the "loved" grounds one of the section's central exhortations. Even more broadly, then, designating them as God's beloved has implications for all the instructions of vv. 12–14. The manner of life these verses set out manifests love, the overarching Christian virtue.

The five-member virtue list in the second half of v. 12 parallels the five-member vice lists of vv. 5 and 8. The virtues in v. 12 are not precise opposites of the vices of either previous list, but they do identify the attitudes that should reign within the church as believers rid themselves of vice. All the virtues in v. 12 involve relations with others; they are not just personal qualities that bring honor to their possessor. This virtue list sets believers apart from the surrounding culture. While some outside the church viewed most of these characteristics favorably, the list is far different from the four cardinal virtues of Greek culture: wisdom, bravery, sobriety, and fairness (see Barth and Blanke 418). This implicit distancing from the surrounding culture is part of Colossians' strategy for helping the readers understand their new identity, precisely as it reinforces the boundary between believers and nonbelievers. Significantly, all the virtues mentioned in the list are characteristics that Paul attributes to God or Christ. Such a list implies that the church must live out the character of God as they have experienced who God is in Christ.

The first virtue in v. 12, "heartfelt compassion," is emphatic not only by its placement at the beginning of the list, but also because the writer uses two words to express it (*splanchna oiktirmou*). *Splanchnon* literally means the inner parts of the body.[42] In the LXX, these inner parts represent the seat of the emotions (e.g., Prov 26:22; 2 Macc 9:5; see also *T. Sim.* 2.4; *T. Zeb.* 2.4). Throughout biblical usage *splanchna* takes on the meaning of compassion or pity. In 2 Cor 6:12, it points to the emotion of a person's innermost parts, to the heart, and has the nuance of compassion. In some places it even functions as a synonym of *agapē* (Phil 2:1; see H. Köster, *TDNT* 7:548–59; Spicq, *TLNT* 3:273–75). *Oiktirmos* is the emotion of pity. The LXX sometimes uses it as a

---

41. This designation is also rare in the Old Testament, especially for Israel. There is a reference to Abraham as God's beloved in 2 Chr 20:7 LXX (cf. the LXX addition to Daniel at 3:35). The LXX also speaks of "beloved Israel" in Deut 32:15 and Isa 44:2. In both these passages, modern translations supply the proper name Jeshrun in place of the LXX rendering of "the beloved." "Beloved" does not seem to be an epithet that the original Old Testament writers used for Israel, though they often affirm that God loves Israel.

42. In classical Greek *splanchnon* referred to the parts given the gods at a sacrifice and so also to the whole sacrifice.

synonym for *eleos* (mercy; e.g., Neh 1:11; 9:19; Ps 24:6 [25:6E];.see R. Bult-mann, *TDNT* 5:160). When *splanchna* and *oiktirmou* are combined (with *oik-tirmou* a genitive dependent upon *splanchna*), the phrase denotes a deeply felt mercy or compassion. This first virtue, then, requires believers to treat others with heartfelt and merciful compassion, just as God showed them compassion by making them "beloved."

The second virtue listed in v. 12 is goodness (*chrēstotēs*). This term has the general meaning of honesty or respectability. According to Spicq (3:514), this is the virtue mentioned most often in extant funerary inscriptions; evidently, many prized this attribute highly. When *chrēstotēs* is attributed to rulers, it means that they are magnanimous. When used of a god, it describes that god as favorably disposed toward a worshiper. Within Judaism, it designates God's "gracious disposition and attitude" (K. Weiss, *TDNT* 9:489–91). Since God has shown this disposition to believers, they must reflect it in their relations with one another.

The most surprising member of this list is "humility" (*tapeinophrosynē*). Humility is not a virtue in Greco-Roman culture (see W. Grundmann, *TDNT* 8:1–6; Bevere 206). Yet on occasion, writers employ the cognate adjective *tapeinos* in contrast to hubris, or to denote simplicity in opposition to ostenta-tion (Plutarch, *Ant.* 735; cited by Spicq, *TLNT* 3:370). Still, *tapeinophrosynē* usually has a derogatory connotation, indicating lowliness or weakness. It is yet more surprising to see humility in this list of virtues because Colossians employs the same term in a derogatory sense in 2:18, 23 to describe the vision-aries' practices. Furthermore, the term appears only seven times in the New Tes-tament (though various cognate forms occur), with five of those in the Pauline corpus. Of those five, three appear in Colossians. Clearly Colossians uses the term in two different senses. While the readers must eschew the humility that the visionaries practice in their rituals, they should adopt an attitude of humil-ity in relation to one another in the context of the church. Thus, Colossians rede-fines humility so that it pertains to relations among believers within the community rather than to relations with heavenly beings.

In a Jewish context, however, *tapeinophrosynē* commonly has a compli-mentary sense. The LXX often makes *tapeinophrosynē* a virtue, referring to a person's attitude in relation to God. Grundmann explains this difference from common Greek usage by observing that within Greek culture, the free (and powerful) person was the ideal; but in Judaism, humans recognize their depen-dence upon God and live as God's servants (W. Grundmann, *TDNT* 8:11–12).[43]

---

43. *Tapeinophrosynē* appears as a virtue in Jewish literature in Job 5:11; Prov 3:34; 2 Esdr 8.48–52; *T. Benj.* 5.5; Philo, *Her.* 29.269. Job 5:11 and Prov 3:34 use the cognate *tapeinos* to express the same idea. Similarly, the covenanters at Qumran referred to themselves as the humble (1QS 2.24; 5.3).

Thus humility expresses the proper and necessary attitude toward God. The early church adopted this understanding of the proper relationship to God. The early use of humility to describe Christ's coming into the world in human form (see Phil 2:5–7) secured its place as a virtue for believers. To adopt the attitude of humility, therefore, conforms one's behavior to the example of Christ. This framework for humility defines it as a willingness to put the good of others before one's own good, to seek the advantage of the other even when it means accepting disadvantage for oneself. The competition over spiritual status that Colossians opposes makes this understanding of humility particularly salient (MacDonald 140). By including this virtue, Colossians rejects the visionaries' whole approach to spirituality. At the same time it advocates a manner of life that runs counter to the dominant cultural understanding of the good life. It promotes a manner of life that takes the self-giving Christ as its pattern. Thus, Colossians expands and reorients the meaning of humility.

The fourth virtue in this list is gentleness (*prautēs*). Classical Greek culture recognized gentleness as a social virtue. In the Hellenistic period some saw it as weakness, but others used this word as the opposite of uncontrolled anger. Thus many in the broader culture continued to view it as a virtue (Bevere 208). Yet *prautēs* seldom appears in inscriptions and papyri. It belongs to literary Greek rather than common language (Spicq, *TLNT* 3:160). When Paul uses *prautēs* in 2 Cor 10:1 to speak of "the gentleness of Christ,"[44] he gives it a meaning that many in the wider culture would have rejected because it designates the opposite of a powerful presence. In 1 Cor 4:21, Paul makes it the opposite of coming to the Corinthians with a rod to force them to behave acceptably. There he pairs *prautēs* with love, as he links it to graciousness in 2 Cor 10:1. The writer of Ephesians (4:2) pairs gentleness with humility, apparently seeing a close connection between these two virtues, which appear together in Col 3:12. Gentleness is another characteristic that the readers must exercise in the context of their community life. *Prautēs* extends the previously mentioned virtues by adding nuances of forbearance (BDAG 861). So this fourth virtue in the list moves us toward the specific instructions about patience and forgiveness in v. 13. Gentleness does not imply that believers should refrain from correcting one another. After all, the basic purpose of Colossians is to keep the church from adopting harmful practices and to correct those who are considering taking them up. Instead, the gentleness spoken of here designates an attitude and demeanor that allows its possessor to offer correction in ways that can be received constructively and also to accept correction, even unjustified correction, in ways that contribute to the good of the community (see Lindemann 60–61; Dunn 229).

The fifth and final virtue of the series in v. 12 is patience (*makrothymia*). A rare term in classical Greek, its earliest uses indicate a sense of resignation. But

---

44. The NRSV, among other translations, renders *prautēs* as "meekness" in this passage.

by the first century it has more the sense of steadfastness in the midst of troubles (J. Horst, *TDNT* 4:375–76). In the LXX it appears only in Wisdom literature, where it often relates to God's restraint or postponement of punishment (Bevere 209–10; J. Horst, *TDNT* 4:382). Paul also speaks of God's patience in withholding a full response to wickedness (Rom 2:4; 9:22). Patience, then, is an aspect of God's graciousness to all people. The conduct of God's people toward one another should reflect this divine patience. The focus in Col 3:12 is not on patience needed to endure trouble while awaiting the Parousia. Rather, this instruction tells the readers how to live together as God's people; they must not become uncaring or hardened in the disagreements that plague their church, but must remain patiently steadfast in their gracious treatment of one another, even in the midst of a serious dispute.

Three of the five virtues in v. 12 also appear in the list of the fruits of the Spirit in Gal 5:22–23 (i.e., goodness [NRSV: kindness], gentleness, and patience). This overlap suggests that the early church recognized these characteristics as a significant part of the life that believers should adopt. The emphasis on relations within the community in the Colossians list implies that the writer has tailored it to fit the letter's occasion, even as he incorporated conventional elements. Overall, this list calls readers to imitate Christ, the one who exemplifies all the virtues in the list.

As we have noted, Colossians commends some virtues that the broader culture acknowledged, though they would not receive the prominence they have here. Other virtues mentioned here, however, run counter to Greco-Roman values. Nevertheless, each of these virtues is at home within Judaism. This is not surprising, because the church received its understanding of God and ethical conduct from Judaism and its Scriptures. Even the virtues affirmed in the cultural environment take on new meanings in the church because in this context they reflect the character of the God to whom Scripture and the life of Christ give witness. Both the transformation of culturally acknowledged virtues and the adoption of virtues not prized in the social world of the early Christians indicate that this letter addresses and helps to form a community that is distinct from the surrounding culture. This distinctiveness forms a part of their identity as God's chosen, holy people. The distinctiveness of this life becomes even more apparent in v. 13, as the writer provides an explicit motivation for his instructions.

In v. 13, the general exhortations of the virtue list give way to more specific instructions about the readers' conduct toward one another. While the virtues of v. 12 designate the attitudes that the readers should adopt, v. 13 translates those attitudes into concrete behaviors in which they must engage within the church. Verse 13 uses two participles to delineate specific behaviors that embody those virtues ("put up with" and "forgive"). These participles may express the means or manner by which the virtues are expressed, or they may be imperatival. Since they are dependent on the imperative "put on" (v. 12), I read them as imperatives that continue the force of that initial verb (as do most interpreters; e.g., Aletti 237; MacDonald 140). Either way, these participles continue the exhortation of v. 12 by instructing the readers to adopt these behaviors as the appropriate manifestations of those virtues and of their identity as God's chosen.

The first exhortation of v. 13 commands the readers to "put up with one another." This instruction indicates that the exhortations of vv. 12–13 do not suggest a sentimental notion that everyone must like every other person. This command instructs believers to express in action the attitudes and characteristics listed in v. 12—even in their relations with those they disagree with and do not like. Since this church has been engaged in arguments about spirituality, this instruction may not have been an easy one to put into practice. Believers must bear with those who are disagreeable and unlikable. The diverse nature of the church's membership may have produced further difficulties. Like other Pauline churches, this church includes people from different social classes and ethnic groups. Such differences produced many conflicts within the Pauline churches, as both the undisputed and disputed Pauline Letters demonstrate (notably, 1 Corinthians and Ephesians). Whatever the reasons for their tensions, community members must put up with one another by acting in accord with the virtues listed in the preceding verse. After all, whatever personal differences existed between members, they have all been granted a common identity as God's chosen and beloved.

The second imperative participle pushes beyond enduring the other person, for the readers must also forgive fellow believers any offenses they may have committed. The phrasing of this exhortation suggests that there are genuine offenses to forgive (O'Brien 202). In a context of disputes about spirituality— especially in view of the tendency of polemical argumentation in the first century to include scandalous accusations about one's opponent—the presence of legitimate complaints is not surprising. Nevertheless, whatever the offense, they must continually forgive their fellow believers. The use of the present tense for both "forgive" and "put up with" suggests continual action. Such forgiveness does not mean that readers should be indifferent to evils or injustices done within the community. That there is something to forgive indicates that the offense is real. But believers must not allow the offense to blind them to fellow believers' value. When they recognize this value, they must forgive. Perhaps such forgiveness suggests that readers must learn to distinguish between the person and the evil that one commits (Pokorný 171–72).

Colossians supplies a specific warrant for the exhortation to forgive one another. Believers must forgive one another in response to, and in imitation of, the forgiveness they have received. This expression of the gospel's message is notable on three counts. First, the writer says that "the Lord" forgave them. "The Lord" here refers to Christ, as it always does in Colossians (and nearly always in Paul, with the exception of quotations from the Old Testament). But identifying Christ as the one who forgives makes this a singular statement. Throughout the Pauline writings, it is God who forgives through the work of Christ. Perhaps Christ's close identification with the work of God in creation and redemption throughout this letter allows the writer to attribute forgiveness, as well, to Christ. If Colossians designates Christ as the one who forgives, this exhortation to "forgive one another" calls the readers once more to emulate the one with whom they have been raised and whom they have "put on." Even if "the Lord" refers to God, Colossians urges its readers to pattern their behavior after the gracious treatment they have received in Christ.

The writer's choice of verbs constitutes a second notable feature of this statement. Here Colossians uses *charizomai* for forgiveness rather than *aphiēmi*, the verb that New Testament writers more commonly use to speak of forgiveness. This use of *charizomai* may highlight "the gracious nature of the pardon" they have received (O'Brien 202, citing its use in Luke 7:42). *Charizomai* has the more general meaning "to give graciously" (BDAG 1078–79), rather than specifically "to forgive," in most of its twenty-two appearances in the New Testament.[45] Paul uses this term to refer to forgiveness among fellow believers (2 Cor 2:7, 10), but nowhere in the undisputed letters does it apply to God forgiving anyone. Indeed, Paul seldom uses the language of forgiveness to describe salvation. Even when he uses the image of justification (a legal metaphor), the undisputed letters do not speak of divine forgiveness with either *charizomai* or *aphiēmi*, except in a quotation of Ps 32:1 (in Rom 4:7). Use of *charizomai* to describe divine forgiveness in Colossians suggests that believers should exercise graciousness as they forgive one another.

The third significant point about this call to forgive fellow Christians in imitation of the Lord is its close connection to a main theme of the letter. Although it seldom occurs throughout the Pauline corpus, *charizomai* in the sense of forgiveness appears three times in Colossians, twice here in 3:13 and earlier in 2:13, where God, in raising believers together with Christ, forgives their trespasses. The language in 3:13 intentionally echoes the affirmation of forgiveness in 2:13 and thus ties this exhortation to a primary theme of the letter. A central purpose of Colossians is to assure its readers of their place with God, particularly that God has forgiven them in Christ. Assurances of forgiveness and of the present possession of God's blessings stand out as constant themes of the letter, while it rejects the teaching that requires visionary experiences as proof of a relationship with God or as the place where God grants that relationship. It is particularly appropriate, then, to ground the command to forgive others in the forgiveness that believers already possess; the warrant provides backing for the

---

45. Outside its three uses in Colossians, *charizomai* denotes the act of forgiving only in Luke 7:42, 43; 2 Cor 2:7, 10; 12:13; and Eph 4:32 within the New Testament.

exhortation and reminds the Colossians of a central affirmation of the letter. This reference to forgiveness also shows that the ethical instructions of Colossians are intimately related to the earlier parts of the letter.

Verse 14 calls love a *syndesmos* (bond). This designates love either as the virtue that binds together all the preceding virtues or as what binds the community together. Clearly love—both God's love for them and the love they have for one another—does bind the community together. But since v. 14 continues the thought (even the sentence) begun in v. 12, it specifies another thing the readers are to put on. The context, then, indicates that love is the virtue that binds the other virtues together.[46] Thus, love is the primary virtue that encompasses all the attitudes and conduct that Colossians exhorts believers to adopt in vv. 12–13.

By calling love a bond, v. 14 may continue to develop the clothing metaphor ("put off [take off]"/"put on" in 3:8–9, 10, 12), because *syndesmos* sometimes stands for the band (or belt) that holds together one's clothes (LSJM 1701). Furthermore, the beginning of v. 14 may be translated either "above all these" or "over all these." The latter translation fits well with identifying "bond" as a belt. If the clothing metaphor remains in view, Colossians makes love the virtue that holds all the virtues together, as a belt holds one's clothes. But whether the writer intends to extend the metaphor, does so by accident, or has left it behind, the point remains the same: love is the basic Christian virtue that enables the exercise of all the others.

Understanding *syndesmos* as the bond that holds together the other virtues does not make love an individualistic virtue (contra O'Brien 203–4), because believers must exercise this love in the church. To be sure, all the virtues of v. 12 describe characteristics that individuals possess, but they must be exercised in the community. As each person lives in love, the church comes to exemplify all these virtues and values.

Some interpreters reject the idea that Pauline thought admits a hierarchy of virtues, with love at the top (e.g., O'Brien 203). While Paul does not mention love as often as we might expect, when he does mention it, love has primacy. Paul elevates love in both 1 Cor 13, where love is greater than faith or hope, and Gal 5:22, where it is the first "fruit of the Spirit" listed. Similarly, Col 3:14 gives love a crowning position.[47]

Love plays a large role throughout Colossians. It appears first in the thanksgiving. Pauline thanksgivings rarely mention the love that a letter's recipients

---

46. Some philosophical schools used this image of the "bond" to name friendship as the virtue that holds the others together (see MacDonald 141).

47. If one opts for translating the beginning of v. 14 "and above all these," this position of "love" is even clearer.

possess, but Colossians does so twice (1:4, 8).[48] The thanksgiving also calls
Epaphras "beloved" (1:7). The writer reminds the Colossians that they now
reside in the kingdom of God's "beloved Son" (1:13) and then that they are
bound together in love (2:2). When 3:12 begins the current section by calling
the Colossians those whom God loves, it picks up this thread. Now in v. 14, the
writer exhorts them to live out the love they possess and the love in which they
have been enveloped. The proximity of the reference to God's love for them
suggests that this exhortation calls them to mirror God's love in their conduct
within the church.

Love, then, binds together Christian virtues and thus leads to "perfection"
or maturity (*teleiotēs*). This mention of "perfection" may echo language that the
visionaries claim for themselves and others who attain visions. Mystery religions used cognates of *teleiotēs* to refer to those who were initiated through
obtaining their mystical experiences. Thus, this language designated those who
had attained a spiritual status above others. There is no solid evidence that the
teachers opposed by Colossians used the term, but this meaning was current in
the readers' environment. Thus, Colossians may intimate that perfection comes
not from exalted spiritual experiences but from exercising love within the
church. Whether or not the expression bears this nuance, it makes love the epit-
ome of the other virtues; it is the virtue that leads to the spiritual advancement
and maturity of both individuals and the community.

[15–17] The exhortation takes a new turn at v. 15. It no longer utilizes the
metaphor of clothing and no longer lists virtues for the readers to adopt. Verses
15 and 16 also shift from the second-person-plural imperative to the third-
person-singular imperative, with God's gift as the formal subject rather than
the readers themselves: "Let the peace of Christ rule in your hearts." Verse 17
returns to a second-person imperative so that the readers' actions are again the
focus: "Do it all in the name of the Lord Jesus." Each of these three verses has
a single basic exhortation that it expands upon.

When v. 15 mentions the peace of Christ, it draws on the claims of sovereignty
made for Christ in the first two chapters, as well as in 3:1, where Christ is seated
at God's right hand, the place of power. Christ made peace by overcoming the
powers that oppose God's will (1:13, 20; 2:15) and once held the readers captive.
Colossians proclaims that believers have been taken into the realm of Christ's
peace and thus experience its blessings and freedoms. Now the writer exhorts
them to let the peace that Christ creates exercise sovereignty in their lives. In a
context in which Rome claims to have brought peace to the world through the

48. No undisputed Pauline letter directly gives thanks for the love that the recipients possess.
First Thessalonians comes the closest when it gives thanks for their labor of love (1:3). The
extended thanksgiving of Ephesians also gives thanks for the recipients' love (1:15–16).

imposition of its rule, Colossians reminds its readers of the very different peace into which God has brought them. This reference to the peace of Christ reminds them that they are residents of a different kingdom. As citizens of Christ's kingdom, they enjoy the blessings that Christ gives. Indeed, the call to "let the peace of Christ rule in your hearts" sounds more like a grace to be received than a value to be promoted (Aletti 240) because this peace is not something they accomplish but something they receive. Still, this is an exhortation; they must appropriate the gift and allow the peace of Christ to reign fully in their hearts.

The peace of Christ possesses two aspects beyond the peace that Christ's victory over the powers brings. First, being brought into the realm ruled by Christ gives the believer an inner peace that comes through knowledge of one's relationship with God. Throughout the letter, Colossians works to strengthen this sense of peace and confidence in its readers in order to oppose the visionaries' claims that they need something more. The second aspect of this peace is that it must show itself in their relations within the church; they must live in peace with their fellow believers. In the light of the communal nature of all the previous and following exhortations, the call to let peace reign in their hearts includes an exhortation to manifest Christ's peace in their dealings with others, as the image of being called in "one body" intimates. This peace with one another grows out of their participation in the peace that Christ gives. Again, the gift and the demand are inseparable.

Colossians does not just encourage its readers to let Christ's peace be present in them; it also urges them to let it "rule" in their hearts. The verb *brabeuō* appears only here in the New Testament, though closely related words do appear. Most significantly, Col 2:18 uses a compound made from this verb (*katabrabeuō*, also a New Testament *hapax legomenon*) to describe the visionaries' judgments against those who do not have visions. Probably use of *brabeuō* in 3:15 deliberately echoes that earlier term and contains an implicit rejection of the posture of condemnation it pictures, while inviting the readers to embody a dramatically different way of being (Hay 133; Aletti 240). The peace that Christ brings, not spiritual competitiveness, should constitute the reality and determine the attitude that directs their lives.

Colossians locates this peace in their "hearts." Greek writers often use "heart" (*kardia*) to speak of the seat of moral, emotional, and intellectual life. It is the place where one feels and thinks, judges and makes moral decisions. It is also the place where these various functions can be integrated (J. Behm, *TDNT* 3:608–12; MacDonald 141). At other times, as in Col 2:2, the heart stands for the whole person. In 3:15, *kardia* probably has the whole person in view, perhaps with specific reference to one's emotional state and moral judgment.

Yet, since believers have been "called *into* the peace of Christ," Colossians has much more than an emotional state in view. The peace of Christ designates a realm established by the work of Christ, by his conquering of opposing forces and his establishing of a good relationship between God and believers. Believers have been transferred into this state of peace with God and security from the powers that control the cosmos. Because they now reside in that space, they have peace in their hearts and must strive for it within their church. This peace differs radically from the peace that Rome imposes, and this statement reminds the readers that they must live lives that stand in opposition to the values and standards of the world around them. The power of Christ enables them to take this stand with peace in their hearts.

The use of "call" language ("into this peace you were called") returns attention to believers' identity as God's chosen (3:12). Language of calling also bears other powerful, political shades of meaning in the first century. *Klēsis* (calling) was the term used for an official summons to a Roman assembly, particularly the calling of a particular group into the assembly. Groups were sometimes determined by social status, sometimes by tribal identity or geographic place of origin. The order of the calling determined the value of one's vote. Those called first had the most influence because they could determine the outcome. Subsequent groups were called only when the vote was too close after the initial groups had cast their votes. The Romans arranged the groupings so that those in power usually controlled the outcome of votes.[49] Colossians gives believers a high rank because their calling is into the peace of Christ.

Debate over whether the reference to "one body" in v. 15 points to the universal church (e.g., Schweizer 208; Harris 166) or the local congregation (e.g., O'Brien 205; Dunn 234–35; Hay 133) misses the main point that Colossians is making. The writer uses the preposition *en*, rather than *eis*, with "one body." Use of *en* suggests that the readers were called *in* one body, not *into* one body. If Colossians has the political meaning of "call" in view, saying they are called *en* one body means that they all received the same calling together, without distinctions that derive from social or ethnic status.[50] Thus, the mention of one body takes up the theme of 3:11, where the writer asserts in a more detailed way that social and ethnic distinctions are irrelevant in the realm of Christ. Again, this sets the reign of Christ against the rule of Rome. In the peace of Christ, there is a single calling to all, without reference to the matters that determine one's status and value in Greco-Roman culture. Thus, believers receive their place within the realm of Christ's peace in a way that counters the values around them and simultaneously commits them to a different manner of life. Furthermore, this peace of Christ not only shapes their observable behavior but also rules in their hearts and so forms their inner selves.

---

49. See Lily Ross Taylor, *Roman Voting Assemblies: From the Hannibalic War to the Dictatorship of Caesar* (Ann Arbor: University of Michigan Press, 1966), 107–13.

50. I thank James Bury of Harding University for his June 2005 correspondence about "calling" and the use of the preposition *en* in this passage.

Verse 15 ends with an exhortation to "give thanks" that employs unusual wording (literally, "be thankful"). *Eucharistos* appears only here in the New Testament, though closely related words are common. In broader usage this term often appears in inscriptions as the recipient's response to a benefaction (Harris 166, citing MM 268). While this reference to thanksgiving prepares for the references to worship that follow in vv. 16–17, it has a broader reference. Expression of thankfulness (*eucharistoi*) is the appropriate response to having received the benefaction of the peace of Christ, and to the divine gift of forgiveness (*echarisato*) that makes it possible (v. 13). Believers have been set free from the powers that oppressed them and have been admitted into this alternate reality in which they receive new life and identity; the only appropriate response is a life imbued with giving thanks.

The tension between claiming allegiance to an alternative reality and living in the world as it currently exists again comes into view here. Giving thanks was one of the primary functions of the worship offered other gods (Schubert 91; Standhartigen 1999, 243). In this, Christian worship fits the model of Greco-Roman religions. But just as Colossians transformed the conventional understandings of Greek virtues, so here giving thanks relates to an alternative reality and manifests itself in unexpected ways. One of those differences appears in v. 16, which indicates that Christian worship is not just communication between the person and God, but should also contribute to the life of the community.[51]

Verse 16 begins with a second overarching exhortation: "Let the word of Christ live richly in you." This exhortation parallels that of v. 15. As v. 15 spoke of the peace of Christ, so v. 16 speaks of the word of Christ. Both verses use the third-person imperative rather than the second person that appears in the rest of the section's exhortations. Verse 16, however, narrows its attention to the church's worship.

Colossians includes instruction about worship among these exhortations because worship comprises a central aspect of believers' communal life, the aspect of their lives that chapter 3 has kept in view to this point. Colossians also needs to provide instruction about the church's worship because the problems with the visionaries involve worship practices. Verse 16 provides one of our few glimpses of early Christian worship. This glimpse indicates that proclamation (the word of Christ), teaching, singing of various sorts, and giving thanks all played a role in the church's worship.[52]

51. While it is true that worship of other gods was sometimes done for the good of the city or region, noncivic worship was a more individualistic affair.

52. Of course, 1 Cor 12–14 allows us to see other aspects of worship in Pauline churches. The pictures in the two letters are fully compatible.

The ambiguous expression "the word of Christ" may point to the proclamation about Christ, the teaching of Jesus, or the voice of the risen Christ in the worshiping community (Standhartigen 1999, 243; cf. MacDonald 142–43). Emphasis falls on the first and third options, though the earthly Jesus' teaching has a place within the gospel proclamation about him and perhaps also in the message that the risen Christ communicates to the church. All the themes that Colossians develops involve teaching about the place and work of Christ. Thus, v. 16 characterizes the church's proclamation as a message primarily about Christ. This message about Christ brings relationship with God and enables proper worship.

The imperative of v. 16 ("Let the word of Christ live richly in you") involves something that is already present in the community, just as the imperative of v. 15 did. The word of Christ (whether the gospel or Spirit-inspired utterance) is present as a gift of God. In some ways this gives the readers a secondary place in the request. Barth and Blanke (426) go so far as to say that it is really a request to God. But Colossians directs its exhortation to the readers; they must allow this gift to indwell them richly. That is, they must permit this gift of God to permeate their lives so that it determines everything about them, particularly the way they conduct themselves in worship, including discerning what does and does not (e.g., elements of angelic worship) belong in worship for it to please God.

This word of Christ lives in them individually and corporately, just as the peace of Christ has both an individual and a corporate aspect. The word of Christ that genuinely and richly lives in a person will be heard in the community so that it enriches the whole church. At the same time, the Word living in the community enables the individual's reception of it. The context of worship orients the exhortation of v. 16 toward the corporate reality, the word of Christ experienced by the church in worship. This corporate reality deepens the individual's experience of Christ's word.

The rest of v. 16 details ways that the word of Christ should live in and among believers. This word manifests itself in "teaching and admonishing," done "with all wisdom." Wisdom characterizes both teaching and admonishing. Colossians mentions wisdom more often than any other Pauline letter except 1 Corinthians. In the face of claims about knowledge gained in extraordinary experiences, Colossians asserts that all wisdom is in Christ (2:3) and charges that the visionaries' teaching has only the appearance of wisdom (2:23). In 3:16, the writer exhorts his readers to allow the wisdom that he prays they will be filled with (1:9) to determine the ways they relate to one another in the church's teaching and worship.

The participles "teaching" (*didaskontes*) and "admonishing" (*nouthetountes*) may function as imperatives (so BDF 468.2), but participles related in such a manner to verbs seldom function as imperatives. It is preferable to construe these as temporal adverbial participles bearing the sense "*as* [*when*] you teach and admonish."[53] Thus, one of the ways the word of Christ comes to expression—springs to life—among the Colossians is through their teaching and admonishing of one another. Teaching (*didaskontes*) involves instruction in the faith, both in what Christians believe and in how they should live. The content of Colossians suggests that such teaching includes beliefs about God, Christ, believers' place in Christ, and their relationship with God. It also includes what those teachings reveal about acceptable understandings of spirituality within the church. Colossians' instructions in ethics address every aspect of believers' lives to help the letter's readers discern how to negotiate their lives in the world, even as they reject its value system. The differences between the church and the dominant cultural values extend into matters of personal, social, and communal ethics.

Admonishing (*nouthetountes*) extends beyond instruction by including warning and correction. Admonition does more than inform, for it intends to influence a person's will and to improve one's spiritual condition (J. Behm, *TDNT* 4:1019). It can also have the nuance of encouragement. In this verse, admonition does include encouragement because it takes place through singing in worship.

Both 3:16 and 1:28 have participial forms of teaching and admonishing and speak of carrying out these tasks "with all wisdom." These parallels, along with other features of 3:16, suggest some important things about the organization of Pauline churches and their understanding of ministry. Colossians 1:28 describes Paul's ministry in the same terms that 3:16 uses to describe the ministry of the whole church, both teaching and admonishing. The ministry of all believers shares this central function of apostolic ministry. Colossians urges the whole congregation to undertake the ministry of proclamation, teaching, and warning as its appropriate work. This suggests a mutuality rather than a strict hierarchical structure within the church. There is no one group responsible for teaching, warning, and encouraging; instead, all have the commission to engage in these tasks.

This impression about internal church structure gains strength when we note that Colossians does not mention designated leaders in worship. The responsibility for leading worship, as for the teaching and admonishing of the community, falls to all believers, not just a few who are vested with authority over

---

53. In sense, if not in grammatical analysis, this interpretation acknowledges the point of Daniel B. Wallace, who contends that these two participles express the means or mode by which the word of Christ should live among those gathered for worship (*Greek Grammar beyond the Basics: An Exegetical Syntax of the New Testament* [Grand Rapids: Zondervan, 1996], 652). Thus, the word of Christ lives among them *through* their teaching and admonishing of one another. The syntactical issue is that the plural "you," not the singular "word," engage in the activities indicated by the (plural) participles *didaskontes* and *nouthetountes*. Furthermore, it seems unlikely that the author thinks that the word of Christ dwells among the readers *only*, or perhaps even primarily, through these activities.

others. This glimpse of the church's worship suggests that church structures have not yet developed into a rigid hierarchy. This distinctive element of the church's life in the realm where Christ rules again sets it apart from the realm ruled by Rome. Dominance, power, and status do not function as the accepted means of organizing the life of the church; rather, all have responsibility for the well-being of each of the others in the group. This understanding of community and worship helps to set the context for reading the household code that follows in 3:18–4:1.

The teaching and admonishing that give voice to the word of Christ come to expression in worship through "psalms, hymns, and spiritual songs." While the author may intend clear distinctions among these musical types, the specifics are lost to current readers. The use of these terms in the LXX and among first-century writers indicates the difficulty one faces in trying to distinguish among them. Josephus uses both hymn (*hymnos*) and song (*ōdē*) to refer to the psalms of Scripture. While the LXX designates most of the compositions in the book of Psalms as psalms (*psalmos*), it calls some songs (e.g., Ps 6). Psalms and hymns both commonly refer to praise of God or the gods in Judaism as well as in other Greco-Roman religions. As Dunn observes, the evidence cannot support the claim that the word "psalms" refers only to those found in the Old Testament, while hymns refers to new Christian compositions (Dunn 238, contra Lightfoot). Paul's uses of *psalmos* in 1 Cor 14:26 to speak of the compositions each member wants to share in worship demonstrates that *psalmos* can refer to more than the biblical psalms. Furthermore, Revelation incorporates biblical psalms into new songs in the church's worship (e.g., Rev 19:1–8; cited by MacDonald 143; cf. "new song" in Rev 5:9–10, 12–14). So any definitive distinction between the biblical psalms and songs composed by the church is untenable. Colossians' mention of psalms probably includes those in the Old Testament book of Psalms, but was not limited to that. In general, "song" is the broadest of these three terms, often referring to music that has no religious content. The LXX, however, uses this word only for a song of praise to God. Since no sharp distinctions among these terms emerge, perhaps the inclusion of all three provides another example of Colossians' tendency to repeat an idea for emphasis.

The adjective "spiritual" may modify only songs or all three kinds of musical works. Since the first two terms are more commonly connected with religious compositions, "spiritual" could apply only to "songs" and so more precisely designate the kinds of songs in view (Fee 654). But the context probably renders such a clarification unnecessary. Still, its location at the end of the list of three types of compositions may suggest that it attaches primarily to the final term. Whether associated with one or all three, "spiritual" characterizes the songs as prompted or inspired by the Spirit. These songs speak the word of Christ. That they are inspired by the Spirit does not necessarily indicate that they are glossolalic (spoken in a "tongue"), even though other New Testament texts may recognize such singing (e.g., 1 Cor 14:13–16). Even if the visionaries' worship experiences have included worship in the tongues of angels, the experience of God's presence in v. 16 does not seem to include that type of singing. Singing in a tongue would not fulfill the purpose of teaching and admonishing the community, because the church would not be able to understand the message of something sung in a tongue (cf. 1 Cor 14:2–4, 15–17). Therefore, singing in a tongue is probably not in view here (Fee 654 n. 71).

A textual variant makes understanding the next prepositional phrase of v. 16 more difficult. The text reads, *en* [*tē*] *chariti* ("with gratitude" or "with grace"). While the stronger textual evidence suggests that the article *tē* should be present, it creates interpretive difficulties. The term *charis* can mean "grace" or "gratitude," with the former being its more-common meaning. When *charis* appears with the article elsewhere in the New Testament, it never means thanksgiving or gratitude, the meaning nearly all modern English translations give it here. Thus, New Testament usage strongly favors the meaning of "grace," even though BDAG lists this passage as an example of *charis* meaning "gratitude" (1080). But if *charis* means "grace" in Col 3:16, it shifts the focus from the act of the one singing to God's attitude toward the one singing. Thus, it refers to the way believers stand in the grace of God, as they sing because of that gift (Fee 654–55).

Outside the New Testament, *charis* does refer to thanksgiving offerings to gods (LSJM 1978–79 and Suppl. 312). Moreover, the context of Col 3:15–17 supports rendering the phrase "with gratitude," because thanksgiving is a running theme in these verses. This contextual consideration bears sufficient weight to counter the otherwise consistent New Testament usage (so O'Brien 210; Barth and Blanke 429). *En* [*tē*] *chariti* also stands structurally parallel to the phrase "with all wisdom" of the preceding clause; both come before the participle(s) they modify. This also supports understanding the phrase to mean "with gratitude," because "with all wisdom" expresses the manner in which believers should teach and admonish, just as "with gratitude" expresses the manner in which they should sing. Though there can be no certainty, these contextual clues and syntactical parallels[54] favor the translation "with gratitude." The phrase signals that the Colossians' singing should express an attitude of thankfulness. This posture in worship thus gives concrete expression to the more general exhortation to give thanks in v. 15.

The congregation's singing (whether out of God's grace or, as seems probable, with gratitude) is offered "in your hearts." This phrase also appears in v. 15, where "the peace of Christ" is to "rule in your hearts." (In Greek the wording of the phrases is exactly the same.) *Kardia* (heart) again probably refers to one's whole being and so indicates that the singing should express the attitude

---

54. Schubert (92–93) notes how often one finds symmetry in the sentences of Colossians.

of one's whole self. Some interpreters argue that "in your hearts" means *silently* because Hellenistic writers see silent prayer as the highest form of thanksgiving to God (e.g., Standhartigen 1999, 244–45). Such a meaning might help the writer counter the visionaries' claims about the superiority of their worship practices; nevertheless, this nuance seems unlikely. If the singing is silent, it cannot fulfill one of its important purposes in this passage. Besides expressing thanks to God, Colossians says that this singing should teach and admonish those who hear it. This can only happen if the person sings aloud (Barth and Blanke 428; Fee 655).

Singing in worship has an important communal function, but its ultimate goal is to honor God. Thus, v. 16 ends by explicitly identifying God as the recipient of these songs. In the midst of a decidedly christocentric passage, Colossians makes God the ultimate object and audience of worship. This is consistent with v. 17—indeed, with all of Colossians, which envisions Christ as the one through whom believers come to God, are related to God, and praise God. Even as Christ is the agent of creation and redemption and the one in whom believers live and find their identity, God remains the primary actor in all of these things and thus the one to whom praise is ultimately due.

Verse 17 provides a fitting conclusion for vv. 12–17 and, at the same time, introduces the household code that follows. Its universal exhortation expands the believer's responsibilities beyond worship and life within the church; it insists that life in Christ involves the whole of one's existence: "And everything you say and do, do it all in the name of the Lord Jesus." The universal scope of this exhortation parallels the universal proclamation at the conclusion of 3:5–11. The elaboration of things believers must *avoid* (vv. 5–11) ended with the declaration that Christ is the all-determining factor in the eschatological reality; now the description of the way of life that believers must *adopt* (vv. 12–16) ends with the exhortation that they live fully in that eschatological reality by conforming their every act to the will of Christ. The all-encompassing nature of the proclamation and the exhortation rests on the exalted understanding of Christ found throughout Colossians. Since Christ is above all creation and is the head of the church, the lives of believers must entirely conform to their identity in Christ.

The sentence's construction indicates how emphatically Colossians wants to claim that every aspect of life falls under the lordship of Christ. In the first clause of the sentence, the verb "do" (*poiēte*) appears along with "everything." But in the next clause, the word "everything" appears a second time, while the reader must supply the imperative verb ("do"). This emphatic "everything" stretches beyond the immediate focus of the preceding verses so that the exhortation includes everything involved when one "put[s] on the new" person that has been created in Christ. Believers must subject their whole existence to the will of Christ.

Since the most immediate context for v. 17 concerns worship, what they "say and do" (literally: "in word or deed"; cf. RSV) may include a reference to liturgy and ritual. If so, the command to say and do "everything . . . in the name of the Lord Jesus" counters any attention to angelic worship. All worship—indeed, all of life—must be conducted only in the name of the Lord Jesus. But the focus has shifted: the writer's attention is no longer the worship setting but the whole of life.

Believers must utter every word and perform every deed "in the name of the Lord Jesus." This phrase draws on the LXX's use of the expression "in the name of the Lord," which appears at least eighteen times,[55] in addition to other related uses (e.g., "in his holy name" or "in the name of God"). The phrase bears different nuances depending on the context: Solomon speaks of those who pray in the name of the Lord (1 Kgs 8:44), and Jonathan and David swear by the name of the Lord (1 Sam 20:42), but it often means that one speaks or acts with or by the authority of God (e.g., 2 Sam 6:18; 1 Chr 16:2; Ezra 5:1). Colossians uses the phrase in this last sense. Believers should conduct their lives in ways that demonstrate their recognition of Christ's lordship. His position authorizes the manner of life they should embody. Everything they say and do, they do through Christ's authority. This imbues all of life with deep significance because the believer's life becomes an embodiment of the gospel's proclamation of the lordship of Christ. Every act of the believers' communal, social, and personal life should not only recognize and conform to their identification with Christ but also be an act that the lordship of Christ authorizes.

Emphasis on Jesus as Lord helps to prepare for the household code of 3:18–4:1, which repeatedly refers to Jesus as "Lord." This identification of Jesus relativizes the claims imposed on believers by the surrounding culture. In every aspect of life, believers owe ultimate allegiance to the true Lord, Christ.

Verse 17 ends with an exhortation to give thanks to God the Father. We have noted the important role that expressions of gratitude play in Greco-Roman religions. This, in part, reflects the patronage system by which the whole of the society operated. In this system the more powerful person helped the less powerful and in exchange expected expressions of thanks and deference that enhanced the patron's social position. When religion mirrored this understanding of social relations, those granted a gift by a god saw themselves under obligation to give appropriate thanks to that god (MacDonald 151). The call to thanksgiving in Colossians likewise constitutes the believer's response to the gifts God has given. This third reference to thanksgiving in the space of three verses reveals that Colossians views thanksgiving as an important element of

---

55. "In the name of the Lord" (*en onomati*) appears in Josh 9:9; 1 Sam 17:45; 20:42; 2 Sam 6:18; 1 Kgs 8:44; 18:24, 32; 22:16; 2 Kgs 2:24; 1 Chr 16:2; 21:19; 2 Chr 18:15; Pss 19:8 (20:7E); 117:26 (118:26E); 123:8 (124:8E); 128:8 (129:8E); Sir 47:18; and Mic 4:5.

Christian worship and life; it comprises a significant part of the life orientation that the letter advocates. When readers recognize all that God has given them in Christ (including all that the visionaries say the readers lack), the only proper response is thanksgiving.

Apart from greetings, thanksgivings, and doxological material, the New Testament seldom refers to "God the Father" in the way Colossians does here. Outside such sections, when New Testament writers call God "Father," they usually insert "and" between the two words. Colossians 3:17 lacks this "and." The absence of the conjunction "and" may intensify this expression of the believer's relationship with God: God is known to believers as their Father. Perhaps designating God as Father in v. 17 reflects the kind of relatedness to God that Colossians wants readers to know they possess because of their identity in Christ. Thus, they give thanks to the God who has brought them into God's own family and as Father has made them heirs, a key aspect of what it meant to be a father in Greco-Roman culture. In that setting, the father determined who received an inheritance and what that inheritance would be. Colossians has already asserted that God has made believers heirs (1:12) and will reaffirm this particularly for slaves in the following section (3:24). Calling God "Father" reintroduces this element of the blessings that believers possess because they have identified with Christ, the "beloved Son" (1:13).

Again, it is notable that for all the attention Colossians gives to the place of Christ, believers direct their thanksgiving through Christ to God. As in much of this letter, Christ serves as the mediator between God and the world or between God and those who now have the intimate relationship with God that allows them to call God their Father.

Verses 12–17 continue the letter's explication of the exhortation to "Focus your intent (or more woodenly, "set your minds"; 3:2 NIV) on things above." These verses also fill out the practical implications of the believer's new identity formed in the image of Christ (3:10–11). This new life includes adopting particular virtues and specific ways of acting that enhance the quality of the community's life. The way God has treated them in Christ sets the pattern for this manner of life, as the explicit example of forgiveness demonstrates (v. 13). These exhortations have both an individual and a communal aspect: the peace of Christ should rule in their hearts in such a way that it shapes their community; the word of Christ should live in and among them so that their praise to God also edifies the church. Finally, the writer asserts that all of life must conform to the new identity that believers have been granted in Christ. This universal exhortation concludes the letter's initial description of the way of life they should adopt (vv. 12–16), as well as the conduct they must reject (vv. 5–11). In addition, v. 17 introduces the following household code, which gives instructions on how Christians should comport themselves in the world beyond the bounds of the church.

Excursus 3: Reading the Household Code

The section composed of 3:18–4:1 comprises a separate unit that has a distinct literary form. Martin Luther labeled this section the *Haustafel*, the household table or instructions, because it gives instruction about how various members of a household should relate to one another. The section stands out from the exhortations that surround it to such an extent that it could be removed and the reader would notice no gap in the flow of the letter from 3:17 to 4:2. Yet this table of instructions is an important part of the letter. Colossians is the earliest of seven such registers of duties within the New Testament. Thus, it may give us some insight into the use of this form in the early church.

Nearly all who have investigated the literary form of the household code trace it back in some way to Aristotle's comments on household management. Though some have argued that the church created this literary form, most agree that the church adapted it from similar forms employed in the first century. The question then largely becomes What group mediated this tradition to the early church? Martin Dibelius (48–51) argued that the household codes in the New Testament draw on a form already present in the early church and tap into ethical traditions in Hellenistic, particularly Stoic, philosophy. Furthermore, he argued, the church only slightly Christianized them by adding phrases such as "in the Lord." Schweizer, Lohse, and Crouch (among others) look more specifically to Hellenistic Judaism as the place from which the church adopted these codes. They cite the comments in Philo and Josephus on the management of the household as evidence of this connection (Josephus, *C. Ap.* 2.189–209; Philo, *Hypoth.* 7.3; *Decal.* 165–67). The early church certainly faced some of the same criticisms leveled against Judaism and so would have similar reasons to address some of the same issues involving the household. Balch (25–31), however, concludes that we must place both the comments of Jewish writers and the New Testament codes in the context of the broader Greco-Roman discussions of household management. This strategy uncovers some distinctive things about the New Testament codes (e.g., the direct address to subordinates, particularly slaves). These distinctive elements suggest that the New Testament codes are not directly dependent upon these other sources for their precise form (see Hartman 1988, 227–30). The codes probably draw on a preexistent topos, a "paraenetic scheme," but do not rely on a precise literary form (*Gattung*; Gehring 229–30).

Interpreters have increasingly recognized that we must place the New Testament codes in the context of Rome's concerns (specifically, the concerns of its elites) about maintaining the structure of society in the face of what they perceived to be the growing presence of nontraditional cults (MacDonald 2003, 17). Indeed, writers such as Dionysius of Halicarnassus (ca. 60 B.C.E.–7 C.E.) concern themselves with keeping the influence of foreign cults out of Roman observances and celebrations. Concomitantly, evidence suggests that various cults felt the need explicitly to affirm their support of traditional values. We will return to these matters below.

Beyond the study of their development as a literary form, the household codes have attracted attention because of their content. Interpreters have evaluated them in radically different ways. Do they prescribe the pattern of family life for all times? Or should they be rejected because they surrender core values of Jesus and Paul, and therefore dramatically compromise the early church's egalitarianism? Thus, while some discover in the codes the divinely ordered hierarchy of the family, others reject them as oppressive. Yet other interpreters argue that we need to seek out their liberative elements to make these codes useful and relevant today (e.g., Mollenkott 37–58).

A clearer reading of this material in Colossians will emerge if we better understand the situation(s) this code addresses. Interpreters have often envisioned a situation more conditioned by their own context than by that of the church in the last half of the first century. Placing Colossians and its instructions to members of the household within their social and political context, as well as their religious context, will point us toward reading them as directives that have encoded meanings intended to be understood only by persons in the church. We turn first, then, to a description of the constructions of households and their meaning in the first-century Greco-Roman world.

The household was the primary social setting of the early church, especially the Pauline churches. While some churches probably met in the small apartments (*insulae*) within the city, most seem to have met in larger houses of wealthier members (Gehring 73; Osiek and Balch 1997, 16–17). The various mentions of households that include dependents and other features common to larger households indicate this setting. References in Acts to church meetings in households (e.g., Acts 12) confirm that households served as a primary gathering place for the church. This setting required the church to situate itself within the structures of a central social institution. Sometimes this led to confrontations with the usual organizational structure of the household, as some of the conflicts of 1 Corinthians demonstrate. When such conflict arose, the solutions the church adopted would not have gone unnoticed by their neighbors. The high population density of ancient cities would not have allowed anonymity.[56] Since the household was a central location for the church's life, we need to understand that institution's traditional social organization and cultural meaning.

According to Aristotle, the smallest household included a master and slave, a husband and wife, and a father and children (*Pol.* 1.3), the three groupings Colossians' household code addresses. In the Greco-Roman world, many saw the household as the cornerstone of society. Aristotle had said that the state was made up of households (*Pol.* 1.13). In many ways it was a microcosm of the larger society and its structures of governance. As Standhartinger (2003, 93) puts it, the household was the "nucleus of the state." Unlike households in industrial societies, the ancient household was primarily a center of production rather than consumption (Osiek and Balch 1997, 42). Households included places for conducting business and producing goods. Poorer artisans (far more numerous than persons with the larger households) often lived in the back room or loft of their business. Wealthier people often had public areas in their houses where the head of the household conducted business. So there was little separation of business and private life. Any change in the way a household functioned, then, would come to the attention of a wider public, not just members of that household.

The household also served as a place of worship. As Osiek and Balch (82) observe, every kinship group was a worshiping group. Worship of the same gods helped bind the group together. Typically, the gods of the household were the gods of the head of the household. Particularly Roman homes had altars for the veneration of the family deities

---

56. Hubbard (423 n. 49) cites estimates of ancient Rome's population density at 300 people per acre and for Antioch, 137 per acre. We may compare that with the population density of New York City today, which stands at about 37 people per acre.

and protectors (cf. from an earlier time Gen 31:19, 34–35; Judg 17–18; 1 Sam 19:13–17). Daily rituals (prayers and sacrifices) were sometimes events in which all members of the household, including slaves, were expected to participate. The religious character of the household also had a civic element. Households participated in and supported the worship of the gods of the city and the empire. Many writers of the period interpreted refusal to participate as unpatriotic and as a sign of potential rebellion. Tacitus (as a prelude to relating events of ca. 70 C.E.), for example, criticizes those who join Judaism because their conversion leads them to renounce their country and hate all the gods (*Hist.* 5.5). This sort of criticism would have been even more emphatic against the church because, unlike Judaism, the church did not have an ancient history attached to a recognized tradition.

Given the public meaning and religious nature of the household, many viewed deviations from the expected pattern with suspicion. In civic society under Rome, everyone was expected to know one's proper place and to stay within it (Downing 364). Rome viewed transgressions of social expectations and boundaries as dangerous, as actions that invited social unrest (Brown 567). The early empire was acutely concerned about social unrest and feared that unsupervised gatherings might foment unrest. Trajan (imperial reign, 98–117 C.E.) even refused to allow the city of Nicomedia to organize a volunteer fire department because its members would meet without sufficient imperial observation, that is, in a setting in which they might criticize the empire (Pliny the Younger, *Ep.* 10.50). Trajan was worried that any kind of association might become a base for rebellion (Portefaix 149). This concern for stability extended to encouraging the stability of family structures (MacDonald 2003, 17). The Roman Senate passed laws setting the age at which upper-class children had to marry and encouraging childbearing. Peace in the civil sphere was impossible, some asserted, without proper order in the household (e.g., Stobaeus, *Flor.* 2.7 [quoting Arius Didymus]; Josephus, *C. Ap.* 2.188–210; cf. Appian [*Bell. Civ.* 4.13–30, 34], who characterizes a time of civic chaos by noting how relations within the household were violated; see Standhartinger 2003, 94). In this setting, any changes in a household's operation would have invited scrutiny from its neighbors and possibly from civic authorities.

Within the household, women generally lived under the authority of the husband or *paterfamilias*. But within this structure, wives occupied a position of authority themselves. Women were responsible for the internal workings of the household, which might include some of the production of the family business. Free women in a well-situated household would have commanded the slaves who lived and (with others) worked in the home and its extended business. The household was the domain of women (Osiek, MacDonald, and Tulloch 136). In the household, women were masters, and when there was no male (e.g., when a woman was a widow), some women even functioned as a *paterfamilias*. Women were sometimes in charge of considerable wealth and so wielded influence that extended beyond the physical confines of the household. Still, most women remained under the power of a male, usually either their father or their husband. Rome exerted considerable effort to maintain this traditional order of the family—both in Rome itself and in the lands it conquered—as a means to maintain civic order.

One of the ways a wife accepted the authority and governance of a husband was by adopting his gods. A wife was expected to participate in the worship of the husband's family deities. In a polytheistic environment, this seldom caused a problem because offering veneration to new gods did not preclude worship of other gods. Within Roman households, women took leading roles in the observances directed to these family gods and family spirits. In addition, wives taught the children about the family gods and provided other forms of religious education (MacDonald 2003, 20; Osiek, MacDonald, and Tulloch 94). For a woman to refuse to adopt the husband's gods or to refuse to participate in their veneration would have been a direct challenge to the husband's authority and to the social structure of the household. Indeed, such conduct might well be viewed as subversive to public order (Carter 25–26; Lincoln 1999, 101).

Our understanding of the places of children in ancient households has been even more influenced by modern culture than have our ideas about women in ancient households. Children were basically possessions of their parents in Greco-Roman culture. Though many frowned upon the practice by the first century, infanticide was common, particularly if the child was female or not physically whole. Children could be sold into slavery, imprisoned, or beaten if that was their father's will. Dionysius of Halicarnassus boasts that Roman law gave fathers the right to treat their sons in nearly any way they saw fit, even reselling them into slavery as many as three times (*Ant. rom.* 2.26.4–27.2). It is crucial to note that this power over a child did not end when the child reached adulthood. Children were expected to defer to their parents' will and judgment throughout their lives. Though he may exaggerate, Dionysius says that a father could have his son put to death even if that son had become an important magistrate (*Ant. rom.* 2.26.4–5). The deference due to parents included the sphere of religion. Children, both sons and unmarried daughters, were to venerate the gods of the father (Lincoln 1999, 101). This obligation extended into the time of the children's adulthood. Such common worship helped bind the family together. Thus, Dionysius chronicled Rome's aversion to admitting foreign cults and rites (*Ant. rom.* 2.19.1–4).

Slaves had the fewest rights of any member of a household. In the ancient world, slavery was not racially based. People often became slaves when their cities or regions lost a war. Many were born into slavery, because children born to slave women automatically became the property of the mother's owner. Aristotle had spoken of slaves as living tools, as less than human (*Pol.* 1.4). Masters assigned their slaves all kinds of work. Some had demeaning work, while others held influential positions within the household—even beyond, when they represented their owner. Enslaved people often possessed many skills. Some were employed as personal physicians and as house philosophers. In this latter role they might serve as teachers of the householder's children. Others, though, were employed in hard physical labor or forced into prostitution. Slaves commonly earned a salary, and some slaves even owned slaves of their own and conducted private financial affairs. Slaves were often manumitted at some point in their lives.

Still, in a culture that placed a high value on honor, slaves enjoyed none. Aristotle asserted that slaves had neither deliberative faculty nor moral virtue (*Pol.* 1.13). Masters determined all the conditions of their slaves' lives. Not only could slaves be assigned any task; they were also sexually available to their masters and so lacked full control over their sexual activity.[57] Slaves were used for sex often enough that postbiblical Christian writers made explicit allowance for those violated, even on a continuing basis, so that they could be members of the church (e.g., Hippolytus, *Trad. ap.* 16.15). Thus,

---

57. For extended treatment of this question, see MacDonald 2007, 94–113.

the church concluded that when a master required sex from a slave, this did not constitute adultery on the part of the slave. The practice of using slaves for sex was so common that there had to be explicit instruction to reject from church membership a master who kept a slave as a concubine, unless he was willing to marry her (*Trad. ap.* 16.16).

Slaves, like others in a household, were expected to adopt the gods of the *paterfamilias* (Osiek and Balch 1997, 82–83; Lincoln 1999, 101). In some ways this bound them to the welfare of the household they served. Refusing to worship the master's gods violated cultural expectations and constituted insubordination. Some in power worried that allowing slaves to worship foreign gods would lead to treachery among them (Portefaix 150). Given the vast numbers of slaves, Rome constantly feared slave rebellions and so opposed anything that might encourage or permit instigating unrest.

One other matter must concern us as we think about the positions of those whom the household code of Colossians addresses. Interpreters usually assume, and occasionally comment explicitly, that the code addresses people in households where the *paterfamilias* was a believer. This assumption is probably incorrect. It is true that Acts often presents entire households converting to the church. In such cases, slaves and perhaps close financial dependents might convert along with the family. But the tendency of Acts to emphasize the respectability of the church probably leads its author to exaggerate the numbers of conversions that follow that pattern. Because Paul plied a trade when he entered many cities as a missionary, he would have come into contact with many people outside the circles of the wealthier householders. Slaves and freed people, along with artisans and businesspeople of varying levels of economic success, would compose the bulk of his audience. His gospel's message, which regarded status categories as having been relativized (male/female, slave/free: see Gal 3:27–28; 1 Cor 12:13), would have had a special appeal among people with low social status. Such a message would be less appealing, however, to those with greater wealth, even though many suffered status inconsistency because their place in society could not rise to match their financial means (Meeks 1983, 21–23). While most churches met in the homes of wealthier individuals, most members would have come from the poorer strata of the city. Evidence from the second century supports this conclusion. Celsus accuses Christians of drawing only from those who are poor and uneducated or from women and children (Origen, *Cels.* 3.44, 55, 59). While this is a polemically motivated exaggeration, the church's membership probably included a majority drawn from these elements of the population.

If many, perhaps a majority, of those addressed belonged to households that have nonbelievers as their heads, the code sounds quite different than it does if we assume that these wives, children, and slaves have believers as the heads of households. If the household head is not a member of the church, the code must set out a way of practicing the faith and surviving in the type of household we have described above. In such households, some expectations irreconcilably conflict with what church membership demands (e.g., worship of only God). People in these households must find ways to remain faithful to God while living in a situation that seemingly requires them to violate that faith.

Before turning to the codes themselves, we must also consider the social and political position of the church as a whole. Interpreters have typically read New Testament texts as purely religious documents produced by a group that eschewed confrontation with the Roman Empire. Though this perspective has some validity, interpreters have increasingly realized that the early church (and before that, probably Jesus himself) used language that would have been heard as dissent from the empire's rhetoric about itself and the good things it brought to the world. Much New Testament language echoes language the empire used in its propaganda and, not least, in settings that included emperor veneration.

Perhaps chief among the phrases that sounded political (and had political implications) is "kingdom of God" or "kingdom of Christ." Such language appears in some of the earliest New Testament writings (e.g., 1 Thess 2:12), and the Synoptic Gospels constantly attribute it to Jesus. The phrase "kingdom of God" envisions an alternative structure of governance for the world. In Philippians, Paul expands this image as he writes to believers living in a Roman colony that included a settlement of Roman army veterans. He proclaims that members of the church have an alternative citizenship to that of Rome (Phil 1:27). Other Pauline language also echoes claims that Rome makes for itself: "gospel," "savior," and "peace," to name the most obvious. Paul uses this language to such an extent that, according to Georgi (157), he writes Romans in active "political aggression." While Colossians does not rise to that level, its discussion of the overcoming of the powers and the subjection of all things to Christ clearly has political and social implications. Colossians makes these implications more explicit in 1:13 when the writer says that believers have been transferred into a new kingdom, the kingdom of God's Son. Maier (325–26) finds the reference to the Roman triumph in Col 2:15 another unmistakable parallel with imperial ideas. In this passage, however, Christ, not a Roman general, triumphs over his enemies.

Given that Pauline churches did not include members of the empire's elite, its members all belong among those subject to Rome's will. The wealth of a few ameliorated the effects of this subjection, even working to the economic advantage of some, but all remained subject to the power of Rome. Joining the church increased the alienation that grew from this disadvantageous position because believers associated themselves with a group that explicitly distanced itself from the beliefs and values of the surrounding world. That is, the Pauline church belongs in the category of a sect, a group that sets itself apart from its culture. The church had a strong countercultural outlook that made it seem threatening to outsiders. Even the church's devotion to a single (foreign) god seemed ominous. When church members removed themselves from the worship of the gods of the city, they made themselves suspect because of the close connection that people in the first century drew between patriotism and religion (see the inscriptions cited by Gordon 136).

To be sure, this countercultural stance did not lead the Pauline churches to seek the immediate overthrow of the Roman Empire or other basic structures of society.[58] They did, however, recognize that society's structures and modes of operation violated God's will.[59] The only way they envisioned these structures changing depended on a catastrophic intervention of God. On the other hand, they did begin to organize their

58. Dale Martin (148) comments that Paul does not advocate revolt but does deconstruct the political and cultural structures in such a way that he undermines their supports.

59. Although Rom 13:1–7 acknowledges that the government's role of maintaining order accomplishes an aspect of God's will, this passage does not constitute an endorsement of the empire's values and structures. The passage's support of these functions of the government

intrachurch relations in ways that better reflected the values of the gospel. But when this manner of living became public, it made them even more suspect in their cultural environment.

To sustain its existence, the church not only needed to oppose the justifications that Rome espoused for its claims to bring peace and security to the world; it also required a competing metanarrative. A metanarrative is an account given to make sense of the world. Such accounts include stories that explain why the world works as it does and why its adherents are in the place they find themselves. Rome's metanarrative included claims that the gods had placed the Romans over the world for the good of the world (*Res. gest.* 12–13; Appian, *Bel. Civ.* 5.130).[60] Thus, those who oppose Rome oppose the will of the gods.

The church's competing metanarrative must explain how it can be a socially marginalized and sometimes persecuted group if they are truly the "people of God" who have come to understand the will of God. The story of Christ's death and resurrection serves this purpose, for it recalls that the exaltation of Jesus comes only after his suffering at the hands of those in power. This becomes the paradigm for the church's worldview, a central element of its metanarrative. Just as the powers of the world opposed Jesus, they now oppose people who believe in him. Though Christ defeated those powers through his crucifixion and resurrection (as Colossians proclaims in 1:15–20 and elsewhere), they refuse to acknowledge their defeat. Thus, in their refusal, those powers sustain the structures of the world that oppose God and God's people. So the church must exist in a setting that involves confrontation with both culture and empire.

The place in which the members of the first-century church find themselves in relation to the empire and the surrounding culture, combined with this counter-metanarrative, makes some of the insights of postcolonial reading useful for interpreting the New Testament, particularly Colossians and its household code. Rejecting the metanarrative of the dominant power is central to the resistance oppressed or dominated people offer (Horsley 2003, 93). When Colossians advocates an alternative account of the cosmos, that account will influence the way its readers understand themselves and their lives. Wilson (224) shows that ethical exhortation in the ancient setting strove to give its hearers a conceptual framework that made sense of the thought behind the instructions. This insight encourages us to examine the way in which Colossians' ethical instructions, including the household code, enable readers to make sense of the letter's claims about Christ's sovereignty.

The work of James Scott provides important insights that illuminate the functions of the household code in Colossians. In his study of the resistance that dominated peoples mount against structures supporting their oppression, Scott (4, passim) argues that subordinated groups develop what he calls a "hidden transcript." This "hidden transcript" reveals what the subordinated people really think, as opposed to the "public transcript" that reflects the views of those in power. This hidden way of speaking expresses what

---

appears in a letter written to a church in the capital of the Roman Empire. To suggest anything less than obedience where possible would have subjected the members of that church to unnecessary persecution.

60. See Zanker 1988 for ways this claim was made in various public images.

the subordinated cannot say explicitly in public because it would constitute open confrontation with those in power and so bring them punishment. Scott (118–19) finds that subordinated groups develop their own counterideologies (e.g., counter-metanarratives) and their own systems of "countermores."[61] While they cannot publicly articulate their alternative understanding of the cosmos without painful repercussions, the oppressed often find ways to express their outlook in public settings in ways that only others in their own group will understand. That is, they find ways to use public language acceptable to the powerful, language that their compatriots understand as expressions of a counterideology. The subjugated peoples do not incur the wrath of the dominant because the dominant do not understand the full message when it is disguised in this way. Even in settings where those in power can overhear, therefore, the subordinates' worldview may find voice—but only if one's ears are properly attuned.

To a considerable degree, the early church found itself in the kind of setting that Scott describes. Most of its members came from subordinate social locations. Membership in the church, a new and exclusive religion, compounded the stress that their social rank entailed. The church's rhetoric and imagery articulated an alternative understanding of the cosmos that opposed Rome's metanarrative. The church did not directly oppose governmental or civic authorities. It did, however, express its counter-metanarrative in the kinds of communities it formed. Since countercultural and subordinated (or persecuted) groups must also develop a system of morality that reflects their outlook, the church had to construct guides for conduct, both within the church and in relation to outsiders, those who belonged to the dominant culture. How could the church express its values in its relations with nonchurch people and institutions? The household codes represent an attempt to do so. The household code instructs church members about how to behave in the public eye so that the church's life (and that of its members) is sustainable.

If Scott is right about the ways subordinated peoples express their views, the household code in Colossians may encode meanings that only insiders were able to hear; church members will hear things in the code that run counter to the most straightforward reading of persons who are not attuned to the countervailing message. What might it mean for wives to be subordinate "as is fitting in the Lord" when this exhortation appears only a few lines after the letter asserts that in Christ the status presupposed by this marriage arrangement has been relativized to the point that no one is accorded special status? The tensions between what the code *seems* to require and what Colossians proclaims about the cosmos and believers' place in Christ, as well as some statements within the code itself (see the commentary below), indicate that something other than the usual straightforward reading is in order. Nearly all commentators acknowledge that the instructions in the household code stand in tension with other material in Colossians, even that such tensions exist within the code itself. (I will address some of these problems in the commentary.) If Colossians employs a "hidden transcript," however, there is a greater measure of congruence between the letter's proclamation and its exhortation. This reading makes good sense in the historical and social context, and it has the advantage of recognizing the letter's internal consistency. The church was not in a position to reorient the culture or to explicitly reject many of its demands. Its members do,

61. Scott (199) also notes that millennial imagery is often part of the counterideology. The church uses exactly such language in its metanarrative.

however, reinterpret those demands so that their lives within that culture gain a new meaning.

Various clues within the code itself commend reading it "against the grain." Among the most striking is the identification of slaves as heirs (Müller 274–75; Standhartinger 2003, 96; 2000, 129–30). Such an identification would be not only unexpected but in some places even forbidden. Yet in 3:24, Colossians tells household slaves that they are heirs of God. In the sentence that immediately follows, moreover, Colossians asserts that masters are also slaves (4:1). The combination of these cultural dislocations requires us to attune our hearing in unaccustomed ways. These statements, among others, suggest that this table of instructions involves more than the surface meaning suggests.

3:18–4:1 The Household Code

At first glance, the connection between the surrounding sections and the table of instructions in 3:18–4:1 appears tenuous. In fact, if this unit were removed, the letter would still read quite smoothly. Still, these instructions play an important role in the letter because they give the specifics of how to live out the more-general exhortations that precede and follow them. The code explicates the admonition of v. 17 that the recipients do "everything in the name of the Lord Jesus."[62] The code's instructions bring us into contact with the realities that the church faced in the world of the first century and give a glimpse of the ways it navigated the challenge of that setting. As is true of all ethical instructions in the Pauline Epistles (indeed, the whole Bible), these instructions address the particular setting of the letter's recipients. The author might give quite different instructions in another setting. The contextual nature of such instructions is clear in Paul's practice of accepting and not accepting money from his churches. In the context of the Corinthian church, Paul says it would violate the gospel for him to accept money (1 Cor 9:1–23; 2 Cor 11:7–15). Yet he thanks the Philippian church for the many times they have sent him support (Phil 4:10–20). This difference indicates neither inconsistency nor development; rather, it shows that Paul, and after him the writer of Colossians, fitted his instructions and his application of the gospel to the particular church he was addressing. So too here, the instructions in the household code address the circumstances of this church in particular. That other New Testament writers and later Christians also take up the form of the household code (e.g., Eph 5:21–6:9; 1 Pet 2:18–3:7), with some variations in the specific instructions, does not alter the contextual nature of the directives found here. The table of instructions in Colossians presents what its author saw as the most appropriate application of the gospel in this church's situation.

---

62. Even the form of this reference to Christ (i.e., "Lord Jesus") points the reader to the discussions of lordship of various kinds in 3:18–4:1.

Two contexts must guide the reading of the instructions in this table of exhortations: the literary context and the social context. Although some interpreters assume that all (or most of) the people addressed by the code belong to households in which the *paterfamilias* (head of the household) is a member of the church, nothing in the text supports this assumption. From the beginning, the church enjoyed a more ready reception from the less privileged, including slaves, the poor, and women. We should expect, then, that many who heard this code belonged to households where belonging to the church created problems for them (see above, *Excursus: Reading the Household Code*). In such situations, the *paterfamilias* would have been concerned to hear that his slaves were meeting with a group that undermined the accepted boundaries separating status groups, or that his wife had joined a group encouraging women to become public leaders. Thus, the setting of the code carries with it the suspicion that the church aroused among the more powerful when their subordinates met without proper supervision. A second important social context is the gathering of the church itself. In the Colossian setting, this is a place where a woman named Nympha is recognized as a leader in the church (4:15). So women have places of status and leadership in the churches that Colossians addresses. The church provided a space in which members of the lower classes and women could experience a real leveling and even reversal of social status (Heen 144). Such a group gave reason for masters, fathers, and husbands to worry about their subordinates' participation in it.

In the literary context, Colossians has proclaimed that Christ is the ruler of the cosmos because he has defeated and subjugated the powers that now control the world. This proclamation implies that the structures those other powers authorize are in jeopardy. The assertions of believers' existence in a new humanity (3:9–10) and their citizenship in the kingdom of Christ (1:13) would support any suspicions outsiders might have. And finally, 3:11 makes the revaluation of societal structures explicit when it says that in Christ there is no Greek or Jew, no slave and free. Such proclamations can only sound threatening to outsiders who hold positions of authority and power. What Downing (363–64) notes about Gal 3:28 is equally true for Col 3:11: putting such a proclamation into practice in society "would be seen as deliberately subversive." For the church to survive, without its members suffering excessively, it must avoid direct confrontations with the demands of cultural and civic structures, confrontations that its proclamation seems to make inevitable.

Several other elements of the literary context should also shape our reading of the code. As already noted, only a few lines after the household code ends, Colossians names Nympha as a leader of the church (4:15). Such prominent mention of a woman in a leadership role might make nonbelievers wary. Nympha's leadership surely would have influenced how the church heard the exhortation about the submission of wives. In yet closer proximity to the code,

the writer admonishes the Colossians to act wisely toward those who are outside the church (4:5). This injunction marks a clear boundary between those in
and those not in the church and indicates that church members must remain cog-
nizant of the watching eyes of outsiders. In some ways, therefore, the code must
enact the wisdom that is to inform their relations with outsiders.

The household code, then, must give its readers a way to navigate a world
that does not recognize the lordship of Christ or accept its implications for the
structuring of relationships within the world. This table of instructions enables
the recipients to rethink how to be faithful, how to understand their situation,
and how to live in a way that does not bring unnecessary hostility or persecution—and perhaps, at the same time, maybe even bring others to the church.
When nonbelievers criticized the early church, one of their complaints was that
church membership led subordinates to fail to accept their proper place within
the household (e.g., Celsus in Origen, *Cels.* 3.55). Householders and civic
authorities took appropriate behavior within the household seriously because
they saw the household as the foundation of society. Instability in the household could lead to social and civic instability and unrest. Therefore, the elements of the church's teaching that would subvert the culture's values and
structures had to be carefully interpreted and perhaps even masked from those
who might misread them.

Distinctive elements of the household code stand out, even as it repeats some
conventional expectations. Perhaps the most profound feature is the way this passage puts everything under the lordship of Christ. Being "in Christ" governs all
of life. There are no less than seven references to Christ as Lord in the nine verses
of the household code. This should alert readers that the writer is advocating a
dramatically different approach to life. It is also striking that the code addresses
the subordinate person in each of its parts. Thus it speaks to them as moral agents
who are responsible for their conduct within the limits imposed by their subordinate position in the social structure. In succession the code addresses three relationships within the household. Each time it addresses the social inferior before
turning to the more powerful. Even as the household code takes up these conventional categories, it sets out an alternative vision of society.

3:18 Wives,[a] submit to your husbands as is fitting in the Lord. 19 Husbands,
love your wives and do not be embittered toward them.

20 Children, obey your parents in all things, because this is pleasing in
the Lord. 21 Fathers, do not provoke your children, so that they may not
become discouraged.

22 Slaves, obey your earthly[b] masters in everything.[c] Do not serve, like
people-pleasers, only when being watched, but with sincerity of heart, out
of reverence for the Lord. 23 Whatever you do, work wholeheartedly as
for the Lord and not for humans, 24 because you know that you will

receive from the Lord the reward of the inheritance. Serve the Lord Christ, 25 for the unrighteous person will receive recompense for the unrighteousness he has committed, and status will not count in this judgment. 4:1 Masters, grant slaves justice and equality, because you know that you too have a Master in heaven.

a. The Greek word is *gynaikes*, a word that also means "women." Likewise, the word translated "husbands" is also the term for men (*andres*). Greek does not have specific words for wife and husband. Both the context and the commands indicate that vv. 18–19 address wives and husbands.

b. The phrase *kata sarka* ("according to the flesh") is here rendered "earthly."

c. P[46] lacks *kata panta* ("in everything"). Perhaps its copyist recognized the radical demand that this seems to impose and the conflict inherent in obeying an earthly master "in everything" and yet claiming that one's true master is Christ, and thus deliberately left it out of the text.

[3:18–19] The household code couches its instructions in the present imperative. This tense suggests that the writer intends these commands to be a continuing part of the way these people relate to one another within these relationships. Thus, these behaviors are to become characteristics of believers' comportment in these various stations within the household.

The household code begins with a brief exhortation to wives and then one to husbands. Thus it starts with the central relationship in the household. In Greco-Roman culture, wives were expected to accede to the husband's authority in all things that related to the way the household was perceived from outside (see above, *Excursus: Reading the Household Code*). The wife even adopted the husband's gods and in the Roman context taught the children about those gods and other spiritual powers. Furthermore, she took a leading role in worshiping them within the household. Even though she wielded significant authority within the household in relation to slaves and others who worked in and for the household, a wife usually remained under the legal authority of her husband (or some other male). The exceptions to this would have been some widows and perhaps a few women among the elite and the wealthy.

The code first instructs wives to "submit to" (*hypotassesthe*) their husbands. While this may sound a bit gentler than the following command that children "obey," there is probably little substantive difference, at least in practice (Lincoln 655). Wives were expected to obey their husbands. A number of interpreters place this command in the context of other Pauline uses of the verb *hypotassō* to argue that it does not indicate the wife's inferiority, and to observe that Paul elsewhere uses the term to direct the attitudes and behavior of both subordinate and dominant persons (e.g., O'Brien 221–22). Others assert that Pauline usage pictures this submission as voluntary (Pokorný 180; Barth and Blanke 434). At the same time, however, some see a limit to this submission:

the writer surely must not have included worshiping the husband's gods (Barth and Blanke 434–35). But this religious expectation was an important part of the wife's submission in the first-century world. Moreover, a substantial number of the subordinates addressed in this code would have belonged to households headed by nonbelievers. Given this setting, the next phrase of v. 18 is extremely important.

The phrase "as is fitting in the Lord" is not just a slight Christianization. This phrase reveals the full meaning of the exhortation. It serves as the defining aspect of the command, not as its basis. That is, it redefines "submit" in a radical way. The idea of what is "fitting" draws on some philosophies of the period. For example, Stoics argued that everyone should live according to the structure of the cosmos. Colossians' addition of "in the Lord" does not make conforming to the present world order a Christian duty (contra Pokorný 180), nor does it show that the author accepts a hierarchy of creation that places husband over wife (contra O'Brien 222). Instead, this phrase must be heard in the context of the status leveling proclaimed in 3:11 and of a house church that has a woman exercising a leadership role. It must also be heard as a message to wives who have nonbelieving husbands.

In this constellation of contexts, the tension between the exhortation ("wives, submit to your husbands") and its qualification ("as is fitting in the Lord") could not be missed. All are one in Christ and must adopt the same virtues, yet this exhortation does not seem to express those beliefs. No one-sided submission is appropriate to what is "fitting in the Lord." "In the Lord," wives should submit, but so should husbands, if readers take 3:11 seriously. Thus the phrase "in the Lord" is a cue to readers that while the structures of the world remain in place and while they must exist within them, those structures stand in tension with their existence in Christ.

This new understanding of existence and submission does not just apply when wives may be called on to worship other gods. Heard as a "hidden transcript" (see *Excursus: Reading the Household Code*), the qualification of submission with "as is fitting in the Lord" tells wives that while they must continue to submit outwardly, particularly if their husbands are nonbelievers, they should recognize the incongruity of that requirement with the lordship of Christ. Such a qualification reveals a different understanding of the world, and that understanding entails a different structuring of relationships. Still, women must live in the world as it exists. (Cf. 2 Kgs 5:18–19, which allowed significant compromise.) So wives of unbelievers must continue to obey their husbands if they and the church are to survive. Only a few decades after Colossians, we have evidence of the difficulties women faced if their church membership was discovered by their husbands, or if that membership began to change the ways they related to their husbands (Justin, *2 Apol.* 2; Tertullian, *Ux.* [*To My Wife*] 2.4–7).

Within Christian households, the outward form of the household would also need to continue to reflect the structure of other households. Failure to maintain this appearance would bring the same kinds of criticisms from those outside that any deviation within the homes of wives of unbelievers would bring. Judaism faced criticism from outsiders for subverting the household structure, as Josephus's apology reveals (*C. Ap.* 2.25–28). In response, he contends that Jewish families do adhere to the proper household structure. Colossians' instruction seems to have the same kind of apologetic purpose. It instructs wives to live in ways that will not bring disrepute or suspicion on the church. Even within Christian households, the perceptions of outsiders must remain a concern. Thus, even where being "in Christ" has transformed relationships, as much outward conformity as possible would remain a necessity.

Verse 19 addresses husbands. These husbands certainly are believers. No other husbands would hear the letter read or heed its content if they heard it. The initial command to husbands in v. 19 is that they "love" their wives. While treatments of household management in the Greco-Roman world did not include the importance of love, other discussions of marriage did (e.g., Plutarch, *Conj. praec.* [*Advice to Bride and Groom*] 142F–143A). Thus this is not a unique injunction. Still, it stands apart from the conventional discussions of household management, where the expected exhortation was that husbands rule wives wisely (Thompson 93). Furthermore, in the immediately preceding instructions about proper living, Colossians has identified love as the virtue that binds the others together (3:14). The call to love should therefore be heard with a distinctively Christian meaning. In the larger context of Pauline writings, this command to love might even constitute a call to mutual submission (so Barth and Blanke 437, citing 1 Cor 13 and Eph 5:21). Christian love does not make subordination of wives easier (as Lincoln 655 asserts); instead, it calls for a new understanding of the relationship. The rest of v. 19 hints that this love involves substantial reorientation of the marriage relationship.

The second part of the command to husbands enjoins them not to "be embittered" toward their wives. This is a strange exhortation if the code sustains the traditional structure of the household. If wives submit and husbands command, then it is wives who might be embittered, not husbands.[63] After all, if they are told in one breath that the distinction between men and women no longer determines status and in the next that they must submit, it could provoke bitterness in *wives*. This exhortation, however, addresses husbands. The injunction makes the best sense in the context of a reorientation of the household. If the husband

---

63. Lincoln (655) understands this expression to mean that husbands are not to act out of bitterness. This would be a very unusual, even unknown, meaning of this verb. Neither does the meaning of "do not be harsh" (Barth and Blanke 437) fit the term.

is no longer the lord of the household, but lives with his wife in mutual sub-mission, his relative lack of power might well generate bitterness within *him*. This gives us a glimpse into the world of Christian households that was not on display to their neighbors and could not be given full expression without arous-ing the ire of those neighbors. When husbands and wives live "as is fitting in the Lord," it changes their relations of authority. The husband's surrender of authority inherent in this new way of life could easily engender bitterness on his part since he was accustomed to a relationship that gave him superiority. This command, then, instructs husbands to live this new life in love, a love pat-terned after the self-giving of Christ and of Paul (1:24–2:4), without allowing their surrender of authority to produce bitterness toward their wives.

[20–21] The writer next addresses children and parents. As the earlier dis-cussion of the household has indicated (see above, *Excursus: Reading the Household Code*), children were expected to remain obedient to parents throughout their lifetime. Fathers possessed great power over children, even after the children became adults, at least in the ideals set out in the literature of the period. Discussions of household management often treated the subject of children. Thus, it is not surprising to find them in this table of instructions. First-century writers saw the behavior of children in relation to parents as a matter of civic concern. Again, one of the criticisms leveled against Jews was that their children were disobedient (see Tacitus, *Hist.* 5.5; Josephus, *C. Ap.* 2.28, 31). Since the early church was so closely associated with the synagogue,[64] the church may have provoked the same kinds of criticisms. Such criticisms are even more likely when we remember that this exhortation also addresses adult children (so also Barth and Blanke 439; Lincoln 655). If children abandon the gods of their family, even as adults, many people of the first century would view this as an act of disrespect and disobedience.

Josephus emphasized the value placed upon children within Judaism, remarking that Jews do not allow abortions or infanticide and commenting on the importance of educating them (*C. Ap.* 2.25–26). He also stressed the demand that children honor and obey their parents. The charge that the church targeted children (see Origen, *Cels.* 3.44, 55, 59) indicates that the church con-tinued to value children as it moved into non-Jewish settings. Consistent with such an approach, Colossians addresses them as members of the community—still keeping in mind that the address includes both adult and minor children.

Colossians instructs children to obey their parents (not just their fathers) in all things. While the verb "obey" (*hypakouō*) may not express a stronger idea than the instruction for wives to submit (*hypotassō*), the addition of "in all things" makes the command emphatic. The writer supports this command with

---

64. The recipients of Colossians in particular seem to have remained related in some way to the synagogue, because they are considering observance of the Sabbath.

the assertion that such obedience is "pleasing in the Lord." This grounding of obedience probably draws on the commandment to honor one's parents, one of the Ten Commandments (Exod 20:12; Deut 5:16) and a command that remained important in the first century (Josephus, *C. Ap.* 2.28, 31). In this section of Colossians, however, the "Lord" designates Christ, rather than God, as in the original command. Both the context and the form of the expression confirm this identification. One would expect the phrase to read "pleasing *to* the Lord." Instead, it says "pleasing *in* the Lord." Children must obey their parents because they live in the sphere governed by Christ (O'Brien 225). This sphere includes expectations about the proper way to conduct themselves in relation to parents. Their participation in the new life calls them to obey their parents.

Such instruction coheres well with cultural expectations but could prove problematic for children within the church if their parents are not believers. Unbelieving parents might well forbid, or at least oppose, participation in the church for both minor and adult children—a command that children surely must not obey. Thus, they would be faced with an unresolvable tension between participation in Christ, which requires obedience to his lordship, and the demand of a parent that they separate themselves from the church. For the writer of Colossians, allegiance and obedience to Christ must take precedence, which means that obedience to parents in "all things" turns out to be more limited than it sounds. As in the case of wives, children who hear the support offered for the command will also hear a cue that both defines its limits and fills in its content. The phrase "*in* the Lord" supplies this signal; even as they obey their parents, children must remain within that sphere. Ironically, remaining in that sphere means that they must at times disobey their parents.

While children must obey their "parents," vv. 20 and 21 explicitly addresses only "fathers." This reflects the cultural setting in which fathers possessed the greater power and authority over their children. The writer may, however, continue to have both parents in mind because "fathers" sometimes functioned as a general reference for parents (so Schweizer 223, citing Heb 11:23 Gk.). Whatever the reference, the persons addressed are within the church. Thus, Colossians is addressing the dominant person in the household structure, the one who has some latitude in structuring the relationships.

Whether the instruction is to both parents or only to fathers, the command emphasizes the *responsibility* of the person in the position of power, not his (or their) authority. "Fathers" are not to provoke or irritate their children. Various Greco-Roman writers commented on the ways the head of the household should exercise authority differently with different kinds of subordinates (e.g., Aristotle, *Pol.* 1.12; see also *Eth. Nic.* 5.6.8–9). The proper way to treat slaves was different from the way one commanded children, and both of these were different from the way one exercised authority in relation to one's wife. Recognizing and practicing diverse ways of relating to various members of the household was part of the art of being the head of the household. It was an exercise of wisdom that not only helped the household to operate smoothly but also enabled other household members to understand and fill their roles at that moment and into the future. This was particularly true for sons, who must learn to be heads of their own households.

The final part of v. 21 gives the reason "fathers" should not provoke their children. "Fathers" should relate to their children in ways that do not lead them to be "discouraged." It is tempting to read this justification within a modern, psychologizing framework so that it means the child may lose the courage to become one's own person (as does Schweizer 224). The proper contexts for reading this support of the command, however, are first-century ideas about households and the situation of this letter's recipients. In the broader setting of Greco-Roman treatments of household management, proper treatment of children prepares them to undertake their roles in society.

In the church setting, however, something more specific is probably in view. Children in households where the head of the household is a church member would probably endure social stigmatization, possibly even persecution. Belonging to the strange and unpatriotic sect (which the church seemed to be) would create a difficult situation for the children of believers. Continual harassment would be difficult to bear and might cause children to abandon the church. This is probably the kind of discouragement Colossians has in mind. Thus, "fathers" should relate to their believing children in ways that help them remain faithful to the church. This consideration might lead the household to exercise great care about any unnecessary and observable deviations from the norm. The household may reject participation in civic religious festivals, including but not limited to emperor veneration, but they need not flaunt other differences because these could provoke retaliation from those around them.

This delicate situation requires fathers to exercise great care as they relate to their children so that they do not inflame intrafamily conflicts. Relations within the family must also reflect each person's participation in the realm governed by Christ and be modeled on his self-giving love. Thus, "fathers" must seek ways to cultivate relationships with their children that are appropriate to this realm, whether or not the family faces pressure from outside forces.

Again, we see something of how a believing household had to negotiate a hostile environment. Parents who were church members had to think about how a household should live out the lordship of Christ as a household in such a way that they did not drive away their own children. The provocations or irritations that fathers should avoid include not only their direct treatment of their children, but also the household's engagement with the surrounding society.

[3:22–4:1] Colossians addresses slaves at greater length than any other group within the code. Perhaps this is because there were so many slaves in the church or because it was harder for them to continue in their subordination after their incorporation into a community proclaiming that the relative status of slave and free is insignificant. The instructions to slaves include, even highlight, a number of such irreconcilable tensions. Some statements within this section demonstrate that slaves should understand themselves in ways the social structure would deem inappropriate, yet these slaves must continue to obey their masters. While reading these instructions, we must keep in mind the situations some slaves faced. Slaves not only lacked status, but also were available for whatever uses their masters might want them for, including sexual acts. This puts slaves in an impossible position when they are commanded to maintain certain standards of sexual conduct, yet lack control over their own sexual behavior (see above, *Excursus: Reading the Household Code*). The code addresses slaves who find themselves in such difficult circumstances. We must listen for ways in which these slaves and the whole church would have heard these instructions.

New Testament writers do not advocate the abolition of slavery and do not insist that householders within the church free their slaves. This is not because abolishing slavery was unimaginable. According to Philo (*Prob.* 79), the Therapeutae and the Essenes rejected the ownership of slaves because it is an outrage to equality and violates the laws of nature. The distinction between these groups and the church, though, is that the church chose to stay engaged with the world. Given the economic system of the first century and the large slave population, remaining engaged with the world entailed accepting the institution of slavery. Since the abolition of slavery was certainly not in the hands of the enslaved, and the church probably counted more slaves than masters among its members, the church was not in a position to abolish slavery. Furthermore, any call to end slavery would have been a political provocation prompting swift and violent repression. So the desire to continue engagement with society combined with the imposed cultural system left no room for public enactment of the leveling of status affirmed earlier in the letter (3:11). Slaves who know their true worth and status as members of Christ must continue to serve their owners and to do so as inferiors. This incongruity remained inescapable. Yet, even the direct address to slaves hints that the church perceived and valued them differently than most others did.[65]

The initial command to slaves not only exhorts them to obey their masters but also highlights the basic incongruity in their lives as it refers to their owners as "earthly [literally, 'according to the flesh'] masters" (cf. Barth and Blanke 445; Dunn 253–54). This description of their masters implies—with emphasis!—that slaves have a higher allegiance than that to their earthly masters.[66]

65. Balch (46–47) comments on how unusual it is for slaves to be addressed in such contexts.

66. Schweizer (224) remarks that the emphasis on Christ as Lord is what makes it necessary to refer to these owners as "according to the flesh."

Those owners are "lords" only in the realm that is marked by rebellion to the true Lord of the cosmos, Christ. Yet slaves must obey "in all things." Again, even the definition of the masters as "according to the flesh" suggests that this obedience "in all things" has limits. The direct address to slaves indicates that they will remain a part of the church. They must, then, disobey any demand that they discontinue their attachment to the church (cf. Barth and Blanke 446). Thus, while the command to obey masters coheres with cultural expectations, its identification of the owner imposes a boundary on "all things."

The rest of v. 22 indicates that slaves cannot withdraw from the world and neglect their assigned tasks, even if they can get away with it. They must accomplish their work in a trustworthy fashion. First, they must not do their work only when "being watched." The vivid and exceedingly rare term *oph-thalmodoulia* appears here for the first time in ancient Greek.[67] Perhaps the author of Colossians coined this word, as he may have invented the word *ethe-lothrēskia* in 2:23. Whatever its origin, it means that slaves should engage their work with an attitude that most did not expect of slaves. Slaves must not do as little as possible to avoid punishment but behave in a trustworthy manner.

Slaves should not serve only when being watched, because they should not be "people-pleasers" (*anthrōpareskoi*). They should not perform their tasks only to gain favor with their owners. This statement may simply extend the preceding statement so that Colossians urges them to show "complete commitment" to their earthly masters (MacDonald 157). Not being "people-pleasers," however, may indicate that they undertake their work without deception because they do not work simply to please their earthly masters. They do not perform their tasks well to receive rewards from their masters "according to the flesh" but because they seek to please their true Lord (cf. Lohse 160; Barth and Blanke 446). When the LXX uses *anthrōpareskos* (people-pleaser) in Ps 52:6 (53:5E; cf. *Pss. Sol.* 4:7, 8, 19), it explicitly draws a contrast between those who seek to please God and those who want to please humans. Similarly, Colossians contrasts those who seek to please God with those who seek the favor of human masters by working only while being watched. This contrast becomes explicit in the following statements.

Colossians instructs slaves to obey their masters with "sincerity of heart," that is, with honesty or with genuineness in their service. They do not commit themselves to this service because they fear retaliation from the earthly owner, but out of respect for the Lord. *Kyrios*, "the Lord," continues to refer to Christ. Only Christ's evaluation of their behavior ultimately matters. "Fearing the Lord" points not just to judgment but also to the reality that believers live every aspect of their lives in the presence of the Lord.

---

67. The only other time this noun appears for over a century is in Eph 6:6.

Verse 23 renews the exhortation of 3:17, which introduces the household code. Verse 17 instructs all believers to do "everything in the name of the Lord Jesus." Verse 23 exhorts slaves to do all their work as though it were done for the Lord rather than for human owners. The exhortation to do everything in life as service to Christ gives new meaning to the service that slaves must render to their earthly masters. While outwardly this exhortation demands conformity to conventional cultural and legal expectations, Colossians infuses that conformity with new meaning. This admonition does not encourage slaves to see slavery as God's will, but rather provides them with a new way to *interpret their required obedience*. All believers, and here particularly slaves, live the whole of their lives as servants of Christ. This higher allegiance to Christ relativizes the claims that any earthly owner can make on slaves. The author of Colossians relieves some of the tension between slaves' proclaimed status in the church and their bondage when he instructs them to perform their service for the Lord rather than for earthly masters. At the same time, however, he radically shifts the reason for their obedience to the earthly master. Slaves do not serve because they are inferior in status or worth, but because the required work can bring honor to Christ if performed as service to Christ.

At this point we should remember that the slave had no choice about being a slave. Though slaves were commonly manumitted at some point in their lives (often around the age of thirty), during their enslavement obedience was the only option that did not bring punishment to the slave and suspicion or persecution to the church. The only thing the writer of Colossians can do is offer an alternative interpretation of the slave's experience. This interpretation makes Christ the slave's true owner. Dale Martin's study of slavery in the Greco-Roman world indicates that slaves could be people with substantial authority and power if they had a powerful master. Managerial slaves of the emperor, for example, wielded great power. Colossians attaches the slaves it addresses to the most powerful master of all: Christ. In the next two verses, this new ownership becomes even more explicit. Being slaves of the Lord of the cosmos would mean a significant change in their perception of their own status. Yet the expectation that believers commit their entire lives to God in Christ holds for all members of the church, not just slaves. In some ways, slaves thus become the paradigm for all who do "everything in the name of the Lord Jesus" (cf. Nash 46–47). The perspective that identifies Christ as the true master of all believers subverts the Roman system of slavery, even as slaves must remain within it.

Verse 24 offers a surprising assurance to slaves, declaring that because they are "in Christ" they will receive an inheritance from God. The term this verse uses for repayment (*antapodosis*) more often means retribution in the sense of punishment (as it often does in the LXX), but it occasionally stands for payment of a reward, as it does here.[68] Thus, God will respond to the injustices and indignities that they currently suffer as slaves. Perhaps the writer uses this word to contrast implicitly what slaves usually expect (punishment) with what they actually receive as servants of the Lord (MacDonald 158).

The substance of that repayment is even more surprising: it is an inheritance. Since slaves were not counted as persons, they were not usually heirs (Standhartinger 2003, 95; Dunn 257). Only under exceptional circumstances (e.g., when there were no children to receive the inheritance, see Gen 15:2–3 and Matt 21:38) would slaves, inherit anything substantial. So, to promise slaves an inheritance, therefore, injects a "reversal of cultural expectations" (MacDonald 158). In several places, the New Testament itself contrasts heirs and slaves (Matt 21:35–38; Rom 8:15–17; Gal 4:1; see Barth and Blanke 448). Such contrasts demonstrate how deep-rooted the expectation was that slaves did not inherit. Yet Colossians promises them an inheritance. This promise shows that these instructions to slaves are not a matter of simple adherence to cultural expectations. Giving slaves the status of heirs, Colossians signals a reorientation of the structure of society. The new construction of reality opposes the outward circumstances that the recipients of Colossians face in the conduct of their daily lives (Müller 274–75). They all have to continue to exist in the structures that currently dominate the world, but they do so knowing that they are heirs, heirs of God. At this juncture, others may not treat them with the dignity appropriate to their identity; but this is temporary. The promise of recompense—indeed of an astonishing reward—assures slaves that God will not allow their current treatment to be the final word.

This reference to an inheritance also ties these instructions to earlier themes in the letter. Colossians 1:12 reminds all the letter's recipients that God has made them suitable recipients of the "inheritance of the saints." The requirement that slaves continue in their current place in society does not negate this hidden status. Their adoption as children of God cannot yet be seen in the structures of the cosmos; thus they remain slaves. But the future act of God will reveal their true worth and status. Colossians reminds the very persons whom society disdains of their true and ultimate status: they are heirs of God and will receive the inheritance from God.

The final verb in v. 24 may be an indicative or an imperative. Most translations understand it as an indicative and so translate, "You serve the Lord Christ."[69] Many commentators, however, render this as a command: "Serve the

68. O'Brien (228) observes that Col 3:24 is the term's only occurrence in the New Testament. It does, however, appear in Codex A in Rom 2:5, and, as O'Brien comments, the closely related word *antapodoma* appears in Luke 14:12 and Rom 11:9.

69. Translations that render the statement in this way include the NRSV, RSV, NIV, NJB, and KJV. An exception to this is the NAS, which renders it as an imperative. The NEB is more ambiguous, perhaps leaving open either option. It translates: "Christ is the Master whose slaves you must be." MacDonald (152) is among the interpreters who translate the statement as an indicative.

Lord Christ" (e.g., Lohse 161; Schweizer 226; O'Brien 228; Hay 146). As a command, it would resume the imperative of v. 23 ("work . . . as for the Lord"). Reading this verb as an imperative also has the advantage of easing the transition to the remarks about judgment in v. 25.

Whether the verb is indicative or imperative, the point remains basically the same: slaves perform their work for Christ rather than for their earthly owner. Their allegiance lies with that true lord, not the usurper who is close at hand. Even the construction of the clause places the emphasis on the identity of the true master, since the words "the Lord Christ" appear before the verb. The way the writer refers to Christ also highlights this perspective; these slaves serve "the Lord Christ." This way of referring to Christ is very unusual in the Pauline corpus. Pauline Letters include many references to "the Lord," to "the Lord Jesus," and to "the Lord Jesus Christ," but only here and in Rom 16:18 does "the Lord Christ" appear. Romans 16, like Colossians, includes the motif of judgment and the verb *douleuō* ("to serve"). In Colossians, the appellation "the Lord Christ" emphasizes his status as the one whom God appointed to defeat the dominating powers and to rule over the cosmos. This sets Christ in sharp contrast to other masters. If they are lords, he is *the* Lord who is above all and to whom all will give account. The stature of this Lord dwarfs that of all other lords; God has appointed this Lord to rule the cosmos and subdue the forces that oppose God's will. Thus Christ is the true master and judge of all.

This claim that slaves who are members of the church serve Christ (which is inherent in a command to "serve Christ") again reorients the service they render. They are not merely slaves of earthly masters but members of the household of the ruler of the cosmos. If slaves in the emperor's household often wielded considerable power and commanded deference because of who their owner was, slaves of the true ruler of the entire cosmos must enjoy even higher status. Such an affirmation does not encourage slaves to accede to the evaluations the world accords them or to be passive, as though their slavery to earthly masters is what God wants. As slaves of the Lord Christ, they belong ultimately to a different master, the master who "owns" all who are in the church and who is ruler of the whole cosmos. Thus Colossians reinterprets the obedience that slaves must give to earthly owners. If masters use these words to hold slaves in subservience, they misunderstand (and misuse) this letter's radical reorientation of the slave's service and life.

Verse 25 supports the self-understanding that the end of v. 24 asserts, as the connecting particle "for" (*gar*) shows. Slaves must recognize Christ as the Lord because he is the one coming in judgment. While v. 25 does not name Christ explicitly, the passive verb *komisetai* ("will receive recompense") points to God as the actor, and in Colossians, Christ is the one through whom God acts in the world.

With a direct warning, the author addresses people who act "unrighteously." The preceding context indicates that this statement primarily addresses slaves. This reminder of God's judgment warns slaves not to act unjustly toward their earthly owners, even though their true Lord is Christ. Despite their difficult position, they remain responsible for their behavior, particularly their behavior toward their masters. Since Christ conducts judgment without regard for social position, slaves must act as responsible agents, even if their owners do not recognize their personhood. Even this word of warning runs counter to the culture's evaluation of slaves, because it recognizes them as moral agents.

Since v. 25 concludes the section addressed to slaves and immediately precedes the exhortation addressed to masters, this reminder about judgment may also apply secondarily to masters. At the least, when the writer identifies the sin that God will judge as acts of injustice, slaves could hear a word of consolation. God will hold the earthly owners who abuse them responsible for their unjust actions, just as slaves will be held responsible for theirs. So slaves can rest assured that any unjust treatment they endure will receive a fitting response from God. Their suffering does not go unnoticed and will not remain unrequited. The assertion that judgment will be meted out without regard for status also means that God holds slaves and owners to the same standard of justice.

The exhortations addressed to slaveholders in 4:1 are only about one-third as long as the instructions addressed to slaves. This may be because there are more slaves than owners in the congregation (Lohse 162; O'Brien 231–32; but MacDonald [159] asserts that this is not necessarily so). Dunn (259) suggests that the brevity of the instructions may be less significant if we remember that this is the third time the writer addresses the head of the household. The section to slaves may also be longer because slaves need more help in interpreting the situation in which they find themselves in the world. The incongruity between their place in the world and their identity in Christ is the most acute. Even though the exhortations to owners are brief, they contain some of the most radical statements in Colossians' household code.

Immediately following the direct address to masters, the words "justice"[70] and "equality" appear in the text and so stand in an emphatic position. "To slaves" then follows "equality," with the verb appearing last in the sentence.[71] Colossians instructs masters to grant their slaves "justice and equality." These are radical demands. The usual translations of 4:1 mask the radical nature of the verse by translating these terms with a phrase such as "justly and fairly" (NRSV, NAB; similarly NIV, NJB, NEB). Lohse (162) reads the terms in this way, saying that the verse forbids abuse of slaves and commenting that popular

---

70. The term translated "justice" here ([*to*] *dikaion*) is a cognate of "unrighteous [person]" (*ho adikōn*) in the previous verse.

71. The word order is, "Masters, justice and equality to slaves grant."

philosophers of the era sometimes perceived a mutual relationship between justice and equality. Some scholars who adopt this interpretation assert that the writer would probably not give "equality" its full meaning in this context (e.g., O'Brien 232; Dunn 259–60; MacDonald 159).[72]

Isotēs, however, appears twice in Philo with the sense of equality in discussions of slavery. Once he notes that the Essenes refuse to own slaves because it is an outrage against equality (*Prob.* 79). The second time Philo uses the term, it is in connection with keeping the Sabbath. He observes that on the Sabbath free people undertake ignoble tasks usually assigned to slaves, and they engage in these tasks as acts of remembering equality. He comments further that this marks a step toward a more virtuous society (*Spec.* 2.68).[73] As early as 1885, H. A. W. Meyer (377–78) recognized the radical nature of the demand to accord "equality" to slaves, though he asserted that masters practice this equality as an act of Christian brotherhood and that it constituted a call not for the abolition of slavery but for "kindly treatment" within the slave system.[74]

It is correct that treating slaves as equals would be impossible in the legal and cultural system of the first century (Dunn 259–60), but this is precisely what Colossians demands from owners. This is one of the clearest places where this table of instructions intentionally signals opposition to the system it seems to support (Standhartinger 2000, 129). If masters would truly accord justice and equality to slaves, then slaves would no longer be treated as slaves. If masters and slaves are equals, there can be no justification for slavery. Therefore, this command to slaveholders subverts the system that the previous verses seem to support. This exhortation to masters recognizes the fundamental contradiction between owning slaves and being "in Christ."

This statement about the treatment of slaves also supports the reading I have given the entire code, since the letter's subversive point of view surfaces momentarily while it addresses the privileged. The code enjoins the necessary conformity to societal norms while at the same time indicating to those within the church that this construction of society stands at odds with the true identity of persons forced to conform. Such a revaluation of slaves cannot be lived out fully in Greco-Roman culture without withdrawing from society (as the Essenes did) or increasing the risk of hostility or persecution.

72. Barth and Blanke (450) cite Aristotle's understanding that what is "just" means what is lawful and equitable. Yet Aristotle significantly does not use the same term to refer to what is "equitable" that Colossians uses in 4:1. Aristotle uses *epieikēs* in his contrast with *dikaios* (*Eth. Nic.* 9.10.1–8), while Colossians uses *isotēs* in conjunction with *dikaios*. Aristotle argues that what is "equitable" is superior to what is "just" because it leads a person to go beyond the letter of the law. When Colossians uses *isotēs*, it goes beyond even a call to "equity," which could be linked to a person's social status.

73. These passages from Philo are cited by Standhartinger 2003, 96 n. 16.

74. Meyer (378) further applied this only to slaves within the church.

At the very least, however, slaveholders in the church must dramatically reorient their thinking about and valuing of their slaves, and this must lead to new ways of treating them, ways that recognize their equality before God and in the church. These masters have, after all, just heard the author identify slaves as heirs.

Colossians 4:1 concludes by reminding slaveholders that they also have a master. The assertion that masters are also slaves eliminates the most basic distinctions of identity and status that separate slaves and owners. Their relationship, then, must be different from that experienced by slaves whose owners do not belong to the church. Such a revaluation of status, however, does not automatically mean that master and slave are completely equal, because some well-placed slaves actually own slaves of their own. Still, both remain slaves. The writer of Colossians reminds slaveholders that their (heavenly) owner demands that they act with justice and equality toward their fellow slaves, even if they own those fellow slaves. This standard of treatment invalidates the relationship of owner and slave. Owners must, then, find ways to enact justice and equality in their interactions with their slaves. But they must do this in ways that do not flaunt the change to the detriment of the church.

Colossians locates the owner of the earthly slaveholders in heaven. This location does not distance that ultimate master but draws attention to his exalted place as judge of all. The reference to Christ abiding in heaven echoes the preceding verse's mention of judgment for those who act unjustly.[75] Thus, earthly masters must conduct themselves in the knowledge that their own master will judge them with righteousness, without regard for their social status.

This word to masters concludes the table of exhortations to particular members of the household. Its outlook should influence how we read the entire code. It levels the inequities in the relationship of master and slave and demands radical revaluations of status. Without overtly rejecting the structures of the household, the code invalidates all their supports. The various caveats inserted in the code direct us to read it "against the grain," viewing its calls for conformity as a public concession necessary for continuing existence and for ongoing mission success—or in the words of 4:5, as a summons to live "wisely in relation to those outside." Yet the code's numerous qualifiers indicate that its readers (both subordinate household members and those with power) should recognize that what the social structures require violates the true identity and status they have received in Christ. Furthermore, the persistence of those structures demonstrates the continuing power of forces that, though defeated by Christ, have not yet surrendered their grasp on the world. In this situation, all believ-

---

75. The use of the cognates for justice (*dikaios*) and injustice (*adikos*) strengthens the connection between 3:25 and 4:1.

ers look forward to the full realization of the "kingdom of [God's] beloved Son" (1:13). During this in-between time, the church must exercise wisdom among those who do not accept the lordship of Christ.

4:2–6 Concluding Exhortations

Colossians 4:2–6 presents a collection of somewhat general exhortations. These broad admonitions bring the body of Colossians to a close. Their more general nature does not indicate that these admonitions are random. Indeed, many of them relate to important themes in the letter. As the author has repeatedly linked the Colossians to Paul's ministry, he now urges them to pray for the success of Paul's efforts to make known the mystery of Christ that has been so important in Colossians. This directive makes the actions of the church and Paul's mission interdependent. Also, the exhortations of 4:2–6 again take up the call for the readers to give thanks. Just as the orientation of the believer's whole life includes thanksgiving in 3:15 and 3:17, so also the prayers in 4:2 incorporate thanksgiving. Thus, the passages that precede and follow the household code summon readers to give thanks.

The shift from more specific instructions to broader admonitions is not unique to Colossians. Similar series of exhortations following more specific instructions appear in 1 Thess 5:12–22 and Gal 5:26–6:6. The instructions in Col 4:2–6 apply to the whole church, rather than addressing various members according to their station in life, as did the instructions of the household code. Even as these concluding exhortations address the whole church, they provide context for understanding the household code because the injunction to "live wisely in relation to those outside" (4:5) shows that the church stands in tension with the surrounding world.

The exhortations in 4:2–6 fall into two sections: vv. 2–4 address Paul's commission and the Colossians' support of it, while vv. 5–6 deal with the Colossians' life among nonbelievers (cf. Barth and Blanke 451). The two subsections have a parallel structure. Both have an imperative followed by two participles and a phrase with the verb *dei* ("it is necessary"). Thus, there is a clear organization and flow to these final instructions.

4:2 Devote yourselves to prayer, staying alert in it and giving thanks. 3 At the same time, pray also for us, that God might open a door of the Word for us so that we may tell[a] of the mystery of Christ,[b] for which indeed I am in prison. 4 Pray that I might make it known, as I must tell of it. 5 Live wisely in relation to those outside, redeeming the time. 6 Always speak graciously; let your words be seasoned with salt, because you know how necessary it is to give an answer [about your faith] to everyone.

a. Codex A adds *en parrēsia* ("boldly") here, but this addition has no earlier support.

b. The original hand of B substitutes *theou* ("of God") for *christou* ("of Christ") here. Only the significantly later Codex L and some translations support this alternative reading; therefore, the reading in the text is secure.

[4:2–4] This concluding section of admonitions begins by exhorting readers to "devote" themselves to prayer. This directive enjoins the church to call on God in prayer constantly. It remains unclear whether Colossians intends to admonish them to engage in prayer regularly or to adopt a prayerful attitude in all they do (Barth and Blanke 452). Either way, this continuous prayer does not consist of requests for particular needs, but of the act of being in the presence of God, offering praise and thanksgiving. The believers' devotion to prayer presupposes that God constantly remains open to them, welcoming them into the divine presence and receiving their praise and their requests. Such access to God assumes that believers do not need the spiritual experiences that the visionaries offer because they already have access to God.

In addition to being "devoted" to prayer, they must "stay alert in it." This exhortation builds on the more general exhortation; it takes the form of a participle that depends on the initial imperative, and thus continues its imperatival force. This admonition entails more than not being careless in prayer (contra Abbott 296). In the New Testament, the verb "stay alert" (*grēgoreō*) and its cognates commonly have an eschatological nuance. "Staying alert" or "watching" often denotes that believers should conduct their lives in light of the coming Parousia (e.g., Matt 25:13; Mark 13:34–37; Luke 12:36–38; see Schweizer 231–32). Many interpreters deny this force to the word in Col 4:2 because the second coming plays a smaller part in Colossians than in many New Testament writings (e.g., Lohse 165). Colossians does point its readers to the coming judgment, however, and does so in the immediate context. The two preceding verses, which address slaves and masters (3:25; 4:1), both refer to eschatological judgment. Since end-time events appear in the context, the image of staying alert does allude to that future coming of Christ. Prayer helps believers maintain readiness for the Parousia by keeping their focus on God and God's will.

At the same time, their watchfulness in prayer probably also alludes to their need to be on watch against the false teaching (Barth and Blanke 452). Given the attention that Colossians has devoted to helping its readers avoid the visionaries' teaching, this admonition in its closing lines probably keeps that goal in sight. Furthermore, their relationship with God depends on remaining faithful to the apostolic message (1:23). Attention to final judgment and the necessity of avoiding the harmful teaching, then, are inseparable in Colossians.

These constant and watchful prayers should include thanksgiving. For Colossians, thanksgiving is a part of the believer's response to God's gifts (2:7;

3:17). The injunctions to give thanks that appear immediately before and after the household code intimate that readers should participate in the particulars of life as believers with a joy and thankfulness coming from their sure possession of God's blessings. However difficult their lives may be in those mundane settings (and 4:5–6 suggests some problems, as do the tensions within the household code), believers can give thanks for the blessings they now possess and for the coming of God's justice for them, as well as for those who abuse them. The act of remembering the blessings experienced in Christ and giving thanks for them will also inoculate readers against the visionaries' teaching because those teachings and experiences will seem of little value in light of the blessings they already possess (Barth and Blanke 452).

The exhortation to general prayer in v. 2 gives way to instructions about a particular request in v. 3. The second imperatival participle dependent on "devote yourselves" narrows the focus to Paul's ministry: Colossians instructs its readers to "pray also for us." The "us" here may include the company with Paul (Timothy, Epaphras, and those mentioned in the closing greetings) or just Paul himself, since Colossians shifts to the first-person singular by the end of the verse. This prayer does not consist of personal requests for Paul or his companions, however, but of entreaties on behalf of the progress of the gospel.

Colossians has Paul ask the readers to pray that "God might open a door of the Word for us." The metaphor of the open door was known in the ancient world, often meaning freedom to act or live as a person desires (e.g., Epictetus, *Diatr.* 2.1.19). In this passage, however, it involves removing any hindrances that hold back the gospel (cf. 1 Cor 16:9; 2 Cor 2:12). More specifically, the request may ask that God remove hindrances in the hearts of unbelievers, or that Paul be allowed to preach in prison, or that he gain freedom and so continue his work, or even that God will use Paul's preaching to reveal the "mystery" (for a more extensive list of possible meanings, see Barth and Blanke 453). The focus is on the advance of the message rather than on Paul's living conditions. The writer may think that the gospel can advance whether Paul is in or out of prison; indeed, in a pseudonymous letter, the writer may think that the gospel has advanced precisely through Paul's imprisonment and martyrdom.

The progress of "the Word" depends on God. Though Paul preaches the message, people receive it through an act of God. This explicit identification of God as the one who enables reception of the gospel fits the context of an admonition to pray. The readers ask God to remove whatever hindrances stand in the way of others coming to faith in Christ.

As MacDonald observes, this passage and the whole of Colossians assume an atmosphere of church growth. The church, Paul, and God act to spread the message throughout all the world (1:5–6, 23; see MacDonald 171). In 4:3, the church's prayers support this evangelistic effort. The call to prayer also binds the church and Paul together as supplicants before God. Both are dependent upon God's acts. This request may, then, reinforce the earlier affirmation of the oneness of all believers in Christ (3:10–11).

The desired prayer petitions God to open "a door of the Word." The Word stands for the gospel message about God's saving acts in Christ. Colossians has included both creation and redemption in these acts of God (1:15–20). This Word takes in Christ's defeat of hostile powers and the forgiveness that believers receive through Christ (2:13–15). Colossians defines "the Word" as "the mystery of Christ," that is, as the mystery that has Christ as its content. In the context of a dispute about experiences received in visions, Colossians defines the gospel message as a mystery, but a mystery with a specific content. Christ's identity and mission, and what God has done through him, constitute this mystery. The gospel message that the readers received through Paul's emissary contains the mystery that brings them relationship with God. This mystery of Christ also provides the basis for their thanksgiving.

As God opens the door that inclines hearers to the gospel, so God enables the one who proclaims the message. The Colossians are to pray that God will open the door so that Paul is able to "tell of the mystery." God's opening the door, therefore, entails divine action upon both the recipient and the preacher. In Paul's circumstances, the Colossians' request is to include giving Paul the courage to speak this message. Verse 3, then, has Paul ask for God's assistance in the proclamation. Thus, the writer has Paul acknowledge his dependence on God for courage in proclaiming the Word and for the way hearers receive that Word.

Verse 3 concludes by informing the readers that Paul is in prison. When 1:24–2:5 detailed Paul's willingness to suffer for the church, particularly for those the letter addresses, it did not mention that Paul was currently in prison. In 4:3, however, Paul suffers imprisonment for his preaching of the gospel. This mention of imprisonment specifies one aspect of Paul's suffering for the gospel and reminds the readers of his reliability as a leader and teacher. When Paul suffers for the gospel, he also suffers for those who receive that message. By asserting that Paul suffers both for the gospel and for the readers, Colossians draws the readers' own faithfulness into the progress of the gospel. This reference to his imprisonment certainly echoes the earlier construction of Paul's ethos. As its exhortations draw to an end, Colossians reminds the readers that they should accept these instructions because they come from Paul, the one who suffers for the gospel and for them. The importance of this image of Paul as the apostle who willingly suffers for the church again becomes evident as the letter draws to a close. Colossians mentions his imprisonment here and again at the very end of the letter; the letter therefore leaves readers with the image of Paul suffering for them.

Colossians does not say where Paul is in prison. Leading hypotheses include Rome, Ephesus, and Caesarea. Which is more likely depends on where one places Colossians within the ministry of Paul. If the letter is pseudonymous, it is impossible to determine what imprisonment the writer has in view, if he has a particular one in mind at all. The important thing, however, is not where Paul is incarcerated but the fact that he is. The mention of imprisonment serves as a support to Paul's authority, not simply as a biographical detail. Even if Paul is the author, the reference to his suffering for the gospel enhances his ethos so that readers will follow his directives.

Colossians 4:3 does not envision Paul's imprisonment as a hindrance to the spread of the gospel but as an embodiment of the gospel, as one of the ways God uses Paul to proclaim Christ (Barth and Blanke 454). Paul's imprisonment does not impede the proclamation; God can open the door despite, perhaps even because of, Paul's present conditions (Lohse 165).

Verse 4 asks the Colossians to pray that God will enable Paul to "make known" or "reveal" this mystery. This unusual way to refer to proclamation of the gospel suggests that Paul, or at least his preaching, serves as a means of revelation. Perhaps he also embodies that revelation through his imprisonment (Lindemann 70). The author may choose the word "reveal" for Paul's proclamation because he has just called the gospel a mystery, something that must be revealed. The language of revelation also implies that Paul's message has a divine origin. This implication again lends authority to the letter and its teachings.

Paul is not only willing to proclaim "the Word"; he is also under compulsion to do so. Colossians has Paul say, "I must tell of it." Paul's apostolic mission requires him to proclaim the mystery. By asking readers to pray that Paul might fulfill his commission, the writer again draws them into the ministry of Paul and makes them participants in his work. They came to the mystery through Paul's work, and now they must support that work with their prayers so that others may enjoy the blessings they possess. In this way, they become "co-responsible for the success of this apostolic commission" (Lohse 165). Their prayers strengthen Paul's efforts on behalf of the gospel; they strengthen Paul, even as he willingly suffers for them.

The injunction to pray in vv. 2–4, then, has several aspects. Devotion to prayer keeps believers ready for judgment and also equips them to reject false teaching. This prayer includes giving thanks for all that God has given them and for the future blessings of the Parousia. The prayers of believers offer requests not just for themselves but also for Paul and the progress of the gospel. Thus, their prayers look beyond their own well-being to the incorporation of others into the "mystery." This summons to prayer, therefore, also ties readers to the Pauline mission and its teachings.

[5–6] Verses 5–6 devote attention to the way believers should conduct their lives in a world that rejects their beliefs and values. These instructions presuppose that the church's life sets it apart from others in society and that this difference often provokes hostility. Believers must not only conduct themselves wisely in this situation, but also be ready to offer reasons for their distinctiveness. Thus, even as they pray that the gospel will come to more and more people, they continue to live in a world dominated by forces that oppose that very gospel and so oppose the life that flows from it.

Verse 5 begins with the exhortation "Live wisely." This admonition picks up a theme that appears throughout the letter and may form an *inclusio* with 1:9–10, where the writer prays that readers will have knowledge of God's will "in all . . . wisdom" (Dunn 265). Colossians also mentions wisdom as a quality that believers should possess in 1:28; 2:3; and 3:16. Now the author indicates that the wisdom believers receive from God must show itself in their manner of life. This wisdom must determine the believer's whole life. The ethical instructions provided by the letter comprise an important part of this wisdom.

New Testament exhortations commonly use the word *peripateō* for "live" (e.g., 1 Cor 7:17; Gal 5:16; Eph 4:1). Literally, this word means to "walk around," but it often functions as a metaphor for one's conduct of life (see the comment on 3:7 above). Beyond this common usage, the writer may use *peripateō* to suggest an active image for the believer's life. Believers do not simply passively move through the world while avoiding immoral conduct; instead, they actively and "visibly demonstrat[e] the fruits" of their new existence in Christ (MacDonald 172).

Colossians identifies a particular arena in which believers should exercise wisdom in their lives: "in relation to those outside." Labeling nonbelievers "outsiders" sets the church apart from the rest of the world in no uncertain terms. It reflects a sectarian outlook that marks a clear divide between those in the church and those not in it. This perspective is a corollary of believers' recognition that they possess a knowledge of the mystery of Christ that unbelievers do not have (Dunn 265). As citizens of the kingdom of God's Son, members of the church are different from their neighbors. Believers must not minimize this difference or act as though the difference has few consequences. Their membership in Christ should reorient their entire lives. Even when believers conform to expected behaviors, they do so from such different motives (i.e., out of service to God through Christ) that they remain distinctive. This distinctness does not, however, mean that they abandon the world or physically separate themselves from it. Rather, they live out this difference in the midst of life.

This distinction between believers and nonbelievers bears two implications. First, believers experience this distinction in the form of *opposition*. The message of Christ's defeat of the powers already demonstrates that the structures of the world are hostile to God's will and to God's people. People outside the church embody and advocate a different set of values, values that often contradict and oppose those believers hold. The values of the unbelieving world do not allow the church to put fully into practice its own beliefs and commitments.

For example, they could not fully enact the leveling of social and ethnic differences that 3:11 advocates. Even if they enact their beliefs only in the context of the gathered church, they set themselves apart from others. Outsiders would often regard as subversive the behaviors that their participation in the "new self" requires, conduct that would therefore incite opposition (see above, *Excursus: Reading the Household Code*). Wisdom with respect to outsiders, then, includes discerning how to live in ways that do not provoke unnecessary opposition and difficulty. Yet the differences remain clear to all.

Designating nonbelievers as outsiders suggests, second, that believers live in a setting where their lives serve as a *demonstration of God's will*. The church remains in contact with society in part to draw others into a community that honors God. Believers serve as lights to others, as guides to who God is and what God wants for the world (cf. Phil 2:15–16; see Barth and Blanke 455, who also cite Matt 5:16). Even in a hostile setting, therefore, an element of evangelism remains. Believers' witness to God should draw others to God, even though their manner of life exhibits a strangeness that requires explanation. The church's opposition to the values of the surrounding culture must not lead it to withdraw from conversation with people who do not presently accept its way of being. This conversation itself, even if it involves danger, may begin to transform that outside world, as the next clause of v. 5 may intimate.

The final exhortation of v. 5 calls readers to "redeem the time." The verb *exagorazō* comes from the commercial sphere, where it means "to buy" or "to buy back," sometimes to buy back a person from slavery or danger. Outside the realm of commerce, it takes the meanings of delivering someone from danger and of making the most of an opportunity (BDAG 343).

In v. 5, the participle *exagorazomenoi* ("redeeming") may express the purpose ("so that you may redeem the time") or the result ("and so you redeem the time") of believers living wisely in relation to outsiders. The brevity of this unqualified expression allows several interpretations. It may simply mean that believers should not idly waste the time God has given them (Lohse 168); however, this exceedingly general meaning seems unlikely. Two other meanings provide more probable explanations of the phrase. It may constitute a call to missionary activity (MacDonald 172; BDAG 343), a reading suggested by the phrase's position within the sentence. In Greek, "those outside" (*tous exō*) comes between the two injunctions in v. 5 ("Live wisely in relation to those outside" and "redeeming the time"). While the preposition *pros* ("in relation to"), which governs "those outside," joins primarily to the preceding command, it also qualifies the following participle so that unbelievers remain in view. Thus, believers are to use the time they have to introduce others to the mystery that gives new life. Even in the midst of opposition, they should use their evangelistic opportunities to invite others into the blessings they have in Christ. Therefore, the phrase expresses a purpose of living wisely.

A second possible meaning of "redeeming the time"—and one that also understands it as expressing purpose here—has it depict living in recognition of the coming eschaton. The use of *kairos* for "time" supports this reading because this term commonly (though not always) has an eschatological nuance in the New Testament (Barth and Blanke 456; Dunn 265–66). I have already noted the presence of eschatological notices in 3:25; 4:1–2. This exhortation picks up that underlying theme, reminding the Colossians that they must live in the midst of an unfriendly world while keeping their eyes on God's final act. Such a reference to the end does not require readers to think that the Parousia is imminent, only that its coming is certain. This injunction, then, reminds its readers of their accountability to God.

Perhaps the best reading of the expression "redeeming the time" combines these options. The phrase urges believers to invite others into the blessings that will be fully realized in that consummating act of God. Thus, living in light of Christ's return means not turning away from outsiders but embracing the task of evangelism.

Verse 6 instructs the community about how to communicate with "those outside." Colossians exhorts its readers to "speak graciously." This communication continues to have the dual purpose of defending one's behavior as a believer and inviting others into the church. Continuing the instructions about how to relate to unbelievers, this admonition encourages believers to engage them with courtesy and kindness. Engagement with even hostile outsiders must reflect the new life that believers possess in Christ. Such exchanges must manifest the "new self." Colossians exhorts readers to speak their words *en chariti*, literally, "with [or in] grace." Following its common usage, *charis* here clearly means "gracious." Yet it is difficult to hear this phrase within Pauline circles without detecting an echo of Paul's proclamation of the grace (*charis*) that Christ mediates to the church (Dunn 266). Still, the primary meaning is that believers' conversations with unbelievers must not project an attitude of superiority, but instead convey the goodness that believers experience through the gifts God has given them.

The phrase "seasoned with salt" confirms the translation "gracious" (instead of "with grace"), because this well-known idiom means "pleasing" (Plutarch, *Mor.* 514E–F; see Lohse 168–69; MacDonald 173). This pleasing speech also has missionary intent. Believers do not turn their backs on the world, but neither do they join it. Instead, they invite others, through gracious and pleasant speech, to join their community. The inviting nature of their speech does not suggest that they are on good terms with those who wield power over them (contra Dunn 267); indeed, the evangelistic intention of gracious speaking reaches beyond those who already find the conduct and teaching of the church attractive. Gracious speech in difficult circumstances, particularly when experiencing persecution, is powerful testimony to the gospel. Paul's own preaching in prison demonstrates that seeking to proclaim the gospel successfully does not require the absence of hostility. And as Tertullian will later assert, "The blood [death] of martyrs is the seed of the church" (*Apol.* 50:13).

The final phrase of v. 6 could be read as a directive that concerns only friendly inquiry into the substance of the faith (Dunn 267). But given the immediately preceding reference to Paul's imprisonment for the gospel and the whole letter's recognition that the powers that control the cosmos also oppose Christ, this reading is unlikely. The readers' gracious speech must be able to explain to outsiders—even the suspicious and hostile—why people in the church believe and act as they do. The form of the phrase imposes an obligation: they must "know how necessary [*dei*] it is to give an answer." This exhortation applies to all members of the community; all must prepare to tell about their faith. And they must prepare to answer "everyone." In light of the preceding household code, "everyone" includes unbelieving husbands, parents, and masters, perhaps also unbelieving wives, children, and slaves. It may even extend to the visionaries (MacDonald 458 n. 20). Particularly those in places of authority over others (husbands, parents, and masters) may be expected to pose sharp questions about what the church teaches and why.

Persecution does not play as large a role in the context of Colossians as it does, for example, in 1 Peter or 1 Thessalonians, but 4:2–6 suggests strongly that opposition, hostility, or perhaps even physical persecution is present and shapes the ways Colossians' readers must negotiate life in the world (MacDonald 173–75). The requirement to "give an answer" implies that unbelievers are questioning the allegiances and behavior of church members. These questions sometimes do more than inquire about the faith, for they may challenge the readers' very participation in the church. Colossians, then, exhorts every believer to be ready to offer an explanation for one's new orientation to life and new communal engagements. This response is a part of what it means to live wisely, so it will be a response that speaks the truth, but does so in a gracious rather than a confrontational manner. Given the church's marginal position and the low status of so many of its members, this path both enables the continuing existence of the church as a group and makes membership as inviting as possible under the circumstances.

The closing exhortations of 4:2–6 concentrate on relationships with outsiders. In vv. 3–4, outsiders are in view as Colossians urges readers to pray for the success of Paul's missionary efforts. Then, in vv. 5–6, the efforts of the Colossians themselves in relation to outsiders become the focus. They must act wisely toward outsiders to minimize hostile opposition and draw others to the church and the blessings it enjoys. A clear tension exists between the church's existence as a group that stands apart from the surrounding culture and the church's evangelistic efforts. Believers must remain distinct and separate, yet at the same time they must remain open enough to invite others into the community of faith.

This tension between distinctness and the appeal to invite outsiders into their fellowship further elucidates the tensions evident in the household code (3:18–4:1) and the vice and virtue lists (3:5, 8, 12). Both these sets of exhortations include some elements that the culture accepts and some elements that are countercultural. The general exhortations of 4:2–6, then, serve as an effective conclusion to the whole hortatory section that begins in 3:1, and to the entire letter body. Believers securely possess a new life in Christ, but they must embody that life in a setting where most people reject their beliefs about God and how God wants them to live. To negotiate life faithfully in such a setting, believers must devote themselves to prayer for God's help (4:2) and learn to "live wisely" (4:5). Such wise living will minimize the threat of persecution and attract others to the church.

The concluding exhortations of 4:2–6 bring the body of the letter to a close. The greetings that follow confirm that Paul and his coworkers have the good of the Colossians at heart and give instruction about sharing this letter with others (and reading a letter dispatched to another church). These greetings encourage readers to accept the instructions given throughout the letter, thereby reinforcing its exhortations to live out their faith in the church and in the world.

COLOSSIANS 4:7–18

Final Greetings and Instructions

Colossians has completed the main argument of the letter with its redefinition of "seeking the things above." The instructions and exhortations in 3:1–4:6 filled "Seek the things above" with a meaning that coheres with the letter's understanding of what Christ's life, death, and resurrection have accomplished for believers. Now the writer ends the letter with greetings to the Colossians from Paul's companions and some closing words from Paul. The writer intersperses these greetings with instructions that allow us a glimpse into the developing recognition of the authority of the Pauline Letters.

Ancient letters often included greetings to and from common acquaintances. Since means of communication were few, many writers took advantage of the opportunity to greet friends and family when they sent a letter to someone known by both parties. These short greetings may include comments about events in the life of either person (e.g., a birthday) or a term of endearment (e.g., "loving wife"). Such greetings sometimes also indicate the social and economic connections the writer has established in the area from which he writes or in the locale of the recipient(s). The greetings in Colossians mention people from widely differing places on the social spectrum, including a slave, a physician, and a woman wealthy enough to host the church in her house. So they reveal something of the diversity within the Pauline churches (Thompson 103).

4:7 Tychicus, the beloved brother and faithful servant and fellow slave in the Lord, will tell you everything about my circumstances. **8** This is the reason I am sending him to you, so that you may know about my situation and so that he may encourage your hearts. **9** [With Tychicus] I am sending Onesimus, the faithful and beloved brother, who is one of you. They will tell you everything about my situation.

10 Aristarchus, my fellow prisoner of war, and Mark, the cousin of Barnabas (about whom you received the command, "If he comes to you, receive him"), send you greetings. **11** So does Jesus, called Justus. These are the only Jews[a] among my fellow workers for the kingdom of God. They have been a comfort to me. **12** Epaphras, one of your own, and a slave of Christ Jesus,[b] sends his greetings to you. He is always struggling in prayer[c] for you, praying that you may stand perfect[d] and fully convinced in all the will of God. **13** For I testify about him that he has labored strenuously for you and for those in Laodicea and those in Hierapolis. **14** Luke, the beloved physician, sends his greeting to you, as does Demas.

15 Greet the brothers and sisters in Laodicea, particularly Nympha and the church that meets in her[e] house. **16** Now when you have read this letter, make sure that the church in Laodicea reads it, too, and that you also read the letter to Laodicea. **17** And tell Archippus: "Attend to the ministry that you have received in the Lord, so that you may fulfill it."

18 I, Paul, send my greeting with my own hand. Remember my chains. Grace be with you.

a. Literally, "those who are from the circumcision."

b. Both ℵ and B have *christou Iēsou* ("of Christ Jesus"), the reading in the UBS text. However, P[46] has only *christou* ("of Christ"). These readings are about equally probable, but perhaps the shorter reading can account for the addition of *Iēsou* more readily than the longer reading can account for its deletion.

c. The text has the plural "prayers," but the sense is that he regularly prays fervently for them. Reflecting the plural, one might translate the phrase "in [his] prayers."

d. In 1:28, I translated the same term, *teleios*, as "complete." The context here favors "perfect." See the comment on 4:12–13 below.

e. The manuscript evidence for the pronoun that follows Nympha is divided. Codex B has a feminine pronoun (*autēs*), which indicates that Nympha was a woman; however, D has the male pronoun, which indicates that this householder is male. Codex ℵ changes the pronoun to the plural "their" (*autōn*). Given the reticence of ancients to identify women as heads of households, the reading with the feminine pronoun is most likely to have produced the others.

Many Pauline Letters include greetings from those with Paul; even pseudonymous letters adopt this form. The greetings in Colossians, however, are more extensive than in any Pauline letter except Romans, and the longest in relation to the size of the letter. The long list of greetings in Romans enhances Paul's credibility because he had never been to that church. By naming contacts whom the recipients know and trust, Paul encourages the Roman church to accept him.

The less extensive, but still substantial, list of associates in Colossians serves multiple purposes. First, the inclusion of greetings from known associates of Paul lends plausibility to the attributed authorship. The greetings in Colossians overlap significantly with those in Philemon, thus providing Colossians a specific setting within Paul's ministry.

Second, when greetings to or from associates appear in pseudonymous letters, they probably point us to leaders known to the second generation of the church. They include known associates of Paul, some of whom probably remained active in the churches that received the letter. Inclusion in such a greeting would have enhanced the named person's status within the church in the present. Thus, the authority of the apostle both supports the teaching the letter advocates and buttresses the positions of the people it places in the immediate company of the apostle. Rather than sending the author's own greetings to people as Paul does in Romans, Colossians has Paul's associates send greetings to the church. The attention Colossians gives to those who send greetings suggests that they represent the apostle's teaching (Pokorný 189–90). Hübner (117–18) suggests that the author of Colossians knows the people he mentions in the greeting, and that they are not only still living but also have given permission for their names to be mentioned in the letter. If this is correct, then Colossians may be a project of the Pauline circle rather than of a single author. But such hypotheses remain speculative (as Hübner recognizes).

[7–9] The greetings section in Colossians begins by naming the two people who are delivering the letter, Tychicus and Onesimus. They do not send greetings themselves, since they would be present when the letter is read, but rather receive recommendations. Readers need to view the people delivering the letter as reliable and trustworthy because they not only deliver the letter but also read and interpret it for the church. Furthermore, they will convey additional information about Paul. In the context of a letter written after Paul's death, these recommendations bolster the status of Tychicus and Onesimus (or perhaps those who have followed them) within the community.

Verse 7 opens with the assurance that Tychicus will provide the Colossians with additional information about Paul. This is the earliest of five New Testament mentions of Tychicus (cf. Acts 20:4; Eph 6:21; 2 Tim 4:12; Titus 3:12).

While this is a fairly common name, the same Tychicus is probably in view in all these places because the texts do not distinguish him from any other Tychicus. The references to him in Acts and the disputed Pauline Letters suggest that he became an important associate of Paul late in Paul's ministry; Paul never mentions Tychicus in the undisputed letters. Acts makes Tychicus a member of a group that accompanied Paul on a journey from Ephesus to Troas (through Macedonia). Perhaps it was in connection with that mission that he became an integral part of Paul's company. Acts also identifies him as an Asian (i.e., from modern Turkey). This associates him with the region that includes Colossae and Ephesus (which is important in other references to him) and so makes his presence in this letter particularly apt.

The mention of Tychicus adds verisimilitude to the claim of Pauline authorship. At the same time, it identifies Tychicus as an associate of Paul who knows more about Paul than his letters convey. This relationship positions him to help the community find its way in Paul's absence. In addition to his knowledge of Paul, Colossians ascribes other important attributes to Tychicus. First, he is a "beloved brother." Since Paul often uses "brother" to refer to fellow believers, this appellation does not indicate any relationship with Paul beyond what he would have with other church members. Still, this title suggests the closeness of relationships within the Pauline churches and reflects the way Paul constructs the community as a fictive kinship group. Church members are not merely friends; they are also members of the same family. This construction of a new family locates believers within a new social structure that has both demands and privileges: they must respond to the needs of one another as kin, because they have all become heirs of the inheritance that God grants through Christ. Therefore, the title "brother"[76] grants believers a new identity within the family of God. At the same time, this way of understanding the community may also have encouraged the adoption of the Greco-Roman household's hierarchical structures within the church.

Tychicus is not just a brother but also a *beloved* brother. This makes his association with Paul more personal, yet it does not set him in a unique position, because Colossians also calls Onesimus, the next person mentioned, a "beloved brother." Still, this designation indicates that Paul knows them as more than just fellow believers and has more than a good working relationship with them; they are especially close to him and his mission.

---

76. Where it appears in Colossians (e.g., 1:2), I have translated the plural "brothers" (*adelphoi*) as "brothers and sisters." Paul and Colossians intend to include all believers with the term "brothers." Use of the masculine without mentioning "sisters" reflects the masculine orientation of the language of these writers. At the same time, identifying them all as brothers situates them to receive God's inheritance in a way that identifying some as sisters would not, because males were the primary heirs in Greco-Roman culture.

Colossians next calls Tychicus a "faithful servant." The adjective "faithful" may apply to both "servant" and the next noun, "fellow slave." Whether it attaches to both or only "servant," it indicates that Tychicus is reliable in service to the readers and to God. Paul commonly uses *diakonos* (servant) to speak of those engaged in ministry. As early as the time of Philippians, however, *diakonos* sometimes designates an office within a church (Phil 1:1). In this Colossians passage, it does not refer to a specific position. While commentators have often wondered whether Tychicus's ministry primarily serves Paul or the church, the latter coheres better with use of the term in the Pauline Letters. In either case, this language links Tychicus with Paul's ministry and so grants him legitimacy as a representative of Paul and of Paul's views once Paul is gone (cf. MacDonald 178).

The title "servant" as a designation for one engaged in ministry signals something important about the way Paul envisions leadership in the church. A servant of the church works for the good of others rather than expecting others to meet one's own needs or conform to one's own desires. Both Paul and the Synoptic Gospels call leaders in the church servants, and even slaves. This terminology suggests a vision of leadership that runs contrary to the ways most envisioned and exercised leadership in the first century. Instead of seeking honor and deference, leaders in the church must serve the needs of others.

The writer makes this understanding of leadership more emphatic with the third title he assigns to Tychicus, "fellow slave" (*syndoulos*). This title intensifies the implication of servitude in relation to the community. The story Matthew (20:20–28) and Mark (10:35–45) tell of the disciples' dispute about who would be greatest, which is initiated by the request of James and John to hold the two highest offices, elucidates this escalation. In this story Jesus tells the disciples that if they want to be leaders in the kingdom, they must be servants (*diakonoi*), and anyone who wants to hold the highest position must become the slave (*doulos*) of all. The designation *doulos* makes willingness to serve others emphatic.

Tychicus is a slave of Christ and a fellow slave with Paul. Some slaves owned by the wealthy and powerful held positions of significant power and authority. They conducted their owner's business and so wielded real power and influence. But Colossians does not call Tychicus a slave "*of* the Lord," but "*in* the Lord." Perhaps this suggests that he serves as a slave of the church within the realm determined and ruled by Christ. So he serves the community according to the values of God's kingdom. Still, this title designates him as a leader, even as it defines how leadership should be practiced in the church.

The term "fellow slave" appears in the Pauline corpus only here and in Col 1:7, where it applies to Epaphras. Colossians relates Tychicus to both Paul and Epaphras when it uses this term to describe him, thus according to Tychicus the same status that it grants the founder of the recipients' church, who is an associate of Paul. This raises both to the status of being coworkers with Paul.

"Slave," then, both elevates and lowers the status of the one who bears the designation. The slave serves in the Lord's realm and serves with Paul, but is still one who serves others. Such a designation demands humility even as its bearer possesses significant authority. Clearly, that authority is derivative, primarily from Christ, but also through association with Paul.

The commendation of Tychicus continues as v. 8 delineates his mission to the Colossians: he is coming to tell them about Paul and to "encourage" their hearts. The first part of the task again indicates that Tychicus knows more about Paul than what the letter contains. In the context of the letter's narrative, Tychicus knows about Paul's imprisonment and other personal affairs. In the context of reading this letter after Paul's death, however, this association intimates that Tychicus knows Paul and Paul's gospel. Thus, he can help the church remain faithful as it seeks answers to its current questions. Notably, Colossians returns to the plural "us" at this point, so that what Tychicus knows about includes not just Paul but also the circle around Paul.

The second purpose of Tychicus's visit is to strengthen and encourage the readers in their faith. *Parakaleō* ("to encourage") can mean to "comfort, encourage, beseech," or "strengthen." In the context of Colossians, with its exhortation to maintain allegiance to the apostolic message, emphasis falls on the meanings "encourage" and "strengthen." The immediate context also suggests this nuance because knowledge about Paul's circumstances will bring the readers encouragement even as it strengthens their resolve to remain faithful to his teachings. The task of strengthening the readers' resolve to persevere in fidelity to Paul's teaching identifies Tychicus with a central purpose of this letter and with the mission of Paul more broadly. Thus, even his assigned task supports his position within the church.

Verse 9 contains a briefer commendation for Onesimus, probably indicating that Onesimus occupies a secondary position in this mission. Onesimus was a common name for slaves, perhaps because its meaning ("useful") seemed particularly apt for one born into slavery (O'Brien 248). The connections between the greetings in Colossians and those in Philemon suggest that the Onesimus in Colossians is the same slave who prompted Paul to write the letter to Philemon.

The author identifies Onesimus as a brother but not as a servant or slave, as he designated Tychicus. Rather than showing sensitivity about the status of Onesimus as a slave (or perhaps, by the time Colossians is written, as a former slave), the writer refrains from using this title because Onesimus does not have the same kinds of connections with the Pauline mission that Tychicus does. Still, he is "faithful and loved." Thus, he remains a reliable fellow believer, even if he does not hold a position of leadership within the Pauline mission.[77] If

---

77. Pokorný (191), however, asserts that there is no real difference in the ways these two are named.

Colossians' readers connect the occasion of this letter and that of Philemon, Onesimus has only just become a member of the church.[78] In that case, placing him among the leaders of the movement would be inappropriate.

The writer notes that Onesimus is from Colossae, so the recipients know him. This mention of Onesimus probably indicates that he became a leader of the church in western Asia Minor (as later and somewhat contradictory sources indicate; see, e.g., *Const. ap.* 7.46, where he is bishop of Berea; Ign. *Eph.* 1.3–4, where an Onesimus not explicitly related to Philemon is bishop of Ephesus). Even this reference to him in a secondary position places him immediately in Paul's circle and thus supports his status within the church. After all, while he is secondary to Tychicus, Paul commissions him to tell the readers about "everything here." This includes more than information about Paul's affairs in prison (cf. Abbott 299). In a time after Paul's death, it points primarily to his teaching and manner of life.

[10–11] In vv. 10–11, fellow workers of Paul send greetings to the Colossians. Following this common custom allows the author to identify the people mentioned as intimates of the apostle and so to support their authority as leaders. Identifying them as Jews also bolsters their status because the early Gentile church regarded being Jewish as a valuable credential for a teacher (see 2 Cor 11:21–22).

Aristarchus, the first coworker mentioned, also sends greetings in Philemon (v. 24). Elsewhere in the New Testament, Aristarchus appears only in Acts, where he comes from Thessalonica and is a traveling companion of Paul; he accompanies Paul as he journeys through Macedonia and again as he begins his trip to Rome (19:29; 20:4; 27:2). Colossians seems to number him among Paul's coworkers who are Jewish. Aristarchus evidently became a significant person in the last stages of Paul's ministry, at least as Acts presents it.

Colossians calls Aristarchus a "fellow prisoner of war" (see G. Kittel, *TDNT* 1:195–97, and the commentators below). Paul uses this vivid description for only three other people: Epaphras (Phlm 23) and Andronicus and Junia (Rom 16:7). While Paul sometimes uses military language, this turn of phrase is difficult. Since Paul describes only three other people as "fellow prisoner of war," some interpreters imagine that these three took turns voluntarily living in prison with Paul (Lightfoot 236; Barth and Blanke 478–79; Dunn 275; among others). No evidence other than this single term supports this unlikely explanation. Still, this descriptor must signal more than simply that each is a believer (Dunn 275). If Acts 19:29 accurately reports the result of the riot in Ephesus incited by the silversmith Demetrius, then Aristarchus was seized and brought into the theater

---

78. In that context, it may be important to say that the runaway slave is now trustworthy (so Lightfoot 235). Alternatively, calling both him and Tychicus "faithful" may imply a contrast to the rejected teachers (Thurston 1999, 48).

by a crowd. In that case, calling him a prisoner of war could allude to this event (MacDonald 180).[79] The emphasis, however, falls on Aristarchus's participation in the battle against the powers of evil (Thurston 1999, 48; Thompson 105). Colossians identifies him as a coworker of Paul who endures difficulties because of his participation in that ministry. While that association may involve imprisonment, the epithet "fellow prisoner of war" emphasizes his more general willingness to stand for the faith in the midst of opposition. In this, he models the behavior that Colossians urges on its readers in the face of the teaching rejected by the letter.

Colossians associates Mark, the second person to send greetings to the readers, closely with the Pauline mission by counting him among Paul's companions. Acts recalls a tradition of Mark falling into disfavor with Paul and so not accompanying Paul on a mission trip (Acts 12:25; 15:37–40). Although Acts asserts that this disfavor resulted from Mark's previous performance in the mission field, it probably has more to do with the dispute in Antioch at which Paul and Barnabas disagreed (Gal 2:11–14). Colossians' identification of Mark as a cousin of Barnabas may suggest either that he was not as well known to the readers as the other individuals mentioned in the letter or that they knew of more than one Mark. No evidence, however, points to a different Mark with whom they might confuse Barnabas's cousin. Still, the writer may insert this clarification to avoid confusion because the name "Mark" was common in the Greco-Roman world. If the Mark of Acts was a different person, the mention of this Mark as a coworker in Colossians might be less strange. On the other hand, associating him with Barnabas might further strengthen Mark's position in the church. This close association of Mark with Paul also intimates that Paul and Barnabas reconciled their most important theological differences.

While Mark receives commendation, he is not traveling at Paul's behest. So Colossians pictures Mark as having a good and cooperative relationship with Paul, but not as a member of Paul's mission team. It is not impossible that Mark belongs within the Pauline group but has not yet been given an assignment. Still, the instructions about "receiving" Mark seem to come from someone other than Paul. Thus, Colossians adds Paul's support to instructions someone else has given at a previous time. The readers are to "receive him," a reception probably entailing financial support as well as acceptance of his leadership. This mention of Mark reinforces his status among the readers. Accepting his leadership also means listening to his teaching. The author of Colossians, then, affirms that Mark will bring authentic teaching, teaching that supports the message of the letter.

---

79. Hübner (118–19), while seeing the term figuratively, notes that the philological arguments favor understanding it as a reference to a literal imprisonment, even though some argue that Paul would more likely use *syndesmos* for a fellow prisoner.

The third person to send greetings is Jesus Justus. Like others at the time (e.g., Paul), this person has taken a Romanized name. This name may signal his commitment to faithful obedience to God because it means "the Just," an appellation that identifies him as a person who is faithful to the law. Beyond his identification as Jewish and the mention of his double name, we know nothing about this person, who appears nowhere else in the New Testament. The readers, however, probably know him as an associate of Paul and perhaps as a leader of the church in their region. Thus, mention of him supports his leadership.

In a somewhat mournful tone, v. 11 reports that the three people just mentioned are the only Jews among Paul's coworkers. The tone echoes the grief Paul expresses for his own people in Rom 9–11. Paul, of course, recognized the validity of the way the Jerusalem church lived its faith, but Colossians hints at the writer's disappointment that more Jews did not participate in the propagation of the gospel among Gentiles. This passage may show how difficult it was for the church to accept as authentic the diverse embodiments of the gospel that various cultural and religious identities of converts required. Accepting the radical divergence of practice between Paul's Gentile churches and the Torah-observant Jerusalem church was a continuing challenge for the early church. The emphasis on church unity in Ephesians may be a further development of the sentiment conveyed by this verse.

These Jewish coworkers are "a comfort" to Paul. This may mean that they offer some relief to his worry about the many who do not turn to the gospel (Barth and Blanke 482) or that they offer comfort in the conduct of his ministry. The term used for comfort (*parēgoria*) appears only here in the New Testament. Outside medical contexts, it primarily means "consolation" or "comfort," often in the face of death (Lightfoot 239, who cites Plutarch *Mor.* 56A [*Adul. amic.*]; 118 [*Cons. Apollo*]; 599B [*Exil.*]; Lohse 173 n. 29, who cites gravestones, among other materials). These fellow Jews, then, offset some of the deep grief that Paul feels about the rejection of the gospel by so many in Israel. The term may also intimate that Paul's circumstances are so dire that he is facing death and so experiences the presence of these coworkers as a deep comfort. This nuance intensifies Paul's plea for the readers to follow the letter's instructions (Thurston 1999, 49). If it is written after Paul's death, it may also picture these leaders, and others like them, as the people who honor Paul's memory by continuing his teaching (Pokorný 193).

These fellow Jews are Paul's coworkers "for the kingdom of God." The phrase "kingdom of God" appears only eight times in earlier writings of the Pauline corpus.[80] In six occurrences, it refers to the consummation at the eschaton (1 Cor 6:9, 10; 15:50; Gal 5:21 [all four of which speak of inheriting or not

---

80. It appears a total of 14 times in the Pauline corpus, including two instances in Colossians (1:13; 4:11), then also in Eph 5:5; 2 Thess 1:5; 2 Tim 4:1, 18.

inheriting the kingdom]; 1 Cor 15:24; 1 Thess 2:12). Despite this Pauline usage, interpreters often assert that the phrase has lost the full force of its eschatological character in Colossians (e.g., Lohse 172; Hübner 119–20). But the earlier use of "kingdom" in Colossians sets the expression squarely in an eschatological, even apocalyptic, framework. In 1:13, God has rescued believers from evil powers and transferred them into "the kingdom of his beloved Son." While Colossians does not stress the imminence of the end, its interpretation of the place of believers in the world is fully eschatological and apocalyptic. Thus in 4:11, the "kingdom of God" refers to the realm in which Christ rules and in which believers experience the initial blessings of the end time. This corresponds to Paul's use of "kingdom of God" in Rom 14:17.

[12–13] Among those who send greetings, Colossians describes Epaphras at greatest length, and he alone sends an individual greeting rather than being part of a group that greets the church. This singles him out as the most important person who greets them. As the founder of the church in Colossae, Epaphras has a special relationship with them. Furthermore, he is a Colossian ("one of you"). We could capture the sense of this expression with the rendering "Your Epaphras." Verses 12–13 affirm and strengthen the close relationship between Epaphras and the readers. Colossians does not explain why Epaphras is not returning with the people who are delivering the letter. Some speculate that he himself is in prison (Hay 161).[81] If the letter is pseudonymous, mention of Epaphras surely serves to strengthen his authority through this commendation by Paul.

The designation "slave of Christ" further strengthens Epaphras's position. Colossians (1:7) has already designated him a "fellow slave" of Paul and so bound him to the Pauline mission. The title "slave of Christ" without the prefix *syn* ("fellow") may enhance Epaphras's status. Though Paul calls himself a slave of Christ on occasion, he seldom assigns this title to others. The only exception is Timothy. In the greeting of Philippians, Paul calls both himself and Timothy "slaves of Christ." This title does not make Epaphras equal to Paul (contra Barth and Blanke 482–83), but it does elevate his stature. It indicates his extraordinary relationship to Christ and his service to the Colossians. It may also mark him as one who carries out some apostolic functions. Epaphras is not an apostle of the whole church, but in many ways he is "their apostle," sent to bring the gospel to Colossae (Pokorný 193, following Marxsen; Lightfoot 239) and perhaps to the surrounding region as well (see the discussion below). The designation "slave of Christ" secures his authority; he is the one who possesses apostolic teaching and holds an extraordinary position of authority.[82] At the

---

81. Schweizer (240) even speculates that Epaphras is one of the people who remain in prison with Paul voluntarily. As noted above, the evidence for such voluntary imprisonment is very weak.

82. O'Brien (255) correctly notes that it is going too far to see in this commendation a conferring of apostolic authority.

same time, it continues a tradition of defining leadership in the church in a countercultural manner (see the comment on 1:7–8 for the combination of authority
and humility possible in the designation "slave").

The letter highlights Epaphras's ministry of intercessory prayer. He does not
simply pray for the readers, but does so constantly and with an intensity
described as "struggling." The writer has applied the same image to Paul's ministry on behalf of the Colossians in 2:1. This link again associates the ministry
of Epaphras with Paul's and at the same time emphasizes the importance of the
subject about which he prays. To have someone so personally related to them
praying with such intensity and constancy adds significant weight to his request
(MacDonald 181).

Epaphras prays that the readers may "stand perfect and fully convinced in
all the will of God." This language ties together the prayer of Epaphras and the
readers' rejection of the teaching opposed by the letter. The teachers have cast
in doubt the readers' certainty of salvation and their knowledge of God's will.
As we have seen in connection with 2:6–23, these teachers demand new practices that they say will lead to full salvation and fuller understanding of what
God wants. Throughout the letter, the writer assures the Colossians that they
already possess all the blessings of God because they have been raised with
Christ. Even those blessings that can be actualized only after death are already
reserved for them in the presence of God, so they need no other spiritual experiences and no mystically attained knowledge of God. Epaphras's prayer supports these claims to salvation and relationship with God, because the object of
his prayer is their recognition that they already possess these gifts.

The petition that the readers may "stand perfect" uses the passive voice in
Greek. Instead of "perfection" being a goal that the readers pursue, it is a gift
that Epaphras asks God to grant to them. Again, this stands in contrast to the
striving that the other teachers enjoin as a means to attain special spiritual experiences. *Teleioi* ("perfect") may also be translated "mature" or "complete," but
given the striving that the visionaries advocate and the letter's emphasis on fullness, the translation "perfect" better fits the immediate context. This does not
imply that the readers have reached moral perfection (as the many exhortations
in Colossians demonstrate), but it does affirm that they fully possess the blessings of God. Epaphras does not pray that God will give them this status as a
new possession, but that God will confirm and strengthen them in what they
already have.

Epaphras's second prayer request also admits two understandings. The verb
plērophoreō may mean "to completely fill" or "to fully convince." Either understanding would address the problems the visionaries are causing. If this verb's
perfect passive participle (*peplērophorēmenoi*), which is parallel with the preceding "perfect" (*teleioi*), asks primarily that the readers be completely filled
(so O'Brien 254), it would intimate that the readers do not need the visionar-

ies' regulations to attain this fullness. But since present possession of fullness has been an important emphasis of the whole letter, a petition that they be filled would run counter to this central affirmation. Still, the passive voice indicates that this filling is an act of God accomplished for the Colossians rather than something that they attain through their own striving.

The better rendering, however, is "fully convinced." Colossians asserts repeatedly that believers already possess forgiveness and relationship with God and that they need no supplemental experiences or knowledge to obtain them. Epaphras prays earnestly that they will become convinced that they fully possess these blessings. Since they already have knowledge of all of God's will, they need only to recognize this gift so that the visionaries cannot tempt them to strive for experiences designed to attain something else. Therefore, Epaphras's prayer amounts to a request that the letter be a success, that the readers realize the futility of accepting the visionaries' teaching because they already have everything God purposes for them.

Enlisting the prayers of the Colossian church's founder adds a powerful inducement for complying with the letter's instructions. Epaphras may have founded the churches of both the supposed audience of the letter and the actual initial readers. In any case, the readers know him as an important and reliable leader. Knowing how strongly he feels about the letter's main issue, and the great struggle he has engaged for the cause, should incline the readers to adopt the letter's outlook.

Verse 13 strengthens the commendation of Epaphras with an oath formula. Even in Paul's circumstance of imprisonment, he witnesses how great a struggle Epaphras endures for the readers. So the apostle commends Epaphras's work. His willingness to suffer for the letter's recipients provides an additional and powerful reason for them to listen to Epaphras. Ancient rhetoricians recommended that speakers demonstrate their suffering or willingness to suffer for the audience as a means of increasing their credibility and persuasive force (see the comments that introduce 1:24–2:5 above). Epaphras has shown his love for the Colossians not only by founding their community but also by suffering for them.

Epaphras did not just work for them; he also "labored strenuously" (*polyn ponon*). The term *ponos* appears only three other times in the New Testament, all of them in Revelation (16:10, 11; 21:4), but it appears more often in the LXX. The term means difficult or strenuous labor and sometimes refers to struggling in battle (Abbott 302; LSJM 1448).

The text does not explain what the strenuous toil of Epaphras involves, but it certainly includes his struggling in prayer, mentioned in the previous verse (Lightfoot 240). The writer likely expects readers to envision other activities as well, such as his work in founding and sustaining their communities—particularly if Epaphras adopted Paul's method of supporting himself through manual labor while establishing churches. A bit closer to hand, perhaps the toil also involved imprisonment and constant travel (Schweizer 240–41). Still more relevant to the letter's argument, the difficult work may involve opposition to false teaching, particularly that opposed in the letter. Whatever the readers may have known or imagined about the specifics of this labor is less important than the image of Epaphras suffering and working for the good of the readers.

This portrait of Epaphras's work and suffering both reflects common means of persuasion in the first century and conforms his ministry to Paul's. The image of Paul developed in 1:24–2:5 emphasizes the ways he has suffered for the readers and for the whole church. This patterning of Epaphras's ministry after Paul's legitimates the work of Epaphras and strengthens his authority. This pattern does not indicate that Epaphras carries on the apostolic mission, as Pokorný argues (193), but it does show his willingness to accept the same kinds of sacrifices that Paul endures for the readers.

Epaphras undertakes this strenuous labor for the churches in Laodicea and Hierapolis, in addition to those in Colossae, an extension of his ministry that also parallels Paul's ministry. When Colossians mentions the difficult struggles Paul undertakes for the church, it is not only for the Colossians but for all believers whom he does not know (2:1). In 4:13, Epaphras's arduous toil, his evangelistic and pastoral ministry, engages a population beyond his home city. His toil throughout the region legitimates his ministry for all the churches in the area, not just those the letter identifies as its recipients. This helps to establish or maintain his authority in the wider church, at least across the Lycus valley.

This verse may provide a glimpse of the letter's actual target audience rather than just of the named recipients. Whether the letter is written before or after the devastation of Colossae by the earthquake in 60–62 C.E., the mention of these other churches suggests that Epaphras's ministry extends beyond Colossae to the churches of the whole region and intimates that all these churches should heed his—and the letter's—instructions. Verse 16 explicitly draws these surrounding churches into the audience addressed by the letter. Mention of these churches suggests that they face the same teaching that Colossians rejects.

[14] The final greetings to the letter's recipients come from two people about whom the writer says little: Luke and Demas. Philemon 24 includes both among Paul's coworkers; 2 Tim 4:11 contains the only other reference to Luke in the New Testament. There Luke alone remains with Paul in the midst of difficult circumstances.[83] Colossians identifies this faithful companion and coworker of Paul as the "beloved physician." This occupation either locates Luke among persons of some wealth or indicates that he was a slave who had been educated to be someone's personal physician. If the latter is the case, he has probably by

83. The Luke mentioned in Colossians is not the Lucian of Rom 16:21. Lucian is identified as a Jew, while this Luke is a Gentile; Paul has already named all those with him who are Jewish. Neither is there reason to identify Luke with the Lucian of Acts 13:1.

now gained his freedom. Colossians offers no hint about which of these characterizations of Luke is more probable. Early twentieth-century commentators sometimes imagined that Luke served as Paul's personal physician (e.g., Abbott 302). Lightfoot (241) even suggested that he joined Paul when the apostle became ill in Galatia (Gal 4:13–14) and then stayed with him. But nothing here or elsewhere in the New Testament suggests that Luke gave Paul extended medical attention.

Along with the "we" sections in Acts, this reference to Luke has led many interpreters to identify the Luke mentioned in Colossians as the author of the Gospel of Luke and Acts. While this tradition is ancient (Eusebius [4th cent.] attributes the view to Papias [late 1st cent.]), no other evidence supports it. Interestingly, this is the second person who sends greetings to the Colossians whom Papias later identified as the author of a Gospel. The mention of Mark and Luke in Colossians and the attribution of a Gospel to each indicate that they were well known in the late first-century church. The appearance of their names in Colossians increases their status and may have been a factor in the tradition's eventual ascription of Gospels to them. They must also have been leaders of the church in the area that Colossians addresses.

The final person who greets the readers is Demas. He is the only person who sends greeting for whom the letter does not add a word of commendation. Demas also appears only two other times in the New Testament, Phlm 24 and 2 Tim 4:10. In this final reference, 2 Timothy contrasts him with the faithful Luke. Colossians' relative silence about Demas should not be interpreted as foreshadowing his later defection. The lack of commendation may indicate only that Paul does not know him as well (Dunn 283; Hay 161) or that the recipients do. Whatever the reason for the reference's brevity, including him among those who greet the readers strengthens his position as a leader in the church; he is a person to whom the readers should pay careful attention. He is, moreover, a person with direct and personal attachment to the apostle and so to his teachings. If the writer of 2 Timothy later expresses dissatisfaction with the use Demas has made of that position, this earlier text still associates him with Paul.

[15–17] In the final sentences before his signature, Paul sends his own greetings to various parties. This is the only Pauline letter that asks one church to greet another church (Hay 162). Perhaps this should not be surprising, because these cities were only about ten miles apart, and therefore the churches located in these cities may have known each other well (Dunn 283). The people greeted in vv. 15–17 are all residents of Laodicea.

The first greeting addresses all Christians in Laodicea, then the writer singles out a particular house church. Although some argue that the greeting of this one church means that its members are the only ones holding out against the visionaries' teaching (e.g., Pokorný 194) and others that it is the only church where the writer knows the leader (Dunn 284), these suggestions probably overreach the text. If the letter intends to address the whole region and was written after the destruction of Colossae, it is unlikely that the writer knows the name of only one host of a church. Perhaps the mention of Nympha's house suggests that all the churches of Laodicea sometimes meet at her house. This would imply that her house is large enough to accommodate the gathering of Laodicea's various house churches on special occasions. But we do not know why Colossians singles out this church. Still, by referring to it in this way and associating it and its leader with Paul, the writer positions it as a leader among the churches of Laodicea.

Identifying the leader of this church has been a problem since at least the fourth century. The spelling of the noun *Nymphan* allows that it can be either masculine or feminine, with only the placement of the accent indicating which gender it is. Our earliest textual witnesses do not contain accent marks. Determination of the gender of the household's owner, then, depends on the pronoun that follows the word "house" (*oikon*). Early manuscripts differ widely: Codex Vaticanus (B, from the 4th cent.) has the feminine pronoun and so identifies Nympha as a woman, but as early as the fifth century, the masculine pronoun appears and thus identifies this householder as Nymphas, a male. Other witnesses, including the fourth-century Codex Sinaiticus (ℵ), avoid the problem by having a plural pronoun so that the church meets in "their house." The culturally shaped expectations of interpreters have often had as much to do with their decisions among these options as has the evidence itself. Late nineteenth- and early twentieth-century interpreters expected only male leadership and therefore identified this leader as male (e.g., Lightfoot 242–43; Abbott 303–4). In the mid-twentieth century, Lohse (174) says it is not possible to decide which is correct. Later in the twentieth century, the consensus shifted so that most scholars now identify this householder as female. This last conclusion follows the usual canons of textual criticism, because the feminine pronoun accounts best for the other readings. Copyists were less likely to change the masculine to a feminine pronoun and also less likely to feel a need to convert it to a plural pronoun if it were masculine. Thus, this verse indicates that the leading house church, and the one Colossians strengthens by explicitly mentioning it, has a woman as its leader.

Nympha is probably a widow who possesses a significant household because she maintains it independently. This probably means she has significant wealth (Dunn 284–85). This measure of wealth opens the possibility that she has been a sponsor of the Pauline mission. No evidence beyond her mention in this verse supports this speculation, but it might explain why Colossians mentions the church that meets in her house. Notably, Colossians accepts the leadership of a woman as a matter of course, requiring no explanation or comment (Hay 162). This note, therefore, provides evidence that women held leadership positions in the Pauline churches even after Paul's death. This is yet another place where tension emerges between the social patterns that the household code *seems* to require and alternative patterns that Colossians elsewhere advocates and supports. The household structure of this exemplary church appears to be incongruent with that suggested by a straightforward reading of the household code.

Beyond greeting the Laodicean churches, the writer exhorts the Colossians to share this letter with them and also to read the letter sent to Laodicea. This reference to a letter to the Laodiceans has prompted many to search for it. Some have identified it with other canonical writings (e.g., Lightfoot [244] identified it with Ephesians, as did Marcion in the 2nd cent., according to Tertullian, *Marc.* 5.17.1). Failure to find a letter to Laodicea moved one early reader to compose one. This letter is little more than a pastiche of Pauline phrases and ideas and is certainly from a later time. Some readers have argued that the letter mentioned was from the Laodiceans to Paul (John Chrysostom mentions that some hold this view, in *Hom. Col.* 12, on 4:12–13; Calvin 361). But there would be little reason to urge the readers of Colossians to consult correspondence directed *to* Paul. Others hypothesize that Epaphras wrote the letter to the Laodiceans because Paul would have no reason to greet the Laodiceans in Colossians if he had written them at the same time (Lohse 174–75 n. 47; Anderson 436–40). But since nothing indicates that the Laodicean letter was written at the same time as Colossians, the most natural reading remains that Colossians has in mind a letter written by Paul. All these hypotheses assume that Paul wrote Colossians.

On the assumption that Colossians is pseudonymous, Lindemann (36) argues that Colossians is actually written for the church in Laodicea and that this exhortation for the Laodiceans to read it intends to assure its application to the real intended readers. This hypothesis leaves open the question of why Paul sends them greetings (Hübner 121). On the other hand, it may help explain why Colossians mentions the church at Nympha's house. If that church actively rejects the teaching the letter opposes, then a word commending it supports both its own standing and its advocacy of the letter's views. But certainty here remains impossible. Rather than being written for the churches in the single city of Laodicea, Colossians may have been written for another church in the region or for the region more generally. The evidence does not allow more specificity than the general conclusion that it was probably intended for churches in the Lycus valley.

More important than identifying the letter to the Laodiceans is what this statement about exchanging letters shows for the emerging use of Pauline Letters in the early church. The multiple house churches within a city or a region shared Paul's Letters almost from the beginning. Paul assumes or sets in motion this circulation of his letters in 1 Thess 5:27, where he instructs the readers to share the letter with "all the brothers" (NIV). This statement directs recipients to read the letter to those in or around Thessalonica who hold the views about the Parousia that the letter seeks to correct, and thus probably alludes to house churches beyond the one(s) that first received it. Another indication that Paul's

Letters circulated even during his lifetime appears in the greeting of Galatians, where Paul addresses the church*es* of Galatia (1:2). Still, Col 4:16 provides the clearest evidence for the intentional distribution of Pauline Letters beyond their original addressees. This passage provides our first hint that the church would or had already begun to develop a collection of Pauline Letters. The practice of exchanging and collecting Paul's Letters indicates that their readers believed these writings had relevance beyond the single church to which Paul originally wrote them. To take this step, the church must have accorded these writings a measure of authority. The instruction to trade letters with Laodicea was an early step in the process that would eventually lead to viewing these letters as Scripture. Perhaps this exhortation to exchange letters itself hastened the collection and the church's recognition of the authority of the Pauline Letters. Yet it is clear that the readers of Colossians already grant substantial authority to Pauline Letters (Hay 166); that is the only reason the author of Colossians would attribute this letter to Paul.

Colossians gives one further exhortation to its readers before the final signature: encourage Archippus in his ministry. Archippus appears only one other time in the New Testament, in the greeting of Philemon, where Paul identifies him as a fellow soldier. He seems, therefore, to have been a coworker in Paul's ministry at some point. The relationship of Archippus to Philemon (whether his son, the head of the household, or the owner of Onesimus and so the real addressee of the letter we call Philemon) remains unclear. At the time of Philemon, however, he apparently hosts the house church of which Philemon was a member. Colossians may envision Archippus as a resident of Laodicea because the text mentions him after referring to the church in that city (4:16).

Colossians calls the readers to charge Archippus to fulfill a ministry, a *diakonia*. Though this term refers to the office of deacon as early as Philippians (1:1), Paul also uses it more generally for ministry, both his own and that of others. Colossians uses *diakonia* with this more general meaning, with no implication that Archippus holds the office of deacon.

Archippus has a particular ministry to fulfill. While his task seems specific, it also has an ongoing character. The readers must encourage him to accomplish it because he has been given this task "in the Lord." Therefore, Christ authorized this ministry. This commendation of Archippus, in the form of an exhortation to encourage him to fulfill his ministry, strengthens his position within the church. Colossians uses the same language in this exhortation that it used to speak of possessing the fullness of God's blessings (2:10): Archippus must "fulfill" this ministry. Furthermore, *plēroō* is the same verb that Colossians used to describe Paul's ministry in 1:25, where he "fulfill[s] the word of God." Perhaps this phrasing indicates that Archippus's task includes leading the church to reject the teaching that Colossians opposes and contending for the views that Colossians advocates (cf. MacDonald 184). That is, he must defend the understandings of Christ, church, and salvation for which this letter argues.[84] In the context of an argument about these issues, particularly if the visionaries do not intend to oppose Paul, the apostle's support of Archippus constitutes a powerful tool.

Colossians directs its readers to exhort Archippus to fulfill his ministry. Whatever authority the letter may provide for him, he does not possess it independently or as an individual. Here is an indication of the collaborative nature of Paul's ministry, even as those around him remembered it after his death. This exhortation indicates that the whole church works to encourage and support the accomplishment of the tasks of ministry, including those set before their leaders. Even more important for Colossians, this exhortation draws readers into the circle of those who agree with the writer's message; they must support the people whom Paul supports. Supporting the ministry of this associate of Paul almost necessarily means accepting the teaching he advocates.

[18] The final verse of Colossians contains a signature formula and final farewell. As in some genuine letters of Paul, Colossians ends with a notice that Paul is now picking up the pen (1 Cor 16:21; Gal 6:11). This reflects his common practice of using a secretary or amanuensis to transcribe his letters as he dictated them (see also Rom 16:22, where the secretary sends his own greeting). The signature adds a mark of authenticity that 2 Thessalonians tries to exploit to the fullest, asserting that this signature is present in all Paul's Letters and serves as their mark of authenticity (3:17). Colossians does not make such claims or draw more attention to the signature than what we find in the undisputed letters. Explicit mention of the signature could be important for Pauline Letters because most of their recipients heard them read rather than reading the letters themselves. Of course, a signature would be useful only if the reader possessed the original letter. Once Paul's Letters were being copied and exchanged, the signature would be in the same hand as the rest of the letter. If Colossians intends to address a community other than one in Colossae, that community would expect to have a copy rather than the original. Thus, they would not be able to verify the signature. Its mention does, however, add weight to the claim of authenticity. So from whatever hand, the purported signature both authenticates the message and carries authority.

The short and (reportedly) personally penned section of Colossians contains one request, that the readers remember Paul's status as a prisoner. On the assumption that Paul is the author, this request asks them to remember him in prayer or, less likely, to send him support (Dunn 289). On the assumption that the letter is written after Paul's death, other emphases predominate—though they may be present even if Paul did compose the letter, because "remembrance" can take multiple forms (see O'Brien 260). A reference to Paul's

---

84. Hay (163–64) suggests that the mission is to interpret Colossians to the Laodiceans.

imprisonment recalls the lengthy discussion of his suffering for the readers (1:24–2:5). Mention of his suffering for them (his "chains") reemphasizes this element of Paul's ethos and thereby encourages readers to trust him and to grant him authority. As noted in connection with 1:24–2:5, rhetoricians recognized reminding an audience of ways the speaker had suffered for them as a means for eliciting their agreement. More specifically, many granted the witness of martyrs particular authority (Dunn 289; see the comment on 1:24 above). This statement also reminds readers of the connection that Colossians makes between Paul's sufferings and Christ's. Lightfoot (245) notes that this allusion to his imprisonment is similar to Gal 6:17, where Paul tells the readers not to cause him problems because he bears the marks of Christ's sufferings in his body. These mentions of Paul's suffering serve similar rhetorical functions; they remind readers that Paul cares enough about them to suffer and that he believes so deeply in the gospel that he endures persecution for it. Colossians' reminder of the suffering of Paul supplies a final authentication of the letter's message. The readers should obey the commands in this letter not only because the message comes from one who possesses apostolic authority, but also because that apostle loves them so deeply that he suffers for them and for the whole church. This final exhortation, then, reinforces the letter's appeals for readers to accept its message.

The letter ends with a short wish of grace for the readers. Letters of the period often ended with a brief, sometimes one-word, wish for the health of the recipient(s). This form appears in the letter from the Jerusalem church leaders inserted in Acts 15:23–29, which ends with the word "Farewell" (*errōsthe*). Paul replaces this closing wish with a benediction of grace for the readers. In all the undisputed letters except Romans, Paul invokes the "grace of the [our] Lord Jesus Christ" over the readers. Colossians contains a shortened version of the prayer, one that does not explicitly connect Christ to this grace. It says simply, "Grace be with you." Within the Pauline corpus this shortened form appears only here and in the Pastorals. Even though abbreviated, it still shifts the focus of the concluding wish from physical health to the well-being of the entire person or the entire community. It also recalls the letter's conviction that God is known in the church primarily as the God who grants the gifts of forgiveness and reconciliation to the community of God's people. Though the writer does not reaffirm it in the closing prayer-wish, for Colossians this grace is mediated to the church and the world through Christ.

The greetings and exhortations that bring Colossians to a close reveal that the ministry of Paul was a collaborative enterprise involving a network of evangelists and house churches. The personal relationships of those coworkers supported the authority of Paul, and their relationship with Paul bolstered the standing of the coworkers at home and in the broader church. The particular people whom Colossians mentions in its closing greetings suggest that the writer has made use of Philemon. But beyond this, mention of many or all of these people establishes them as reliable leaders in Paul's absence. This is not apostolic succession as the later church would think of it, but it does create a cadre of leaders who know and understand Paul and so have the assumption of authority. Their authority, however, comes not solely from Paul but also from their own ministries. Most of the people mentioned must have been known to the actual readers of Colossians. This would be the only reason to create such an extensive list of people who are with Paul in his imprisonment. Such contact with Paul, when combined with his direct or implicit commendation, legitimates the ministry of these known church leaders. Their leadership, in turn, supports acceptance of the teaching of Colossians.

While combating the visionaries' teaching, Colossians has set its Christology and ecclesiology in a cosmic context. Colossians presents Christ as creator and ruler of the whole cosmos and as initiator and head of the church. It is "in Christ," indeed through being identified with Christ, that believers receive God's gifts in their fullness. Through baptism, without further ritual requirements, believers attain identification with Christ. Because they are identified with Christ, certainly Christ should determine the whole of believers' lives. Christ so permeates all aspects of life that being "in Christ" determines how believers conduct themselves in their specific social locations. Thus, even the household code testifies to the lordship of Christ over all of life.

In the argument of Colossians, the most important affirmation is that because believers have been incorporated into and identified with the Christ who is over all, they need no dramatic spiritual experience to bring them to God or to demonstrate that they are God's people. The identity given them in baptism assures them of forgiveness, of the closest relationship with God, and of their status as coheirs with Christ. Nothing a vision can offer them compares with or supplements the position or blessings they already enjoy in Christ. No powers or additional rites can bring them better knowledge of what God wants or greater access to God's blessings. Through their acceptance of Christ in baptism, they are the holy and elect of God, who have been securely "transferred into the kingdom of [God's] beloved Son." They can be certain that Paul's concluding prayer will be answered, since what he asked for, they already possess, and its continued possession is the gift of being in Christ. So indeed, grace will be with them.

INDEX OF ANCIENT SOURCES

INDEX OF AUTHORS

INDEX OF SUBJECTS